REVOLUTIONARY
PEDAGOGIES

REVOLUTIONARY PEDAGOGIES

Cultural Politics, Instituting Education, and the Discourse of Theory

Peter Pericles Trifonas, EDITOR

ROUTLEDGEFALMER
A MEMBER OF THE TAYLOR & FRANCIS GROUP
NEW YORK LONDON

Published in 2000 by
Routledge
29 West 35th Street
New York, NY 10001

Published in Great Britain by
Routledge
11 New Fetter Lane
London EC4P 4EE

RoutledgeFalmer is an imprint of the Taylor & Francis Group.

Library of Congress Cataloging-in-Publication Data

Trifonas, Peter Pericles, 1960–
    Revolutionary pedagogies: cultural politics, instituting education, and the discourse of theory / [edited by] Peter Pericles Trifonas.
        p. cm.
    Includes bibliographical references and index.
    ISBN 0-415-92568-1 (hb: alk. paper) — ISBN 0-415-92569-X (pb: alk. paper)
    1. Critical pedagogy. 2. Education—Political aspects. 3. Education—Social aspects. 4. Education—Philosophy.

LC196.R48 2000
370.11'5—dc21   99-056409

To my parents, Panagiotis and Martha, whose immeasurable sacrifice and love taught me that to live is but to learn; the joyful inspiration of their ancient wisdom is confirmed each and every single day by the miracle of my own children, Peirce, Anthi, and Yanni.

Contents

III   THE DISCOURSE OF THEORY

Acknowledgments

I would like to thank Gayatri Spivak, Jacques Derrida, Peter McLaren, Henry Giroux, John Willinksy, Roger Simon, Nicholas Burbules, Doug Kellner, Michael Apple, Patti Lather, Bill Pinar, Denise Egéa-Kuehne, Jo-Anne Dillabough, Cameron McCarthy, and Greg Dimitriadis, who have participated in this anthology, for their support of this project and for the generous contributions of their texts to the collection. I have learned much from their work and have been inspired by the gift of their friendship.

Heidi Freund has provided valuable insight into the task of editing this book as well as tremendous reserves of patience while it was transformed into its present form. Thank you.

I would like to express my gratitude to Elefteria Balomenos for reading portions of the manuscript and for assisting in the writing of the introduction.

This book would not have been possible without a fellowship from the Social Sciences and Humanities Research Council of Canada and a Connaught Grant from the University of Toronto.

Introduction

How does contemporary critical theory encounter pedagogy? radicalize it? revolutionize it? make it revolutionary? This is the central question, among others, that this volume seeks to address. It does so by highlighting the work of contemporary theorists who are also very well known for their revolutionary teaching and the radicality of what they have taught with respect to cultural politics, instituting education, and the discourse of theory. Although this characterization of the chapters presented in this volume is self-consciously forefronted by the title of the anthology (and any title worthy of the appellation "title" should surely thematize the heterogeneity of a body of work so as to do just that!), the text does not speak only to those who have embraced the ethical value of opening the empirico-conceptual and epistemic limits of one's work and oneself to the risk of less than canonical modes of thinking. It also addresses those who would wholeheartedly blame contemporary theorizing for all that is perceived to be "wrong" with the state of the humanities and the social sciences today. By containing the idiomatic values of such arguments within the thematic trajectory of this titular enframing of the topic, the essays sustain a probing articulation of the tensions among the discursive spaces and the real-world dimensions of an interdisciplinary nexus of theory that informs and manifests practice in the application of ideas. For any engagement or identification with a theoretical position or direction (for instance, a theorem, a system, a methodology, a "proof," an ideology, an argument) implies the critical outworking of an academic responsibility to uphold an obligation owed to the search for truth at all costs. This is what *makes* theory practice and provides a justifying principle, a principle of reason for what we think, do, and write. The collection converges upon specific interpretations of the obligation we have to respond responsibly to the alterity of those we teach for beyond ourselves. The interplay between texts I have included thereby challenges us to reflect upon and to reexamine the logic and the boundaries of "thought" and "action," "theory" and "practice," and what comprises and displaces the opposition of these two entities in the name of revolutionizing pedagogy, radicalizing the normative limits of its ethics so as to make it more responsive to the difference of an Other.

Of course, the relating of "idea" to "performance" and vice versa is most certainly nothing new, especially as it relates to the teaching body and a body of teaching. As I have said, the desire motivating the appearance of this text is not to offer yet another treatise containing polemics on why one should be "for" as compared to being "against" theory in the pursuit of achieving discreet pedagogical purposes, objectives, and ideals. No matter what the ethico-ideological impetus behind such a stance may be, there is no fruitfulness in taking either an offensive or a defensive posture for the sake of simply protecting the lineage, direction, and territory of a disciplinary ground from the contaminating effects of its Others. For in choosing sides, one reinstitutes the ideological errors of those familiar divisions, epistemic and methodological, that do nothing more than promote and entrench the institutional conflicts (skirmishes and wars) between otherwise interrelated and complementary faculties and induce artificial distinctions grounding the differences among areas of study—for example, the theoretical versus the practical, the scientific versus the artistic, the cognitive versus the aesthetic, the rigorous versus the undemanding, the male-oriented versus the female-oriented, the required versus the elective, and so on. The quest for validation, in each and every case, is worked out at the expense of recognizing the openings of an interdisciplinary logic—a pragmatico-interpretative space beyond the oppositionality of binary thought—that would defy the historicity of an institutional axiomatics aimed at the calculation and realization of a single, teleological destination. For it is the myopia of a repression of the desire to trailblaze, to forge new directions and paths of inquiry, thinking and teaching, that risks the danger of separating theory from practice for the sole purpose of policing boundaries and orienting the ends of research and of education. This would lead to the abdication of academic responsibility to the truth of the Other that we cannot already know and results in the instauration of a "pointless pedagogy" grounded *on, of,* and *for* the rationality of its own reason. Its logic remains, in effect, a prisoner to the fulfillment of its own faith and faithfulness in the laws and rules it upholds *without exception* by being negatively positioned toward what it must deny as Other in order to keep intact the right of its self-approving integrity. A pointless pedagogy is not aimless, that is, without purpose or direction. It is, however, conceptually and performatively unquestioned (what is its point?) and therefore both unqualified and underdetermined, yet curiously enough also overqualified and overdetermined, in the limits of its responsivity by offering no opening toward a recognition of what it might exclude as being unlike itself. A pointless pedagogy—signifying everything and nothing through its lack of an affirmative response to anything outside of itself—has no hope or possibility of realizing the horizons of other teachings whose alterior truth it cannot but deny.

None of the texts collected in this volume is guilty of doing this—that is, of promulgating a closure of response and responsibility in favor of a strategic exclusions intended to work in defense and support of a single-minded theory of/and/as practice. And this is what makes the particular thematic trajectory or "theoretical jetty" of each essay "radical" and "revolutionary" (even "topical" when we relate it back to the title) by articulating a path toward an alterior ground for enacting a reactionary and inclusive pedagogy aimed at the ethical reconstruction of education and its institution via an intensification of academic responsibility. So there is a common thread weaving together the heterogeneous strands of thinking represented here. The anthology gathers together the texts of theorists and educators whose practice has and is struggling to rethink the ethics and politics of dominant modes of knowledge and their pedagogical forms of expression that have operated within the institutional purview of a traditional system of education to locate the epistemic and performative parameters of its scene of teaching along a normative axis of response and responsibility. In essence, this is what gives the book its ethical and transformative impetus: another way to put it would be its reconstructive and therefore revolutionary bent. That is, it engages the form and content of seemingly benign dimensions of what has been protected under the aegis of an existing codification of social infrastructures and their prevailing cultural conditions as the "knowledge worth knowing."

How do the transdisciplinary sites of the discursive engagement of critical theory with pedagogy confront the ethico-political consequences of (post)modern social practices as active forms of cultural politics? How does this confrontation of critical theory and pedagogy with the field of social and cultural practices redefine the bounds of pedagogy and the instituting or institution of education? How does the discourse of theory affect our responsibility to rethink and revolutionize what it means to teach, to learn, to know? In short, how is the idea of the "revolutionary pedagogy" possible, or not, and what forms does it take when it is applied to the scene of teaching and learning, including research, as an active means of transforming the cultural historicity of educational praxis? In essence, these are the guiding questions that this edited book addresses by isolating the need to renegotiate the formative grounds of knowledge across three areas constituting the sites of its pedagogical articulation: Cultural Politics, Instituting Education, and the Discourse of Theory. On the one hand, the essays contained in this collection can be read as individual texts that stand very much alone as examples of groundbreaking work done within these interdependent areas of inquiry. On the other hand, each chapter relates to the other by being interdependent upon arguments that link and extend these contested sites of knowledge production in order to take up the question of the ethico-political interpellation and radicalization of the scene of teaching and learning toward a revolutionizing of pedagogy.

The first section, on Cultural Politics, deals with questions regarding the formation of subjectivity as the basis for a pedagogical reconfiguring of what it means to be a subject from competing and complementary points of view, for example, ethnicity, race, gender, sexuality, and class.

Gayatri Chakravorty Spivak, in "Diasporas Old and New: Women in the

Transnational World," takes up the question of the future of feminist theory. The struggle of women in relation to the displacement of subjectivity that has resulted from the increased migrancy of labor due to global economic restructuring is the focus of the chapter, as the sociocultural manifestations of a new economic citizenship are examined with respect to the problem of a universalization of feminism. There is a listing of what injustices the transnational inspires and also how, by removing the obstacles preventing the actualization of border crossings it is feasible to assure the possibility of the sustainable development of capitalism through the movement of bodies over space and time. Spivak attends to the difficulties of reading sociopolitical and economic contexts serving to unite women from the new diasporas of the transnational marketplace with women of developing nations and the difficulties of achieving international solidarity among feminists in the name of the subalterned, the disenfranchised, and the abused. The chapter ends with a never-ending syllabus—one to be permanently under erasure—and some suggested readings for a course in global feminist theory that enacts the movement toward realizing a transnational perspective necessary for a reconfiguring of the roles and identities of women across the changing definitions of citizenship, state, and nation constantly working themselves out through the economically driven conditions of diasporas old and new.

In "Strange Fruit: Race, Sex, and an Autobiographics of Alterity," William F. Pinar blurs the dividing line between race and gender. The purpose of the quest is to revisit life stories that are not his own but have influenced the integrity and integration of his thinking and being as a subject. The hope Pinar augurs is to reformulate the boundaries of self and other. The intersections of race and homosexuality form the starting point for an inquiry into *currere,* or curriculum inquiry conceived as a type of social psychoanalytics, which brings together Pinar's voice with the narratives of others as autobiographics of alterity will enmesh with and disambiguate their dimensions through the articulation of the differential effects on the subjective present by a time past. Pinar engages the disturbing history of violence against black males in America and outlines the pathological dimensions of racism exemplified in the phenomena of lynching and the mutilation of sexual organs and other body parts. What causes such acts of hatred and ritualistic cruelty that are focused on race and gender but also imply a fear of sexuality and difference? How can we explain the psychic drives of this traumatic behavior in American culture, beyond explanations resorting to an identification of neurasthenia based solely on object relations and the binary formation of subjectivity? In one sense, answering these questions is the crux of Pinar's chapter but like Spivak, he prefers only to begin upon the path of exploring the historicity of subject formation and otherness as the radicalization of difference by pointing to a direction of study he is and will be doing (really has been doing) for some time via the autobiographics of alterity called *currere.* The chapter thus foreshadows a curriculum of research constructed to answer a larger and more pressing question in trying to set the theoretical and practical groundwork for conceiving the possibility of what Franz Fanon called a "new man."

In "All-Consuming Identities: Race and the Pedagogy of Resentment in the Age of Difference," Cameron McCarthy and Greg Dimitriadis present a dialogue of our times that illuminates the divergent forces involved in the formation of a cultural consciousness which is ill at ease within its insatiable appetite for material assets. The chapter illustrates how the rituals of contemporary culture and its ideology allow for a clear-sighted affiliation of interests through which subjectivity is defined in relation to the comfort of an illusion of belonging to a community and knowing one's place in it. McCarthy and Dimitriadis argue that this image of identity forms a niche that prefigures and limits one's vision of the dimensions of the lifeworld and is ill at ease with the reality of a subject's appetite for material and social assets so prevalent in the political economy of modern day global capitalism. The sense of self is realized through the commodification of desire and the obsessions and excesses it produces as identity is worked out via the consumption of popular culture. Thus, for McCarthy and Dimitriadis, subjective appetites and perspectives inevitably exist, albeit subsumed among the influences of the pop culture industry which is mapping and recodifying the signs of difference on a global scale. Through this reign of images that are consumed and all-consuming, identity is manifest according to an obsession or fetishization of object relations occupying the subject. Popular culture—as conceived in this chapter—serves to propel affiliations and disassociations of convenience, necessity, and urgency in the desire to meet the real and affective constraints of time and appetite. The scarcity of resources creates and reinforces the limit of accessibility that marks a rift in race relations and racial animosity based on policy discourses reducing equality of opportunity, for example, access to education and to a fair-game, market-based economy structured around strategies of competition and meritocracy.

Roger Simon discusses the importance of a public memory as a transactional space, not for the consolidation of national memory but for mobilizing practices of remembrance-learning in which one's stories might be shifted by the stories of others. In "The Touch of the Past: The Pedagogical Significance of a Transactional Sphere of Public Memory," Simon argues that memories become transactional when they enact a claim on us, providing accounts that interrupt one's self-sufficiency essentially by claiming an attentiveness to an otherness that cannot be reduced to a version of our own stories. Such memories are not limited by practices of identity and identification. Within a transactional sphere of public memory, possibilities exist to enact a memorial relation to others quite different from ourselves. One condition under which this may occur is in one's encounter with testimony, understood as a multilayered communicative act, a performance intent on carrying forth memories through the conveyance of a person's engagement between consciousness and history. Testimony is always directed toward another, attempting to place the one who receives it under the obligation of a response to an embodied singular experience not recognizable as one's one. But there are different ways in which witnesses to testimony may respond to its transactive address. Two different forms of sensibility in this regard are discussed: the spectatorial and summoned. The first responds to testimony as if it were a document to be understood, felt, and judged. The second requires that one accept co-ownership of the testimony-witness relation and the burden of being obligated to testimony beyond one's instrumental concerns, opening oneself to the force of testimony that may call one's very practice of listening and responding to it into question. How this might be so and what the pedagogical importance of such a practice of listening might be is discussed in relation to listening to testimony given by members of the Sayisi Dene First Nation as they provide accounts of the 1956 forced removal of their peoples from their homelands by the Canadian government. An argument is made that listening may become a mode of thought when it is structured within a double attentiveness which calls into question our sufficiency to hear what is being spoken. In such listening/thought is the possibility of having Sayisi Dene stories shift our own, a shift that is necessary to any future reconstruction of First Nations–Canadian relationships.

The second section, on Instituting Education, takes the analysis further into the question of what it means to teach and the ethics of pedagogy, the valuations of its institutions, and the movements for and against visions of equitable educational reform, whatever these may be, for example, critical pedagogy, deconstruction, poststructuralism, or postmodernism.

Jacques Derrida takes up the question of the scene of pedagogy in "Where a Teaching Body Begins and How It Ends." This text was originally produced from the notes taken at an organizational meeting of the Research Group on the Teaching of Philosophy (GREPH) and was published in a book about the teaching of philosophy that included contributions by Michel Foucault and Michel Serres, among others. In it, Derrida deconstructs the function of the teaching body in the institution by reflecting upon the curricular expectations of his own pedagogical role as *répétiteur,* or an instructor who taught the history of philosophy in such a way as to render its repetition during examination possible, while he was at the École Normale Supérieure. The chapter essentially offers an example of the political implications and applications of deconstruction by outlining how the GREPH should conduct its battle against the Haby Reform, an edict that threatened the eradication of the teaching of philosophy in the French high school system and afterwards. Derrida offers a genealogy of the historical formation of the teaching body of philosophy in France. As a statement of how to operationalize, motivate, and sustain an ethical and political resistance to the declarations of the state, the text uses this inherited model of teaching to show how it is upheld and depends on the system of education that it in turn advocates and reinforces. In this sense, the text is historically important because of the insight it gives us into the mission of the GREPH and the extent of Derrida's involvement within the radical scope of this pedagogical interest group. It also establishes what many in North America have denied or ignored: the ethics and politics of deconstruction articulated via Derrida's work on the institution of education.

"Technologies of Reason: Toward a Regrounding of Academic Responsibility" builds upon facets of Derrida's work on the institution of education undertaken after his involvement with the GREPH. It concentrates upon the ethics of deonstruction as a way to reconfigure academic responsibility. In this chapter, my own, I have taken up the question of the grounding of reason within the university by reading a text by Derrida, "The Principle of Reason: The University in the Eyes of its Pupils," which asks (and I am paraphrasing somewhat): Is the university's reason for being rational? Which is another way of asking us—those who teach and learn within and without its walls—to reflect upon the nature of our academic responsibility in upholding the tradition of the *Universitas*. In many ways, Derrida's text is a genealogy of the history of reason and its transformation to a scientifico-technical rationality that owes much to Heidegger. The chapter pays close attention to the Heideggerian line of Derrida's argument that develops via the images of the ground/abyss of reason as metaphors for the principle of reason as a principle of foundation and self-evidence. This is the basis of academic responsibility that is unquestioned and taken for granted. Derrida's text exhibits the union of constation and performativity it exemplifies in saying what it does and doing what it says. "The Principle of Reason" was a lecture given on a bridge over the gorge at Cornell University. And this, of course, is not insignificant but central to the argument of my chapter.

Peter McLaren takes the binary logic or "reason" of racialization that juxtaposes the Other against the color white and relates it to the ethical predicament of the instituting of education at a time of global expansions and interconnectivity when capitalism has been essentially self-validated and self-congratulated as the spectre of a democracy to come. "Unthinking Whiteness: Rearticulating Diasporic Praxis" is in itself a reactionary stance toward maintaining an ignorance of how sociopolitical forms of repression rooted at the cultural foundations of our institutions impinge upon the ethical and material fabric of our everyday lives. The recodification of capitalism by the rise of technology, McLaren argues, has made it impossible to ignore the changes to what we know as democracy and schooling that have brought out challenges to the concept of self and Other, including an acceptance of whiteness as the semiotic marker of subjectivity and humanity. Racism is thus linked with capitalism and its ethics of exclusion based on the historicity of imperialist

economic imperatives evident in the contemporary global marketplace that originally brought the non-Western Other to the West. For McLaren, the struggle for
democracy requires a radicalization of the political imaginary or an envisioning of
citizens as more than clients and consumers. The chapter ends with the discussion
of critical pedagogy and an ethical imperative beyond communitarianism. It is becoming more and more obvious that an uncomplicated notion of a community un-
responsive to difference allows no social transformativity to take place, as the ideal
of community and belonging must be maintained at the expense of subjective
agency, of freedom, and of the Other.

Henry Giroux, besides being arguably the most recognizable advocate of critical
pedagogy, is also well known for his texts on postmodern education and cultural
studies. This work is extended here in this book. In this chapter, "Postmodern Education and Disposable Youth," the aforementioned themes are readdressed but
taken in a new direction, as the deprecating hype around the meaning of postmodernism and its nonessentialist recoding of the values of reason is brought face to
face with a serious discussion of what postmodernism entails for pedagogy in ethical terms. The argument of this text is firmly entrenched within the discourse of
theory, but the domain of inquiry is the current state of schools and schooling and
the possibility of configuring a radical democratic project that would recognize
manifestations of alterity beyond the modernist reason and logic of rejecting difference. Giroux analyzes the political and economic rootedness of social and cultural
conditions that have produced hybrid states of subjectivity he identifies as border
youth, urbane nomads, literally and figuratively, who must be recognized in both
their marginal position and contingency to the world of fixed meanings and representations. The postmodern does not exacerbate the dislocation of identity as much
as it offers the possibility of explaining and understanding it and, of course, using
this insight to inform the institution of education and intensify the responsibility of
its pedagogical manifestations both in form and in content. Toward this end,
Giroux goes on to discuss the representation of popular culture in some recent controversial films to analyze and illustrate how variations of the image of border youth
are played out in public by the media and can be used to enact an ethical pedagogy
that is more responsive to alterity in the postmodern age.

"Multiple Literacies and Critical Pedagogies: New Paradigms" is a statement
about rethinking contemporary pedagogical practices with respect to the multicultural evolution of society. In many respects, it is a complement to the chapters in
this section that precede it because it extends the theme of reason and rationality in
the instituting of education and concretizes the need for the teaching body to open
itself up to the use of nontraditional methods of reading and writing. Referring to
media literacy as the key for coping with the breakneck speed of technological
innovations invading the scene of teaching, Kellner argues for a critical pedagogy

that is both deconstructive and reconstructive in its quest to meet the pedagogical challenges of difference. The chapter outlines the effects of technological transformations—procedural refinements and epistemological redefinitions—that have forever altered the process of reading and writing by taking into account and accounting for the revolutions in teaching they require and inspire as an intersubjective exchange and recoding of experience.

The last section deals with the Discourse of Theory or the responsibility of the representational practices that have framed how the call for educational reform is expressed as forms of thinking, writing, and research. Is style or form as important as content? Part III is a meditation from various points on what this question means and has meant for the revolutionizing of pedagogy and educational research and the problems of ethical and political polarization or conflict that the discourse of theory has revealed.

Michael Apple, in "The Shock of the Real: Critical Pedagogies and Rightist Reconstructions," frames the problems of unifying the discourse of theory in the proliferation of meanings given to critical pedagogy. The internal struggles of like-minded left-wing theorists have opened a gap for the New Right's reconstructions of emancipatory education that have lead to the instauration of an image of plain, commonsensical approaches to education. For Apple this is doubly alarming because not only is a new orthodoxy being constructed by an appeal to the need for obvious and clear-cut standards, but it is being inaugurated using some of the same data, examples, and discourse that are now part of the established vernacular of critical pedagogy, for example, its concern for achieving a utopic state of free and equal individuals. This rhetoric is, Apple argues, vague and disjointed at best, even contradictory to its emancipatory premises, because it is not directly tied to real transformations in the material realm of sociocultural and politicoeconomic practices or to what affects schools and teachers on a day-to-day basis. The result is that education has shifted to the right. Apple discusses strategies and methods for altering this disturbing path in a radical way by asking critical pedagogy to ground its discourse in the realities of those it wants and needs to identify with it, thereby making a more effective push toward the realization of democratic schools.

In "The Limits of Dialogue as a Critical Pedagogy," Nicholas Burbules rethinks the emancipatory potential of dialogue. In essence, the chapter is about the limits of communication and the responsibility in/of response. He has written much on this subject, but this essay is an extension and deepening of his previous work on dialogue that takes into account those factors inhibiting the possibility of understanding the Other and coming to terms with an alterity we cannot begin to comprehend yet must accept. Burbules covers the history of dialogue since Plato and ends up in the postmodern era of identity politics and difference. The milieu of the breaking down of sign-sense relations and its aftermath of multiple sites of meaning negotiation marks the point where discourse is a situated practice. He is then able to analyze and complicate the decontextualized model of dialogue that posits an ideal vision of the clear exchange of information in light of current theorizing.

John Willinsky discusses what the use of new information technologies, such as data mining and Knowledge Discover Databases (KDD), will do to the old theory/practice debate, as those who stand up against theory begin to find that their case for the accessibility and practicality of applied research is being seriously eroded by the efficiency of centralized and automated data mining of commercial and government databases supplemented by built-to-order research. In "The Social Sciences as Information Technology: A Political Economy of Practice," he discusses the ramifications of this hypothesis. It is suggested that the politics of theory and in the social sciences will become just that, as we engage, to give it a slightly sci-fi flavor, in the coming struggle over the function and control of these knowledge-generating analytical and synthetic engines. Call it "Automation in Theory" or perhaps "Automata Theory"; Willinsky implies we need a political economy of practice and offers us one to consider.

In "Responsible Practices of Academic Writing: Troubling Clarity II," Patti Lather looks at the politics of the call for clarity in language through the case histories of women with HIV and how the impossibility of testimony complicates rather than reduces the impact of texts as catalysts for response or analysis. Her concern is with the "limit questions," that is, those interrogations that lead to a complication of the values of responsibility in response to a text. The question of clarity and meaning—the sign-sense dyad—is coupled with the question of reading and writing and what we owe to the Other in the process of representing experiences we cannot ever hope to translate or record faithfully. Lather discusses the ethical dilemma of writing her research of women with HIV and the problems of creating a text that would do justice to the heteroglossia of the dialogue between the researchers and the participants of the ethnography.

In "Degrees of Freedom and Deliberations of 'Self': The Gendering of Identity in Teaching," Jo-Anne Dillabough critiques from two related feminist perspectives the foundations of the theoretical discourse that upholds the concepts of "teacher professionalism" and "professional identity" as they are currently manifest in the field of teaching. In the first instance, feminist critiques of liberal democracy are drawn upon to expose the gendered assumptions which underlie dominant conceptions of the "professional" teacher. Dillabough pays particular attention to the now-dominant view of the teacher as a rational and instrumental actor, and its gendered dimensions are explored. Second, the gender dualisms which reside at the heart of the concept and discourse of "teacher professionalism" are identified and discussed. The discussion is then widened to examine the role of gender politics in shaping the epistemological premises upon which teacher professionalism is developed and its more formative role in the exploitation of women teachers' labors. Drawing upon examples of current feminist research and her own preliminary empirical data, Dillabough concludes the chapter by presenting an alternative conceptual framework for assessing the gendered nature of identity-formation in teaching.

I CULTURAL POLITICS

Gayatri Chakravorty Spivak

DIASPORAS OLD AND NEW
Women in the Transnational World[1]

What do I understand today by a "transnational world"? That it is impossible for the new and developing states, the newly decolonizing or the old decolonizing nations, to escape the orthodox constraints of a "neo-liberal" world economic system which, in the name of "Development," and now "sustainable development," removes all barriers between itself and fragile national economies, so that any possibility of building for social redistribution is severely damaged. In this new transnationality, what is usually meant by "the new diaspora," the new scattering of the seeds of "developing" nations, so that they can take root on developed ground? Eurocentric migration, labor export both male and female, border crossings, the seeking of political asylum, and the haunting in-place uprooting of "comfort women" in Asia and Africa. What were the old diasporas, before the world was thoroughly consolidated as transnational? They were the results of religious oppression and war, of slavery and indenturing, trade and conquest, and intra-European economic migration, which, since the nineteenth century, took the form of migration and immigration into the United States.

These are complex phenomena, each with a singular history of its own. And women's relationship to each of these phenomena is oblique, ex-orbitant to the general story. It is true that in transnationality their lines seem to cross mostly, though not always, in First World spaces, where the lines seem to end; labor migrancy is increasingly an object of investigation and oral history. Yet even this tremendous complexity cannot accommodate some issues involving "women in the transnational world." I list them here: (1) homeworking, (2) population control, (3) groups that cannot become diasporic, and (4) indigenous women outside of the Americas.

Homeworking involves women who, within all the divisions of the world and in modes of production extending from the precapitalist to the post-Fordist, embracing all class processes, do piecework at home with no control over wages; and thus absorb the cost of health care, day care, workplace safety, maintenance, management; through manipulation of the notion that feminine ethics is unpaid domestic labor ("nurturing") into the meretricious position that paid domestic labor is munificent or feminist, as the case may be. The concept of a diasporic multiculturalism is irrelevant here. The women stay at home, often impervious to organizational attempts through internalized gendering as a survival technique. They are part (but only part) of the group necessarily excluded from the implied readership of this essay.

"Population control" is the name of the policy that is regularly tied to so-called aid packages, by transnational agencies, upon the poorest women. As workers like Malini Karkal, Farida Akhter, and many others have shown, the policy is no less than gynocide and war on women.[2] It is not only a way of concealing overconsumption—and each one of us is on the average twenty to thirty times the size of a person in Somalia or Bangladesh; but it also stands in the way of feminist theory because it identifies women with their reproductive apparatus and grants them no other subjectship.

For "groups that cannot become diasporic" I turn to the original definition of the "subaltern" as it was transplanted from Gramsci:

> . . . the demographic difference between the total . . . population [of a colonial state] and all those who can be described as the "elite." Some of these classes and groups such as the lesser rural gentry, impoverished landlords, rich peasants . . . upper-middle peasants [and now some sections of the urban white- and blue collar work force and their wives] who "naturally" ranked among the "subaltern," [can] under certain circumstances act for the "elite". . . . —an ambiguity which it is up to the [feminist] to sort out on the basis of a close and judicious reading.[3]

Large groups within this space of difference subsist in transnationality without escaping into diaspora. And indeed they would include most indigenous groups outside Euramerica, which brings me to the last item on the list of strategic exclusions above. Womanspace within these groups cannot necessarily be charted when we consider diasporas, old or new. Yet they are an important part of "the transnational world."

What I have said so far is, strictly speaking, what Derrida called an *exergue*.[4] It is both outside of the body of the work of this paper and the face of the coin upon which the currency of the Northern interest in transnationality is stamped. This brief consideration of the asymmetrical title of the conference can lead to a number of labyrinths that we cannot explore. I cut the meditation short and turn to my general argument.

Nearly two years later, as I revise, I will linger a moment longer and inscribe the "groups that cannot become diasporic" more affirmatively, as those who have stayed in place for more than thirty thousand years. I do not value this by itself, but I must count it. Is there an alternative vision of the human here? The tempo of learning to learn from this immensely slow temporizing will not only take us clear out of diasporas, but will also yield no answers or conclusions readily. Let this stand as the name of the other of the question of diaspora. That question, so taken for granted these days as the historically necessary ground of resistance, marks the forgetting of this name.

When we literary folk in the U.S. do multiculturalist feminist work in the areas of our individual research and identity, we tend to produce three sorts of thing: identitarian or theoretist (sometimes both at once) analyses of literary/filmic texts available in English and other European languages; accounts of more recognizably political phenomena from a descriptive-culturalist or ideology-critical point of view; and, when we speak of transnationality in a general way, we think of global hybridity from the point of view of popular public culture, military intervention, and the neocolonialism of *multi*-nationals.

Thus from our areas of individual research and identity group in the United States, we produce exciting and good work. If we place this list within the two lists I have already made, it becomes clear that we do not often focus on the question of civil society. Hidden and transmogrified in the Foucauldian term "civility," it hardly ever surfaces in a transnationalist feminist discourse. In a brilliant and important recent essay, "The Heart of Ex-Nomination: Nation, Woman and the Indian Immigrant Bourgeoisie," Ananya Bhattacharjee has turned her attention to the topic.[5] But in the absence of developed supportive work in the transnationalist feminist collectivity, this interventionist intellectual has not been able to take her hunch on civil society as far as the rest of her otherwise instructive essay.

In an ideal democratic (as opposed to a theocratic, absolutist, or fascist) state, there are structures other than military and systemic or elective-political from which the individual—organized as a group if necessary—can demand service or redress. This is the abstract individual as citizen, who is "concretely" recoded as the witness, the source of attestation, in Marxian formulation the "bearer," of the nation form of appearance. This "person" is private in neither the legal nor the psychological sense. Some commonly understood arenas such as health, education, welfare, and social security, and the civil as opposed to penal or criminal legal code, fall within the purview of civil society. The individual who can thus call on the services of the civil society—the civil service of the state—is, ideally, the citizen. How far this is from the realized scene, especially if seen from the point of view of gays, women, indigenous and indigent peoples, and old and new diasporas, is of course obvious to all of us. However, it is still necessary to add that, within the definitions of an ideal civil society, if the state is a welfare state, it is directly the servant of the individual. When increasingly privatized, as in the New World Order, the priorities of the civil society are shifted from service to the citizen to capital maximization. It then becomes increasingly correct to say that the only source of male dignity is employment, just as the only source of genuine female dignity is unpaid domestic labor.[6]

I write under the sign of the reminder that the other scene, sup-posing any possible thought of civil societies (which is itself race-class-gender differentiated between South and North) of an almost tempoless temporizing, negotiating with the gift of time (if there is any), is not this.[7] It is our arrogant habit to think that other scene only as an exception to the temporizing focused by the Industrial Revolution, which I pursue below.

I began these remarks by saying that transnationality has severely damaged the possibilities of social redistribution in developing nations. Restated in the context of the argument from civil societies, we might say that transnationality is shrinking the possibility of an operative civil society in developing nations. The story of these nations can be incanted by the following formulas since the Industrial Revolution: colonialism, imperialism, neocolonialism, transnationality. In the shift from imperialism to neocolonialism in the middle of this century, the most urgent task that increasingly backfired was the very establishment of a civil society. We call this the failure of decolonization. And in transnationality, possibilities of redressing this failure are being destroyed. I do not think it is incorrect to say that much of the new diaspora is determined by the increasing failure of a civil society in developing nations.

Strictly speaking, the undermining of the civil structures of society is now a global situation. Yet a general contrast can be made: in the North, welfare structures long in place are being dismantled. The diasporic underclass is often the worst victim. In the South, welfare structures cannot emerge as a result of the priorities of the transnational agencies. The rural poor and the urban subproletariat are the worst victims. In both these sectors, women are the superdominated, the superexploited, but *not in the same way*. And, even in the North, the formerly imperial European countries are in a different situation from the U.S. or Japan. And in the South, the situations of Bangladesh and India, of South Africa and Zaire are not comparable. Political asylum, at first sight so different from economic migration, finally finds it much easier to recode capitalism as democracy. It too, then, inscribes itself in the narrative of the manipulation of civil social structures in the interest of the financialization of the globe.

Elsewhere I have proposed the idea of the rise of varieties of theocracy, fascism, and ethnic cleansing as the flip side of this particular loosening of the hyphen between nation and state, the undermining of the civil structures of society. Here I want to emphasize that, as important as the displacement of "culture"—which relates to the first word in the compound, "nation," and is an ideological arena—is the exchange of state, which is an abstract area of calculation. Women, with other disenfranchised groups, have never been full subjects of and agents in civil society: in other words, first-class citizens of a state. And the mechanisms of civil society, although distinct from the state, are peculiar to it. And now, in transnationality, precisely because the limits and openings of a particular civil society are never transnational, the transnationalization of global capital requires a poststate class system. The use of women in its establishment is the universalization of feminism of which the United Nations is increasingly becoming the instrument. In this reterritorialization, the collaborative nongovernmental organizations are increasingly being called an "international civil society," precisely to efface the rôle of the state. Saskia Sassen, although her confidence in the mechanisms of the state remains puzzling, has located a new "economic citizenship" of power and legitimation in financial capital markets.[8] Thus elite, upwardly mobile (generally academic) women of the new diasporas join hands with similar women in the so-called developing world to celebrate a new global public or private "culture," often in the name of the underclass.[9]

Much work has been done on the relationship between the deliberate withholding of citizenship and internal colonization. In her "Organizational Resistance to Care: African American Women in Policing," Mary Texeira has recently cited Mike Davis's idea of the "designer drug-busts" in Los Angeles as "easy victor[ies] in a drug 'war' that the LAPD secretly loves losing."[10] Michael Kearney shows vividly how the U.S. Border Patrol keeps the illegal migrants illegal on the Mexican border.[11] The state can use their labor but must keep them out of civil society. In Marx's terms, capital extends its mode of exploitation but not its mode of social production. In Amin's, the periphery must remain feudalized. In Walter Rodney's, underdevelopment must be developed.[12]

In other words, are the new diasporas quite new? Every rupture is also a repetition. The only significant difference is the use, abuse, participation, and rôle of women. In broad strokes within the temporizing thematics of the Industrial Revolution, let us risk the following: like the Bolshevik experiment, imperial and nationalist feminisms have also prepared the way for the abstract itinerary of the calculus of capital. "Body As Property" is an episode in "The Eighteenth Brumaire of Bella Abzug."

The study of diasporic women and the ambivalent use of culture in access to a national civil society is a subject of immense complexity whose surface has been barely scratched in terms of such cases as the *hijab* debates in France. What is woman's relationship to cultural explanations in the nation-state of origin? What is "culture" without the structural support of the state? And, as I have been insisting, the issue is different for women who are no longer seriously diasporic with reference to the modern state. This difference was brought home to me forcefully when a new diasporic student of mine, because her notion of citizenship was related to getting citizenship papers, was unable quite to grasp the following remark by Jean Franco: " The imperative for Latin American women is thus not only the occupation and transformation of public space, the seizure of citizenship, but also the recognition that speaking as a woman within a pluralistic society may actually reinstitute, in a disguised form, the same relationship of privilege that has separated the intelligentsia from the subaltern classes."[13]

Franco is suggesting, of course, that even women who resist and reject their politico-cultural description and collectively take the risk of acting as subjects of and agents in the civil society of their nation-state are not necessarily acting for all women.

In the case of *Martinez vs. Santa Clara Pueblo,* where by tribal law the mother cannot claim child custody because her divorced husband belongs to another tribe and the Supreme Court refuses to interfere, Catherine MacKinnon invokes, among other things, the matriarchal tribal laws of yore.[14] A transnational perspective would have allowed her to perceive this as the colonizing technique of all settler colonies: to create an artificial enclave within a general civil society to appease the rising patriarchal sentiments of the colonized. As the Women's Charter of the ANC pointed out forty years ago, invoking culture in such contexts is dangerous.[15]

I have suggested above that the boundaries of civil societies mark out the state but are still nationally defined. I have further suggested that a hyperreal class-consolidated civil society is now being produced to secure the poststatist conjuncture, even as religious nationalisms and ethnic conflict can be seen as "retrogressive" ways of negotiating the transformation of the state in capitalist postmodernization. Feminists with a transnational consciousness will also be aware that the very civil structure *here* that they seek to shore up for gender justice can continue to participate in providing alibis for the operation of the major and definitive transnational activity, the financialization of the globe, and thus the suppression of the possibility of decolonization—the establishment and consolidation of a civil society *there*, the only means for an efficient and continuing calculus of gender justice *everywhere*.

The painstaking cultivation of such a contradictory, indeed aporetic, practical acknowledgment is the basis of a decolonization of the mind. The disenfranchised new or old diasporic woman cannot be called upon to inhabit this aporia. Her entire energy must be spent upon successful transplantation or insertion into the new state, often in the name of an old nation in the new. She is the site of global public culture privatized: the proper subject of real migrant activism. She may also be the victim of an exacerbated and violent patriarchy which operates in the name of the old nation as well—a sorry simulacrum of women in nationalism. Melanie Klein has allowed us the possibility of thinking this male violence as a reactive displacement of the envy of the Anglos and the Anglo clones, rather than proof that the culture of origin is necessarily more patriarchal.[16]

The disenfranchised woman of the diaspora—new and old—cannot, then, engage in the *critical* agency of civil society—citizenship in the most robust sense—to fight the depradations of "global economic citizenship." This is not to silence her but rather to desist from guilt-tripping her. For her the struggle is for access to its subjectship of the civil society of her new state: basic civil rights. Escaping from the failure of decolonization at home and abroad, she is not yet so secure in the state of desperate choice or chance as even to conceive of ridding her mind of the burden of transnationality. But perhaps her daughters or granddaughters—whichever generation arrives on the threshold of tertiary education—can. And the interventionist academic can assist them in this possibility rather than participate in their gradual indoctrination into an unexamined culturalism. This group of gendered outsiders inside are much in demand by the transnational agencies of globalization for employment and collaboration. It is therefore not altogether idle to ask that they should think of themselves collectively not as victims below but agents above, resisting the consequences of globalization as well as redressing the cultural vicissitudes of migrancy.

This, then, is something like the situation of diasporas, and, in that situation, of our implied reader. The image of the classroom has already entered as a sort of threshold of description for the latter. Therefore we might well speak of classroom teaching. The so-called "immediate experience" of migrancy is not necessarily consonant with transnational literacy, just as the suffering of individual labor is not consonant with the impetus of socialized resistance. In order that a transnationally literate resistance may, in the best case, develop, academic interventions may therefore be necessary; and we should not, perhaps, conflate the two.

Even if one is interventionist only in the academy, there are systemic problems, of course. And I do not intend to minimize them. It is again because of constraints on time that I am reminding ourselves only of the methodological *problems*. The first one is that the academy operates on the trickle down theory, with rather a minor change in the old dominant, which is that the essence of knowledge is knowledge about knowledge, and if you know the right thing your mind will change, and if your mind changes you will do good. I know how one must fight to change the components of academic knowledge. Nonetheless one cannot fall into the habit of mere descriptive ideology-critical analyses—incidentally often called "deconstruction"—and reproduce one's own kind in an individualistic and competitive system in the name of transnationalism. We must remind ourselves that knowledge and thinking are halfway houses, that they are judged when they are set to work.

Perhaps this can break our vanguardism that knowledge is acquired to be applied. I have tried to suggest that setting thought to work within the U.S. civil structure in the interest of domestic justice is not necessarily a just intervention in transnationality. Thus we confront an agenda as impossible as it is necessary.

It is in the spirit of such speculation that I will move now to some thoughts about intervention only in the academy. In the fall of 1993 I attempted to teach a course on global feminist theory. I will share with you some of the lessons I learnt during the semester. My earlier examples from Jean Franco and Catherine McKinnon are from that class, from the Latin and North American weeks respectively.

This is a list-making kind of essay. This part too will be a list of problems. The book list is long and I will pick only a few items on it. I have generally assigned collective responsibility for the problems. Of course that was not always the case. What I say will seem simple, but to implement what we proposed to ourselves and to make a habit of it is difficult, certainly more difficult than inspirational political talk in the name of transnationality that silently presupposes a civil structure.

Starting with Ifi Amadiume's *Male Daughters, Female Husbands,* we had our first problem: the internalization of European-style academic training.[17] All but one student was against Eurocentrism. But they valued noncontradiction above all else. (Students who come to my poststructuralism seminar can be coerced into relaxing this requirement. But global feminism is a tougher proposition. And, given the subdivision of labor in my institution at the moment and the reputation of the English Department, there were no Black students.) Amadiume, a Nigerian diasporic in London, wasn't doing too well by those standards. The only alternative the class could envision was the belligerent romanticization of cultural relativism. What seems contradictory to Europeans may not to Africans? Nigerians? Ibos? I am not an Africanist and have been faulted for wanting to study African feminism in a general course. But even to me these relativist positions seemed offensive.

A combination of this impatience with illogic hardly covered over with relativist benevolence has now become the hallmark of UN-style feminist universalism.[18] I think it is therefore counterproductive today to keep out resistant nonnatives or nonspecialists from speaking on the obstacles to transnational literacy as they arise with reference to different points on the map. At any rate, I learned to propose that we look always at what was at stake, a question that seemed to be much more practical than the litany of confessional or accusatory, but always determinist, descriptions of so-called "subject-positions."

I did not of course have the kind of insider's knowledge of Amadiume's place in the African field that I would have had if I had been an African or an Africanist. It did however seem fairly clear from Amadiume's text that she was pitting her own academic preparation in the house of apparent noncontradiction against "my knowledge of my own people":

When in the 1960s and 1970s female academics and western feminists began to attack social anthropology, riding on the crest of the new wave of
women's studies, the issues they took on were androcentrism and sexism.
[She cites Michelle Rosaldo, Louise Lamphere, and Rayna Reiter, among
others.] The methods they adopted indicated to Black women that white
feminists were no less racist than the patriarchs of social anthropology whom
they were busy condemning for male bias.

If we take the magnitude of her predicament into account, we can look at the book
as a strategic intervention.

Another problem that some found with Amadiume and that was to surface
again and again through the semester with reference to material from different geographical areas was that the traditional gender systems seemed too static and too
rigid. Once again, I asked the class to consider the politics of the production of theory. Amadiume is an anthropologist by training. Africa has been a definitive object
of anthropology. Oral traditions do not represent the dynamism of historicity in a
way that we in the university recognize. And orality cannot be an *instrument* for
historicizing in a book that we can read in class. I reminded myself silently of Derrida's tribute to the mnemic graph in orality: "The genealogical relation and social
classification are the stitched seam of arche-writing, condition of the (so-called oral)
language, and of writing in the colloquial sense."[19] Neither Amadiume nor her
readers have at their command the memory active within an oral tradition as a
medium. The only kind of thing we are capable of recognizing is where the technical instrument is European and the references alone are bits of "ethnic" idiom, such
as Mnouchkine's *Oresteia*, or Locsin's *Ballet Philippine*. But Amadiume is *questioning* the European technical instrument, from within, with no practical access to the
instrumentality of her tradition, which makes a poorer showing in a medium not
its own.[20] Of course, the traditional gender system will seem "too static" by contrast
with the system we fight within.

In addition, as I have pointed out, traditional gender systems have been used to
appease colonized patriarchy by the fabrication of personal codes as opposed to imposed colonial civil and penal codes. They have also been the instrument for working out the displaced envy of the colonized patriarchy against the colonizer. We
must learn to look at customary law as a site of struggle, not as a competitor on a
dynamism count. This became most evident in our readings on Southern Africa.

But let me linger another moment on the question of what is at stake: who is
addressed, within what institution? The class seemed to be most comfortable with
the work of Niara Sudarkasa (Gloria A. Marshall) from the Department of Anthropology at the University of Michigan, a woman from an old U.S. diaspora, produced through a reputable U.S. university, who has taken a name from her cultural

origin and is explaining that cultural material to other U.S. tertiary students. I am not asking us to denigrate the evident excellence of her work. I am asking us to consider that our approval comes from the comfort of a shared cultural transcription, cultural difference domesticated and transcoded for a shared academic audience. Reading Filomena Steady's *Black Women Cross-Culturally*, I asked the students to read the notes on contributors as texts: what is at stake, who is addressed, what institution, *cui bono*?[21]

Given the difference, for example, between the liberal University of Cape Town and the radical University of the Western Cape, I could not dismiss out of hand a Black man teaching customary law at the former institution as yet another academic. Indeed, the inventive constitutional transmogrification of customary law in some Southern African feminist constitutionalist work, in order that the frontage road to the highway of constitutional subjectship can be left open for the subaltern woman, attempts to face the contradiction which Jean Franco signals. We must learn to make a distinction between the demand, in itself worthy, for the museumization of national or national-origin "cultures" within the instrumentality of an alien and oppressive civil society, and these attempts to invent a gendered civility. In this latter struggle, civil concerns within the new nation under duress must be aware of the threat of economic transnationalization, whose euphemistic description is "Development," capital D, and the lifting of the barriers between international capital and developing national economies euphemistically known as liberalization. Let us, for example, look at the warning issued by Mary Maboreke, Professor of Law at the University of Zimbabwe:

> Zimbabwe attained independence on 18 April 1980. . . . As of 1 October 1990, Zimbabwe abandoned its strict trade controls over trade liberalization. . . . [T]he new economic order flash[es] a warning light. . . . All the gains made so far would vanish. . . . Analyses of how deregulation programmes affected women should have been done before the problems arose. It is now rather late to demand the necessary guarantees and protections. As it is we have lost the initiative and are now limited to reacting to what authorities initiate.[22]

Unless we are able to open ourselves to the grounding feeling, however counterintuitive, that First World diasporic women are, by the principles of the case, on the other side from Maboreke, we will not be able to think transnationality in its transnational scope, let alone act upon it. We "know" that to ground thinking upon feeling cannot be the basis of theory, but that "is" how theory is "judged in the wholly other," that "is" the "ghost of the undecidable" in every decision, that "is" how the "truth" of work is set or posited [*gesetzt*] in the work(ing), that is why logocentrism is not a pathology to be exposed or corrected, that is how we are disclosed and effaced in so-called human living; we cannot get around it in the name of academic or arty antiessentialism.

When a prominent section of Australian feminists claim uniqueness by virtue of being "femocrats," namely being systemically involved in civil society, we can certainly learn from them, but we might also mark their "sanctioned ignorance" of the Southern African effort, sanctioned, among others, by themselves and us.[23] Some of us in the class pointed out that faith in constitutionality was betrayed after the Civil Rights struggle with the advent of the Reagan-Bush era. This certainly seems plausible in the U.S. context. But this too is to universalize the United States as ground of evidence, one of the banes of United Nations feminism. Academic efforts at thinking global feminism must avoid this at all costs. The ungendered and unraced U.S. Constitution was and is widely supposed to be the first full flowering of the Enlightened State. To be foiled by its conservative strength is not to be equated with the attempt to put together a new constitution in Southern Africa—Zimbabwe, Botswana, Namibia, and now South Africa—and to strive to make it gender-sensitive from the start. If the U.S. experience is taken as *historically* determining, it is, whether we like it or not, Eurocentric. Philosophically, on the other hand, a persistent critique—that the subject of the Constitution is the site of a peformative passed off as a constative, that the restricted universalism of all ethno-customary systems share in some such ruse, that all contemporary constitutions are male-reactively gendered—seems appropriate from those who have earned the right to practice it, so that a constitution is seen as dangerous and powerful; as a means, a skeleton, a halfway house.[24]

I have repeatedly suggested that the word "Development" covers over the economics and epistemics of transnationality. "Women in Development" can be its worst scam. Nowhere is this more evident than in Southeast Asia. This taught us (in the class) the importance of checking the specificity of imperial formations in our consideration of the woman of each region. For it is in the clash and conflict of imperial subject formation, indigenous/customary law, and regulative psychobiographies (the history of which we cannot enter without a solid foundation in local languages) that the track of women in the history of the transnational present can be haltingly followed.

In the case of Southeast Asia, for example, we have to follow the uneven example of U.S. imperialism and the culture of development proper—export-processing zones, international subcontracting, post-Fordism and how it reconstitutes women. Aihwa Ong helped us see how the conventional story of colonialism and patriarchy will not allow us to solve the problem.[25] Her most telling object of investigation is so-called examples of mass hysteria among women in the workplace, and her analytical tool is Foucauldian theory. Although Ong herself is impeccable in the politics of her intellectual production, she, like the rest of us, cannot be assured of a transnationally literate audience in the United States in the current conjunctures. The habit of difference between using "high theory" to diagnose the suffering of the exploited or dominated on the one hand, and a self-righteous unexamined empiricism or "experiencism" on the other produces the problem of recognizing theory when it does not come dressed in appropriate language. Foucault is full dress, and we had less difficulty in gaining mastery over our material by way of his speculations when used by a developing-nation-marked U.S. diasporic, especially since the instructor's position of authority was also occupied by a similar subject, namely, Gayatri Spivak. When we resist this within the U.S. field, our only route seems to be an altogether antitheoreticist position, privileging anything that is offered by nongovernmental activists and their constituencies, not to mention writers who describe them with a seemingly unmediated combination of statistics and restrained pathos. I cannot, at this fast clip, walk with you through learning and earning the right to discriminate among positions offered by "participants." Let me simply say here that out of all the good and fact-filled books on Southeast Asia we read, when we encountered, at the end of Noeleen Heyzer's painstaking book, *Working Women in South-East Asia,* full of activist research, words I am about to quote presently, we had difficulty recognizing theory because it was not framed in a Heideggerian staging of care, or a Derridean staging of responsibility.[26] But here *is* theory asking to be set into—posited in—the work (at least, as long as we are in the classroom) of reading, a task that would inform—and indeed this is what I have been trying to say in these crowded pages—an impossible and necessary task that would inform the overall theme of the conference where these words were first uttered beyond the outlines of the diasporic subject into transnationality; and make indeterminate the borders between the two.

> Women are culturally perceived as really responsible for tasks associated with the private sphere, especially of the family. . . . It is . . . in the public sphere that bonds of solidarity are formed with others sharing similar views of the world. . . . [Yet] many cultures perceive the need to "protect" women from being exposed to these. . . . [By contrast, t]he task ahead is certainly to spread the ethics of care and concern. This concern entails an alternative conception or vision of what is possible in human society . . . a vision in which everyone will be responded to. . . .

Let us linger a moment on the possibility of rethinking the opposition between diaspora and globality in the name of woman, *if* we can all recognize theory in activist feminist writing (since in the house of theory there is still a glass ceiling). In

Situating the Self, Seyla Benhabib is clearly looking for a more robust thinking of responsibility to supplement masculinist political philosophies that radiate out from social needs and rights thinking.[27]

She cannot, however, conceive of the South as a locus of criticism. Her companions are all located in the North:

> Communitarian critics of liberalism like Alasdair MacIntyre, Michael Sandel, Charles Taylor and Michael Walzer . . . [f]eminist thinkers like Carol Gilligan, Carole Pateman, Susan Moller Okin, Virginia Held, Iris Young, Nancy Fraser, and Drucilla Cornell . . . [p]ostmodernists, . . . by which we have come to designate the works of Michel Foucault, Jacques Derrida and Jean-François Lyotard. . . .

Following the Euro-U.S. history of the division between public and private as male and female, her particular prophet is Carol Gilligan. She cannot find responsibility except in the private sphere of the family and perhaps, today—though one cannot readily see why this is specifically modern—in friendship. She cannot, of course, recognize an altogether more encompassing thought of responsibility in what she calls "postmodernism."[28] But neither "postmodernism" nor Benhabib can acknowledge the battering of women in their normality by way of notions of responsibility.[29] It is left to women like Heyzer to recognize that responsibility—the impossible vision of responding to all—has the greatest chance of animating the ethical in the public sphere of women in development when it becomes another name for superexploitation, precisely because in such a case feminine responsibility is conveniently defined, by the enemy, as it were, within the public sphere.[30] Here the incessant movements of restricted diasporas become more instructive than the cultural clamor of Eurocentric economic migration.

When Lily Moya, thwarted in her attempt to move from subalternity into organic intellectuality, runs away into Sophiatown and says, "the witchdoctor is menstruation" and "My life was a transfer," even so astute a writer as Shula Marks looks for a diagnosis.[31] In the comfort of our fourth-floor seminar room, we were learning to recognize theory in unconventional representations, "philosophy in the text of metaphor."[32] Moya's propositions were to us as much of a challenge as "man is a rational animal."

On page 129 of *Beyond the Veil,* a common Arabic women's expression is quoted: *Kunt haida felwlad.*[33] It is rather a pity that Fatima Mernissi translates this as: "I was preoccupied with children." If we translate this literally as "I was then in boys," we a get a theoretical lever. "Boys" for all "children" packs the same punch as "man" for all persons. And if we take that "in" and place it against the gynocidal thrust of the International Council on Population and Development connected to capital export and capital maximization—the correct description of transnationality—we come to understand the killing schizophrenia which these women suffer, caught in the unresolved contradiction of abusive pharmaceutical coercion to long-term or permanent contraception on the one side and ideological coercion to phallocentric reproduction on the other.[34] And *devenir-femme* in Deleuze's and Guattari's *Capitalism and Schizophrenia* can then undergo a feminist reinscription which is parasitical to the authors' *pouvoir-savoir*.[35]

I touch here upon the crucial topic of the task of the feminist translator as informant. Diaspora entails this task and permits its negligent performance. For diasporas also entail, at once, a necessary loss of contact with the idiomatic indispensability of the mother tongue. In the unexamined culturalism of academic diasporism, which ignores the urgency of transnationality, there is no one to check uncaring translations that transcode in the interest of dominant feminist knowledge.

I began these remarks with a list of the groups that a title such as ours cannot grasp. I then rewrote their name as "those who have stayed in place for more than thirty thousand years," as the limit to the authorized temporizing of our civilization as leading to and proceeding from the Industrial Revolution, the experience of the impossible that opens the calculus of resistance to transnationality. I suggested then that we are called by this limit only by way of battered and gender-compromised versions of responsibility-based ethical systems. Just as for the women of each geopolitical region, we have to surmise some network of response or reaction to hegemonic and/or imperialist subject-constitutions; to distinguish the heterogeneities of the repositories of these systems one calculates the moves made by different modes of settler colonizations. And out of the remnants of one such settlement we were able to glean a bit of theory that gave the lie to ontopology and to identitarian culturalisms.

This lesson in theory is contained in the philosopheme "lost our language," used by Australian aborigines of the East Kimberly region.[36] This expression does not mean that the persons involved do not know their aboriginal mother tongue. It means, in the words of a social worker, that "they have lost touch with their cultural base." They no longer compute with it. It is not their software. Therefore what these people, who are the inheritors of settler colonial oppression, ask for is, quite appropriately, mainstream education, insertion into civil society, and the inclusion of some information about their culture in the curriculum—under the circumstances, the only practical request. The concept-metaphor "language" is here standing in for that word which names the main instrument for the performance of the temporizing that is called life. What the aboriginals are asking for is hegemonic access to chunks of narrative and descriptions of practice so that a representation of that instrumentality becomes available for performance as what is called theatre (or art, or literature, or indeed culture, even theory).[37] Given the rupture between the many languages of aboriginality and the waves of migration and colonial adventure clustered around the Industrial Revolution narrative, demands for multilingual education would be risible.[38]

What will happen to the woman's part in the lost "software," so lovingly described by Diane Bell in *Daughters of the Dreaming*, is beyond or short of verification.[39] For "culture" is changeful, and emerges when least referenced. This lesson I have learned, for example, by way of the displacement of the scattered subaltern anticolonialist ghost-dance initiative among the First Nations of the North American continent in the 1890s, then into political protest within the civil society at Wounded Knee in the 1970s and its current literary/authentic multiculturalist feminist transformations in Silko's *Almanac of the Dead*.[40]

For reasons of time, appropriate also because of my unease about academic identity politics in these transnationalizing times, South Asia, the place of my citizenship, the United States, the source of my income, and Northwestern Europe, the object of my limited expertise, remained blank on the first time of these remarks. And, apart from reasons of time at this second time, these omissions still seem appropriate. We certainly enjoyed reading some texts of Italian feminism.[41] But it was remarkable that, although diasporic Third World women offer large-scale support, through homeworking, to Italy's postindustrial base, and Benetton is one of the leaders in the field of post-Fordist feminization of transnationality, these women and this phenomenon were never mentioned. The class discussions of civil society around the Italian feminists' expressed concerns were therefore interesting, especially since we followed up Swasti Mitter's documentation in her own work on economic restructuring in general.[42] Lack of time will not allow me to touch on the new postcoloniality in post-Soviet Asia and the Balkans; nor on the reasons why East Asia defeated me. These two complex issues do not fit within the broad lines I have laid out. Here's why, briefly.

The historical narratives which constituted "the Balkans" and "inner Asia" as regions are, in themselves, profoundly dissimilar. Yet, by way of their unified definition as Soviet Bloc, and thus their equally single dismantling, albeit into a disclosure of their heterogeneous historicity, they *seem* similar. Our temporizing is organized not only around the Industrial Revolution but also around single-nation empires. To see the uneven sovietization of the "Soviet Bloc" in terms of the precapitalist multinational empires as well as the Asian bloc, we must examine the difference betwee Lenin's and Stalin's versions of imperialism and nationalism.[43] Although the unifying bulldozer of financialization is at work in the pores of the Balkans and the Transcaucasus—USAID building a "civic society" in Bosnia, the IMF pressuring Armenia to settle the Nagorno-Karabakh issue before loans are assured—the general question of the diaspora, as perceived by remote-control bleeding-heart feminism, is so patheticized by the human interest that can fill in the loosened hyphen between nation and state that questions of transnationality cannot be considered within a general feminist conference or course. Inner Asia, by contrast, seems only too ready for anthologization into feminism. This may be a result of the existence of a small Russianized corps of emancipated bourgeois women in this sector. But who will gauge their separation from the subaltern, from Asian Islam—how, in more senses than one, they have "lost their language" without being in the almost tempoless temporizing of the aboriginal limit? A new sort of subaltern studies is needed there, for which the appropriate discipline is history and an intimate knowledge of the local languages an absolute requirement. This is all the more necessary because this region's "liberation" comes concurrently with the United Nations' consolidation for a culturally relativist feminist universalism making the world ultimately safe for Capital. My minimal attempts at tracking this region's preparation for the Fourth World Women's Conference organized by the United Nations at Beijing (1995) increases a conviction that the constitution of "woman" as object-beneficiary of investigation and "feminist" as subject-participant of investigation is as dubious here as elsewhere. I have not the languages for touching the phenomenon. And therefore it fits neither my syllabus nor our title.

And East Asia. As controlling capital, often a major player with the North. As superexploited womanspace, one with the South and its nonelite networks. Hong Kong unravelling the previous conjuncture, territorial imperialism, the mark of Britain. China unravelling a planned economy to enter the U.S.-dominated new empire. Economic miracle and strangulation of civil society in Vietnam. New World Asians (the old migrants) and New Immigrant Asians (often "model minorities") being disciplinarized together. How will I understand feminist self-representation here? How set it to work? How trust the conference circuit? A simple academic limit, marked by a promise of future work.

To end with a warning. In the untrammeled financialization of the globe which is the New International Order, women marked by origins in the developing nations yet integrated or integrating into the U.S. or EEC civil structure are a useful item. Gramsci uncannily predicted in his jail cell that the U.S. would use its minorities in this way.[44] And remember Clarice Lispector's story, "The Smallest Woman in the World," where the pregnant pygmy woman is the male anthropologist's most authentic object of reverence?[45] It is as if these two ingredients should combine. An example:

A little over a decade ago, I wrote a turgid piece called "Can the Subaltern Speak?" The story there was of a seventeen-year old woman who had hanged herself rather than kill, even in the armed struggle against Imperialism, and in the act had tried to write a feminist statement with her body, using the script of menstruation to assert a claim to the public sphere which could not be received into what may be called a "speech act." Hence I lamented about this singular (non)event: "The subaltern cannot speak." Her name was Bhubaneswari Bhaduri.

Bhubaneswari's elder sister's eldest daughter's eldest daughter's eldest daughter is a new U.S. immigrant and has just been promoted to an executive position in a U.S.-based transnational. This too is a historical silencing of the subaltern. When the news of this young woman's promotion was broadcast in the family amidst general jubilation I could not help remarking to the eldest surviving female member: "Bhubaneswari"—her nickname had been Talu—"hanged herself in vain," but not too loudly. Is it any wonder that this young woman is a staunch multiculturalist, wears only cotton, and believes in natural childbirth?

There are, then, at least two problems that come with making the diaspora definitive: first, that we forget that postnationalist (NGO) talk is a way to cover over the decimation of the state as instrument of redistribution and redress. To think transnationality as labor migrancy, rather than one of the latest forms of appearance of postmodern capital, is to work, however remotely, in the ideological interest of the financialization of the globe.

And, secondly, it begins from the calculus of hybridity, forgetting the impossible other vision (just, perhaps, but not "pure") of civilization, "the loss of language" at the origin.

Meaghan Morris had apparently remarked to Dipesh Chakrabarty that most trashings of "Can the Subaltern Speak?" read the title as "Can the Subaltern Talk?" I will not improve upon that good word. I will simply thank Meaghan Morris for her witty support, as I will thank Abena Busia, Wahneema Lubiano, Geraldine Heng, Cassandra Kavanaugh, Ellen Rooney, Rey Chow, Jean Franco, and others for making the syllabus possible; and the members of my seminar at Columbia in fall 1993 and at the University of California-Riverside in spring 1994 for teaching me with what responsibility we, women in a transnational world, must address ourselves to the topic: "Diasporas Old and New."

An Unfinishable Syllabus: Always to be Updated

Spivak   Feminist Theory   Fall 93

I. Sub-Saharan Africa

Ifi Amadiume, *Male Daughters, Female Husbands: Gender and Sex in African Society* (London: Zed Books, 1987).

Filomina Chioma Steady, ed., *The Black Woman Cross-Culturally* (Rochester, NY: Schenkman, 1981), Introduction and essays by Sudarkasa, Aidoo, Urdang, Gugler, Pala, Hine and Wittenstein, Terborg-Penn, Staples.

II. N. Africa

Assia Djebar, *Women of Algiers in Their Apartment* (Charlottesville, VA: University Press of Virginia, 1992).

Fatima Mernissi, *Beyond the Veil: Male-Female Dynamics in Modern Muslim Society* (London: Al Saqi, 1985).

III. S. Africa

Susan Bazilli, ed., *Putting Women on the Agenda* (Cape Town: Ravan Press, 1991), Introduction and essays by Zama, Ginwala, Mabandla, Nhlapo, Gwagwa, Maboreke, Gawanas, Dow.

Shula Marks, ed., *Not Either an Experimental Doll* (Bloomington, IN: Indiana University Press, 1987).

IV. S. Asia

Bina Agarwal, ed., *Structures of Patriarchy: State Community and Household in Modernizing Asia* (London: Zed Books, 1988), essays by Agarwal, Schrijvers, Phongpaichit, Srinivasan.

Kumkum Sangari and Sudesh Vaid, eds., *Recasting Women: Essays in Colonial History* (New Delhi: Kali for Women, 1989), Introduction and essays by Chakravarti, Mani, Banerjee, Kannabiran and Lalitha, Chatterjee, Tharu.

V. South-East Asia

Noeleen Heyzer, *Daughters in Industry: Work, Skills and Consciousness of Women Workers in Asia* (Kuala Lumpur: Asian and Pacific Development Center, 1988), Chap. 1 (pp. 3–32), Chaps. 8, 9, 10, 11 (pp. 237–326), Chap. 13 (pp. 356–384).

_____, *Working Women in South East Asia*, Introduction and Chaps. 1, 4, 7, 8.

Saskia Wieringa, ed., *Women's Struggles and Strategies* (Aldershot, UK: Gower Publishing, 1988), Introduction and Chap. 5 (pp. 69–89).

Aihwa Ong, *Spirits of Resistance and Capitalist Discipline: Factory Women in Malaysia* (Albany, NY: SUNY Press, 1987), Chaps. 7, 8, 9, 10 (pp. 140–221).

VI. West Asia

Leila Ahmed, *Women and Gender in Islam: Historical Roots of a Modern Debate* (New Haven, CT: Yale University Press, 1992).

Smadar Lavie, *Poetics of Military Occupation: Mezeina Allegories of Bedouin Identity* (Berkeley, CA: University of California Press, 1990).

VII. Australia

Diane Bell, *Daughters of the Dreaming* (Minneapolis, MN: University of Minnesota Press, 1993).

Kaye Thies, *Aboriginal Viewpoints on Education: A Survey in the East Kimberley Region* (Needlands, Australia: University of Western Australia, 1987).

Selections from John Frow and Meaghan Morris, eds., *Australian Cultural Studies* (Champaign-Urbana, IL: University of Illinois Press, 1993).

Selections from *Australian Feminist Studies*.

VIII. Latin America

Elisabeth Burgos-Debray, ed., *I, Rigoberta Menchu: An Indian Woman in Guatemala* (London: Verso, 1984).

Juan Flores et al., eds., *On Edge: the Crisis of Contemporary Latin American Culture* (Minneapolis, MN: University of Minnesota Press, 1993), essay by Franco.

Jean Franco, *Plotting Women: Gender and Representation in Mexico* (New York: Columbia University Press, 1992).

Jane Jaquette, *The Women's Movement in Latin America: Feminism and the Transition to Democracy* (Boulder, CO: Westview, 1991), Introduction and pp. 72–148, 185–208.

NACLA Report on the Americas 27.1 (1993), pp. 19, 46–47.

Elizabeth Jelin, *Women and Social Change in Latin America* (London: Zed Books, 1990), Introduction and Part I, Chap. 2.

Selections from Heleieth Saffioti, *Women in Class Society* (New York: Monthly Review Press, 1978).

Steady, *The Black Woman Cross-Culturally,* essay by Nunes.

IX. U.S.

Judith Butler, *Gender Trouble: Feminism and the Subversion of Identity* (New York: Routledge, 1990).

Patricia Hill Collins, *Black Feminist Thought: Knowledge, Consciousness, and the Politics of Empowerment* (New York: Harper, 1991), Chaps. 2, 5, 6, 10.

bell hooks, *Black Looks: Race and Representation* (Boston: South End, 1992).

Catharine MacKinnon, *Feminism Unmodified: Discourses on Life and Law* (Cambridge, MA: Harvard University Press, 1987).

Steady, *The Black Woman Cross-Culturally,* Part II, Chaps. 2–6.

X. Italy

Sheila Allen and Carol Wolkowitz, *Homeworking: Myths and Realities* (London: Macmillan, 1987), pp. 170–171.

Paola Bono and Sandra Kemp, eds., *Italian Feminist Thought: A Reader* (London: Blackwell, 1991), Introduction and pp. 33–208, 260–283, 310–317, 339–367, Chronology.

Rosi Braidotti, "The Italian Women's Movement in the 1980s," *Australian Feminist Studies* 3 (Summer 1986).

Patricia Cicogna and Teresa de Lauretis, eds., *Sexual Differences: A Theory of Social-Symbolic Practice* (Bloomington, IN: Indiana University Press, 1990).

Mirna Cicogna, "Women Subjects and Women Projects,*" Australian Feminist Studies* 4 (Autumn 1987).

Swasti Mitter, "Industrial Restructuring and Manufacturing Homework: Immigrant Women in the U.K. Clothing Industry," *Capital and Class* 27, 47–49, 62, 75–76.

Selections from Enzo Mingione, "Social Reproduction of the Surplus Labor Force: The Case of

Italy," in Nanneka Redclift and Mingione eds., *Beyond Employment* (London: Macmillan, 1985).

XI. North-West Europe

Parveen Adams and Elizabeth Cowie, eds., *M/F* (Cambridge, MA: MIT Press, 1990), pp. 3–5, 21–44, 134–148, 274–282, 315–327, 345–356.

Frigga Haug and Others, *Female Sexualization: A Collective Work of Memory* (London: Verso, 1987).

Toril Moi, ed., *French Feminist Thought: A Reader* (London: Blackwell, 1987), essays by Beauvoir, Leclerc, Delphy, Kristeva, Irigaray, Le Doeuff, Kofman, Montrelay.

Denise Riley, *Am I That Name? Feminism and the Category of "Women" in History* (Minneapolis, MN: University of Minnesota Press, 1988).

XII. Post-Soviet Eurasia

Mary Buckley, *Perestroika and Soviet Women* (New York: Cambridge University Press, 1992).

Nanette Funk and Magda Mueller, eds., *Gender Politics and Post-Communism: Reflections from Eastern Europe and the Former Soviet Union* (New York: Routledge, 1993), Introduction and essays by Todorova, Harsanyi, Siklova, Kiczkova and Etela Farkasova, Milic, Duhacek, Bohm, Dolling, Adamik, Fuszara, Lissyutkina.

Helena Goscila, ed., *Fruits of Her Plume: Essays on Contemporary Russian Women's Culture* (Armonk, NY: M.E. Sharpe, 1993), essay by Ivanova.

Barbara Holland, ed., *Soviet Sisterhood* (Bloomington, IN: Indiana University Press, 1985), essays by McAndrew, Allott, Holt.

Selections from Gregory Massell, *Surrogate Proletariat* (Princeton, NJ: Princeton University Press, 1977).

Selections from R. Aminova, *The October Revolution and Women's Liberation in Uzbekistan* (Moscow: Nauka Publishing House, 1977).

Appendix

XIII. East Asia

(For lack of time, this area was not covered. What follows is a working bibliography on China which I will have to work through. Only one work and one journal covering Japan are included. Because the next time I teach this course student suggestions will allow me to shorten the reading list, I hope to be more inclusive).

Ray Chow, *Writing Diaspora: Tactics of Intervention in Contemporary Women's Studies* (Bloomington, IN: Indiana University Press, 1993).

Ono Kazuko, *Chinese Women in a Century of Revolution* (Stanford, CA: Stanford University Press, 1989).

Tonglin Lu, ed., *Gender and Sexuality: Twentieth-Century Chinese Literature and Society* (Albany, NY: SUNY Press, 1993).

Yayori Matsui, *Women's Asia* (London: Zed Books, 1989).

Janet W. Salaff, *Working Daughters of Hong Kong* (Cambridge, UK: Cambridge University Press, 1981).

Selections from *U.S.-Japan Women's Journal.*

Margery Wolf and Roxane Witke, *Women in Chinese Society* (Stanford, CA: Stanford University Press, 1975).

Notes

1. This chapter is the text of a talk delivered at Rutgers University in March 1994. It was previously published in another form in *Textual Practice* 10.2 (1996), pp. 245–269. The dynamic of women in diaspora is so fast moving that it is hopeless to attempt to "update" this. The reader might want to check Spivak, "'Woman' As Global Theatre: Beijing 1995," *Radical Philosophy* 75 (Jan-Feb 1996), 2–4, for the line of revision that I would take. Increasingly and metaleptically, transnationality is becoming the name of the increased migrancy of labor. To substitute this name for the change from multinational capital in the economic restructuring of the (developed/developing) globe—to recode a change in the determination of capital as a cultural change—is a scary symptom of Cultural Studies, especially feminist Cultural Studies.

2. As I will show later, the complexity of Farida Akhter's position is to be understood from the weave (or text-ile) of her work, not merely her verbal texts, which are, like all translations, not a substitute for the "original." Let me cite, with this proviso, Akhter, *Depopulating Bangladesh* (Dhaka: Narigrantha, 1992), and Malini Karkal, *Can Family Planning Solve the Population Problem?* (Bombay: Stree Uvach, 1989). The scene has been so Eurocentrically obfuscated that I hasten to add that this is not a so-called "pro-life" position, but rather a dismissal of Western (Northern) universalization of its domestic problems in the name of woman. See also Spivak, "Empowering Women?" *Environment* 27.I (Jan-Feb 1995), 2–3.

3. Ranajit Guha, "On Some Aspects of the Historiography of Colonial India," in Guha, ed. *Subaltern Studies: Writings on South Asian History and Society* (Delhi: Oxford University Press, 1982), p. 8.

4. Jacques Derrida, "White Mythology: Metaphor in the Text of Philosophy," in *Margins of Philosophy,* Alan Bass, trans. (Chicago: University of Chicago Press, 1982), p. 209.

5. In *Public Culture* 5.1 (Fall 1992).

6. For the usual debate on civil society between left and right, see Justin Rosenberg, *The Empire of Civil Society: A Critique of the Realist Theory of International Relations* (New York: Verso, 1994), and Ernest Gellner, *Conditions of Liberty: Civil Society and Its Rivals* (New York: Allen Lane, 1994).

7. I use "sup-pose" (rather than "pre-suppose," which presupposes the subject's agency) here in what I understand to be Derrida's sense in *The Other Heading: Reflections on Today's Europe*, Pascale-Anne Brault and Michael Naas, trans. (Bloomington, IN: Indiana University Press,

1992), p. 76. The word *suppose* is unfortunately translated "presuppose" in the English version. The imaginary map of geo-graphy as we understand it today has been traced by pushing the so-called aboriginals back, out, away, in. The story of the emergence of civil societies is sup-posed in that movement.

8. Saskia Sassen, *On Governance in the Global Economy* (New York: Columbia University Press, 1996.

9. The argument about feminist universalism propagated through the United Nations is beginning to invaginate this essay in its current revision. I am now convinced that the recoding of transnationality (an economic phenomenon) as people moving across frontiers is part of this propagation: capital being recoded into capital-ism. I have proposed elsewhere these United Nations initiatives in the name of woman have produced feminist apparatchiks whose activism is to organize the poorest women of the developing world incidentally in their own image ("train them to be women," in Christine Nicholls's bitter, felicitous phrase) primarily in the interest of generating research fodder according to the old dominant: the essence of knowledge is knowledge about knowledge. As part of this endeavor, some large U.S.-based organizations secure funds for nonelite NGOs in order to enrich their own databases or to redirect the latters' energies toward activities favored by the former: ideological manipulation of the simplest sort, rather like buying votes in the interest of "economic citizenship." Recently I have twice heard this kind of activity described by two different people as "working with" these NGOs. Here again the academic diasporic or minority woman thinking transnationality must be literate enough to ask: *cui bono*, working *for* whom, in what interest? In "The Body as Property: A Feminist Re-Vision" (in Faye Ginsburg and Rayna Rapp, eds., *Conceiving the New World Order,* Berkeley, CA: University of California Press, 1995), Rosalind Pollack Petchesky almost quotes Farida Akhter, a Bangladeshi activist, for a few lines, only to substitute Carol Pateman, whose "critique" seems to her to have an "affinity" with Akhter but to be "more systematic and encompassing" (395). Not content with silencing Akhter by substitution, she then proceeds to provide a "feminist" alternative to such "essentialism" by way of ethnography (New Guinea tribal women can't be different from women exploited by post-Fordism in Bangladesh!), sixteenth-century Paris, "the early-modern European origins of ideas about owning one's own body" among the women of the British Levellers, and, finally, the work of Patricia Williams, the African-American legal theorist. Here is her version of Akhter:

> Farida Akhter, a women's health activist and researcher in Bangladesh, condemns "the individual right of woman over her own body" as an "unconscious mirroring of the capitalist-patriarchal ideology . . . premised on the logic of bourgeois individualism and inner urge of private property." According to Akhter, the idea that a woman owns her body turns it into a "reproductive factory," objectifies it, and denies that reproductive capacity is a "natural power we carry within ourselves." Behind her call for a "new social relationship" with regard to this "natural power" of woman lies a split between "the natural"

woman and "the social" woman that brings Akhter closer to the essentialized embrace of "difference" by radical feminists than her Marxist framework might suggest. (pp. 394–395)

In *Capital I*, Marx writes that the pivot of socialist resistance is to understand that labor *power* is the only commodity which is the site of a dynamic struggle (*Zwieschlächtigkeit*) between the private and the socializable. If the worker gets beyond thinking of work as *Privatarbeit*, or individual work, and perceives it as a potential commodity (laborpower) of which s/he is the part-subject (since laborpower is an abstract average), s/he can begin to resist the appropriation of surplus value and turn capital toward social redistribution. As a person who is daily organizing struggles against transnationalization, Akhter expects familiarity with this first lesson of training for resistance. The trivial meaning of the proletarian is that s/he possesses nothing but the body and is therefore "free." If one remains stuck on that, there is no possibility of socialism, but only employment on the factory floor. This *Zwieschlächtigkeit* between "private" and "social" (labor and laborpower) is Akhter's "split between the 'natural' and the 'social.'" Notice that, in keeping with Marx, she uses "power," where Petechesky substitutes "woman." And indeed, there is a bit of a paradox here: that the "natural" in the human body should be susceptible to "socialization"! Why is Akhter speaking of a "reproductive power?" Because, as a person working against the depredations of capitalist/individualist reproductive engineering, she is daily aware that reproductive labor power has been socialized. When she calls for a "new social relationship," she is using it in the strict Marxist sense of "social relations of production." New because the Marxist distinction between all other commodities and laborpower will not hold here. The produced commodities are children, also coded within the affective value form, not things. U.S. personalism cannot think Marx's risky formulation of the resistant use of socialized laborpower, just as it reduces Freud's risky metapsychology to ego psychoanalysis. Further, since its implied subject is the agent of rights-based bourgeois liberalism, it cannot think of the owned body from the proletarian perspective, as a dead end road. It can only be the bearer of the "abstract" legal body coded as "concrete." (It is of course also true that U.S.-based UN feminism works in the interest of global financialization, a.k.a. Development. Here I should say of Petchesky what I have said of Brontë and Freud in "Three Women's Texts and a Critique of Imperialism," in Henry Louis Gates, Jr., ed., *"Race," Writing and Difference* [Chicago: University of Chicago Press, 1985], p. 263; and in "Can the Subaltern Speak?" in Cary Nelson and Lawrence Grossberg, eds., *Marxism and the Interpretation of Culture* [Champaign-Urbana, IL: University of Illinois Press, 1988], pp. 296–297. Akhter expresses similar sentiments more simply in "unconscious mirroring.") Incidentally, it is also possible that the split between "natural" and "social" is that split between species-life and species-being that the young Marx brings forward and displaces into his later work as that between the realm of freedom and the realm of necessity: the limit to planning. But it would take the tempo of classroom teaching to show how U.S.-based feminism cannot recognize theoretical sophistication in the South, which can only be the repository of an ethnographic "cultural difference." Here suffice it to say that Carol Pateman, with respect, is certainly not a more "systematic and encompassing" version of this. And you cannot answer the demand for a new social relation of production in the New World Order (post-Soviet financialization, patenting of the DNA of the subaltern body for pharmaceutical speculation, and so on) by citing anthropology and early-modern Europe. Indeed, it is not a question of citing colored folks against colored folks, but of understanding the analysis. But perhaps the worst moment is the use of Patricia Williams. I cannot comment on the ethico-political agenda of silencing the critical voice of the South by way of a woman of color in the North. It should at least be obvious that the abusive constitution of the body in chattel slavery is not the socialization of the body in exploitation. The matrilineality of slavery cannot be used as an effective alibi for the commodification of reproductive laborpower. Williams herself makes it quite clear that today's underclass African-American wants to *feel* ownership of the body in reaction against her specific history and situation. And that situation is the contradiction of the use of chattel slavery to advance industrial capitalism. Patricia Williams writes of this use, this passage within the U.S. juridico-legal system. She cannot be further used to "disprove" the conjunctural predicament of the South. Women in a transnational world—notice Petchesky's use of artistic representation as evidence through the diasporic artists Mira Nair and Meena Alexander, both of Indian origin; not to mention the fact that, in transnationalization, the cases of Bangladesh and India are altogether dissimilar—must beware of the politics of the appropriation of theory.

10. Mike Davis, *City of Quartz: Excavating the Future in Los Angeles* (New York: Vintage, 1992), p. 267.

11. Michael Kearney, "Borders and Boundaries: State and Self at the End of Empire," *Journal of Historical Sociology* 4.1 (March 1991), pp. 52–74.

12. Samir Amin, *Unequal Development: An Essay on the Social Formations of Peripheral Capitalism*, Brian Pearce, trans. (New York: Monthly Review Press, 1976); Walter Rodney, *How Europe Underdeveloped Africa* (Washington, DC: Howard University Press, 1981).

13. Jean Franco, *Plotting Women: Gender and Representation in Mexico* (New York: Columbia University Press, 1992), p. 11.

14. Catherine MacKinnon, *Feminism Unmediated: Discourses on Life and Law* (Cambridge, MA: Harvard University Press, 1987), pp. 63–69.

15. Raymond Suttner and Jeremy Cronin, eds., *Thirty Years of the Freedom Charter* (Johannesburg: Ravan Press, 1986), pp. 162–163.

16. Melanie Klein, *Envy and Gratitude* (London: Tavistock, 1957).

17. Ifi Amadiume, *Male Daughters, Female Husbands: Gender and Sex in African Society* (London: Zed Books, 1987). The passage quoted here on page 11 is from p. 9.

18. A discussion of the impossible situation of the Bangladesh garment industry, caught between World Bank pressure against unionization and post-GATT social dumping, resulting in the fetishization of child labor with a total incomprehension of the situation of urban subaltern children in Bangladesh, drew from a grant-rich "feminist" sociologist colleague, conversant with the depredations upon welfare in New York, the remark that one must of course remember cul-

tural difference! It had quite escaped this intellectual that I was speaking of Northern exploitation, not of some imagined Bangladeshi cultural preference for making children work! It's not much better with Southern academics. A similar discussion in Sri Lanka had elicited from a female graduate student the question: "Is Gayatri Spivak for child labor?"

19. Derrida, *Of Grammatology*, Spivak, trans. (Baltimore, MD: Johns Hopkins University Press, 1976), p. 125.

20. I have tried to describe a similar predicament for myself in "A Response to Jean-Luc Nancy," in Juliet Flower MacCannell and Lara Zakarin, eds., *Thinking Bodies* (Stanford, CA: Stanford University Press, 1994), pp. 39–48.

21. Filomina Chioma Steady, ed., *The Black Woman Cross-Culturally* (Rochester, NY: Schenkman, 1981).

22. "Women and Law in Post-Independence Zimbabwe: Experience and Lessons," Susan Bazilli, ed., *Putting Women on the Agenda* (Johannesburg: Ravan Press, 1991), pp. 215, 236–237.

23. Hester Eisenstein, "Speaking for Women? Voices from the Australian Femocrat Experiment," *Australian Feminist Studies* 14 (Summer 1991), 29–42.

24. Derrida, "Declarations of Independence," Thomas W. Keenan, trans., *New Political Science*, 15 (Summer 1986), 7–15. But here too we must remind ourselves that the feeling/thinking ground is what makes the critique persistent even as it foils it: disclosure, alas, in effacement. All uses of "deconstruction" as verb or noun are practically breached by this double bind. No use talking about infinite regress, for infinite progress is no different, only differant, in(de)finitely.

25. Aihwa Ong, *Spirits of Resistance and Capitalist Discipline: Factory Women in Malaysia* (Albany, NY: SUNY Press, 1987), Chaps. 7, 8, 9, 10 (pp. 140–221).

26. Noeleen Heyzer, *Working Women in South-East Asia: Development, Subordination, and Emancipation* (Philadelphia: Open University Press, 1986). The passage quoted is from pp. 131–132.

27. Seyla Benhabib, *Situating the Self: Gender, Community and Postmodernism in Contemporary Ethics* (New York: Routledge, 1992). The passage quoted is from pp. 2–3.

28. Thomas W. Keenan, *Fables of Responsibility: Aberrations and Predicaments in Ethics and Politics* (Stanford, CA: Stanford University Press, 1997).

29. Frigga Haug's excellent book, *Beyond Female Masochism: Memory-Work and Politics (Questions for Feminism)*, Rodney Livingstone, trans. (London: Verso Books, 1992), indispensable for consciousness raising, legitimizes the European history of the compromising of responsibility-in-gender by a mere reversal. To tease this out for responsibility-based systems requires a different sense of one's own position ("textuality"), a different agenda.

30. I am drawing on a big theme here, which I have merely touched upon by way of the notion of the difference between socialism and capitalism. (See Spivak, "Supplementing Marxism," in Stephen Cullenberg and Bernd Magnus, eds., *Whither Marxism?* [New York: Routledge, 1994], pp. 118–119.) Derrida puts these impossibilities in the place of the figuration of the gift, if there is any. But a thinker like Karl-Otto Apel would simply dismiss them as "utopian" ("Is the Ideal Communication Community a Utopia?" quoted in Benhabib, *Situating the Self*, p. 81). My

"experience" here is of young women working in the garment factories in Bangladesh, displaced from their family, seemingly on a superior footing to the unemployed young men on the street, and yet without any care taken to recode their ethical beings into the public. I admire Carol Gilligan, but to cite her here is an insult, for she must retrain herself with a different group under observation and with the instruction of experts in the field such as Heyzer. *Mutatis mutandis*, I encounter a similar problem with the industry in revising Freudo-Lacanian psychoanalysis in the name of feminist cultural studies.

31. Shula Marks, ed., *Not Either an Experimental Doll: the Separate Lives of Three South African Women* (Bloomington, IN: Indiana University Press, 1987), pp. 207, 209.

32. I am of course reversing the subtitle of that essay by Derrida, which I cited in note 4.

33. Fatima Mernissi, *Beyond the Veil: Male-Female Dynamics in Modern Muslim Society* (London: Al Saqi, 1985).

34. This contradiction is a *gendered* displacement of the broader contradiction, which has been pointed out in David Washbrook's essay "Law, State and Agrarian Society in Colonial India," *Modern Asian Studies* 15.3 (1981), pp. 649–721, that if colonial practice operated in the interest of capitalist social productivity, the indigenous practices within which local capitalisms flourished contradicted that interest. See Ritu Birla, "Hedging Bets: Politics of Commercial Ethics in Late Colonial India," Department of History, Columbia University, dissertation. The contradiction we are discussing is also a *classed* displacement of the earlier contradiction between emancipation and culturalism for women in the colonies.

35. Gilles Deleuze and Felix Guattari, *Anti-Oedipus: Capitalism and Schizophrenia*, Robert Hurley et. al., trans. (Minneapolis, MN: University of Minnesota Press, 1983).

36. Kaye Thies, *Aboriginal Viewpoints on Education: A Survey in the East Kimberley Region* (Needlands, Australia: University of Western Australia, 1987).

37. After the Massacre at Wounded Knee, Sitting Bull's cabin was taken to the 1892 Exposition at Chicago. This is claiming the right to theatre by the dominant, exactly the opposite of what we are commenting on. Or, not quite exactly. For the historically subordinated "had" the language to lose, which the dominant only destroyed. Somewhere in between is Buffalo Bill Cody, who acquired the freedom of Wounded Knee participants so that they could show "Wounded Knee." Today's restricted multicultural diasporists would find in Cody their prototype. It is Capital in the abstract that "frees" the subject of Eurocentric economic migration to stage "culture" in First World multiculturalism.

38. See Gordon Brotherston, *The Book of the Fourth World: Reading the Native Americas through Their Literature* (Cambridge, UK: Cambridge University Press, 1993), and, in the context of contemporary Canadian bilingualist struggle, Merwan Hassan, "Articulation and Coercion: The Bilingual Crisis in Canada, *Border/Lines* 36 (April 1995), pp. 28–35.

39. Diane Bell, *Daughters of the Dreaming* (Minneapolis, MN: University of Minnesota Press, 1993).

40. Leslie Marmon Silko, *Almanac of the Dead* (Harmondsworth, UK: Penguin, 1991).

41. Paola Bono and Sandra Kemp, eds., *Italian Feminist Thought: A Reader* (London: Black-

well, 1991); Patricia Cicogna and Teresa de Lauretis, eds., *Sexual Differences: A Theory of Social-Symbolic Practice* (Bloomington, IN: Indiana University Press, 1990); Mirna Cicogna, "Women Subjects and Women Projects," *Australian Feminist Studies* 4 (Autumn 1987); Rosi Braidotti, "The Italian Women's Movement in the 1980s," *Australian Feminist Studies* 3 (Summer 1986).

42. Swasti Mitter, "Industrial Restructuring and Manufacturing Homework: Immigrant Women in the U.K. Clothing Industry," *Capital and Class* 27, 47–49, 62, 75–76.

43. See Joseph Stalin, *Nationalism and the Colonial Question: A Collection of Articles and Speeches* (San Francisco: Proletarian Publishers, 1975); and V.I. Lenin, *Imperialism, the Highest Stage of Capitalism: A Popular Outline* (New York: International Publishers, 1939). Although Stalin constantly invokes Lenin in order to legitimize himself, Lenin is speaking of the northwestern European single-nation empires and their connections to the march of Capital, whereas Stalin is speaking of the Russian, Ottoman, and Habsburg empires, and the manipulation of their cultures and identities in the interest of forming something like a future new empire. Thus their lines lead toward finance capital and linguistic and cultural politics, respectively; in their current displacements, the economic phenomenon of transnationalization and its reterritorialization into migrant hybridity by multiculturalist diasporists, respectively.

44. See passage quoted in Mahasweta Devi, *Imaginary Maps*, Spivak, trans. (New York: Routledge, 1995), pp. 212–213.

45. In Clarice Lispector, *Family Ties*, Giovanni Pontiero, trans. (Austin, TX: University of Texas Press, 1972), pp. 88–95.

William F. Pinar

STRANGE FRUIT
Race, Sex, and an Autobiographics of Alterity

Introduction

Gender and race conflate in a crisis.
(Henry Louis Gates, Jr. 1996, 84)

As a feminist man, it is clear to me that I must confront my own manhood, understood of course not essentialistically, but historically, socially, racially, in terms of class and culture. The main issue of the twentieth century may have been—may remain—the color line, but this line does not stay within itself, by itself, dividing what would otherwise be a monolith: humanity. The color line traverses other planes, inhabits other problems, especially educational ones. Race and gender intersect and, as Gates (1996) observed, conflate. The racial crisis is gendered, and the crisis of gender is racialized. Within these intersections of race and homosexuality, I want to work autobiographically to perceive the lives of four men and the historical moments they inhabited. In particular, I want to outline the shadows they cast over me and us, European-American men. In so doing, I sleep with bodies of knowledge which might help reconfigure the lived practices of male self-constitution, and, in so doing, reformulate self and other: an autobiographics of alterity. Curriculum understood as *currere* is a form of social psychoanalysis, a complicated conversation with myself and others, the point of which is movement: autobiographic, political, cultural. I employ the method of *currere* in search of a passage out of the impasse that is *fin-de-siècle* America, the impasse in this individual life which shares with others the dilemma of being an American, an American man, an American white man, in my case, an American white man who is queer.

It is clear that autobiography is not just about oneself but also about the Other.

It is, in Leigh Gilmore's phrase, a technology of self-production. It is, as well, a technology of the production of Others. How can we understand this production of the "self" as a gendered and racialized production? How might the European-American male begin to grasp how his masculinity is racialized and how his "race" is gendered? To answer these questions I have undertaken a study of four men whose lives and times span the twentieth century and traverse the Western world. How might such work enable one to reexperience the present in *fin-de-siècle* America? How might an indirect autobigraphy or, to borrow from Gilmore (1994), an autobiographics of alterity, help us to move through racial and gender sediments which contribute to the stasis that is the present moment? To begin we must return to a time past, still in the present

Strange Fruit

> [T]he repeated castrations of lynched black men
> cry out for serious psychocultural explanation.
>
> (Cornel West 1993, 86–87)

On February 20, 1892, in Texarkana, Arkansas, a black man named Ed McCoy (also known as Ed Coy), accused of rape, was lynched by white men (Newton and Newton 1991, 256). Ida B. Wells, a black journalist and teacher of extraordinary courage, was present. Wells, whose offices for her newspaper, the *Free Speech*, had been demolished because it carried editorials that whites considered inappropriate, had undertaken the task of visiting lynching events and investigating their causes. Of course, the primary "cause" tended to be rape, but, as Wells reported, blacks (overwhelmingly black men) were lynched for wife beating, hog stealing, quarreling, "sassiness," and even for no offense whatsoever (Braxton 1989). Rarely was rape in fact a factor.

In her autobiography Wells discusses the rape myth; she reports several cases that discredit it. One of these cases was Edward McCoy's, who had been burned alive that February night in Arkansas. The crime of which he was "convicted" was assaulting a white woman. Wells writes: "He was tied to a tree, the flesh cut from his body by men and boys, and after coal oil was poured over him, the woman he assaulted gladly set fire to him, and 15,000 persons saw him burn to death" (quoted in Braxton 1989, 121).

In McCoy's case, the woman he was accused of assalting turned out to be the same woman with whom he had been sexually involved for "more than a year previous." As the "victim," her white male defenders directed her to start the fire. As she lighted the pyre, McCoy "asked her if she could burn him after they had 'been sweethearting' so long." She could. As was often the case, and as Wells well knew, a "large majority of the 'superior' white men" responsible for the lynching were "reputed fathers of mulatto children" (quoted phrases in Braxton 1989, 121).

Contrary to white opinion of the time, Ida B.Wells knew that lynching was not an occasional excess committed by a few fanatics and extremists. Lynching was central to a gendered system of organized racial terror in America. Many Southern whites participated in or witnessed lynchings. They were supported by legal and other authorities, sanctioned by the news media, ignored (and therefore condoned) by the federal government. Despite six decades of antilynching efforts, federal legislation was never made into law (Zangrando 1980). The allegation of rape was almost always groundless; often the lynching victim was not even the man charged with the crime. For over a century, black men (relatively few black women and very few white people were lynched) were tortured, sometimes burned alive at the stake, often castrated. These were spectacles that were sometimes advertised days in advance by the local papers and sometimes more widely attended than a county fair (Braxton 1989). Seven years after the last recorded lynching in 1959 (Smead 1986), convicted rapist and future presidential nominee Eldridge Cleaver (1968) would poetically link certain sexual themes embedded in lynchings:

> *From "To A White Girl"*
> White is
> The skin of Evil.
> You're my Moby Dick,
> White Witch,
> Symbol of the rope and hanging tree,
> Of the burning cross.
> Loving you thus
> And hating you so,
> My heart is torn in two.
> Crucified. (13)

Evidently the "white girl" is male: Moby Dick, indeed.

In contrast, Audre Lorde (1982) identified with those who were crucified and, Christlike, might rise again:

> I was the story of a phantom people
> I was the hope of lives never lived
> I was a thought-product of the emptiness of space
> and the space in the empty bread baskets

I was the hand, reaching toward the sun
the burnt crisp that sought relief. . . .
And on the tree of mourning they hanged me
the lost emotion of an angry people
hanged me, forgetting how long I was
in dying
how deathlessly I stood
forgetting how easily
I could rise
again. April 20, 1952. (118)

The imagery of lynching—poetry, literature, music, in the minds of white men—was inescapably erotic. The mulatto Joe Christmas in Faulkner's *Light in August*, himself a child of an interracial love affair, was doomed to castration and death by lynching. The white lyncher in James Baldwin's (1965) *Going to Meet the Man* tosses on his bed in sexual frustration before he rises to join the manhunt at dawn. Lynching is the culmination of an interracial love affair in Jean Toomer's (1975) *Cane*. Billie Holiday, the great jazz singer, made famous the indelible image of the "strange fruit" of race and sex in the American South:

Southern trees bear a strange fruit,
Blood on the leaves and blood at the root;
Black body swinging in the Southern breeze,
Strange fruit hanging from the poplar trees.

Pastoral scene of the gallant South,
The bulging eyes and the twisted mouth;
Scene of magnolia sweet and fresh,
And the sudden smell of burning flesh.

Here is a fruit for the crows to pluck;
For the rain to gather, for the wind to suck,
For the sun to rot, for the tree to drop,
Here is a strange and bitter crop.
                    (quoted in Hall 1979, 150)

Lynching, then, was sexualized violence committed against black men by white men (women watched), rationalized by a heterosexual rape threat that turned out to be, almost always, a fantasy. Was lynching, then, in some sense a form a homosexual rape? Is racism, in some way, an affair between men?

Self-Division and the Multiplication of Others

> [I] take the world inside myself.
>
> (Hubert Fichte, quoted in Jones 1996, xiv)

> The world must be placed in the subject in order that the subject
> can be for the world.
>
> (Gilles Deleuze 1993, 26)

It was the Edward McCoy story that gave point to this project. His murder suggested to me that there might be a homoerotic element in white racism. Of course, racism cannot be reduced to its erotic elements. But their elaboration might help to understand our submergence in certain racial and sexual "regimes of reason" (Leitch 1992), regimes which have perpetuated a series of specific oppositions, including black/white, man/woman, and queer/straight. And implied by these oppositions are a series of cultural, political, and educational stalemates, blocking us culturally and politically as we Americans face the close of the twentieth century. If we can move through the blocks that these oppositions create and reproduce, we might begin to move through the stasis of the historical present. Intellectuals might become "bodies of knowledge" rather than bureaucrats of the mind (Pinar 1997). But moving through the psychological blocks to homosexual desire is paramount. As Eve Kosofsky Sedgwick (1990) observes: "Modern homosexual panic represents, it seems, not a temporally imprisoning obstacle to philosophy and culture, but, rather, the latent energy that can hurtle them far beyond their own present place of knowledge" (139). That is my hunch too.

In *Understanding Curriculum* (Pinar et al. 1995) in a postscript to the next generation, I observed that the conceptual unity of the Tylerian period had ended, that the era of curriculum development was over, that the field had been reconceptualized from a form of social engineering to a scholarly field in which theory plays a prominent role. In the contemporary curriculum field, there is no conceptual unity. Rather, there is a series of powerful, and relatively isolated, discourses, regimes of "truth" and "reason." This triumph of the new field will become a problem, a problem suggested by its parallels with the national situation with its tendentious debates and anxieties over immigration and multiculturalism generally. There is a trend toward political, religious, and ethnic balkanization (including, in the 1990s, genocide in the Balkans themselves). As we know from Derrida and Foucault, we can locate this tendency toward oppositions, oppositions which become locked in stasis, arrest, and blocked movement, in the European psyche and its institutional structures, in the self-division of which Christianity itself is both a reflection and provocation, as are imperialism, colonialism, nationalism, racism, sexism, heterosexism, although each of these is, of course, relatively autonomous, each exhibiting singular histories and a separate series of causalties. Each plays multiple roles in the formation of the historical present: *fin-de-siècle* America.

Can the construction of the Other via self-repression and the consequent splitting off, including projection, of these repudiated self-contents onto Others (and then socially codified as racism, misogyny, and homophobia) be located in compulsory heterosexuality? Probably not. Ancient Greece reminds us that homosexuality by itself guarantees neither democracy nor social justice. But in the twentieth century they are not unrelated either. As homosexual repression moves toward the cultural surface to become not only a political issue and an entry into a denied/distorted past, we might rediscover and reexperience the trauma which keeps us trapped in the present. We know this much: in the loss, via repression and sublimation, of homosexual desire and love, which occurred sometime during early Christianity and the last days of Rome, man turned on himself, and on woman, in new and theologically grounded ways. He became liable to split off projective identifications, false but vivid fantasies of differences between what he imagined himself to be and how others appeared to him. While it may have been primarily a political issue to them, the early Christians are to blame. They are responsible for the two-thousand year-old regime of "compulsory heterosexuality." Does the partially clad man on the cross represent the murdered remains of the man we once loved, the father, the son, oneself? All we have now are fragments of memory. Is that why, in the Dutch film *The Fourth Man,* Jesus is replaced with the nearly naked hunk hanging on the mausoleum wall, who is then fellated by his worshipper? The crucifix signs the death of homosexuality, its distorted and denied reappearance in the Catholic Church (the "Boys of St. Vincent" as it were), in enforced heterosexuality, in imperialism, including missionarism, functioning as it did and does now to cover up the avarice of expanding capitalism. Like Sedgwick, I "will argue that an understanding of virtually any aspect of modern Western culture must be, not merely incomplete, but damaged in its central substance to the degree that it does not incorporate a critical analysis of modern homo/heterosexual definition" (Sedgwick 1990, 1).

It becomes clear that "reason" as understood in the traditional (Tylerian) curriculum, in Schwabian, deliberative theory, and in Marxist political theory, remains unaware of its sources and functions to the extent it overlooks its heterosexist origins and elements. A politically enforced heterosexuality, one reproduced by homophobic masculinities, tends to objectify the woman as, per object relations theory (Chodorow 1978), he keeps "her" repressed inside. And for such men, reason becomes, necessarily, an effort to control the self, order the world, and objectify others. It makes racism, sexism, and heterosexism inviting, as the structure of these modes of being-with-others requires a self-division, a cognitive structure, that, in classic Cartesian fashion, divides the world into the thinking self and everything else. And "everything else," as we know, is a "natural resource" for exploitation. The black body becomes cargo, a medium of labor and exchange and desire. The woman becomes sexual object and unpaid laborer (housewife, mother), the homosexual the sinner or deviant, the earth a "natural resource," and the self-divided, self-alienated "heterosexual" male sees all as opportunities for gain in a falsely construed Oedipal competition with other self-divided, self-estranged males. The sentimentalized, "pure," sexually vulnerable white woman who had to be protected by castrating big black brutes: these were all "furniture" in the nineteenth-century white male mind, furniture the imprints of which remain today. Sedgwick (1990) observes:

> It may be, then, that much of the heritage that today sets "sentimentality" and its ever more elusive, indeed, ever more impossible Other at the defining center of so many judgments, political as well as aesthetic, impinging so today on every issue of national identity, postcolonial populism, religious fundamentalism, high versus mass culture, relations among races, to children, to other species, and to the earth, as well as most obviously between and within genders and sexualities—it may be that the structuring of so much cultural work and apperception around this impossible criterion represents a kind of residue or remainder of erotic reactions to the male body, relations excluded from but sucked into supplementarity to the tacitly ethicized medical anthropomorphizations that have wielded so much power over our century. (180)

Through recovery and expressions of homosexual desire a series of oppositions may begin to disappear.

With Jacques Daignault I taught a seminar during June 1991 entitled "Forgetting the Self?" In the theory of autobiography I sketched then, I worked to "forget" what I imagined I knew about myself in order to remember what had been repudiated. Now I work to identify elements I once associated with the Other, both abstract and concrete, historical and embodied, which constitute the social world in which the self takes (imaginary) form. After Leigh Gilmore (1994), I term this theory of *currere* an "autobiographics of alterity." I have chosen four men whose lives and work span the twentieth century in ways which point to intersections among homosexuality, race, cultural renewal, and self-formation, intersections which might point to passages through the historical present, at the *fin de siècle*, at the dawn of the next century, the new millennium. These men become, in a sense, "shadowgraphs." As Søren Kierkegaard wrote, in *Either/Or*, volume I:

> I call these sketches Shadowgraphs, partly by the designation to remind you at once that they derive from the darker side of life, partly because like other

shadowgraphs they are not directly visible. When I take a shadowgraph in my hand, it makes no impression upon me, and gives me no clear conception of it. Only when I hold it up opposite the wall and now look not directly at it, but that which appears on the wall, am I able to see it. So also with the picture which I wish to show here, an inward picture which does not become perceptible until I see it through the external. This external is perhaps quite unobtrusive but not until I look through it, do I discover that inner picture which I desire to show to you, an inner picture too delicately drawn to be outwardly visible, woven as it is of the tenderest moods of the soul.

And so an autobiographics of alterity also might be termed "indirect autobiography." By telling the stories of these four men, I work to honor them while illuminating their "shadows". . . indirectly.

Regressive/Progressive/Analytic/Synthetic

> [T]he speaking subject is also the subject about which it speaks.
> (Michel Foucault 1987, 10)

The plan of a series on an autobiographics of alterity is this: in the first volume I would sketch the outlines of an autobiographics of alterity, employing gendered questions of the racialized Other in the self-formation of the European-American male. To do so I would discuss what I take to be an "imprinting" experience of racism: lynching, and in particular its mangled homosexualized elements that seem so obvious now. Black men were often castrated by white men during these rituals of torture; body parts were sometimes kept as souvenirs, including the penis. Why were black men lynched? As mentioned, a variety of provocations was invoked, but the allegation of rape was the most powerful. It was almost never true; it was almost always a white man's fantasy. If white men obsessed that the black man wanted to rape "his" woman, what can it mean? Could it mean that he has converted his own desire into fear, which was then displaced, projected onto the "woman" next to him, that imaginary white woman of purity and honor? If the white man could be so mistaken about the black man's sexual intentions, does he understand anything about the black man? Perhaps, for example, the white male fear of prison rape is also a fantasy. But the studies show this fear is real: even in majority-white prisons, the overwhelming percentage of prison rapes have been conducted by black males upon white males. And the preference of heterosexually identified black males is not white (or black) male homosexuals, but young white heterosexuals. "Now whitey knows it is his turn" (quoted in Scacco 1975, 52), one black informant said, pointing to the political nature of prison rape. Is this Ed McCoy's revenge? Why would black men conceive of political revenge in sexual terms? Why indeed?

In the second introductory volume I would focus on European male self-formation within the *civitas,* including the modern nation, especially as these developments are racialized and gendered. In volumes 3 through 6, I would portray four historical moments and four men whose characters illuminate many of the issues we European-American men face today. (They are my issues as well. I do not conflate "we" and "I" but I do accept Sartre's concept of the "universal singular," implying that the individual does embody the "situation"—which for Sartre was a meaningful, boundaried space and time of lived experience, individual and historical—in a singular way.) In the raindrop is the ocean, the old proverb reminds.

The first man who embodies in a singular way a specific historical moment (*fin-de-siècle* Europe) is Robert Musil, the Austrian novelist, essayist, and journalist. Musil's novel of a Prussian military school—entitled *Young Torless,* published at the dawn of the twentieth century—will help me to discuss the crisis of European culture, which was also a crisis of European masculinity. I am not a historian; I will not be making claims about history. Rather, I want to unearth—as in a kind of social psychoanalysis—those elements of that cultural and political crisis which signaled the beginning of the end of the age of European hegemony. These issues—among them mind and body, Christian and Jew—have largely disappeared from the European-American male screen of preoccupation. Disappeared perhaps, but not gone: remembering *fin-de-siècle* Vienna may shed new light on our own time. Several of these elements are very familiar—anti-Semitism, fascism—but their relation to homosexual desire and repression is perhaps less known. To underline how this work points to us, I will make the Musil volume also a "tale of two cities." Juxtaposed to Vienna in first years of the twentienth century will be Atlanta, Georgia, where an American version of anti-Semitism and fascism occurred. The occasion was the Leo Frank case. The meaning of these events—the cities, the men, the novel—for us represents a kind of cultural psychoanalysis, located in the "universal singular"—an autobiographics of alterity.

From a depiction of this internal crisis of European culture, I would move in volume 4 to its last imperialist, colonialist gasp—not unrelated to its earlier internal crisis, of course. The location and time of this episode was north Africa in the 1950s and 1960s. From German-speaking Europe—Musil was an Austrian who spent much of his life in Germany and Switzerland—we move to the Caribbean, to France (briefly), and finally to North Africa and the Algerian revolution. The man is—you have no doubt guessed by now—Frantz Fanon. Native to Martinique— what has been termed the the center of African culture in the New World—Fanon received his postsecondary education in France. His astonishing but short life of political activism and intellectual accomplishment was lived out in North Africa, dedicated to the emergence not only of an independent Algeria but also of an Africa freed from colonial subjugation. Fanon knew—if coded in heterosexist terms—about the sexual dynamics of race, writing about them in his *Black Skin, White Masks*, first published in 1952. His portrait of the "wretched of the earth"— first published in 1961—inspired many who would participate in the failed American revolution of the 1960s.

The third moment/man does not follow chronologically the Algerian war of independence. Having studied the crisis, then the collapse, of European empire, I want to back up a bit, to focus on the moment just after World War II, a moment of political opportunity in which socialists, communists, as well as various sectors of the center and right fought hard to sculpt the emergence of postwar Europe. This was for many an optimistic time, a moment defined in large part by the American/European economic expansion, including the trend toward the globlization of capitalism, foreshadowing, as we know now, its (momentary?) triumph worldwide. The cultural costs, the political struggles, a singular and magnificent effort at a European renaissance: these point to the third moment and the third man. The one who embodies them is Pier Paolo Pasolini: filmmaker, novelist, poet, essayist, theoretician.

In volume 6 I would move to the last historical moment in this regressive phase of *currere,* the 1960s, and focus upon the United States. What has been a series of high-risk discursive moves becomes in this phase higher-risk, in no small part because the United States has not yet fully come to grips with this moment. It appears we have moved somewhat out of the country's knee-jerk repudiation of it, but just barely. I want to rescue that moment, to reexperience it, not for the sake of its idealization or sentimentalization, not even for what we think of it now, but for what it was like then. To attempt that, I will focus on the struggle for civil rights, specifically the history of SNCC (Student Nonviolent Coordinating Committee) and the Black Panthers. The man is Eldridge Cleaver, who, perhaps more than any other single individual, evoked the potential, personified the excesses, and was condemned to live out its mangled gendered fate. Many will protest: Cleaver is hardly a "great man," as one might say about Musil, Fanon, and Pasolini. I tend to agree. With the exceptions of Martin Luther King, Jr., and Malcolm X, there were no great men engaged in the fight for a new American nation in the 1960s. (And I need not remind the reader those two men were murdered.) The fight was carried on primarily by the young, and perhaps one reason it failed—there were numerous reasons—was the conspicuous absence of "greatness" in the leadership. I do think Cleaver had a hint of greatness about him—although few can remember that today after his religious and political conversions, his heroin habit—but my interest is not to establish that. Rather I want to portray this complicated, contradictory, and gendered embodiment of this fourth historical moment, an American moment in which politics, culture, and economics become intertwined in a struggle for civil rights, for dignity, for—as Cleaver and others insisted— "manhood."

After completing this regressive phase of *currere*, I would move to the progressive, an imaginary exposition of what the future might be. In this indirect autobiography I want to focus not on what is self-evidently futuristic, for instance, science fiction or upon Toffler-like projections of what might be. Rather, I imagine those themes, constructs, and styles absent in the present configuration of European-American masculinity. So the progressive volume moves through topics and modes of writing that I imagine at play in the future, that is, what is split off, in the imaginary, materially missing in the present. I emphasize the body. As we know, African-Americans, women, queers, children . . . we all have bodies, but the white man has, well, a mind. For him the body is his "tool," often his weapon, sometimes his commodity for exchange in the sexual economy, but it would seem to lack a certain phenomenological and autobiographical reality. Yet it is throughout this absent male body that his subjectivity has been hidden, his manhood etched and expressed. The future might have to do with the body, its prosthesis the computer, and its medication, including illegal drugs. The future—the absent present—has to do with the earthly body, with women, with African-Americans. The present is still his, is still "a man's world," but the future will be otherwise, perhaps.

That is why the progressive focuses on the body. The male body signifies much of what is repressed in the culture of European-American masculinity. To himself, a man's body is invisible. In his self-annihilation he has banished his body and objectified everyone elses. The body is black, it is female, it is queer. The missing body is why homosexual desire is so key; it locates the self-dissociated het-man's spirit where it has been banished: in his body. The homosexual is the socially outcast displacement of his own self-love, self-desire, the nearly naked image of which hangs everywhere in the West: the crucifix. As noted, the scantily clad dead man on the cross represents both the crime that was the Christian-led annihilation of homosexual culture in the West and its punishment: the Church. Homosexual desire becomes the medium of our resurrection: take that man down off the cross, and awaken him with a kiss.

These seven volumes—two introducing the project, four regressive moments/ men, and the one progressive moment—I have worked on somewhat concurrently. Initially these volumes were chapters in one book; they grew too large to be contained within two covers. In order to maintain their sense of sequence and interrelatedness, I have worked on all seven more or less simultaneously. The analytic volumes—there are three planned at this stage—will wait until these are finished, as they do represent analyses of the regressive and progressive moments. The outlines of these three books are visible to me: one will focus on the (gendered, racialized)

American nation, another upon the psychological dynamics of self-divison (emphasizing Lacan), a third on issues of representation. The final volume in the series, the synthetic, will attempt a mobilization of the reformed male self in light of the psychointellectual labor undertaken. It is in one sense a photographic blowup of "curriculum," of curriculum as "complicated conversation," on this occasion, a conversation about masculinity, race, politics, and sexuality.

Conclusion

> [D]oes the relation to oneself have an elective affinity with sexuality, to the point of renewing the project of a "history of sexuality"?
>
> (Gilles Deleuze 1986, 102)

What is the method of *currere*? Its movements are regressive-progressive-analytic-synthetic, moving backward to enlarge the pool of memory, forward to disclose one's fantasies of what is "not yet," then analytically to reincorporate the "new information" in an enlarged, complicated present, synthesized in order to act in the world. The method of *currere*—the Latin infinitive of curriculum—is thereby a strategy for reconfiguring one's self, especially one's relationship to one's "subject matter," one's academic discipline, which is a spiritual, psychological, and political discipline as well. It takes as its starting point that the "self" is a term of convenience, illusory, historically and culturally variable, points of convergence and divergence and emergence across multiples planes: existential, psychological, racial, economic. As a form of educational autobiography, *currere* seeks to enlarge and enliven that conversation—the highly specialized, bureaucratized, formalized conversation—that is the school curriculum.

In this project I want to illustrate this concept of curriculum as a complicated conversation by showing how one's study of the disciplines represents conversations with oneself as well as others. I want to show what phenomenologists might call the "arc of intentionality," with one end point residing in the individual as lived and the other in the readings as quoted, paraphrased, recontextualized, rewritten in these books. In another sense I want to show how intellectual work represents a symbolization of individual psychologial processes and social currents, how the historical moment—as Erik Erickson (1975) indicated—merges with individual life. By showing how four men and four moments in the past century leave their residue in me and how I am present in my characterization of them, I hope to inspire you to think about how you have been formed by events and individuals you would identify as key. How do you "signify" through your intellectual labor? As Leigh Gilmore has shown, autobiographical work—autobiographics—is a process of self-formation. When we think of the regressive moment as enlarging the pool of memory, revealing life history that is already there but forgotten, we must acknowledge that the revelation of this forgotten material changes who it is we experience ourselves to be in the present. Gilmore is right to emphasize how autobiography has been used by the male bird to crow, making it of limited use to women, to those who would consciously employ it as a technology of self-production. In showing how my "shadows"—my "alterities"—can be discerned in these four moments, these four men, I hope to illustrate an autobiographics of otherness, of alterity, that is how the self becomes formed in relation to others. This process of subject formation (both subjectivity and subject matter) is not altogether unrelated to the general phenomenon of "othering," in which fragments of the self are repudiated, repressed, and split off, projected onto others. That is, in no small measure, why the black man appeals to the white man. He is of course appealing in himself, but because he—in his nightmarish fate—became the Rorschach ink blot for Europeans and colonists and their children, because he was vulnerable militarily, he became victimized by the powerful heathens from the North (Davidson 1994). He was forced by violence to conduct himself in accordance with those split-off fragments of the white man, those fantasies which took social form as the black man's "place," his self-formation, his personality, his "white mask" (Fanon 1967).

Missing himself, never content with this wretched process of self-dissociation, the white man was determined to reclaim what he had projected onto, in his fantasy, through his subjugation of, the black man. He tried to reclaim it through slavery, racism, colonialism, all laced with sex, desire, and his own self-loathing. Of course, economics and politics were very much operative in these phenomena . . . but the psychological and sexual elements of these political and economic phenomena must be now excavated. They are terribly important: Would there have been slavery, despite its economic appeal, had not this complex psychocultural and sexual dynamic in Europe been under way, available to intersect with military superiority and cultural predatoriness and economic self-interest? There is no simple answer here, no exact parallel, but very inexact if highly suggestive relations among phenomena of self-formation, social practices, and human tragedy.

There is another point to be made. *Currere* is an educational form of autobiography; here I hope to elaborate a method and content of antiracist, antimisogynist education that is autobiographically structured. White boys need to retrieve those fragments they've attached to Others, and when they do so, they will change. They may still have pale skin, but they'll be "white boys" no longer. They will change sexually, as compulsory heterosexuality, heterosexism, and homophobia are intertwined with racism, misogyny, and the exploitation of the earth.

Jerome Buckley (1984) notes that, overall, formal education tends not to be the subject of the autobiographer. Why? Buckley believes that the reason has to do with autobiography itself, which attempts to describe those efforts of the individual to "find" himself and to establish his identity beyond the confines of institutionalization. Not *just* beyond, I would say. Through the method of *currere* the student might establish himself not only apart from the school, but *through* it. Intellectual life cannot now, at least in the U.S., be easily or sharply separated from institutional life. Intellectual labor represents an instrumentation and symbolization of the autobiographical self, even when it is self-estranged. What I wanted, when I first worked on autobiography in Rochester in the early 1970s, was a method to make life in dead institutions. How could we use these great male edifices to become pregnant but not carry our children to bureaucratic term; rather, to give birth to a new intellectual and social order?

Since Rousseau and the Romantics, pursuit of the subjective life has in part been a defense against what has seemed a soul-destroying objectivism. Such objectivism—positivism—I associate with contemporary European-American masculinity and the fantasy of universal reason. Buckley (1984) notes that an intensifying sense of the social, racial, and gendered dimensions of the self has steadily challenged an isolating (male) solipsism. From the outset, the literature of selfhood, both animated and threatened by its focus, has sought in its positive aspiration a synthesis between self and society, and at its best has achieved a powerful interchange. Black and women's autobiography illustrate vividly this point.

Roland Barthes once mused: "To write on oneself may seem a pretentious idea; but it is also a simple idea: simple as the idea of suicide" (quoted in Crimp 1993, 259). Did Barthes commit suicide? He died a month after he was hit by a laundry van. In a snide obituary in *The Village Voice*, Alexander Cockburn suggested he had killed himself. Aware of Barthes's despair over his mother's recent death, Cockburn speculated that Barthes's own death had been a kind of suicide, a lack of the will to live as a result of that exaggerated attachment to the mother that some straight boys imagine to be a condition of male homosexuality (Crimp 1993). Evidently ignorant of object relations theory (Chodorow 1978), Cockburn did not realize that all men, all women, are, *au fond,* mother-identified.

In the writing of *Camera Lucida,* Barthes's evasion of his own self-constitution (by insisting on the death of the subject) disappeared; he "finally arrived at a concept in defiance of his own theory of the subject." Susan Sontag agreed: "His voice became more and more personal, more full of grain, as he called it." But, Douglas Crimp asserts, the matter is precisely the reverse: "the grain of the voice, as Barthes described it, is not the personal but its opposite, all that is *individual without being personal.* It is the (material) body, not the soul" (quoted passages in Crimp 1993, 271; emphasis added). This would be one consequence of an autobiographics of alterity: an individual who is not individualistic but individuated in his commitment to others.

Postscript

By undertaking intellectual work on masculinity and whiteness, is there a risk one might contribute to processes of recentering rather than decentering them, as well as reifying the terms and their "inhabitants"? This is question Ruth Frankenberg (1997) raises in the introduction to an important new collection of essays on "displacing whiteness." Acknowledging the risk, she replies "there are also tremendous risks in *not* critically engaging whiteness," and, I would add, masculinity. "Among these are," she writes:

> first, a continued failure to displace the "unmarked marker" status of whiteness, a continued inability to "color" the seeming transparency of white positionings. Second, to leave whiteness unexamined is to perpetuate a kind of asymmetry that has marred even many critical analyses of racial formation and cultural practice. Here the modes of alterity of everyone-but-white-people are subjected to ever more meticulous scrutiny, celebratory or not, while whiteness remains unexamined—unqualified, essential, homogeneous, seemingly self-fashioned, and apparently unmarked by history or practice (for example, the notion of "racial-ethnic communities" as synonym for "communities of color"). Third . . . critical attention to whiteness offers a ground not only for the examination of white selves (who may indeed be white others, depending on the position of the speaker) but also for the excavation of the foundations of all racial and cultural positionings. (Frankenberg 1997, 1–2)

Currere, understood as an "autobiographics of alterity," requires us to focus not only upon the production of whiteness and masculinity and their intersections and conflations, but also on their dissolution and reformation. As Fanon knew: "For Europe, for ourselves, and for humanity, we must turn over a new leaf, we must work out new concepts, and try to set afoot a new man" (quoted in Gendzier 1973, 270). Let us begin here, now.

References

Baldwin, James. 1965. *Going to Meet the Man*. New York: Dial Press.

Braxton, Joanne M. 1989. *Black Women Writing Autobiography: A Tradition within a Tradition*. Philadelphia, PA: Temple University Press.

Buckley, Jerome Hamilton. 1984. *The Turning Key: Autobiography and the Subjective Impulse since 1800*. Cambridge, MA: Harvard University Press.

Chodorow, Nancy. 1978. *The Reproduction of Mothering*. Berkeley, CA: University of California Press.

Cleaver, Eldridge. 1968. *Soul on Ice*. New York: Dell Publishing Co.

Crimp, Douglas. 1993. "Fassbinder, Franz, Fox, Elvira, Erwin, Armin, and all the Others." In *Queer Looks: Perspectives on Lesbian and Gay Film and Video*. Martha Gever, Pratibha Parmar, and John Greyson, eds. Toronto: Between the Lines, 257–274.

Davidson, Basil. 1994. *The Search for Africa: History, Culture, Politics*. New York: Random House.

Deleuze, Gilles. 1986. *Foucault*. Foreword by Paul A. Bové, Sean Hand, ed. and trans. Minneapolis, MN: University of Minnesota Press.

Deleuze, Gilles. 1993. *The Fold: Leibniz and the Baroque*. Foreword by T. Conley, trans. Minneapolis and London: University of Minnesota Press.

Erickson, Erik. 1975. *Life History and Historical Moment*. New York: Norton & Co.

Fanon, Frantz. 1967. *Black Skin, White Masks*. Charles Lam Markmann, trans. New York: Grove Weidenfeld. Originally published in French under the title *Peau noire, masques blancs*, copyright 1952 by Éditions du Seuil, Paris.

Fanon, Frantz. 1968. *The Wretched of the Earth*. Preface by Jean-Paul Sartre. Constance Farrington, trans. New York: Grove Press. Originally published by François Maspero, éditeur, Paris, France, under the title *Les damnés de la terre*, 1961.

Faulkner, William. 1987. *Light in August*. New York: Garland.

Foucault, Michel. 1987. "Maurice Blanchot: The Thought from Outside." In *Foucault/Blanchot*, Brian Massumi trans. New York: Zone Books, 7–58.

Frankenberg, Ruth. 1997. "Introduction: Local Whiteness, Localizing Whiteness." In *Displacing Whiteness: Essays in Social and Cultural Criticism*, Ruth Frankenberg, ed. Durham, NC: Duke University Press.

Gates, Jr., Henry Louis. 1996. *Colored People: A Memoir*. New York: Alfred A. Knopf.

Gendzier, Irene L. 1973. *Frantz Fanon: A Critical Study*. New York: Pantheon Books.

Gilmore, Leigh. 1994. *Autobiographics: A Feminist Theory of Women's Self-Representation*. Ithaca, NY: Cornell University Press.

Hall, Jacquelyn Dowd. 1979. *Revolt against Chivalry: Jessie Daniel Ames and the Women's Campaign against Lynching*. New York: Columbia University Press.

Jones, James W. 1996. "Introduction." In Hubert Fichte. *The Gay Critic*. Ann Arbor, MI: University of Michigan Press, vii–xx.

Leitch, Vincent B. 1992. *Cultural Criticism, Literary Theory, Poststructuralism*. New York: Columbia University Press.

Lorde, Audre. 1982. *Zami: A New Spelling of My Name*. Trumansburg, NY: The Crossing Press.

Musil, Robert. 1955 [1905]. *Young Torless*. Preface by Alan Pryce-Jones. New York: Pantheon Books Inc.

Musil, Robert. 1990. *Precision and Soul: Essays and Addresses*. Burton Pike and David S. Luft, eds. and trans. Chicago and London: University of Chicago Press.

Newton, Michael, and Newton, Judy Ann. 1991. *Racial and Religious Violence in America: A Chronology*. New York: Garland.

Penley, Constance, and Haraway, Donna. 1991. "Cyborgs at Large: Interview with Donna Harraway." In *Technoculture*, Ruth Frankenberg, ed. Minneapolis and Oxford: University of Minnesota Press, 1–20.

Pinar, William F. 1997. "Regimes of Reason and Male Narrative Voice." In *Representation and the Text: Re-Framing the Narrative Voice*, William G. Gierney and Yvonna S. Lincoln, eds. Albany, NY: State University of New York Press, 81–113.

Pinar, William F., Reynolds, William M., Slattery, Patrick, and Taubman, Peter M. 1995. *Understanding Curriculum: An Introduction to Historical and Contemporary Curriculum Discourses*. New York: Peter Lang.

Scacco, Jr., Anthony M. 1975. *Rape in Prison*. Springfield, IL: Charles C. Thomas, Publisher.

Sedgwick, Eve Kosofsky. 1990. *Epistemology of the Closet*. Berkeley and Los Angeles: University of California Press.

Smead, Howard. 1986. *Blood Justice: The Lynching of Mack Charles Parker*. New York: Oxford University Press.

Toomer, Jean. 1975. *Cane*. New York: Liveright.

West, Cornel. 1993. *Race Matters*. Boston: Beacon Press.

Zangrando, Robert L. 1980. *The NAACP Crusade against Lynching, 1909–1950*. Philadelphia: Temple University Press.

Cameron McCarthy and Greg Dimitriadis

ALL-CONSUMING IDENTITIES
Race and the Pedagogy of Resentment in the Age of Difference

Introduction

Over the years, we have come to see multicultural-ism—as a set of propositions about identity, knowledge, power, and change in education—as a kind of normal science—as a form of disciplinarity of difference in which the matter of alterity has been effectively displaced as a supplement. On the terms of its present trajectory, multiculturalism can be properly diagnosed as a discourse of power that attempts to manage the extraordinary tensions and contradictions existing in modern life that have invaded social institutions, including the university and the school. At the heart of its achievement, multiculturalism has succeeded in freezing to the point of petrification its central object: "culture." Within the managerial language of the university, culture has become a useful discourse of containment, a narrow discourse of ascriptive property in which particular groups are granted their nationalist histories, their knowledges, and, alas, their experts. Cultural competence then becomes powerfully deployed to blunt the pain of resource scarcity and to inoculate the hegemonic knowledge paradigms in the university from the daylight of subjugated knowledges and practices.

It is mere wish fulfillment, however, to attempt to hold still or at bay the extraordinary social currents unleashed in popular life now bearing down upon the modern subjects that inhabit contemporary industrial societies. These currents can be located, in part, in the destabilizing political economy and cultural imperatives unleashed in the push and pull of globalization and localization. On the one hand, the tensions and contradictions of economic reorganization, downsizing, and instability in the labor market have spawned paranoia and uncertainty among the working and professional classes. On the other, culture and ideology ignite the false clarity of essential place, essential home, and the attendant practices of moral and social exclusionism. These dynamic forces have taken hold in the "body politic," so to speak. They reveal themselves at the level of the subject in terms of excess of desires, unfulfilled appetites, incompleteness and general insecurity, anger and violent passions, frustrations and resentment. At the level of social institutions, these tensions of unfulfillment must be understood as a problem of social integration of difference in a time of scarcity. The educational project then becomes a site of unbridled consumerism—shopping for futures in the context of what C.L.R. James calls "the struggle for happiness" (James 1993, 166).

For cultural critics like ourselves, a key place to read these dynamics is at the level of the popular. We therefore want to take the subject of diversity, knowledge, and power to a place that is normally considered outside the circuit of the education field itself, to the end point and margin of education, to the terrain of popular culture and its pedagogies of wish fulfillment and desire. Desire is understood here as a productive agency of lack, the excess rising below and above needs, the latent wish for totality and completeness in a context of containment, limits, and constraints—power disguised and raw.

In so doing, we want to shift attention from the multiculturalist complaint over current modes of teaching and curriculum, *per se,* to the broader issue of the cultural reproduction of difference and the coordination of racial identities, what Larry Grossberg (1992) calls the organization of affect. We want to look at the problem of diversity and difference in our time as a problem of social integration of modern individuals and groups into an increasingly bureaucratic, commodified, and deeply colonized and stratified lifeworld. All of this raises the stakes for the practices of cultural reproduction and their role in identity formation, foregrounding the connections between the production and reproduction of popular cultural form and the operation of power in daily life. Power is understood here as a modern force in the Foucauldian sense, inciting and producing certain possibilities, subject positions, relations, limits and constraints. Power in this sense does not simply prohibit or repress. It is a force that is dispersed. It circulates. It is not outside relations. It produces relations. It is not simply a question of who or what exercises power, but how power is exercised in the concrete (Hall 1980).

In critical ways as, C.L.R. James argues in *American Civilization* (1993), one can get a better insight into the tensions and contradictions of contemporary society by observing and interpreting popular culture than by analyzing canonical educational texts. James makes this argument in a radical way, in his essay, "The Popular Arts and Modern Society":

It is in the serious study of, above all, Charles Chaplin, Dick Tracy, Gasoline Alley, James Cagney, Edward G. Robinson, Rita Hayworth, Humphrey Bogart, genuinely popular novels like those of Frank Yerby (*Foxes of Harrow, The*

Golden Hawk, The Vixen, Pride's Castle) . . . that you find the clearest ideological expression of the sentiments and deepest feelings of the American
people and a great window into the future of America and the modern
world. This insight is *not* to be found in the works of T.S. Eliot, of Heming-
way, of Joyce, of famous directors like John Ford or Rene Clair. (119)

What James is pointing toward through this revisionary strategy is the fact that
what we call popular culture is our modern art, a modern art deeply informed by
and informative of the crises and tensions of cultural integration and reproduction
in our time.

One of the principal crises of social integration in modern life is the crisis of
race relations. We define racial antagonism in this essay as an effect of the competition for scarce material and symbolic resources in which strategies of group affiliation and group exclusion play a critical role. This crisis of racial antagonism must
be seen within the historical context of the contradictions of modern society and
the rapid changes taking place in the material reality and fortunes of people, their
environments, the institutional apparatuses that govern and affect their lives, their
relations with each other, and their sense of location in the present and in the future. Rapid changes of this kind have meant rapid movement and collision of peoples. And above all, as Arjun Appadurai (1996) has argued, they have necessitated a
diremption of the central site of the work of the imagination from the ecclesiastic
arena of high art and aesthetics to the banality of everyday practices and the wish
fulfillment of the great masses of the people.

These tensions, as one of us has argued elsewhere, must be foregrounded in any
discussion of the resurgence of racial antagonism and the accompanying restless-
ness among the working and professional white middle classes (McCarthy 1998).
In what follows, we try to understand these developments by reading patterns of
recoding and renarration in public life as foregrounded in popular culture and policy discourses. We direct attention in this area to the twin processes of racial simulation, or the constant fabrication of racial identity, through the production of the
pure space of racial origins and resentment (the process of defining one's identity
through the negation of the Other). We look at the operation of these two
processes in popular culture and education. We argue that these two processes operate in tandem in the prosecution of the politics of racial exclusion in our times,
informing key policy debates.

The Public Court of Racial Simulation

Highlighting the centrality of simulation and resentment foregrounds the fact that
American middle-class youth and suburban adults "know" more about inner-city

black and Latino youth through electronic mediation, particularly film and television (for example, the show *Cops*), than through personal or classroom interaction or even through textbooks. Yet these processes are coconstitutive, as school textbooks, like academic books generally, have become part of a prurient culture industry with their high-definition illustrations, their eclectic treatment of subject matter, and their touristic, normalizing discourses of surveillance of marginalized groups. In this sense, education (and multicultural education in particular) is articulated to popular culture in ways that implicate broader cultural imperatives.

The logics here are multiple and complex. Hence critical pedagogues such as Steinberg and Kincheloe (1997) are correct to note the ways in which popular texts and their complex pleasures and pedagogies are elided from dominant classroom culture today, an insight underscored by an important body of work in cultural studies and education (see, for example, Giroux 1996). In this sense, school life is largely divorced from the realities of the popular. However, in another and equally important sense, schools are, in fact, entirely imbricated in the kinds of market logics and imperatives so intrinsic to popular culture. As Andy Green (1997) notes, for example, movements for "school choice" index the ways schools are accommodating, not contesting, dominant discourses of consumer capitalism. These discourses are implicated at all levels of the educational process—from decisions about policy and administration to the situated realities of the classroom. As such, Ruth Vinz notes the "shopping mall" approach to multicultural education so prevalent today, giving a most compelling (hypothetical) example:

> On Monday of a given week, students begin their unit on Native Americans. They learn that Native Americans lived in teepees, used tomahawks to scalp white folks, wore headdresses, and danced together around a fire before eating their meal of blue corn and buffalo meat. By Wednesday of the same week, literature is added as an important cultural artifact; therefore, one or two poems (sometimes including Longfellow's "Hiawatha") represent tribal life of the past and present. By Friday, students take a trip to the Museum of the American Indian with its unsurpassed collection of artifacts and carry home their own renditions of teepees, tomahawks, or headdresses that they made during their art period. (Vinz 1999)

The following week, she notes, students might continue their virtual tour of the globe, moving to, for example, Latin American cultures—"During the second week, students study Latinos. . . . " As Vinz makes clear, dominant approaches to multicultural education evidence a kind of market logic, putting multiple and fabricated cultural products at the fingertips of students to consume in very superficial ways.

In this sense, educational institutions are always in synch with popular culture in terms of strategies of incorporation and mobilization of racial identities. Indeed, we live in a time when "pseudo-events" fomented in media-driven representations have usurped any relic of reality beyond that which is staged or performed, driving, it is crucial to note, incredibly deep and perhaps permanent wedges of difference between the world of the suburban dweller and his or her inner-city counterpart. Daniel Boorstin writes, "we have used our wealth, our literacy, our technology, and our progress, to create a thicket of unreality which stands between us and the facts of life" (Boorstin 1975, 3). These Durkheimian "facts of life"—notions of what, for example, black people are like, what Latinos are like—are invented and reinvented in the media, in popular magazines, newspapers, television, music, and popular film. As critics such as Len Masterman (1990) point out, by the end of his or her teenage years, the average student will have spent more time watching television than he or she would have spent in school. In the United States, it is increasingly television and film that educate American youth about race. Again, popular culture and dominant educational imperatives are mutually articulated in complex ways.

Resentment, Identity-Formation, and Popular Culture

In his *On the Genealogy of Morals* (1967), Friedrich Nietzsche conceptualized resentment as the specific practice of identity displacement in which the social actor consolidates his identity by a complete disavowal of the merits and existence of his social Other. A sense of self, thus, is possible only through an annihilation or emptying out of the Other, whether discursively or materially. These practices of ethnocentric consolidation and cultural exceptionalism now characterize much of the tug-of-war over educational reform and multiculturalism—and the stakes could not be any higher for all parties involved.

Indeed, resentment has become perhaps *the* preeminent trope in which and through which "whiteness" is lived in the U.S. today. Whiteness is an unspoken norm made pure and real only in relation to that which it is not. "Its fullness," as Michelle Fine and Lois Weis note, "inscribes, at one and the same time, its emptiness and presumed innocence" (Fine and Weis 1998, 156–157). Offering a key example, Fine and Weis explore, in telling ethnographic detail, the saliency of resentment for the white, working-class men of Jersey City, New Jersey, and Buffalo, New York, two cities ravaged by deindustrialization. As they note, these men, who have lost the economic and cultural stability of the past, blame "ethnic others" for their condition. While the marginalized black men Fine and Weis interview (as part of the same research project) are more apt to offer critiques of "the system," white men ignore such considerations. Personal resentment reigns supreme. Larger structures, the structures that have traditionally supported and served them, are left uninterrogated and naturalized. Fine and Weis write:

> Assuming deserved dominance, [white working-class men] sense that their "rightful place" is being unraveled, by an economy which they argue privileges people of color over white men in the form of affirmative action, and by pressure from blacks and Latinos in their neighborhoods wherein they feel that their physical place is being compromised. (133)

Hence resentment has become a key way to buck a growing and, for these men, painful tide of difference. This sense of resentment is reinforced and undergirded by several key discourses made available in popular culture and academic circles today, discourses which seek to manage the extraordinary complexities that so mark contemporary cultural life. These discourses have become most salient for white men, but they cannot and have not been so contained. Rather, they proliferate in complex and contradictory ways, offering and enabling multiple effects for differently situated groups and individuals.

We will limit our discussion to four such discourses. First, we would like to call attention to *the discourse of origins* as revealed, for example, in the Eurocentric/Afrocentric debate over curriculum reform. Discourses of racial origins rely on the simulation of a pastoral sense of the past in which Europe and Africa are available to American racial combatants without the noise of their modern tensions, contradictions, and conflicts. For Eurocentric combatants such as William Bennett (1994) or George Will (1989), Europe and America are a self-evident and transcendent cultural unity. For Afrocentric combatants, Africa and the diaspora are one "solid identity," to use the language of Molefi Asante (1993). Proponents of Eurocentrism and Afrocentrism are themselves proxies for larger impulses and desires for stability among the middle classes in American society in a time of constantly changing demographic and economic realities. The immigrants are coming! Jobs are slipping overseas into the Third World! Discourses of Eurocentrism and Afrocentrism travel in a time warp to an age when the gods stalked the earth.

These discourses of racial origins provide imaginary solutions to groups and individuals who refuse the radical hybridity that is the historically evolved reality of the United States and other major Western metropolitan societies. The dreaded line of difference is drawn around glittering objects of heritage and secured with the knot of ideological closure. The university itself has become a playground of the war of simulation. Contending paradigms of knowledge are embattled, and combatants release the levers of atavism holding their faces in their hands as the latest volley of absolutism circles in the air.

For example, Michael Steinberg (1996) tells the story of his first job (he was hired during the 1980s) as "the new European intellectual and cultural historian at a semi-small, semi-elite, semi-liberal arts college" in the Northeast. As Steinberg notes, during a departmental meeting he unwittingly contradicted the hegemonic hiring practices of his new institution by "voting for the appointment to the history department of an African Americanist whose teaching load would include the standard course on the Civil War and Reconstruction." Several minutes after the meeting, one of the white academic elders of this Northeastern college informed Steinberg that: (a) his function as a European intellectual was "to serve as the guardian of the intellectual and curricular tradition"; (b) that he should "resist at all costs the insidious slide from the party of scholarship to the party of ideology"; and (c) that if he "persisted in tipping the scales of the department from tradition to experimentation and from scholarship to ideology," he would be digging his own grave, insofar as his own, "traditionally defined academic position would be the most likely to face elimination by a newly politicized institution" (105). Unwittingly, Steinberg had been thrown pell-mell into the war of position over origins in which the resources of the history department he had just entered were under the strain of the imperatives of difference.

A second resentment discourse at work in contemporary life and popular culture is *the discourse of nation*. This discourse is foregrounded in a spate of recent advertisements by multinational corporations such as IBM, United, American Airlines, MCI, and General Electric (GE). These ads both feed on and provide fictive solutions to the racial anxieties of the age. They effectively appropriate multicultural symbols and redeploy them in a broad project of coordination and consolidation of corporate citizenship and consumer affiliation.

The marriage of art and economy, as Stuart Ewen (1988) so defines advertising in his *All Consuming Images,* is now commingled with the exigencies of ethnic identity and nation. At one moment, the semiotic subject of advertising is a free American citizen abroad in the open seas, sailing up and down the Atlantic or the translucent aquamarine waters of the Caribbean sea. In another, the free American citizen is transported to the pastoral life of the unspoiled, undulating landscape of medieval Europe. Both implicate a burgeoning consumer culture undergirded by the triumph of consumer capitalism on a global scale.

Hence the GE "We Bring Good Things to Life" commercial (which is shown quite regularly on CNN and ABC), in which GE is portrayed as a latter day Joan of Arc fighting the good fight of American entrepreneurship overseas, bringing electricity to one Japanese town. In the ad, GE breaks through the cabalism of foreign language, bureaucracy, and unethical rules in Japan to procure the goal of the big sell. The American nation can rest in peace, as the Japanese nation succumbs to superior U.S. technology.

Third, there is *the discourse of popular memory and popular history*. This discourse suffuses the nostalgic films of the last decade or so. Films such as *Dances with Wolves* (1990), *Bonfire of the Vanities* (1990), *Grand Canyon* (1993), *Falling Down* (1993), *Forrest Gump* (1994), *A Time to Kill* (1996), *The Fan* (1997), *Armageddon* (1998), and *Saving Private Ryan* (1998) foreground a white middle-class protagonist who appropriates the subject position of the persecuted social victim at the mercy of myriad forces—from "wild" black youth in Los Angeles (in *Grand Canyon*), to Asian store owners who do not speak English well (in *Falling Down*), to a black baseball player living the too-good life in a moment of corporate downsizing (in *The Fan*). All hearken back to the "good old days" when the rules were few and exceedingly simple for now-persecuted white men.

Joel Schumaker's *A Time to Kill* is a particularly good example here, offering key pedagogical insight about social problems concerning difference from the perspective of the embattled white suburban dweller. The problem with difference is, in Schumaker's world, symptomatic of a crisis of feeling for white, suburban, middle classes—a crisis of feeling represented in blocked opportunity and wish fulfillment, overcrowding, loss of jobs, general insecurity, crime, and so forth. The contemporary world has spun out of order, and violence and resentment are the coping strategies of such actors.

In *A Time to Kill*, Schumaker presents us with the world of the "New South," Canton, Mississippi, in which social divides are extreme, and blacks and whites live such different lives that they might as well be on separate planets. But this backwater of the South serves as a social laboratory to explore a burning concern of suburban America: retributive justice. When individuals break the law and commit acts of violent antisocial behavior, the upstanding folks in civil society, the film argues, are justified in seeking their expulsion or elimination. The film thus poses the rather provocative question: When is it respectable society's "time to kill"? Are there circumstances in which retribution, revenge, and resentment are warranted? The makers of *A Time to Kill* say resoundingly "yes!" This answer is impervious to class or race or gender.

In order to make the case for retributive justice, Schumaker puts a black man at the epicenter of this white normative discourse—what Charles Murray (1984) calls "white popular wisdom." What would you do if your ten-year-old daughter were brutally raped and battered, pissed on, and left for dead? You would want revenge. This is a role play that has been naturalized to mean white victim, black assailant— the Willy Horton shuffle. In *A Time to Kill*, however, the discourse is inverted: the righteously angry are a black worker and his family, as two redneck assailants brutally raped and nearly killed his daughter. Carl Lee, the black lumberyard worker, gets back at these two callous criminals by shooting them down on the day of their arraignment. One brutal act is answered by another. One is a crime, the other is righteous justice. Crime will not pay. In this revenge drama, the message of retributive justice is intended to override race and class lines. We are living in the time of an eye for an eye. The racial enemy is in our private garden. In the face of bureaucratic incompetence, we have to take the law into our own hands.

These films are seeped in nostalgia, enmeshed in the project of rewriting history from the perspective of bourgeois anxieties and the feelings of resentment which often drive them. This project is realized perhaps most forcefully in the wildly successful *Forrest Gump.* A special-effects masterwork, this film literally interpolates actor Tom Hanks into actual and re-created historical footage of key events in U.S. history, renarrating the later part of the twentieth century in ways that blur the line between fact and fiction. Here, the peripatetic Gump steals the spotlight from the Civil Rights Movement, the Vietnam War protesters, the Women's Movement, and so forth. Public history is overwhelmed by personal consumerism and wish fulfillment. "Life," after all, "is like a box of chocolates. You never know what you're gonna get." You might get Newt Gingrich. But who cares? History will absolve the American consumer.

Finally, we wish to call attention to *the conversationalizing discourses of the media culture.* From the television and radio talk shows of Oprah Winfrey and Jenny Jones to the rap music of Tupac Shakur to pseudo-academic books such as *The Bell Curve, The Hot Zone,* and *The Coming Plague,* to self-improvement texts such as *Don't Sweat the Small Stuff . . . and It's All Small Stuff,* these examples from popular culture all psychologize and seemingly internalize complex social problems, managing the intense feelings of anxiety that are so much a part of contemporary cultural life. Television talk shows, for example, reduce complex social phenomenon to mere personality conflicts between guests, encouraging them to air their differences before encouraging some kind of dénouement or resolution. Histories of oppression are thus put aside, as guests argue in and through the details of their private lives, mediated, as they often are, by so-called experts. Racial harmony becomes a relative's acceptance of a "biracial" child. Sexual parity is reduced to a spouse publicly rejecting an adulterous partner. Psychologistic explanations for social phenomenon reign supreme and are supported by a burgeoning literature of self-improvement texts that posit poor self-esteem as the preeminent societal ill today. These popular texts and media programs are pivotal in what Deborah Tannen calls *The Argument Culture* (1998) in which the private is the political, and politics is war by other means.

Identities are thus being formed and reformed—"produced," following Edward Said—in this complex social moment, where the "tide of difference" is being met by profound renarrations of history. It is precisely this kind of rearticulation and recoding that one of us has called nonsynchrony (McCarthy 1998). Here we have tried to draw attention to how these complicated dynamics operate in debates over identity and curriculum reform, hegemonic cultural assertions in advertising, popular film, and in the conversationalizing discourses of contemporary popular culture. Further, as we have shown, these discourses are imbricated in an emergent popular culture industry, one that has radically appropriated the new to consolidate the past. This is the triumph of a nostalgia of the present, as "difference" comes under the normalizing logics and disciplinary imperatives of hegemonic power. Diversity, as such, can sell visits to theme parks as well as it can sell textbooks. Diversity can sell AT&T and MCI long distance calling cards as well as the new ethnic stalls in the ethereal hearths of the shopping mall. And sometimes, in the most earnest of ways, diversity lights up the whole world and makes it available to capitalism.

Educational Policy and the Pedagogy of Resentment

Importantly and most disturbingly, we wish to note, this kind of diversity is also increasingly informing—indeed, producing in the Foucauldian sense—educational policy on both the right and left, as evidenced by several key debates now circulating in the public sphere. These debates have had very real material effects on the dispossessed, those quickly losing the (albeit meager) benefits of affirmative action (for example, through California's Proposition 209), bilingual education (for example, through California's Proposition 227—the so-called "English for the Children" initiative), and need-based financial aid. The idea of high-quality (public) education as the great potential equalizer—a good in and of itself—is now being lost to the bitter resentments at the heart of contemporary culture, lost to petty market logics and the freestanding subject-positions so enabled by them. This weak kind of diversity, as noted, is encouraged by a consumer capitalism that is entirely linked to the imperatives of resentment explored throughout. In a particularly stark example of this process, Martin Luther King, Jr.'s, revolutionary dream of the day when his "four little children will . . . live in a nation where they will not be judged by the color of their skin, but by the content of their character," has been appropriated by right-wing commentators such as Shelby Steele (1990) to contest the advances of affirmative action.

How the discourse of resentment has (explicitly) propelled the conservative agenda here is fairly obvious. A new and seemingly beleaguered middle class is looking to recapture its once unquestioned privilege by advocating "color-blind" hiring and acceptance policies (in the case of affirmative action) while forging a seemingly unified—and, of course, white Anglo—cultural identity through restrictive language policies (in the case of bilingual education). Indeed, the consolidation of seamless and coherent subjects at the heart of contemporary cultural media flows (as explored above) has enabled and encouraged the overwhelming public support for and passage of bills like California's Propositions 209 and 227 (in the case of the latter, by a two-to-one margin). These evidence the popular feelings of resentment that Fine and Weis so powerfully document among white working-class men in *The Unknown City.*

Yet these resentments run deep and operate on numerous levels here—hence the tensions now erupting between African-Americans and Latinos *vis-à-vis* many such bills. A recent *Time* magazine article entitled "The Next Big Divide?" explores burgeoning conflicts between African-Americans and Latinos in Palo Alto over bilingual education, noting that these disputes arise in part from frustration over how to spend the dwindling pot of cash in low-income districts. But they also reflect a jostling for power, as blacks who labored hard to earn a place in central offices, on school boards, and in classrooms confront a Latino population eager to grab a share of these positions (Ratnesar 1997, 1). It has been suggested, in fact, that efforts to institute black "ebonics" as a second language in Oakland was prompted by competition for shrinking funds traditionally allotted to bilingual (Spanish) programs. Resentment, spawned by increasing competition for decreasing resources, is key to unraveling the complexities of these struggles, for, as Joel Schumaker tells us, its power transcends both race and class lines.

Perhaps more importantly, however, the discourse of resentment is also informing more seemingly liberal responses to these issues and bills. The importance of public education in equalizing the profound injustices of contemporary American society is increasingly downplayed in favor of discourses about self-interest and the rigid feelings of resentment which undergird them. Affirmative action, thus, is a good because education will keep dangerous minorities off "our streets" by subjecting them to a lifetime of "civilizing" education, crafting them into good subjects for global cultural capitalism. Further, the story goes, affirmative action really helps middle-class women more than blacks or Latinos, so it should—quite naturally— remain in place.

These discourses inform the debate on bilingual education, as well, a debate that has similarly collapsed liberal and conservative voices and opinions. Indeed, bilingual education, many argue, should be supported (only) because it will prepare young people for an increasingly polyglot global cultural economy, hence keeping immigrants and minorities off public assistance, allowing them to compete in an increasingly diverse (in the sense developed above) global community. Cultural arguments are also elided from in and within these positions, for, as many so eagerly stress, bilingual education really helps immigrants learn English and become assimilated faster—a bottom line supported by an ever-present spate of quantitative studies.

Market logics are all-pervasive here and are deeply informed by self-interest and resentment. These forces have shown themselves most clearly in recent decisions to provide less need-based financial aid for higher education to the poor, apportioning the savings to attract more so-called qualified middle-class students (Bronner

1998). Competition for the "best" students—seemingly without regard for race, class, and gender—has become a mantra for those wishing further to destroy educational access for the dispossessed. Indeed, why, many argue, should poor minorities take precious spots away from the more qualified wealthy? The resentment of the elite has now come full circle, especially and most ironically in this moment of unmatched economic wealth. These are not lean, mean times. We live in era of unbridled wealth won, in large measure, for the elite through the triumph of resentment and its ability to dictate public policy.

Conclusion

Resentment, in sum, is produced at the level of the popular, at the level of the textual. Yet its implications run deep, across myriad contexts, including public policy, which is increasingly defined by the logics of resentment. Thus those of us on the left, those wishing to help keep the promise of public education a real one, must question the terms on which we fight these battles. We must question if our responses will further reproduce a discourse with such devastating and wholly regressive implications. As Foucault reminds us, we must choose what discourses we want to engage in, the "games of truth" we want to play. Indeed, what will be our responses to the burgeoning trend of eliminating need-based financial aid policies? What game will we play? And toward what end?

Such questions are crucial and pressing, as this moment is replete with possibility as well as danger. This period of multinational capital is witness to the ushering in of the multicultural age—an age in which the empire has struck back, and First World exploitation of the Third World has so depressed these areas that there has been a steady stream of immigrants from the periphery seeking better futures in the metropolitan centers. With the rapid growth of the indigenous minority population in the U.S., there is now a formidable cultural presence of diversity in every sphere of cultural life. If this is an era of the "post," it is also an era of difference—and the challenge of this era of difference is the challenge of living in a world of incompleteness, discontinuity, and multiplicity. It requires generating a mythology of social interaction that goes beyond the model of resentment which seems so securely in place in these times. It means that we must take seriously the implications of the best intuition in the Nietzschean critique of resentment as the process of identity formation that thrives on the negation of the Other. The challenge is to embrace a politics that calls on the moral resources of all who are opposed to the power block.

This age of difference thus poses new, though difficult, tactical and strategic challenges to critical and subaltern intellectuals as well as activists. A strategy that seeks to address these new challenges and openings must involve as a first condition a recognition that our differences of race, gender, and nation are merely the starting points for new solidarities and new alliances, not the terminal stations for depositing our agency and identities or the extinguishing of hope and possibility. Such a strategy might help us to understand better the issue of diversity in schooling and its linkages to the problems of social integration and public policy in modern life. Such a strategy might allow us to "produce" new discourses as well, especially and most importantly in this highly fraught and exceedingly fragile moment of historical complexity.

References

Appadurai, A. 1996. *Modernity at Large: Cultural Dimensions of Globalization.* Minneapolis, MN: University of Minnesota Press.

Asante, M. 1993. *Malcolm X as Cultural Hero and Other Afrocentric Essays.* Trenton, NJ: Africa World Press.

Bennett, W. 1994. *The Book of Virtues.* New York: Simon and Schuster.

Boorstin, D. 1975. *The Image: A Guide to Pseudo-Events in America.* New York: Atheneum.

Bronner, E. "Universities Giving Less Financial Aid on Basis of Need." *New York Times* June 21, 1998: A1.

Ewen, S. 1988. *All Consuming Images: The Politics of Style in Contemporary Culture.* New York: Basic Books.

Fine, M., and Weis, L. 1998. *The Unknown City: Lives of Poor and Working-Class Young Adults.* Boston: Beacon Press.

Giroux, H. 1996. *Fugitive Cultures: Race, Violence, and Youth.* London: Routledge.

Green, A. 1997. *Education, Globalization and the Nation State.* London: Macmillan Press.

Grossberg, L. 1992. *We Gotta Get Out of This Place: Popular Conservatism and Postmodern Culture.* New York: Routledge.

Hall, S. 1980. "Cultural Studies: Two Paradigms." *Media, Culture, and Society* 2: 57–72.

James, C.L.R. 1993. *American Civilization.* Oxford: Blackwell.

Masterman, L. 1990. *Teaching the Media.* New York: Routledge.

McCarthy, C. 1998. *The Uses of Culture: Education and the Limits of Ethnic Affiliation.* New York: Routledge.

Murray, C. 1984. *Losing Ground: American Social Policy, 1950–1980.* New York: Basic Books.

Nietzsche, F. 1967. *On the Genealogy of Morals.* W. Kaufman, trans. New York: Vintage.

Ratnesar, R. 1997. "The Next Big Divide?" *Time* December 1: 52.

Steele, S. 1990. *Content of Our Character: A New Vision of Race in America.* New York: St. Martin's Press.

Steinberg, M. 1996. "Cultural History and Cultural Studies." In *Disciplinarity and Dissent in Cultural Studies*, C. Nelson and D.P. Gaonkar, eds. New York: Routledge, 103–129.

Steinberg, S., and J. Kincheloe, eds. 1997. *Kinderculture: The Corporate Construction of Youth*. Boulder, CO: Westview Press.

Tannen, D. 1998. *The Argument Culture: Moving from Debate to Dialogue*. New York: Random House.

Vinz, R. 1999. "Learning from the Blues: Beyond Essentialist Readings of Cultural Texts." In *Sound Identities*, Cameron McCarthy et al., eds. New York: Peter Lang.

Will, G. 1989. "Eurocentricity and the School Curriculum." *Baton Rouge Morning Advocate* December 18: 3.

Roger I. Simon

THE TOUCH OF THE PAST
The Pedagogical Significance of a Transactional Sphere of Public Memory

I remember when the people were brought to Churchill, my husband and I watched them being unloaded off the plane at the shores of Hudson Bay. "This is a bad, bad thing for our people," we said. "Somebody's making a great mistake. From here on, they will be suffering. They are not prepared for this." There were no houses for them anywhere. The winter was closing in. I was very saddened by what was happening. I felt, from now on, there'll be nothing but disaster for our people.

—Betsy Anderson

I also remember the time we were moved to Churchill. When our elders say that the people were dumped on the shores of Hudson Bay, they are telling the truth. Some families didn't have tents for shelter, and they had young children, but they were left like that. As the winter set in we had no other way but to live in a canvas tent for the whole winter. My dad eventually built a shack with scrap lumber across the Churchill River where some people were living. We would live there in the winter and come across to the town and summer at the point, Cape Merry. We had a homemade stove made out of a forty-five gallon gas tank. People didn't own proper woodstoves in those days.

—Mary Yassie

We were working at the airport. We were outside, doing casual labor, when the plane landed and the people were unloaded. The plane was a huge aircraft with a round belly. It landed and the people came out one by one. I remember the children crying and the few dogs yelping to get free. Eventually everything and everyone was unloaded and put on a big truck and driven down into town. They were all taken to the point at Cape Merry. There, the people were dumped to fend for themselves on the shores of Hudson Bay. Winter was closing in. Some of the people set up their tents, and some made makeshift shelters for themselves. One of the tents stood out because you could see the shadows of the people who were sitting inside. Already, the feeling of hopelessness was in the air. There was no laughter, no joy, only dead silence. Even the dogs were not moving. The feeling just hung over the people like death.

—Charlie Kithithee

(All quotes from Bussidor and Bilgen-Reinart 1997, 47–48.)

What might it mean to live our lives as if the lives of others truly mattered? One aspect of such a prospect would be our ability to take the stories of others seriously, not only as evocations of responsibility but as well as matters of "counsel." Walter Benjamin (1969) referred to counsel as "less an answer to a question than a proposal concerning the continuation of a story which is just unfolding (86)." For Benjamin, in order to seek and receive counsel, one would first have to be able to tell this unfolding story. On such terms, for the lives of others to truly matter—beyond what they demand in the way of an immediate practical solidarity—they must be encountered as counsel, stories that actually might shift our own unfolding stories, particularly in ways that might be unanticipated and not easily accepted. In what way, then, might stories such as those of Betsy Anderson, Mary Yassie, and Charlie Kithithee be encountered as counsel? In order to explore the possible terms of such an encounter, I will address here the importance of a sphere of public memory as a transactional space, not for the consolidation of national memory but for mobilizing practices of remembrance-learning (Eppert 1999) in which one's stories might be shifted by the stories of others.

The notion of public memory moves remembrance beyond the boundaries of the singular corporal body. Whereas autobiographical memory references the ability to recall previous states of consciousness (including thoughts, images, feelings, and experiences), public historical memory is grounded in a shared pedagogy of "rememory" (Morrison 1987), a decidedly social repetition or, better, a rearticulation of past events suffused with demands of remembrance and learning across generations, across boundaries of time, space, and identifications. As Michael Roth (1995, 8) points out: "talk about memory has become the language through which we address some of our more pressing concerns. This is because in modernity, memory is the key to personal and collective identity. . . . [However,] the psychologization of memory makes it extremely difficult for people to share the past, for them to have confidence that they have a collective connection to what has gone before." In stressing this point, Roth is keenly aware that memory is not just that which contributes to knowledge of the past and/or underwrites a claim to group or communal membership. Quite divergently, memory may become *transactional*, enacting a claim on us, providing accounts of the past that may wound or haunt—that may interrupt one's self-sufficiency by claiming an attentiveness to an otherness that cannot be reduced to a version of our own stories. Such an interruption underscores the potential radical pedagogical authority of memory, in that it may make apparent the insufficiency of the present, its (and our own) incompleteness, the inadequacy of our experience, the requirement that we revise not only our own stories but the very presumptions which regulate their coherence and intelligibility. On such terms, a transactive memory has the potential to expand that ensemble of people who count for us, who we encounter, not merely as strangers (perhaps deserving pity and compassion, but in the end having little or nothing to do with us), but as "teachers," people who in telling their stores change our own.

As I will argue, the substance of such a transactive public memory is informed by the reflexive attentiveness to the retelling or representation of a complex of emotionally evocative narratives and images which define not necessarily agreement but *points of connection* between people in regard to a past that they both might acknowledge the touch of.[1] Certainly, such acknowledgments will always be marked with the contemporary and historical specificities, inequities, and power relations which shape the terms of various everyday lives. But for the moment, what I wish to emphasize here is that the practice of a transactive public memory evokes a persistent sense—*not of belonging but of being in relation to*, of being claimed in relation to the experiences of others. It is thus that a transactive public memory proposes a connection between oneself and what has gone before, a connection that may be other to one's identificatory investments. As Roth (1995) stresses: "the psychogization of memory and the doubts about the possibilities for objective history have combined to create an attitude that lets each person have his or her own history. What may appear to be a benign pluralism (or multiculturalism), however, can actually be another symptom of the continuing privatization (or ghettoization) of our relationship with the past. This form of social amnesia depends on a superficial relativism in which one has no investment in the past that one might share with another" (15).

A transactive public memory places one in relation to the past in its otherness and in its potential connection to oneself as coming after (perhaps emerging out of or against) the past. In this sense, public memory invokes a "kinship" beyond that rendered by biology, tribal traditions, or national histories. Such a form of public memory thus should be in a position to raise the questions: Who counts as our ancestors? Whose and what memories matter—not abstractly—but to me, to you?

What practices of memory am I obligated to, what memories require my attention and vigilance, viscerally implicating me—touching me—so that I must respond, re-thinking my present?

Boundary Work

The boundary of one's historical memories is often defined in reference to experiences within sets of social relations regulated under the regime of "nation" or "tribe"—whether that national or tribal entity be coincident with the terrain of state sovereignty or a diasporic cultural formation.[2] It is not accidental that the historical traces that continue to touch me in significant ways include the 1905 Kishnev pogrom, the mass slaughter at Babi Yar, the genocidal concentration camp universe now recognized by the designation "Auschwitz," the founding of the State of Israel, Baruch Goldstein's slaughter of Muslims at prayer in the Cave of the Makhpela in Hebron, and the recent murder of Yitzhak Rabin. My education and ongoing communal attachments have created identifications which are bound to these and other specific memories, memories with profound implications for how I face reality and live and work with others whose routines and material circumstances provoke memories with very different substances.

However, if the limits of historical memory are fully constrained by notions of identity and identification, the possibilities for transactive public memory are clearly limited. For in such identity-based affiliations begins the refusal to take other people's memories seriously, as of no concern, as having nothing to do with you, as not your responsibility, unless, perhaps, one can forge an identification between one's own troubles and traumas and those of others. It is not difficult to hear a condescending indifference in this refusal of the touch of the past as when, for example, First Nations' land claims are dismissed as the views of "those who wish to impose their memories on us, to have us relive the past and wallow in what has be done rather than live in the present." This refusal is also heard in the studied rage and resentment of those subject to the legacies of imperialism. "You ask us to suffer with you, but your memories are not ours, and your narcissistic lamentations do not bring tears to our eyes" (cited in Finkielkraut 1992). In these words spoken by the defense at the trial of former SS officer Klaus Barbie, one encounters a refusal of the connection between the Nazi genocide of European Jewry and the lives of those subjected to centuries of racist and imperial exploitation (a refusal that falls into an attempt to read the practice of Holocaust memory as an expression of Western racism rather than a supplement to attempts to rupture its continuing presence).

The point here is not that we must transcend our historical specificities and identifications. Rather it is to recognize that a transactive sphere of public memory is a space crosscut with boundaries that serve as both limit and resource for one's capacity to be responsive to the touch of the past and hear the counsel in the memories of others. These boundaries mark my distance from that undergone and spoken of by others. They estrange me from various pasts to which I always arrive too late, reminding me that the time of other people's memories is not my time. Yet these boundaries are not simply the limit of my social imagination condemning me to indifference, voyeurism, or an epistemological violence that can only render the experience of others in terms I recognize or imagine as my own. Rather, these boundaries initiate the terms for the reconstruction of my historical memory (Simon, forthcoming). That is, on these boundaries I can begin to enact my memorial kinship to the memory of another with the recognition of my distance from these memories. And I can accomplish this practice when, as a witness to other people's memories, I attempt to hear and respond to the stories of others in a way which takes cognizance of the strangeness of these stories, their foreign-ness. This is a form of re-memory in which memories of "that which were never my fault or deed" (Levinas, 1998) begin to touch, to interrupt my taken-for-granted performance of the present.

Given the increasingly heterogenous space of the nation-state and the increased human stake in an interdependent global future, national and diasporic formations cannot remain the limit of our concern. Our lives together may indeed depend on questions such as: How, in what sense, and under what conditions might events such as the recent slaughter of Tutsis in Rwanda or the Mohawk uprising in Oka, Quebec, or, less immediately, the Irish Great Hunger or the events of the Middle Passage which instituted slavery in the Americas become "personal" for me? What might be the substance of a point of connection at which I am touched to respond to the memories of others, not in the sense of some meaningless sentiment, a too-easy empathy, or the false nostalgia of a late imperialism, but rather as means of experiencing certain events as part of ongoing relations of power and privilege, the legacy of which I participate in and I am called to transform?

No doubt the institutionalized practices which organize and regulate our encounters with historical memory may severely restrict the terms on which people may hear and learn something of each other's lives. Even when there is interest and responsiveness, these restrictions often diminish the power of the seen and heard to rupture one's performance of the present. Rarely do we engage other people's memories "faced" by others (to cite a concept central to the thought of Levinas), responsible to and claimed by their unthematizable difference in ways that we cannot expect. Thus, if the terms of public memory are to shift, increased attention must be given to practices which confront us, claim us to a memorial kinship because they reside beyond the bounds of the histories which give substance to one's attachments, affirmations, and expectations, confirming who we are and what we know. What might such practices be?

Testimony and Public Memory

Consider for a moment the practice of testimony. The primary purpose of testimony is to convey through multiple expressive forms the historical substance and significance of prior events and experiences. Testimony compromises representations either by those who have lived through specific events or, alternatively, by those who have been told of such lived realities, either directly or indirectly, and have been moved to convey to others that which has been impressed upon them.[3] What I wish to emphasize most about testimony is that it is a multilayered communicative act, a performance intent on carrying forth memories through the conveyance of a person's engagement between consciousness and history (Felman and Laub 1992). Thus, whether across generations or across cultures, testimony is always directed toward another, attempting to place the one who receives it under the obligation of response to an embodied singular experience not recognizable as one's own.

If one listens to testimony receptive to this transactive address, one finds oneself at a point of connection, commanded by a persistent sense of belonging to something or someone that is other to oneself. To be present to testimony, to be responsive as a requested witness (not as spectator, voyeur, analyst, or student), is to be claimed to another in ways that are not reducible to practices of identification or humanistic assertions of empathy. To clarify this position, I shall briefly describe two quite different sensibilities: the *spectatorial* and the *summoned*. The notion of sensibility I refer to here is a particular way of opening oneself to another, of approaching another through a particular embodied cognizance.

A spectatorial sensibility concerns the construction of an observer—one who listens and watches. Limited to neither one's visual nor auditory sense, spectatorial sensibility references a larger, pervasive organization of perceptual engagement, a particular management of the way one attends to another. This sensibility embodies and enacts a capacity to grasp a given testimony within frames of understanding which render it intelligible and meaningful in ways that evoke thought, feeling, and judgment. A spectatorial sensibility is not limited to abstract and objectified forms of historical interpretation. In a spectatorial sensibility one might expect to be informed but also inspired, delighted, disgusted, saddened, and horrified. What is not expected is that one may become obligated[4] and called into question by the summons of another, consigned and challenged by the substance and substantiality of that one who now holds my regard. Thus quite otherwise, experiencing testimony on the terms of a summoned sensibility requires a very different embodied cognizance, one incarnated in notions of touch rather than sight or sound. This is a sensibility that instantiates the proximity of self and another, an Other who calls, who summons me, and who thus puts me under an encumbrance in which I must consider my response-ability.

These two forms of sensibility lead to very different ways of discussing one's response to testimony. They also align themselves quite differently in relation to various forms of public memory. Within a spectatorial sensibility, testimony is generally framed as a document. One might regard this document as partial evidence supporting or refuting a historical argument and/or a display of the constructed character of memory, particularly in relation to traumatic events. In either case, its characterizations are of the order of an observer in relation to a "text." Testimony is apprehended, read or heard, as a document of memory being remembered. But testimony is not only a document; it is a very specifically textured performative act. To repeat an earlier foreshadowed argument, in bearing witness, one always bears witness to someone, so that in speaking, the witness who speaks summons another to witness this speaking. If one accepts this summons, accepts co-ownership of the testimony-witness relation and the burden of being obligated to testimony beyond one's *a priori* instrumental concerns, then one may be said to approach testimony within a summoned sensibility. The contrast between spectatorial and summoned sensibilities suggests not merely that there are different ways of reading or listening to testimony but that there are different ways to live historically, each with contrasting assumptions regarding the relation between remembrance and learning. It is not a matter of attempting to adjudicate which among differing forms of engagement is the superior, reducing remembrance to one correct form. Indeed, one might choose or find oneself impelled to participate at different times in each of these sensibilities. What is important to underscore, however, is that for a public memory to enact its most radical pedagogical potential, it must include both these sensibilities. Why is this so?

In being summoned to a witnessing relation, one remains open to the possibility of unforeseen memory, the possibility of unfamiliar or uncanny connections, connections which may disrupt attempts to comprehend events and their implications for the lives of people affected by them. While this disruption leaves one less secure in negotiating daily life within an assured "history of the present," it also brings forth the possibility of time, the possibility of futurity. Following Levinas on time, the future is *what comes toward the self, ungraspable, outside its possibilities* (see Cohen 1994, 142). In this sense, a community desirous of hope requires a transactive public memory, a sphere of memorial practice that includes the summons to witness past events that are beyond one's memory and in which one has not been directly implicated. More boldly stated, there is no future without such transactive memorial claims, without responsibilities to memories other than one's own, to memories you have no responsibility for but which claim you to a memorial kinship. As Levinas suggests (1987), in this responsibility, "I am thrown back toward what has never been my fault or my deed, toward what has never been in my power or my freedom, toward what has never been in my presence, and has never come into memory" (111). Hope and an ethical pragmatics mix in this responsibility "to a past that concerns me, that 'regards me,' and is 'my business' outside of all reminiscence, retention, representation, or reference to a remembered present" (111–112). This mix of hope and ethics depends on a responsiveness to others that recognizes that the meeting of testimony and witness does not take place "at the same time," that one does not witness the Other as a contemporary. Witnessing, then, is an event of two disjunctive temporalities, an event in which the other's time disrupts mine. Thus, *it is a new time*, an extra-ordinary dis-juncture of I and other, an experience of proximity which initiates an "infinite distance without distance"(Cohen 1994, 147). It is a moral time, a time of non-in-difference of one person to another, of obligation and responsibility to and for the other (Cohen 1994, 149).

It should be clear by now that I am proposing a transactional sphere of public memory as an educative space, a crucial set of actual practices for encountering historical memories on terms that might teach us anew how to live in the present. As an educational space, a transactional sphere of public memory must be instilled with practices that help us attend to the alterity of lives of others. What might such practices be that could encourage the disruptive touch of memories not mine? What pedagogies can we initiate that might shift the sensibilities through which we listen to the stories of others? With these questions, I want to bring these reflections home, in this case, home to Canada. Returning to stories of the Sayisi Dene with which I began, I will further consider what is at stake in memories of that which has "never been my fault or deed."

Listening as a Mode of Thought[5]

The 1996 Royal Commission on Aboriginal People (RCAP) suggested that Canadians are simply unaware of the history of the Aboriginal presence in what is now Canada and that there is little understanding of the origins and evolution of the relationship between Aboriginal and non-Aboriginal people that have led us to the present moment. For this reason, Georges Erasmus, former cochair of RCAP and a former chief of the Assembly of First Nations, has written, "The roots of injustice lie in history and it is there where the key to the regeneration of Aboriginal society and a new and better relationship with the rest of Canada can be found" (Royal Commission on Aboriginal Peoples 1996). It is in regard to this latter prospect, new and better relations between the people of the First Nations and Canadians, that I now wish to address the possibilities inherent in a transactional sphere of public memory.

No doubt what is currently remembered/forgotten of the histories of First Nation–Canadian relations is implicated in permitting (indeed encouraging) Canadians to distance themselves from, and abdicate their responsibility in regard to, the ongoing conditions of injustice that are part of the day-to-day lived experiences of Aboriginal people in Canada. Certainly there is the need for much increased public attention to the history of First Nation–Canadian postcontact relationships, an attention whose hope is a renewed historical consciousness which would have an impact on how Canadians enact their current relations with First Nation communities. However, what remains unclear is the necessary substance of such a historical consciousness and how it might be established. While one surely must start by supporting the inclusion of "postcontact histories" in educational sites such as schools, cinema, broadcast televison, and the Internet, one must also recognize the limits to the provision of history as "information," as if historical narratives were a neutral form of reportage that encouraged the measurement of historical awareness in terms of how many "facts" someone knows about particular past events, personalities, and communal/societal structures.

The publication and distribution of various forms of written and oral testimony have made up one attempt by First Nation communities to contribute to the development of historical awareness and understanding of the history of First Nation–Canadian relations and its impact on the lives lived in its wake. The testimonial record produced in Canada is consistent with efforts by Aboriginal communities worldwide to speak of their own histories and the histories of their subjugation by and resistance to colonial regimes. One aspect of this history has been government-initiated removal of peoples from land they had being living on for centuries. The Royal Commission on Aboriginal People emphasized that much of the shared history between First Nations people and Canadians is one of dispossession and displacement of Aboriginal people from their traditional homelands, homelands crucial to their physical and cultural survival. One compelling chronicle of such a forced dispossession and displacement is Ila Bussidor's (1997) *Night Spirits: The Story of the Relocation of the Sayisi Dene* (written with the collaboration of Üstün Bilgen-Reinart). In *Night Spirits*, Bussidor provides an account of her people's forced removal by the Canadian government from their traditional homelands and hunting grounds in Northwestern Manitoba to the barren shores of Hudson Bay near Churchill. Bussidor not only writes the story of her family as they experienced the relocation but also provides interview excerpts from various Sayisi Dene who bear witness to particulars of this shameful event and its tragic and traumatic consequences. The reports by Betsy Anderson, Mary Yassie, and Charlie Kithithee cited at the beginning of this chapter are a component of this witness. So is the following account by John Solomon of the events of August 17, 1956, when a government-chartered transport plane arrived at Little Duck Lake, Manitoba, to remove the people living there:

The plane came with three white people plus the pilot. They said they came to move the people. The people never replied. We took whatever we could with us, we left behind our traps, our toboggans, our cabins, and we got into that plane. When we got out in Churchill, there were no trees. The wind was blowing sand on everything. We didn't know what to do next. We couldn't do anything there. We couldn't go trapping. We couldn't set a net. There was nothing to hunt. We were in a desperate state. We had nothing to live on. (Bussidor 1997, 46)

Testimonial accounts such as this one have the potential to make a transactive claim on Canadian public memory, one with the possibility of shifting the stories non-Aboriginals tell of themselves and hence possibly renewing the terms on which to build a redefined relationship between First Nation peoples and Canadians. But what could it mean to listen to such testimonies in order to open oneself to the radical pedagogical and political potential of such memories?

While accounts such as those of Anderson, Yassie, Kithithee, and Solomon seem straightforward enough, they can place difficult and serious demands on readers who recognize they are being called to listen to a bearing of witness directed toward themselves, a "telling," a "speaking to" of traumatic events that will always exceed the words spoken. In this sense, no matter how many words we might read of Sayisi Dene accounts, their testimonies will manifest the marks of insufficiency. These marks—inscribed within the texts themselves—are the scars that bear the difficulties of fully rendering the realities of human cruelty and suffering. It is in this limit condition of testimony that the unspoken may be heard, and it is in the practice of attuning to what is not spoken that the possibility exists for listening to become a way of thinking.

The inevitable limits of the testimonial act mean that narratives and images of historical trauma such as that reported by Anderson, Yassie, Kithithee, and Solomon are shot through with absences that, in their silence, solicit questions. Actively attending to transactive claims of such testimonies includes more than their simple comprehension, more than registering a few shocking facts that one did not know, more than chalking up more evidence of a history of injustice. Such listening requires an attentiveness to the questions one feels such accounts solicit, that is, an attentiveness to one's compulsion to pose difficult and, at times, unanswerable questions, which nonetheless impulsively press for responses that *seemingly* (from within one's own entanglement of history and epistemology) promise help in deciphering what is to be heard in a testimonial account. What is sought in such questions typically is attached not to something within the text but rather to something missing from the text. Rooted in one's own insufficiencies, these are not necessarily polite questions. Indeed, it may be troubling to those bearing witness to hear them spoken, particularly so when such bearing witness is self-understood as an attempt to heal the wounds of a traumatic past.

Nevertheless, what is crucial to stress is that such questions are emotional interrogatives on the part of the listener, marks that the testimony heard is breaking the well-ordered frame which regulates our everyday sense of how human relationships take place. Thus it is that more than one non-Aboriginal reader of *Night Spirits* has asked the question (minimally, to themselves): Given the lack of information the Sayisi Dene had as to why they should move, the sudden unexpected arrival of the plane, the short time they were given to collect belongings, the fact that only four white people arrived to initiate the move, and the absence of reports of people being threatened if they resisted being removed, why did the Sayisi Dene get on the plane? Why didn't the people simply refuse to comply with the government agents who told them to do so?

Now we may indeed render this question as not simply impolite or even cruel, but violent and obscene. This is particularly so to the extent that the question initiates a process of revictimization of the Sayisi Dene and works to alleviate government responsibility for the forced removal and its devastating consequences. Arrogantly judgmental, the question more than hints that the Sayisi Dene were passive victims whose passivity is implicated in their own fate. Indeed, in my view, when the genesis of a question such as this is left unexamined, there is little to redeem this form of "curiosity." Alternatively, one may take the pedagogical position that no question is inappropriate and that, indeed, such a question can be taken as a teachable moment for the provision of information regarding the long history of the development of British and Canadian state-structured authority as it imposed itself on and became entwined with the lives of First Nations peoples. However, the provision of information rarely addresses the generative basis of such a question. If information is provided as authorative history which cancels the question, it may, in fact, short-circuit the pedagogical process which takes as problematic one's practice of listening to others.

It is the possibility of a critical, transformative learning that offers listeners the chance to redeem their obscene questions. This learning begins when we view such questions as *symptomatic* of the difficult knowledge (Britzman 1998) contained in the testimony of the Sayisi Dene, knowledge that places a claim on its non-Aboriginal listener and requires a degree of self-reflexivity in order to be responsive and responsible to that claim. Testimonies such as those of Anderson, Yassie, Kithithee, and Solomon carry a surreal quality for those of us who find such experiences unimaginable. In this sense, they lead to the query: How can this be so? How could this have happened? These are questions that can never be totally resolved by historical narrative. In seeking to find some stable frame for undoing the surreal character of what has been heard, further questions are posed in an attempt to make some sense of the events under description. What is crucial to recognize in this is that when attempting to listen responsibly, one may find testimony such as that provided by the Sayisi Dene disrupting one's taken-for-granted sense-making practices. On such terms, testimonies of historical trauma are always at least partially transgressive, bringing into question the central stories and propositional schema which order one's life.

Faced by a testimony whose texture unhinges one's sense of "what and how things happen," one seeks a "shadow text" (Simon and Armitage-Simon 1995, Simon and Eppert 1997) that may recover and reinscribe a lost sense to an testimonial account. Drawing on taken-for-granted knowledge and beliefs in order to provide workable interpretations that make traumatic events and experiences less incomprehensible, shadow texts may be written not only with partial historical knowledge but, as well, with misconceptions, misinformation, myths, projections, and prejudice. Reflecting an inability or unwillingness to sustain attempts to work through, what, in the end, may be unresolvable questions, shadow texts may become simplistic (or worse, racist and sexist) rationalizations which cripple one's capacity to witness testimony. Thus whether and how the writing of shadow texts is attempted implies much in regard to how the obligations of witnessing are enacted. The work of writing shadow texts, of attempting to provide at least some partial explanation or rationalization which might stabilize our understanding of what happened in the past, is an effort to establish a basis on which the memory of a testimony might be claimed. Yet if one is to be open to the transactive claim of historical memories, one must recognize, as Terrance Des Pres (1980, 42–43) suggests, that the survivor is a genuine transgressor, "a disturber of the peace . . . a runner of the blockade . . . erect[ed] against knowledge of 'unspeakable' things. About these [the survivor] aims to speak, and in so doing . . . undermines, without intending to, the validity of existing norms." To evoke through testimony the memory of an injustice that has initiated a traumatic legacy of death and misery is to be caught in a potential disruption to one's understanding of the human possibility inherent in configuration of our present social order, a disruption that may frighten us as participants in that social order, insofar as it "bears witness to our own historical disfiguration" (Felman and Laub 1992, 73–74).

Thus a responsible listening to the testimony of the Sayisi Dene may require that we face up to the question of how we are to hear accounts of First Nation–Canadian history which bear witness to displacement, death, degradation, and "our own historical disfiguration." This is not a matter merely of an individual's readiness or interest to hear such accounts. Certainly, most Canadians will read Bussidor's book without experiencing a loss of significance of their own sense of the social arrangements that inscribe their everyday lives. Perhaps they will be shocked, perhaps they will "weep" (as a promotional statement for *Night Spirits* suggests), and perhaps they may demand that the government atone for its actions through symbolic and material means. But, much more radically, we are still left with the question of how we are to hear and remember the stories of the Sayisi Dene in ways that incorporate them into an intelligible past while recognizing that there is an insistence in their stories which requires reopening the present to reconsideration—in other words, reopening the very historically constituted terms on which we live and that provide for our understanding history. Beyond the usual rhetoric that testimony renders historical abstractions personal and emotional—characteristics that often fail to lift testimony beyond the entrapment of spectacle—testimonial witness does have the potential to break through one's spectatorial notions regarding what constitutes comprehendible narratives of suffering, survival, and resistance. While such notions enable a certain comprehension of stories of colonialization, to the degree that testimonial address astonishes, disturbs, transgresses those it addresses, it provides much more than information previously unknown. It initiates a summons that is simultaneously a possibility for a learning with the potential radically to reorient what is required to face history anew, a learning rooted in what Levinas (1969) refers to as the "traumatism of astonishment" calling what I know and how I know into question.

It is for this reason that symptomatic obscene questions asked in the face of testimony hold enormous pedagogical potential. To actualize this potential means, however, recognizing that such questions arise from the transactive claim on the listener that testimony initiates and that in order to respond responsibly to this claim, we must rethink how to accomplish the act of listening. A responsible listening thus may require a double attentiveness, a listening to the testimony of the one who is speaking and, at the same time, listening to the questions we find ourselves asking when faced by this testimony. It is then that we might ask ourselves, in hearing a testimonial account: Why are we asking the questions we do? Why do we need to know this? In other words, rather than setting our questions aside or simply posing the questions to, for example, the Sayisi Dene, in order to work through a responsible listening one must pose to ourselves questions about our questions, interrogating why the information and explanations we seek are important and necessary to us.

Here, then, is a critical moment of learning. Without prescribing what this learning might be, let us consider a few possibilities. The first consequence of this reflexive turn to consider the grounds of our own questions may be the realization of our own insufficiency to hear Sayisi Dene testimony, our own inexperience and our own historical ignorance. Surely an initial response to this insufficiency would be a responsibility to learn more about what happened to the Sayisi Dene, collecting as much information as one can in regard to the relocation and its consequences. To this, reasonably, would be added further study of the history of First Nations–Canadian relations and how this history is implicated in the event and consequences of the relocation. However, as I have been suggesting, simply acquiring more information will never suffice if one is to respond to the force of a testimonial address, a force which, if acknowledged, puts ourselves into question. Thus we would have not only to try to alleviate our own ignorance but also to transform the very grounds for its existence in the first place. Crucial here would be the recognition that our insufficiency to hear the testimony of another is a *historical* insufficiency, one with structural conditions that hold it in place.

Thus, too, we are challenged to study our own education and limits, beginning to understand how the social arrangements of our lives and the investments that they inculcate are not only incomplete but also deficient, at least in terms of what we need to know to reconstruct the substance of First Nation–Canadian relations. But such a formulation of the learning inherent in questioning our questions is far too limited. Ignorance is not simply a rationally organized state of affairs but is, as well, a dynamic, unconscious structure which fosters resistance to knowledge. Thus an exploration of our own insufficiencies means attending to what presumptions and defences Sayisi Dene testimony elicits. This would be an attempt not only to learn *about* this testimony, but also to learn *from* it by working through the vaguely felt and little understood psychic projections and culturally invested frameworks that order our attention to narratives that speak to "the past in Canada."

The recognition of insufficiency, however, sets only one half of the learning agenda. The other half requires yet another turn in the practice of critical reflection. This is an openness to the possibility that our questions are not really questions at all, but, rather, rhetorical statements based on the premise that we really are able to understand what we are being told, that indeed we have heard of similar things happening before and that we can understand (and judge) Sayisi Dene testimony on these terms.[6] Thus is set another learning task defined as a response to the following questions: What other histories are elicited (perhaps free-associated) by us when hearing Sayisi Dene testimony? How does this displacement of the relocation of Dene onto other histories condense what, in fact, are separate realities? What knowledge and understanding are subjugated in this process of displacement, and what perspective might be gained in it? And what is our relation to these "other" histories, and how is comprehension of Sayisi Dene testimony filtered through our struggles to understand these other instances, particularly those including forced population removal, for example, the Nazi attempt to make Europe *Judenrein*, or the recent Serbian attempt at "ethnic cleansing" in Kosovo?

While such explorations might help further unravel the grounds of our own questioning, critically examining the rhetorical tenor of these questions requires one further step. This would be an attending to the particular historically and culturally structured forms of narrative coherence and reason which have become a precondition for our attention to and making sense of the stories we are told. We

might note how, in listening to certain testimony that is "hard to follow," our attention wanders, contrasting this with the narrative structures of an account that seem
riveting, holding our attention throughout. We might also note to what degree the
"sense of an account" devolves to a judgment as to the persuasiveness and reliability
of the practice of witness. It is not that one can ever completely eliminate the practice of judgment in hearing the stories of another (nor would such an elimination
be desirable) but, rather, that what is at issue is taking full measure of how and why
the terms of our judgments are invoked in the practice of listening, and what this
prevents us from hearing.[7]

In holding together the doubled moments of attentiveness to testimony, one informational, the other reflexive, there is a practice of binding together remembering
and learning. If such a practice is brought to a sphere of public memory, learning in
such a space could be more than knowledge acquisition and remembering more
than the retrieval, recollection, or recall of something past but now forgotten. It
may be objected that the reflexivity I suggest necessary to a transactive public memory is a perverse narcissism that turns an engagement with history toward a concern
with oneself rather than the concerns of the Other. After all, what is important
about the Sayisi Dene testimony is that it makes a claims on us to learn of events
hidden to most Canadians, to hear a story of people who suffered and died unnec-
essarily and as a result of government action, and to work in solidarity with those
Sayisi Dene who are still living the legacy of this event and attempting to recover a
viable and dynamic communal life. The fundamental issue is to recognize an injustice within a demand for justice and to take the measure of what changes must accrue as a result. But what must accrue as a result is not only retributive justice for
the Sayisi Dene but also, as Bussidor and other Dene recognize, a change in the way
non-Aboriginals view their shared history with First Nation peoples. For this
change to happen, we will have to learn to listen differently, to take the measure of
our ignorance, and reassess the terms on which we are prepared to hear stories that
might trouble the social arrangements on which, as Canadians, we presume a collective future. In Benjamin's idiom, we have to learn to take the counsel in stories of
a shared past as told by First Nations people.

Education and Canadian Public Memory

That which is being given in and through the testimony collected in *Night Spirits* is
a memorial inheritance whose importance exceeds the immediacy of one's own
personal engagement with these memories. Bussidor's own testimony and the testimonies collected by her make a claim on Canadian public memory. This is particularly so if we take Canadian public memory as sphere for developing a historical

consciousness—not as an individual awareness and attitude but as a practice, a commitment to and participation in an organized practice of remembrance and learning. Certainly this would be a form of public memory quite different from the reiteration of valued stories which attempt to secure the permanence of collective affiliations and identifications in stable notions of a meaningful past. Rather, I prefer to think of public memory as a sphere of interminable and exacting learning not just where one is informed through remembrance but where one learns to remember anew. What needs to be offered within a practice of public memory is not the sameness of common memory but the discontinuities of an always incomplete remembrance.

On such terms, memory would not be simply a private act but rather a social gesture—a gesture that bears responsibility for the past to the present, reopening the present in terms demanded by a fair hearing of the past. In regard to such a notion of public memory, an educator's responsibility is not only to support the inclusion of forgotten or unknown histories that pertain to our contemporary problems and relationships, but also to help constitute public memory as a pedagogical space by making evident and supporting the critical exploration of the questions, uncertainties, ambiguities, and failures that arise in the process of trying to hear testimonies that speak to these forgotten or unknown histories. That is, in order for Canadian public memory to foster a renewed historical consciousness which would impact how Canadians enact their current relations with First Nations communities, as educators we must try to find ways to define memory-spaces (in schools, in media, in art practice, in Internet-based exchanges) in which stories of speaking and hearing, remembering and learning are exchanged, examined, and understood as the grounds for a critical pedagogical practice of remembrance.

The insistence on the importance of a "public" memory at this moment in Canadian history is a self-conscious response to contemporary inclination toward the privatization of memory. Such an insistence affirms the need for a collective space of remembering and learning quite different from the construction of memory strictly defined on individual terms. One cannot, of course, minimize the importance of personal, local memories. But when we are asked to attend to the testimony of witnesses speaking about experiences that bear on the possibilities of new and better relationships among diverse members of the geographical based political economy we find ourselves within (and may still, acting in concert, at least partially restructure), it is necessary to affirm one's commitment to a public dialogue in which the transactive character of memory is seen as an opportunity for a necessary learning. This would be a learning founded on an *a priori* commitment to attend to the concerns of those who are here, facing us, who, in speaking to us of a shared history, draw near, demanding something of our time, energy, and thought. It is also a learning that recognizes the witness as (to echo the words of

Des Pres) a "genuine transgressor" whose words refuse to be reduced to the terms of prevailing categories and, indeed, are necessary for the invention of new forms of social life.

Sayisi Dene: Testimony and Public Memory

One might argue that the little-known story of the Sayisi Dene must be recovered because it is emblematic of systemic structures of violence enacted within Canadian colonial relations. Indeed, Ila Bussidor herself asks that the story not be heard as unique to the Sayisi Dene. Undoubtedly the Sayisi Dene testimony references a larger picture of the Canadian colonialization of First Nation peoples. No doubt, the death and suffering of the Sayisi Dene must be related to millions of other instances of Aboriginal death and suffering over the last five centuries. But within a renewed Canadian public memory, a story would not need to satisfy the criteria of being emblematic or exemplary in order to be worthy of remembrance. No one's pain should be diminished by saying it is less emblematic, less historically important than anyone else's. Certainly, a "public" memory ought to acknowledge that if remembrance is required for justice to be pursued, then remembrance is required when people have been injured. But it is not simply the fact of victimization that is the force of obligation to remember and attend to Sayisi Dene testimony, its also that they are here, now, addressing us, summoning us to listen and learn not just *about* their story but *from* their story, teaching us in turn how it is that the story they tell is not just about them but about us as well.

The Sayisi Dene live in the present with the ongoing consequences of injustice that have resulted from policies and decisions made by the Canadian and Manitoba governments on behalf of their constituents. To witness the stories of the 1956 forced removal of the Dene, one has to hear about traumatic deaths and sufferings of specific people. The loss and grief, both personal and collective, remain deeply experienced. Amid the lives of real people, justice is no abstraction; it exists in relation to people who have been hurt and requires something be done to support the repair of this hurt. While remembrance does not ensure anything, least of all justice, it can concretize human aspirations to make present a world yet to be realized, thus presenting us with claims of justice and the requirements of compassion.

However, for remembrance to be truly hopeful, something more must be put into play than human aspirations for a better future. This requires attending to practices of remembrance as a difficult learning, a learning that can hold open the present to its insufficiency. To do this, remembrance requires attuning oneself to the power of the Sayisi Dene testimony to rupture our invested understanding of ourselves, our government, and the regulating political, economic, and technological frameworks we unconsciously use to negotiate our world. The trauma that the Dene experienced and the compelling nature of Bussidor's and others' testimonies are such that they refuse to remain assimilated to the terms of dominant historical understanding. Rather, this testimony keeps returning, provoking deep questions about what it means for us to understand the lives of others. It calls us again and again to attend, hear, and respond responsibly, attempting to recognize what of ourselves is tied up with our understanding of the history and contemporary substance of First Nations–Canadian relationships. While the roots of injustice lie in history, we have yet to realize a historical consciousness, as a mode of learning and practice of instantiating living communal memories, that might be capable of supporting the regeneration of new and better relations between First Nations peoples and Canadians. This then is the time and the task.

Acknowledgments

This chapter is drawn from a larger project exploring the relation of testimony and historical memory. Project work has generously been supported by a grant from the Social Sciences and Humanities Council of Canada.

Notes

1. To speak of touch here is to emphasize the primacy of a response that reveals the vulnerability of the self to the approach of another. As Wyschogrod (cited in Jay 1994, 557) has suggested, "touch is not a sense at all; it is in fact a metaphor for the impingement of the world as a whole upon subjectivity . . . to touch is to comport oneself not in opposition to the given but in proximity with it."

2. As Appadurai (1996) comments, "sentiments whose greatest force is in their ability to ignite intimacy into a political sentiment and turn locality into a staging ground for identity, have become spread over vast and irregular spaces as groups move, yet stay linked to one another through sophisticated media capabilities." It is perhaps ironic to note that the practices of globalization have made many diasporic formations increasingly stable and central loci of learning and identification.

3. Note here the importance of not restricting oneself to the legal regulation of what constitutes legitimate testimony, where practices of conveyance of lived realities may often be dismissed as "hearsay."

4. This is not to say an observer operating with a spectatorial sensibility is without obligations. One may be obligated within the norms of historiography, by principles of research ethics, or by a series of *a priori* affiliations and identifications which require attentiveness to what an-

other is attempting to communicate. However, none of these obligations are founded in that instant of regard in which I face another who in that moment addresses me.

5. The thoughts in this section are based on the collective work of Susan Fletcher, Florence Sicoli, Nancy Chater, Lynne Davis, and myself. While their guidance and critique have been essential, they are in no way responsible for the position taken in this paper.

6. One witness, upon viewing a videotape of Ila Bussidor providing testimony to the Royal Commission, exclaimed: "What is new in this? What am I do with this story? Haven't we heard all this before? The Sayisi Dene relocation is just another version of what happened at Davis Inlet" [referring to another incidence of forced removal initiated by the Canadian government].

7. For an extensive example of how the normative structure of judgments, mobilized when listening to testimony, limit what can be heard, see Simon and Eppert 1997.

References

Appadurai, Arjun. 1996. *Modernity at Large: Cultural Dimensions of Globalization*. Minneapolis, MN: University of Minnesota Press.

Benjamin, Walter. 1969. "The Storyteller." In *Illuminations*. Harry Zohn, trans. New York: Schocken Books.

Britzman, Deborah P. 1998. *Lost Subjects, Contested Objects: Toward a Psychoanalytic Inquiry of Learning*. Albany, NY: State University of New York.

Bussidor, Ila, and Bilgen-Reinart, Üstün. 1997. *Night Spirits: The Story of the Relocation of the Sayisi Dene*. Winnipeg: University of Manitoba Press.

Cohen, Richard A. 1994. *Elevations: The Height of the Good in Rosenzweig and Levinas*. Chicago: University of Chicago Press.

Des Pres, Terrance. 1980. *The Survivor: An Anatomy of Life in the Death Camps*. Oxford: Oxford University Press.

Eppert, Claudia. 1999. "Learning Responsivity/Responsibility: Reading the Literature of Historical Witness." Doctoral Dissertation, University of Toronto.

Erasmus, G., and Dessault, R. 1996. "Address for the Launch of the Report of the Royal Commission on Aboriginal Peoples." Museum of Civilization, Nov 21 (unpublished address).

Felman, Shoshana, and Laub, Dori. 1992. *Testimony: Crises of Witnessing in Literature, Psychoanalysis and History*. New York: Routledge.

Finkielkraut, Alain. 1992. *Remembering in Vain: The Klaus Barbie Trial and Crimes against Humanity (European Perspectives)*. Roxanne Lapidus, trans. New York: Columbia University Press.

Jay, Martin. 1994. *Downcast Eyes: The Denigration of Vision in Twentieth-Century French Thought*. Berkeley, CA: University of California Press.

Levinas, Emmanuel. 1969. *Totality and Infinity*. Alphonso Lingis, trans. Pittsburgh, PA: Duquesne University Press.

Levinas, Emmanuel. 1987. "Diachrony and Representation." In *Time and the Other (and Other*

Additional Essays). Richard Cohen, trans. Pittsburgh, PA: Duquesne University Press.

Levinas, Emmanuel. 1998. *Otherwise Than Being or Beyond Essence.* Alphonso Lingis, trans. Pittsburgh, PA: Duquesne University Press.

Morrison, Toni. 1987. *Beloved.* London: Chatto.

Roth, Michael S. 1995. *The Ironist's Cage: Memory, Trauma, and the Construction of History.* New York: Columbia University Press.

Royal Commission on Aboriginal People 1996 Report. Volume 1. "Looking Forward, Looking Back." Ottawa: Canada Communications Group.

Simon, Roger I., and Wendy Armitage-Simon. 1995. "Teaching Risky Stories: Remembering Mass Destruction through Children's Literature." *English Quarterly* vol. 28, no. 1 (Fall): 27–31.

Simon, Roger I., and Claudia Eppert. 1997. "Remembering Obligation: Pedagogy and the Witnessing of Testimony of Historical Trauma." *Canadian Journal of Education* vol. 22, no. 2 (Spring): 175–191.

Simon, Roger I. Forthcoming. "The Paradoxical Practice of *Zakhor*: Memories of 'That Which Has Never Been My Fault of Deed.'" In *Between Hope and Despair: Pedagogy and the Remembrance of Historical Trauma.* Roger I. Simon, Sharon Rosenberg, and Claudia Eppert, eds. Boulder, CO: Rowman and Littlefield.

II   INSTITUTING EDUCATION

JACQUES DERRIDA
Translated by Denise Egéa-Kuehne

WHERE A TEACHING BODY[1] BEGINS AND HOW IT ENDS[2]

[**W**e'll have more than one sign that these notes were not destined, as one says, to be published.

However, nothing was to keep them concealed. What could be more public, fundamentally, and more demonstrable than teaching? What could be more exposed, if not, as is the case here, its staging [mise en scène] or its being put into question again [remise en question]? This is why—and it is my primary reason[3]—I accepted the offer to reproduce these notes without the slightest modification.

But there must have been other reasons since I hesitated for a long time. Indeed what could be the significance of a fragment (more or less arbitrarily cut, as with a massicot) out of one single session—and what is more the first session—bearing more than the others the mark of the inadequacies, the approximations, the programmatic generality delivered before an audience more anonymous and undetermined than ever? Why this session rather than another one, and why my continuous discourse rather than others, rather than the critical exchanges which followed? I could not settle on a response to these questions, but I finally considered that the struggle in which the GREPH is engaged today[4] rendered them secondary; since the proposed session refers essentially to the GREPH, why not seize indirectly [par la bande] this opportunity to make the challenges and the objectives of its work better known?

Other objection, more serious: Was my participation in this book compatible with the very subject these notes will offer for reading, at least in part and indirectly? Should I serve (or make serve) one of these numerous enterprises (here under its immediately publishable form) which multiply skirmishes against the very thing (this being said without suspecting—it is not important— all the intentions of all their agents) from which they draw their existence and whose alibis they foster? More precisely still: Do not the gathering of names, the sorting out of figures, and the exhibition of titles make clear *one of these phenomena of* authority *(well established, already, counterinstitution, even if, considered from different angles, its unity must leave us perplexed and invite the most cautious of investigations) necessarily produced by the apparatus which, on the contrary, it should be a matter of dislocating? The connections between this apparatus and the publishing one are increasingly evident. They constitute precisely one of the objects of research of the* GREPH, *or rather one of its targets, which is why it should articulate its action with that of a group of research and information working on the publishing machine. The subject of what you are reading here is obvious (nondisguised), and indeed consists in calling for such actions, on the job* [sur le tas].

But I am greatly simplifying, we must hurry. The laws of this field are convoluted, and one must handle this problem [s'y prendre] *by attacking them* [en s'en prenant à elles]. *In short, because I take into account the largest amount of data at my disposal, and because it seems to me that the objectives of the* GREPH *mandate it, ultimately I prefer to run the risk of posing here (this time from an internal border) spiraling questions which touch upon the places, scenes, and forces which still enable these questions to present themselves.*

This fragment of the first session opened a sort of counterseminar at the Research Center on the Teaching of Philosophy. This center was instituted at the École Normale Supérieure *two years earlier* [i.e., 1972], *and is distinct in principle from the* GREPH, *with which, of course, opportunities for exchange are abundant.*

The agenda for 1974–1975 includes the following questions:

- *What is a teaching body—philosophy?*
- *Today, what does "defense" mean, and today, what does "philosophy" mean in the slogan "defense of philosophy"?*
- *French ideology and ideologues (analysis of the concept of ideology and of the French ideologues' politico-pedagogical projects around the Revolution).]*

Here, for example, is not an indifferent[5] place.

One should not-forget-it. One should (first, let's attempt just to see if we can pull it off, a discourse without "should," and not only without any apparent "should," visible as such, but without any concealed "should"; I propose that we drive them out of discourses said to be theoretical, even transethical, and even when they do not present themselves as instructional discourses; at bottom, in these last instances, in teaching discourses, the "should"—the lesson given every moment, as soon as one begins to speak—is perhaps, naively or not, all the more declared; a fact which, under certain conditions, can render it powerless faster), therefore one should avoid naturalizing this place.

Naturalizing always comes to neutralizing; or in any case, it comes pretty close to it.

By naturalizing, by pretending to consider as natural what is not and never was, one neutralizes. One neutralizes what? Or rather, to give the impression of neutrality, one dissimulates the active intervention of a force and of an apparatus.

By passing for natural (therefore beyond questioning and transformation) the structures of a pedagogical institution—its forms, its norms, its visible or invisible constraints, its frames, the whole apparatus we would have called *parergonal* last year, and which, while it seems to surround it, it determines it to the very center of its content, and no doubt from its center outward—one carefully covers the forces and the interests which, without the slightest neutrality, dominate, master, impose themselves on the process of teaching from within an agonistic field which is heterogenous, divided, and worked through by an unceasing struggle.

Therefore any institution (again, I am using a word which will need to undergo a certain work of critique), any relation to the institution, calls for, and ahead of time, in any case, implies a choice [*prise de parti*] in this field: taking into consideration, actually considering the actual field, it calls for taking a stand [*prise de position*] and a bias [*parti pris*].

There is no neutral or natural place in teaching.

Here, for example, is not an indifferent place.

A broad analysis (historical, psychoanalytical, politico-economical, and so on, and also somewhere philosophical) would be imperative to define this here-and-now, even though in principle a theoretical analysis is insufficient here, since it becomes effectively "relevant" only for staging [*mettre en scène*] and bringing into play [*mettre en jeu*] he who in practice takes the risk of going as far as displacing the very locus from which he carries out this analysis, even though it is therefore insufficient and interminable as such.

This here-and-now appears immediately as a theater hall [*salle de théâtre*], a movie theater [*salle de cinéma*], or a converted community hall [*salle de fête*] (for reasons of security, and because there were not enough seats in the so-called lecture halls [*salles de cours*] still reserved only a short time ago for a small number of selected "*normaliens*"[6]). Here, in the École Normale Supérieure, in the place where I, this teaching body which I call mine and which occupies a very determined function in what is called the French philosophical teaching body today—I teach, I now say that I teach.

And where for the first time, at least in this direct form, I am about to speak of the teaching of philosophy.

That is to say where, after some fifteen years of practicing what one calls teaching, and twenty three years of civil service, I only begin to systematically question, exhibit, critique (or rather, I start by beginning there, I start by beginning to do it systematically and effectively: it is this systematic character which matters if one's aim is not to settle for verbal alibis, for skirmishes and scratches which do not affect the established system, which no philosopher somewhat alert will ever have omitted, and which, on the contrary, are part of the predominant system, of its very code, of its relation to itself, of its self-critical reproduction, this self-critical reproduction forming perhaps the element of tradition and philosophical conservation, of its constant changing of the guard [*sa relève*],[7] with the art of questioning which will be addressed later; it is this *systematic* character which matters, and its *effectiveness*, which one has never been able to reduce to the initiative of one person only; and that is why, for the first time, here, I link my discourse to the work of a group engaged under the name of GREPH); hence I begin, so late, to systematically question, exhibit, and critique—in the hope of transforming—the borders of that in which I have delivered more than one talk.

When I say "so late," it is not (at least not mainly) to make a scene, and to once more pull the self-rectification stunt, the *mea-culpa* or the bad-conscience-on-exhibit stunt. That would be a gesture for which I could justify at length why I refrain from it. Let us say, to cut it very short, that I never had a taste for it and that I even made of it an issue of taste. Rather, when I say "so late," it is to begin the analysis of both, *at one and the same time*, a delay which, as we know, is not solely mine and cannot be explained solely by subjective or individual insufficiencies, *and* a possibility which today does not open by accident or because of the decision of one person only. And the delay and the awareness one acquires of and from it, under various forms, as well as the beginning of a research (theoretical and practical, as one says) on the teaching of philosophy, all that responds to a certain number of necessities. All that can be analyzed indeed.

But even if it is a question here, after all, neither of individual errors nor of individual merits, neither of dogmatic slumber nor of personal vigilance, let us not take that as an excuse to dissolve into anonymous neutrality what is, once more, neither neutral nor anonymous.

As you know, on several occasions, I have insisted on this: the École Normale should be neither at the center nor even at the origin of the activities of the GREPH. To be sure. But the fact that the GREPH will have seemed at least to begin to locate here must not be omitted; it is in no way fortuitous. That constitutes a possibility, a resource to be exploited; it must be analyzed and brought into play [*mettre en oeuvre*] in all its historico-political bearings. But this possibility also imports its limits. One could go beyond those only on the condition (necessary though insufficient) of taking into account—a critical and scientific account—this hardly contestable fact. Without delay or caution, we will have to keep (theoretically and practically, as one must say) a rigorous account of the role this strange institution still plays, and especially will have played in the cultural and philosophical apparatus of this country. And whatever the bottom line of this account, this role will have been very important; any denial on this subject would be futile or suspect.

On the other hand, declaring that here I will bring only a partial or particular contribution to the activities of the GREPH, without engaging it and especially without orienting it, must not cause the following fact to be misappreciated or subtracted from the analysis (deducted): after having announced it for a long time, I at least appeared to take the initiative, in a seminar I conducted, of instituting the GREPH, and first of all its preliminary proposal [avant-projet], submitted here for your discussion.

That is not fortuitous. I do not call attention to this to mark or appropriate a new institution or counterinstitution but, on the contrary, to turn over a surface, to give back, render,[8] submit a very particular effect which comes with my function in this process.

Consequently, from what I will call, to go fast, my place or my viewpoint, it was evident that the work in which I was engaged—at the risk of new misunderstandings, and by algebra, let us name it the (affirmative) deconstruction of phallogocentrism as philosophy—did not belong in any simple manner to the forms of the philosophical institution. By definition, this work was not limited to a theoretical content, not even to a cultural or ideological content. It did not proceed according to the established norms of a theoretical activity. By more than one trait and at strategically defined moments, it had to resort to a "style" unacceptable for a university lecture body (one did not have to wait long for "allergic" reactions), unacceptable even in places where one thinks oneself foreign to the university. As we know, it is not always inside the university that the "university style" dominates. It may happen that it clings to the skin of those who have left the university, and even of some who never attended it. It can be seen from its borders. Hence this work was grappling with the ontological or transcendental subordination of the signifying body in relation to the ideality of the transcendental signified *and* to the logic of the sign, to the transcendental authority of the signified as well as that of the signifier, therefore with what constitutes the very essence of the philosophical. Thus consequently, from then on, it has been necessary (coherent and programmed) for deconstruction not to limit itself to the conceptual content of philosophical pedagogy, but to tackle the philosophical scene and all its institutional norms and forms, as well as all that renders them possible.

Had it limited itself—which it never did except in the eyes of those who derived

some benefit from seeing nothing—to a simple semantic or conceptual deconstitu-
tion, deconstruction would have but formed a modality—a new one—of the internal self-critique of philosophy. It would have run the risk of reproducing the
philosophical propriety, the relationship of philosophy to itself, the economy of traditional putting into question [*mise en question*].

But in the work awaiting us, we shall have to be wary of all forms of reproduction, of all the powerful and subtle resources of reproduction: among which, if one
can still say that, the form of a concept of reproduction which cannot be utilized
here ("simply") without "broadening" it (Marx), which cannot be broadened without recognizing there the always heterogenous contradiction at work, which cannot
be analyzed in its essential contradiction without posing in all its magnitude the
problem of contradiction (or of dialectic) as philosopheme. Is it with such a
philosopheme (with something like a "Marxist philosophy") that in a "last instance" an effective deconstruction of philosophy can operate?

Inversely, if deconstruction had at the basis neglected the *internal* destructura-
tion of the phallogocentric onto-theology, it would have reproduced the classical
logic of the frame, because of some sudden haste insisting on the primacy of the political, sociological, historical, economic, and so on. And it would have let itself be
guided, more or less directly, by traditional metaphysical schemes. It seems to me
that this is what threatens or limits, at the root, the rare and therefore very valuable
French research projects on the teaching of philosophy, whatever the differences or
oppositions which relate them one to the other. But my reservation here—later I
will try to argue for it by looking at it more closely—does not lead me to fail to recognize, far from it, the importance and the function of trail-blazing [*frayage*] which
the books of Nizan or Canivez, Sève or Châtelet, for example, may have.

Therefore deconstruction—or at least what I have proposed under this name
which is quite as good as any other, but no more—has always had in principle some
bearing on the teaching apparatus and function in general, and on the philosophical apparatus and function in particular and *par excellence*. Without reducing its
specificity, I will say that what begins now is nothing but a stage to pass through
along a systematic trajectory.

No doubt a stage, but which meets a formidable difficulty as if naked (or almost, as one must always say in a gymnastics), a historical and political testing [*mise
à l'épreuve*] of which I would like to indicate right now the principial scheme.

On the one hand: the deconstruction of phallogocentrism as deconstruction of
the onto-theological principle, of metaphysics, of the question "What is?" of the
subordination of all the fields of questioning with the onto-encyclopedic instance,
and so on—such a deconstruction attacks the root of the *universitas*, the root of philosophy as teaching, the ultimate unity of the philosophical, of the discipline of philosophy, or of the university of philosophy as the foundation of any university. The

university *is* philosophy indeed, a university is always the construction of a philosophy.[9] But, it is difficult (but not impossible, as I will try to show) to conceive a program of philosophical teaching (as such) and a philosophical institution (as such) which follow substantially from, or even survive, a rigorous deconstruction.

But on the other hand: concluding from a *project* of deconstruction to the pure and simple, *immediate* disappearance of philosophy and of its teaching and teachings, to their "death" as one would say with the vacuity of someone who today would still ignore what the returns of the dead are all about,[10] would mean once more abandoning the terrain of a struggle to very determined forces whose interest is always to install—according to ways we will have to study, on the places apparently deserted by philosophy, and therefore from then on occupied, preoccupied by empiricism, technocracy, morality, or religion (and all this at once)—a properly metaphysical dogmatism, more vital than ever, to serve forces which have been forever linked to the phallogocentric hegemony. In other words, still going no further than the algebra of this preliminary positioning [*mise en place*], abandoning the terrain under the pretense that one can no longer defend the old machine (and that one has even contributed to its dislocation) would therefore mean that one understands nothing about the deconstructive strategy.

It would mean confining it to a set of *theoretical* operations: immediate, discursive, and finite.

Since the theoretical and discursive operation privileges the philosophical form of discourses, even if deconstruction had already reached some sufficient general results on fundamentals (which is far from being certain, too many indices point to that), this philosophical discourse is itself determined (in effect) by an enormous organization (social, economical, instinctual, phantasmic, and so on), by a powerful system of multiple forces and antagonisms—which deconstruction has itself as its "object" but of which it is also, in the necessarily determined forms it must take, *an effect* (I refer you to what I say about this word somewhere else, in *Positions*[11]).

In this sense it is always unfinished [*interminée*]; and in order not to be reduced to a modern episode of philosophical reproduction, deconstruction can neither be associated with a liquidation of philosophy (triumphant and verbose in one case, embarrassed and still fussy in the other), the political consequences of which have been diagnosed long ago; nor can it hang on to some "defense of philosophy," to some reactive rearguard action which, in order to keep a decomposing body, only makes things easier for these liquidating attempts.

Consequently, as always fighting on two fronts, on two stages, and according to two ranges, a rigorous and efficient deconstruction should at one and the same time develop a (practical) critique of the current philosophical institution *and* engage a positive, rather affirmative, audacious, extensive, and intensive transformation of a teaching said to be "philosophical." No longer a new *plan of the university*, in the eschato-teleological style of what was done under this name in the eighteenth and nineteenth centuries, but an altogether different type of propositions, dependent on and answerable to another logic, and taking into account a maximum of new data of all kinds which I do not undertake to enumerate today. Some of them will rapidly become clear. These offensive propositions would both align themselves with the theoretical and the practical state of deconstruction, and take very concrete forms, the most efficient possible in France in 1975. I will not fail to take my risks and my responsibilities regarding these propositions. And to mark as of now— if the name "Haby"[12] is attributed to the most conspicuous sign of this context— that I will not form an alliance with those who are intent on "the defense of philosophy" as it is practiced today in its French institution; that I will not subscribe to just whichever form of battle "for philosophy," since what interests me is a fundamental transformation of the *general* situation in which these problems are set.

If I brought forth these first remarks on a possible link between the activities of the GREPH and an enterprise of deconstruction, it is not solely for the reasons which have just become evident. It is also in order not to neutralize or naturalize the place which I occupy there, it is even in order no longer to pretend that I discount it, as it may have seemed useful to do sometimes, give or take a few simulacra, of which I would like to reconstitute the logic.

Perhaps it will introduce us to the question of the teaching body.

Within the French National Education system, by immediate priority, my professional function binds me to the École Normale Supérieure[13] where I occupy, under the title of teaching assistant of the history of philosophy, the place which has been defined as that of *agrégé-répétiteur* since the nineteenth century. I want to stop for a moment on the word *répétiteur* to begin discussing the question of the teaching body in respect to what makes it yield to repetition.

As a *répétiteur*, the *agrégé-répétiteur* should not produce anything, at least if produce means to innovate, to transform, to make the novel happen. He is destined to repeat and to make others repeat, to reproduce and to make others reproduce: forms, norms, and content. He must assist students with reading and understanding texts, help them interpret these texts, and help them understand what is expected of them—help them understand what they must respond to and what they are responsible for at each different stage of evaluation and selection, in regard to the contents or the logico-rhetorical organization of their exercises (*explication de texte, dissertation,*[14] or lessons). Therefore, with the pupils, he must make himself the representative of a system of reproduction (no doubt complex, worked upon by a multiplicity of antagonisms, relayed by relatively independent microsystems, and because of its movement, always leaving a sort of parallel circuit connection [*prise de dérivation*][15] whose representatives can, under certain conditions, exploit the system and turn around against it, although at every moment this system is hierarchized and constantly tends to reproduce this hierarchy); or rather, he must be the expert who, supposed to be more familiar with the demand to which he had to yield first, can explain it, translate it, repeat it, and therefore re-present it for the young candidates. This demand is necessarily the demand of what dominates in the system (right now, for convenience's sake, let us call that "power," being understood that I do not simply mean what one generally puts under this word, especially not simply the power of the government or the majority of the moment), represented by the relatively autonomous power of the teaching body, itself delegating its own boards of examiners for *concours*[16] or theses, and its commissions or consultative committees. The *répétiteur* passes for being an expert in the interpretation of this demand; he is not allowed to formulate any other unless he submits it to one channel or the other for the approval of said power, which may-or-may-not-or-cannot-or-does-not-want-to-be-able-to-or-does-not-want-to-want-to let it go through. In any case, it is always the demand of the dominant power which, by contract, the expert commits himself to represent before the candidates; he helps them comply with it, and he does all that in response to the general demand, from which, of course, that of the candidate is not excluded.

To be sure, since this field remains a multiplicity of always overdetermined[17] antagonisms, the transmission belt works and runs through all sorts of resistances, of counterforces, and of leeway or contraband movements. The most apparent effect is thus a series of dissociations in the practices of *répétiteurs* and candidates: one applies rules in which one no longer believes at all or entirely, which one even otherwise criticizes, often violently. The candidate asks the *répétiteur* to initiate him into a discourse whose form and content appear obsolete to one of them or to both—obsolete for reasons which are highly determined and quite familiar to some or again, what one will judge more or less serious as the case may be, proper to a sort of foreign language, modern [*vivante*] or not. In the best of cases, the *répétiteur* and the candidate exchange conniving winks and, at the same time, recipes: "What to say, what not to say, how it must be said or not be said?" and so on, so long as it is understood that we agree no longer to subscribe to the demand which is placed on us, to the philosophy or, let us say for convenience's sake, to the ideology implied in the demand, no more than we acknowledge the competence of those whom the power designates to judge us, according to modalities and aims open to critique. Let us not limit this situation to the "exercises" and to the explicit preparation of examinations and *concours*: it is that of any discourse held in the university, from the most conformist to the most contentious, at the École Normale or elsewhere. By the same token, the *répétiteur* and the candidate break up, dissociate, or split apart. The candidate knows that, most often, he must present a conformist discourse to which he does not subscribe regarding either its form or its content. The *répétiteur* dons his official cap to correct *dissertations* and "repeat" lessons, and to give technical advice in the name of an examination board and canons which in his eyes are discredited. Like the candidates, he severely judges, for example, some reports published by a given examination board; and when either of them happens to address some protests to the General Inspectors[18] or to the chairs of the examination boards, they know from experience that they will quite simply remain unanswered.

Since for few years the *répétiteurs* have been authorized here to hold a seminar in addition to and beside the repetition exercises proper, the *répétiteur* reproduces this division in his "seminar": he tries to help the "candidates" even as he introduces, as if smuggling them in, premises which no longer belong to the space of the general *agrégation*[19] and even undermine that space more or less slyly. Such a dissociation is so well assumed or internalized on both sides that during these exercises, and again partially during the seminars, I for one could almost totally forego involving a research I carry on somewhere else and which can be possibly consulted in publications. I act as if that work did not exist, and only those who read me can reconstitute the web which, of course, though concealed, holds together my teaching and my published texts. In principle, everything in the seminar must begin at a fictitious point zero of my rapport with the audience: as if at every moment, we were all "great beginners." And on these two values (repetition and "great beginners"), we will have to return to seek there a general law of philosophical exchange, a permanent general law whose phenomena will have nonetheless been differentiated, specific, and irreducible through the course of history. This dissociative fiction is well assumed on both sides, give or take a few ruses and detours; once, a short time ago, I happened to hear it said to me, if you will, by two students of the École, whom I quote here not for the sake of the anecdote but for the sake of the symptom. During the course of his studies, one of them said to me: "I decided not to read you in order to work without prejudice and to simplify our relations." And indeed, he seems to have read me after the *agrégation*, and has even quoted me in some of his publications (otherwise remarkable), which would have caused him, he told me, some difficulties with this or that committee before which he was still in a candidate position. His studies finished, and once appointed to the position of assistant at a university in Paris, the other one told me recently that he preferred these publications of mine to that other one and asked me whether I shared his sentiment; as I showed some reticence and some powerlessness to grade my own exercises, he concluded in way of an excuse: "You know, for what it's worth, it is mostly to show you that now I read you." Now, that is to say now that I am no longer a candidate for the *agrégation*, now that the space of repetition no longer runs the risk (or so he believed) of getting blurred, the space where you, the *répétiteur*, had to reflect a code and a program before I, so that in turn, I could reflect them.

By the word program, I do not understand only the one which, every year in the spring, in a rather arbitrary fashion (and in any case according to motives which are never exposed, about which no one ever has to call on anyone to answer for them) fixes and cuts out an individual subject (for example the chair of an examination board), himself lifted out, by ministerial decision, from the teaching body of which he is a member; this lifting out is done behind the scenes and without the initiative of the teaching body itself, and so *a fortiori* without the initiative of the body of the candidates; and the occult character of the ministerial decision is propagated in the occult nature of the co-optation. In any case, the place of this occultation can be clearly located: it is one of the points where a nonphilosophical and nonpedagogical power intervenes to determine who (and what) will decisively and with absolute authority determine the program and the filtering and encoding mechanisms of the whole instruction. When one thinks about the centralistic and militarized structure of the French National Education system, one can see what army movements are triggered in the university and in publishing (there the connecting mechanisms are somewhat more complex but very narrow) by the slightest tremor of the programming device. From the moment the examination board, or the testing apparatus in general, holds such a power from the ministry (for even if it is elected, most of the time it is so only partially, and in fact it takes into account the results from competitive examinations evaluated by an appointed examination board), without ever consulting with the teaching body as such, it can give itself a theatrical representation of its liberty or of its liberalism. In fact, directly or not, it is subjected to the ideological or political constraint, to the real program of the power. And from then on, it necessarily *tends* to reproduce it in its most essential aspects, reproducing its conditions of practice and repelling anything which comes to push aside this order.

Therefore, under the name of program, I do not refer only to the one which seems to drop out of a [clear blue] sky every year, but rather to a powerful machine with complex gears. This machine includes chains of tradition or repetition whose works are not proper to any particular historical or ideological configuration, and which have been perpetuating themselves since the beginnings of sophistry and philosophy—not only as a sort of fundamental and continuous structure which would support some singular phenomena or episodes. In fact, this deeply set machine, this fundamental program is each time reinvested, reinformed, reemployed in its totality by each determined configuration. One of the difficulties of this analysis is due to the fact that deconstruction must not, cannot, simply pick and choose among long and relatively immobile chains on the one hand, and short and rapidly obsolete chains on the other, but it must exhibit this strange logic whereby, at least in philosophy, the multiple powers of the oldest machine can always be reinvested and exploited in a situation never encountered before. It is a difficulty, but it is also what renders possible a *quasi-systematic* deconstruction while and by guarding it against empiricist astonishment. And these powers are not only logical, rhetorical, didactic schemes, nor even essentially philosophemes, but they are also sociocultural or institutional operators, scenes or paths of energy, conflicts of forces utilizing all sorts of agents. Since, of course, when I say, according to so trivial a formula, that power controls the teaching apparatus, it is neither to situate power outside the pedagogical scene (it constitutes itself inside it as an effect of this very scene, and whatever the political or ideological nature of the powers in place around it may be), nor to lead anyone to thinking or dreaming some teaching without power, emancipated from its own effects of power, or liberated of any power external or superior to itself. That would be an idealistic or liberalistic representation with which a teaching body comforts itself efficiently, a teaching body blind to power: that to which it is submitted, that of which it disposes at the locus where it denounces power.

It is twisted enough: doing away with one's own power is not the easiest thing to do for a teaching body, and the fact that it no longer quite depends on an "initiative" or a "gesture," or on an "action" (for example, political, in the coded sense of this word) may indeed belong to this structure of the teaching body which I want to decompose here.

Therefore, inside this field, everywhere where teaching is taking place—and in the philosophical *par excellence*—there are *powers*, representing battling forces, dominating or dominated forces, conflicts and contradictions (what I call *effects of différance*[20]). This is why a task such as the one we are undertaking—and here comes a platitude, the experience of which shows that one must constantly recall it—implies, on the part of all those who participate in it, that they take a political position, whatever the complexity of the strategic relays, alliances, and detours (our Preliminary Project [*Avant-projet*] plays an important part in it, but then again it will have scared away some "liberals").

Therefore there could not be, should not be [*il ne saurait y avoir*] *one* teaching body [un *corps enseignant*] or *one* body of teaching [un *corps d'enseignement*] (teacher/teaching/taught [*enseignant/enseigné*]: we will broaden the syntax of this word, from the corpus which is taught to the body [*corps*] of disciples): homogenous, identical to itself, suspending within itself the oppositions which would occur outside (for example the politics and policies [*politiques*]), and when the opportunity arises, defending PHILOSOPHY IN GENERAL against the aggression of the nonphilosophical coming from outside. Therefore if there is a battle with respect to philosophy, its site cannot be but inside as well as outside the philosophical "institution." And if something were threatened and had to be defended, that too would take place inside and outside, since the outside forces always have their allies or their representatives inside. And reciprocally. It could very well be that the traditional "defenders" of philosophy, those who never have the slightest suspicion as to the "institution," might be the most active agents of its decomposition, at the very moment when they express indignation before those who clamor the death-of-philosophy. No possibility is ever excluded in the combination of "objective alliances," and each step is always booby-trapped.

Defense, body, repetition. Defense of the teaching of philosophy; teaching body (exposed, as we shall see, as a simulacrum of a nonbody reducing the taught body to a nonbody; or inversely, which comes to the same thing, a body reducing a body to being nothing but a body or a nonbody, and so on); repetition: that is what one should reassemble to hold them together in their "system" and under one's gaze if here the task were to think together the ensemble [*penser ensemble l'ensemble*], and to hold it under one's gaze, that is to say if one still had to teach.

What is needed? (What does the aphorism need to become teaching, teacher? And what if sometimes the aphorism were the most violent didactic authority? Like the ellipse, the fragment, the "I say almost nothing and I take it back right away" holding the potential control of the entire withheld discourse, policing before the fact all continuities and all supplements to come?)

One of the reasons I insist on the function of *répétiteur* which occupies me here is that if today this word seems to be reserved to the École Normale, with this air of being behind the times or antiquated befitting any self-respecting nobility, today this function remains active everywhere. This is one of the most revealing and most essential functions of the philosophical institution. On this topic, I will read a long paragraph in Canivez's book *Jules Lagneau, professeur et philosophe. Essai sur la condition du professeur de philosophie jusqu'à la fin du XIXe siècle*,[21] one of the two or three books which, in France, as far as I know, directly tackle certain historical problems of the philosophical institution. An indispensable material is treated there: that is to say also read, selected, and evaluated according to the system of some very determined philosophy, morality, or ideology. We will study them here and attempt to identify them, not only in this or that declared profession of faith, but in these more hidden, more subtle, apparently secondary operations which produce—or powerfully contribute to producing—the thetic effect of any discourse; moreover, this particular one [Canivez's] happens to be a main thesis for a doctoral degree which militates in favor of a sort of liberal spiritualism, eclectic because of its liberalism, even if it happens to condemn Cousin's[22] version of eclecticism. But we know that eclecticism does not exist, at least never as this openness which allows everything to go through. Its name indicates that, overtly or not, each time it practices choice, filtering, selectivity, preference, elitism, and exclusion. The excerpt I announced describes the *teaching of philosophy in the eighteenth century* in France:

"One must not forget that instruction was accompanied by an education inspired from religion. Pedagogical practice always lags behind customs, no doubt because teaching is more retrospective than prospective."[23]

I interrupt my reading a moment for a first digression.

If the "pedagogical practice always lags behind customs"—a proposition which perhaps overlooks a certain heterogeneity of relations in that respect but which appears, globally, hardly contestable—this structure of teaching which lags behind [*retardataire*] can always be interrogated as repetition. This does not exempt us from any other specific analysis but makes us touch upon a structural invariant of teaching. It comes from the semiotic structure of teaching, from the *practically* semiotic interpretation of the pedagogical relation: teaching [*l'enseignement*] delivers signs [*des signes*], the teaching body [*le corps enseignant*] produces (shows and puts forward) signs [*des enseignes*] and, more precisely, signifiers which suppose the knowledge of a previous signified. Referred to this knowledge, the signifier is structurally second. Any university places language in this position of delay or derivation in respect to significance or truth. Now if one places the signifier—or rather the signifier of signifiers—in a transcendental position in relation to the system, that does not change a thing to the matter: by giving it a second life [*un second souffle*], one reproduces here the teaching structure of a language and the semiotic delay of a didactic practice. Knowledge and power remain fundamental. The teaching body, as *organon* of repetition, has the age and the history of the sign, it lives off a belief (but then, what is belief in this case and from this situation?) in the transcendental signified; it lives again longer and better than ever with the authority of the signifier of signifiers, for example of the transcendental phallus. One may as well recall that a critical history and a practical transformation of "philosophy" (one can say here of the institution of the institution) will have, among their tasks, to perform the practical analysis (that is to say effectively decomposing) of the concept of teaching as a trial [*procès*] of significance.

From this digression, I return to Canivez: "Pedagogical practice always lags behind customs, no doubt because teaching is more retrospective than prospective. In a society increasingly secularized [*laïcisée*], secondary education maintained a tradition where Catholicism appeared as an untouchable truth. As Vial wrote, this is indeed a pedagogy which befits a divine-right monarchy (*Trois siècles d'enseignement secondaire*, 1936)."[24]

Again, I interrupt the quote. Canivez's remark, and *a fortiori* Diderot's text which follows, does show that the historical and political field could not be homogeneous at any point in time. An irreducible multiplicity of conflicts among dominated/dominating forces works upon the whole field but also upon any discourse on that field, and immediately [*sur-le-champ*]. Canivez takes a position (like Cousin) in favor of secularization [*laïcité*]. He also notes the contradiction between a society on its way to secularization [*laïcisation*] and the pedagogical practice which outlives it for a long time. At that very same time, Diderot was engaging with others in a struggle which is not yet finished; he also called attention to the political motif concealed under the religious or confounded with it: "Rollin,[25] the famous Rollin has no other goal than to make priests or monks, poets or orators: that indeed is what it is about! . . . It is about giving zealous and faithful subjects to the sovereign; useful citizens to the empire; educated, honest and even amiable individuals to society; good husbands and good fathers to families; letters, and a few men of great taste to the Republic; and edifying, enlightened and peaceable ministers to religion. That is no small objective." (*Plan d'une université pour le gouvernement de Russie, 1775–1776*).[26]

At the time when Diderot writes these words, the body of philosophy professors is far from being—without cleavage and in a homogenous fashion—the servile representation of a politico-religious power, itself worked upon by contradictions. In the seventeenth century, in the archives of the discussions at the university of Paris, one can already find accusations against the independence of some professors, for example against those who would teach in French (we shall have to consider again the importance of what is at stake here). In addition, Canivez recalls that in 1737, professors were ordered to dictate their courses. Furthermore, this was a rule which was recalled rather than instituted. Dictating was synonymous with teaching. "A master [*régent*] could say that he had 'dictated' for ten years in a particular *collège*."[27] The "dictation" of the course repeated a fixed and controlled content, but it was not identical to "repetition" in the narrow sense which we will determine later. When he arrived in a *collège*, the professor had to submit his teaching program to the hierarchy. Sometimes such a "prolusion" took the form of these "inaugural lectures" with which we are familiar still. Also, he often had to submit the totality of his course notes; hence the advantage of a more controllable dictation.

> Gradually, we had moved from reading a text, analyzing it and commenting upon it, to the dictated course, even as the contact with the text grew more remote. First, the course had been a summary of Aristotle's or some scholastic's doctrine, followed by an abstract of the commentary on this doctrine; then it had become an organized copy [*la mise au net*] of the average opinions concerning the content of the philosophical themes exploited by the tradition. Not until the nineteenth century will programs determine questions to be learned rather than authors to be studied.[28]

We will have to see what in fact happens regarding that in the nineteenth century, but let us not go and imagine that the shift to questions radically transforms the pedagogical scene, or that the suppression of the "dictation" ends all dictation.

The program of questions (to be "learned" says Canivez, "question" signifying "title" or "theme"), the list of authors, and any other efficient mechanisms which we will try to analyze, are there to sneak in the dictation, to render it more clandestine and, in its operation, its origin, and its powers, more mysterious.

> In the perspective of old, it did not occur to professors and to their [hierarchic] superiors that course notes could represent some personal work other than by the way they were organized [agencement]. More attention was paid to their errors, their mistakes, and the novel material they might contain, originating in the current fads, than to their vague attempts at originality. The professor is the faithful transmitter of a tradition and not the worker of a philosophy in-the-making. Often, the regents exchanged notebooks which had already been used by their predecessors, or which they had written during their earlier years in the profession, later neglecting the recent contributions from research.[29]

The individual whom Canivez calls "the worker of a philosophy in-the-making," on the margin or outside the dictating institution of philosophy, already devotes himself to a precise, keen, and pointed critique of the teaching power. This is the case of Condillac. He precedes and inspires most of the Ideologues' critical and pedagogical projects during and after the Revolutionary period. We will have to examine all the ambiguities. But already, with a final condemnation of the philosophical university, the last part of his Course on Modern History opposes to this university the institution of the scientific academies, and expresses regrets that the universities do not follow its progress:

> The way to teach still suffers from the centuries during which ignorance was forming its plan: for the universities are very far from having followed the progress of the academies. If the new philosophy begins to gain admittance in them, it still has much difficulty establishing itself there; and if that, it is allowed to get in only on the condition that it will put on some scholastic rags. In order to promote the advancement of knowledge, some establishments were constructed, which one can but commend. But no doubt, they would not have been constructed had the universities been capable of fulfilling this objective. Therefore it seems that there was an awareness of the flaws of education; however, no one provided any remedies for them. It is not enough to construct good establishments: we must also destroy the bad ones, or reform them on the model of the good ones, and even on a better model if it is possible.[30]

The intra-institutional contradiction is such that the defense of the (university) teaching body ["defense" and "body" are Condillac's words; I will emphasize them][31] cannot be made against "the power," against a certain force temporarily in power at that time and already internally dislocated, but against another institution in the process of constituting itself or in progress, a countererection representing another force with which "the power" must reckon and negotiate, to wit the academies.

On the other hand, the abbot Condillac, preceptor of the prince of Parma, whom he is addressing here, condemns this university into which the "new philosophy" was smuggled; he condemns it as *a body*, and a body which *defends* itself, a body whose *members* are subjected to the unity of the body. And in the schools entrusted to religious orders, he sees an aggravation of this phenomenon of a dogmatic body.

> I do not pretend that the way to teach is as vicious as it was in the thirteenth century. The scholastics have removed a few flaws from there, but gradually, and as if in spite of themselves. Left to their routine, they value and hold on to what they are still keeping; and it is with the same passion that they valued and held on to what they have abandoned. They have fought battles in order not to lose anything: they will fight others to *defend* what they have not lost. They are not aware of the ground they were forced to abandon: they do not anticipate that they will have to abandon more still; and had he come two centuries earlier, he who doggedly *defends* the rest of the abuses remaining in the schools, would have *defended* with the same doggedness things he condemns today.
>
> Universities are old and they have the shortcomings of old age: I mean they are hardly designed to correct themselves. Can one assume that professors will renounce what they believe they know, in order to learn what they do not know? Will they confess that their lessons teach nothing, or teach only useless things? No: but like the schoolchildren, they will continue to go to school to fulfill a task. If it gives them enough to live on, then it is enough for them; as it is enough for the disciples, if it consumes the time of their childhood and of their youth. The consideration which the academies enjoy is a spur for them. Besides, their free and independent members are not forced to follow blindly the maxims and prejudices of their *body*. If old people value and hold on to old opinions, young people have the ambition to think better; and it is always they who, in the academies, make the revolutions which are the most advantageous to the progress of knowledge. Universities have lost much of the consideration they used to enjoy; they are less

and less emulated each passing day. A deserving professor is disgusted with himself when he sees that he is confused with the pedants whom the public despises, and when, seeing what he should do to distinguish himself, he considers that it would be imprudent on his part to attempt it. He would not dare change the whole plan of study, and if he wants to hazard only a few minor changes, he has to take the greatest precautions. If the universities have these shortcomings, what will be the case of schools entrusted to religious orders, that is to say, to *bodies* which have a way of thinking to which all its members are forced to subject themselves? [JD's emphasis][32]

I did not quote this long text just to play with its current interest, nor to pick up on all the cleavage lines only which always, and always in a specific manner, share a field of ceaseless struggle with regard to the institution of philosophy. But also—to anticipate a little—Condillac opposes an institution from the standpoint of another institution, another institutional place (the academies), and he does so in the name of a philosophy which, massively, will inspire the pedagogico-philosophical projects during and after the Revolutionary period (we will see the properly Revolutionary episode reduced to almost nothing). Hence, what is essentially at stake here, visible or concealed, is the whole politico-pedagogical history from the nineteenth century on to present days. We shall soon directly begin its analysis. In the eyes of a certain teaching body, Condillac's discourse appears revolutionary or progressivist, and already represents *another teaching body in the making*, an (ideological) ideology about to become, as we say, dominant, itself destined to ambiguous setbacks, to a whole complex and differentiated history, acting as both a restraint and a mover for philosophical critique. In its most formal features, this scheme is also current.

Today, in order to retain only one sign of this ambiguity, let us not forget that, while supporting the progress of modern academies, this critique belongs to the pedagogical relationship between a preceptor and his prince. Furthermore, and this is a more durable feature yet, this critique reproduces an ideal of self-pedagogy for a virgin body, an ideal which supports a powerful pedagogical tradition and finds its ideal form, precisely, in the teaching of philosophy: a figure of the young *man* who, at a very determined age, and at a time when he is totally trained yet still a virgin, teaches philosophy to himself, naturally. The master's body (professor, mediator, preceptor, midwife, *répétiteur*) is there only during the time it takes for its own effacement, always in the process of withdrawing, the body of a mediator simulating its disappearance in the relation of the prince to himself, or for the benefit of another essential corpus which will be discussed later. "From now on, My Lord, it is up to you to educate yourself by yourself. I have already prepared you for that, and even accustomed you to it. Here is the time which will decide what you have to be some day: for the best education is not the one we owe our preceptors; it is the education we ourselves give to ourselves. Perhaps you imagine that you are finished; but it is I, My Lord, who is finished; and you, you have to begin again."[33]

The *répétiteur* effaces himself, repeats his effacement, stresses it while pretending to leave the prince disciple—who in turn must begin again, must spontaneously reengender the *paideia* cycle or, rather, must let it basically engender itself principially as auto-encyclopedia.

Behind the "repetition" in a narrow sense, the one Canivez considers, for example, there is always a repetition scene analogous to the one I wanted to point to with this reference to Condillac. Canivez regrets that the repetition and the *répétiteur* are increasingly absent from current teaching. In the process of a historical analysis which looks descriptive and neutral, he adds as in passing a personal appreciation which, jointed to so many other remarks of this type, constitutes the ethico-politico-pedagogical system of his thesis:

> To the fundamental exercise which the course constitutes, was first added the repetition. One avoided studying in isolation; the professor, the *répétiteur* or a good student, the *décurion*, went over the course again with the student, corrected his mistakes, and explained to him the difficult passages. It was a time for personal exchange between them, a particularly fruitful moment, when its merit was protected and it did not turn into rote learning or a quiz on the discipline. This is one of the exercises which are conspicuously absent in today's teaching.

And after the examination of a *dissertation* at Douai university (1750), here is what was noted, in the well-known style of the reports: "The copies of our current bachelors are not better; they are only more vague and less structured."[34]

The *répétiteur* or the repetition in a narrow sense comes only to represent and determine a general repetition which covers the whole system. The course—"a fundamental exercise"—is already a repetition, the dictation of a given or received text. It is always already repeated by a professor before young men of a determined age (here, I wish to make it clear that this question of age, which it seems to me captures in itself all the determinations—to be quick, let us say psychoanalytical and political—of the teaching of philosophy, will constantly serve as my guiding thread through the next sessions), by a male professor, no need to say, preferably single. The rule of ecclesiastical celibacy, another sign of the sexual scene which will concern us, had been maintained, more or less constraining, in spite of the secularization of culture; and you know what Napoleon's views were in this respect:

> There will be no political stability as long as there is no teaching body based on stable principles. . . . A teachers' corps would come into existence if all

the principals, proctors, and professors of the Empire were subordinate to one or several head officials, just as the Jesuits were subordinate to a general, to provincials, etc. . . . If it were deemed important for the civil servants and the secondary school teachers not to be married, one could reach this state of affairs easily and in a short time . . . the means to obviate all inconvenience would be to set celibacy as a law for all the members of the teaching body, except for the teachers in special schools and in the *lycées*, and for the inspectors. In these positions, marriage presents no inconvenience. But the principals and the masters of studies in the *collèges* could not get married without renouncing their position. . . . Without being bound by vows, the teaching body would be no less religious. [*Instructions to Fourcroy*][35]

One finds this general repetition again (thus represented by the study master or the more advanced body of an alumnus) in the spirit defining the function which occupies me here, in this place which is not indifferent. The *agrégé-répétiteur* has first been, and still remains in certain respects, a student who after the *agrégation* stays on at the École to help the other students—by making them repeat—prepare for examinations and *concours* through exercises, advice, and a sort of assistance; he assists both the professors and the students. In that sense, entirely absorbed in his function of mediator within this general repetition, he is also the teacher *par excellence*. Like in the Jesuit *collèges*, as a rule, it is a good student who has proved his worth and who, on condition that he be single, stays as a boarder in the École for a few years, three or four maximum, while beginning to prepare his own accreditation (his thesis) in order to access the higher ranks of the teaching body. That was the very strict definition of the *agrégé-répétiteur* when I was myself a student in this house. This definition is not altogether obsolete. Yet a complication slightly affected it when, some fifteen years ago, the compromise between two antagonistic necessities created the teaching-assistant body in France. They are civil servants with (under certain conditions) a guaranteed stability in higher education, but without a title or any professorial power. Relatively regularly promoted to the rank of teaching assistants, the *agrégé-répétiteurs* have a tendency to become sedentary in the École; they are authorized to give some courses and to hold some seminars under the condition that they still assume the responsibilities of the *agrégé-répétiteur*. They no longer have to live in the École, and they get married more frequently, which, associated with other transformations, changes the nature of their rapport with the students.

This is where I was heading with this sign. There is nothing fortuitous in the fact that the critique of the university institution is most often done at the initiative of teaching assistants (all that has only a statistical, tendential, and typical value).

That is to say of subjects who, blocked or subordinated by the apparatus, no longer simply have an interest in keeping it, as do the higher ranking professors, nor do they have any insecurity to dread or massive reprisals to fear from it; which distinguishes them from the assistants who are dependent and ask for favors, since they can always lose their position. The pattern is at least analogous in secondary education (which includes a superior body of tenured teachers, an inferior body of tenured teachers, and a body of nontenured teachers). The teaching assistant thus conveys a contradiction and a breach in the system. It is always in places of this type that a front has the best chances of establishing itself. And in the analysis that the GREPH should unceasingly conduct concerning its own possibility or its own necessity, and its limits as well, it will have to take into account these laws and these types, among other things. I just wanted to announce it with a sign.

Therefore, here is not a neutral and indifferent place.

In addition to what I have just recalled, this place is being transformed and dislocated. Here is a first sign of this: the fact that the majority among you does not belong to the École Normale Supérieure and even, if I am not mistaken, admits to being only rather loosely connected to it (let us be satisfied with this euphemism); so this is a first sign and visible here, in a theater hall or movie theater barely transformed into a lecture hall, here in the École Normale Supérieure which transforms itself while resisting its own transformation; here in the place where I—this teaching body which I call mine, a very determined *topos* within the body supposed to teach philosophy in France—today, I teach.

In a sort of contraband between the *agrégation* and the GREPH.

I say that I am only going to make some proposals, always subject to discussion, and that I am going to pose some questions, for example the one which, apparently by my own initiative, I have put on the agenda today, to wit: "What is a teaching body?"

To be sure, anyone can interrupt me, ask his or her "own proper" questions, displace or annul mine; I even ask this with hardly a pretense at sincerity. But, of course, everything seems to be organized for me to keep the initiative I took, or which I had conferred upon myself, and which I could take only by submitting myself to a certain number of complex and systematic normative exigencies of a teaching body, authorized by state representation to confer the title, the right and the means of this initiative. Actually, the contract to which I am referring is even more complicated, but it also demands that I move rather quickly.

When I say that I pose some questions, I feign not to say anything which could be a thesis. I feign to pose something which, fundamentally, would not pose itself. Since a question is not, one believes, a thesis, it would not pose, impose, or suppose anything. That is what builds the teaching body: this pretended neutrality, the non-thetic appearance of a question which poses itself without even looking as if it *poses itself.*

We know that there is no question (the barest, the most formal, the questioning form itself: What is? Who? What? next time we shall recognize there the recourse of recourses for the erection and countererection of institutions) which is not constrained by a program, informed by a system of forces, invested by a battery of determining, selecting, and sifting forms. The question is always *posed* (determined) by someone who, at a given moment, in a language, in a place, and so on, represents a program and a strategy (by definition inaccessible to an individual and conscious control, representable).

In this country [France], each and every time the teaching of philosophy is "threatened," its traditional "defenders" send a warning, to convince or dissuade while reassuring: beware, what you are going to put in question is the possibility of a pure questioning, of a free, neutral, objective, and so on, questioning. An argument without strength or relevance which—no surprise here—has never reassured, never convinced, never dissuaded.

Here, I am here the teaching body.

I—but who?—represent a teaching body, here, at the place where I am, which is not indifferent.

In what respect is it a glorious body?

My body is glorious, it focuses all light. First, that of the projector above me. Then it radiates and draws all the eyes upon itself. But it is also glorious in the sense that it is no longer simply a body. It is sublimated in the representation of at least another body, the teaching body, of which it should be both a part and the whole, a member which allows the assembled body to be seen; which in turn produces itself while effacing itself as the barely visible, quite transparent representation of the philosophical corpus and the sociopolitical corpus, the contract between these bodies [*corps*] never being exhibited on the front of the stage.

From this glorious effacement, from the glory of this effacement, a benefit is drawn, always, of which it remains to know by what means, by whom, and to what purpose. Reckoning is always more difficult than one believes, given the erratic character of a certain remainder. And it also goes for all supplementary benefits drawn from the very articulation of these calculations, for example here, today, by he who says: "I—but who?—represent a teaching body."

His body becomes a teaching body when, as a locus of convergence and fascination, it becomes more than a center.

More than a center: a center, a body at the center of a space exposes itself on all sides, it bares its back, and lets itself be seen by what it cannot see. In return, in the traditional topology, the eccentricity of the teaching body allows both the synoptic watching which covers the field of the taught body with its gaze—each part of which is enclosed in the mass and always surrounded—and the withdrawal, the reserve of the body which does not give itself away, offering only one side to the gaze which yet it mobilizes with its entire surface. It is well known; let us not dwell on it. The body becomes a teaching body and exerts what we shall call, even if it complicates things later, its mastery and its magisterialness, only by playing on a stratified effacement: before (or behind) the global teaching body [*corps*], before (or behind) the taught corpus (here in the sense of philosophical corpus), before (or behind) the sociopolitical body [*corps*].

And we do not understand *at first* what a body is, though we know *afterwards* what these effacements, submissions, and neutralizations mean with their semblance of mastery: what a philosopher would still call the being or the essence of the body said to be "proper" (response to the question "what is a body?") will perhaps come to itself (that is to say to something else) from this economy of effacement.

Each time, this captation by effacement, this fascinating neutralization has the form of a cadaverization of my body. My body fascinates only by playing dead, at the moment when, pretending to be dead, it stands erect with the rigidity of a cadaver: taut, but with no strength of its own. Not disposing of its own life but only of a delegation of life.

I do not call such a scene of cadaverizing seduction a simulacrum of *effacement* through a vague equivalence between the negativity of death and a removal of writing. The effacement, here, is indeed, on the one hand, the erosion of a text, of a surface, and of its textual marks. This erosion is indeed the effect of a repression *and* of a forcing back, of a reactive bustle. The philosophical as such always originates there. On the other hand, and by the same token, by sublime annihilation, the effacement makes disappear the determined features of a *facies*, and of all that which, in the face, cannot be reduced to something vocable and to something audible.

Therefore all the rhetorics of this cadaverizing effacement are relations of *corps à corps*.

The body effects with which I play—but you do understand that when *I* says *I*, you no longer know, already, who speaks and to whom *I* refers, an *I* refers, whether there is or not a teacher's signature, since I also pretend to describe in terms of essence the operation of an anonymous body in teaching transit [*en transit en-*

seignant]—feign to suppose or to make believe that my body is in no way responsible: it would exist, would be *there* only to represent, signify, teach, deliver the signs of at least two other bodies. Which. . . .

Notes

JD identifies the notes included in the original French text.

1. "What American English calls 'the faculty,' those who teach, is in French *le corps enseignant*, the teaching corps (just as we say 'the diplomatic corps') or teaching body." J. Derrida, "The Principle of Reason: The University in the Eyes of Its Pupils," *Diacritics*, 1983, 3–20, 5.

2. Published for the first time in *Politiques de la philosophie*. Other texts by Châtelet, Foucault, Lyotard, and Serres gathered by D. Grisoni, Paris: Grasset, 1976. Reprinted in *Du droit à la philosophie*. Paris: Éditions Galilée, 1990, 111–153.

3. On connotations of the word "reason," especially in the context of the university and education, see "The Principle of Reason: The University in the Eyes of its Pupils," *Diacritics*, Fall 1983, 3–20, especially pages 6–8, and the following quote from Leibniz: "There are two first principles in all reasoning, the principle of non-contradiction, of course . . . and the principle of rendering reason" (7).

4. GREPH: This acronym stands for "Groupe de recherches sur l'enseignement philosophique" (also referred to as "Groupe de recherche [singular in Bennington's English version] sur l'enseignement philosophique" in Geoffrey Bennington and Jacques Derrida, *Jacques Derrida*, Chicago: University of Chicago Press, 1993, 333). Translated as "Research Group on Philosophical Education" (for example, Thomas Pepper, in *Yale French Studies* 77, 1990, 40) or as "Research Group on the Teaching of Philosophy" (for example, Peggy Kamuf, in *Points . . .* , ed. Elizabeth Weber, Stanford, CA: Stanford University Press, 1995, 88, 462, 465, for example). In 1974, Derrida drafted the *Avant-projet* for the foundation of the Groupe de recherches sur l'enseignement philosophique. He describes it in "The Almost Nothing of the Unpresentable," tr. Peggy Kamuf, in *Points. . .* , pp. 78–88. Derrida declares: "GREPH brings together teachers, high school and university students who, precisely, want to analyze and change the educational system, and in particular the philosophical institution, first of all through the extension of the teaching of philosophy to all grades where the other so-called basic disciplines are taught" (88).

5. Although the word *indifférent* has been translated by "insignificant" in other texts, I chose to keep the English term "indifferent" in order to underscore the theme of neutrality developed in this context. See for example, in "Languages and Institutions of Philosophy," a series of four lectures delivered in English as part of the Fifth International Summer Institute for Semiotic and Structural Studies (May 31–June 25, 1984), held at Victoria College, University of Toronto; published in English in "Recherches Sémiotiques Semiotic Inquiry" *RSSI* 4(2): 91–154 (92); in French in *Du droit à la philosophie*. Paris: Éditions Galilée, 1990, 281–394 (284).

6. Students attending the École Normale Supérieure.

7. *La relève* refers to the Hegelian concept of *Aufhebung*, and Derrida's reading of Hegel as presented in "From Restricted to General Economy: A Hegelianism Without Reserve," in *Writing and Difference*, Alan Bass, trans. Chicago: University of Chicago Press, 1978. Hegel uses this term, playing on its ambivalence, to designate, in the dialectical movement, the passage from one state to the other. Any new state is born of the negation of the preceding one; therefore it aims to abolish it. Yet at the same time it conserves it. Thus *Aufhebung* literally means "lifting up," but also embedded in it is the double meaning of conservation and negation. In Derrida's *Margins of Philosophy*, Alan Bass writes: "For Hegel, dialectics is a process of *Aufhebung*: every concept is to be negated and lifted up to a higher stage in which it is thereby conserved." The translation of a word with a double meaning is always difficult, and has to do with the problematics of writing and *différance*. For example, Jean Hyppolite attempts to render *Aufhebung* as both *supprimer* and *dépasser*. Derrida translates it as *la relève*, from the verb *relever* (to lift up, *Aufheben*), also meaning to relay, to relieve, as in one soldier relieving another one on duty (hence the "changing of the guard"). (Thanks are due to John Protevi for pointing out the Hegelian reference).

8. See note 3, and "The Principle of Reason: The University in the Eyes of its Pupils," C. Porter and E.P. Morris, trans. *Diacritics*, Fall 1983, 3–20, especially pages 7 and 8, and the following quote from the translators' note: "to render reason (to give it back, as it were) worked in exchange and concert with to yield reason and to give reason; any one of the three could mean to give grounds for one's thoughts and assertions, but also, to give an account on one's acts or conduct, when summoned to do so" (7–8).

9. A reminder that the theory of knowledge, the essential concern of Plato's reflection, has been considered as the core of philosophy.

10. See Jacques Derrida, *The Gift of Death*, David Wills, trans. Chicago: University of Chicago Press, 1995.

11. Jacques Derrida, *Positions,* Paris: Minuit, 1972, p. 90. JD

12. Haby, Minister of the French National Education under the government of Valéry Giscard d'Estaing, had submitted a proposal which would have curtailed, even possibly eliminated, the teaching of philosophy in the *lycées,* where it is part of the last year curriculum.

13. This text was written in 1972. Between 1960 and 1964, Derrida taught "general philosophy and logic" at the Sorbonne (assistant of Bachelard, Canguilhem, Ricoeur, and Wahl). In 1964, he was admitted to the Centre National de la Recherche Scientifique from which he immediately resigned to accept a teaching position at the École Normale Supérieure to which he had been invited by Hyppolite and Althusser. He was to remain there until 1984: in 1983 he was elected to the École des Hautes Études en Sciences Sociales (as Director of Studies for Philosophical Institutions), where he still teaches.

14. The lengthy and highly formalized written composition on a historical, literary, philosophical, and so on, topic, a part of all secondary and higher education and included in all examinations and *concours* (see note 17).

15. A metaphor using rather loosely the concept of electric parallel circuits. This type of elec-

tric circuit provides more than one path for current, each with a uniform voltage, no matter how many power sources. After the electric current leaves a source, it follows two or more paths before returning to the source.

16. In the French education system, *concours* are highly competitive examinations where candidates are ranked according to their overall results. In particular, these *concours* are used as entrance examinations to all the main schools, especially the Grandes Écoles, including the École Normale.

17. Of relatively recent usage in philosophy, this term refers to "multiple determination." This notion is most frequent in psychoanalysis and in the history of philosophy, where Althusser borrowed the term from Freud (i.e., overdetermination of dream images, where each element of the dream is in fact the expression of several hidden thoughts condensed into one single element) to apply it to the analysis of historical processes. Most often, if not always, we must face complex contradictions, and though the new situation may appear as a resolution of those contradictions, it is in fact "overdetermined." Therefore, the notion of "overdetermination" is a relatively fine analytical tool which helps avoid the dogmatic application of, for example, the Marxist premises.

18. A body within the French National Education system whose responsibility it is to oversee the performance of teachers and administrators at the elementary and secondary levels.

19. The *agrégation* is a highly competitive examination (*concours*) used to select candidates to higher teaching positions.

20. In the context of Hegel's *Aufhebung* (see note 7), Derrida points out that in a word which carries two contradictory meanings, there is always an effect of *différance*. It is this effect of *différance*, this excess of the very trace *Aufhebung*, which the *Aufhebung* cannot *Aufheben*, i.e., lift up, conserve, and negate. See also *"Différance,"* in J. Derrida, *Margins of Philosophy,* A. Bass, trans. Chicago: The University of Chicago Press, 1982.

21. Canivez, Doctoral dissertation, Association des publications de la Faculté de Lettres de Strasbourg, 1965. JD

22. Victor Cousin (1792–1867) was the leader of the French eclectic spiritualist movement.

23. Canivez, 82.

24. Ibid.

25. Charles Rollin (1661–1741) was an educator who wrote a major Traité des Études (1726-1728).

26. Denis Diderot, *Oeuvres complètes,* édition chronologique, tome XI. Paris, Société encyclopédique française et le Club français du livre, 1971, p. 747. JD

27. In the French education system, the general high schools, called *collèges* and *lycées,* prepare students to enter universities. Generally speaking, *collèges* go from sixth grade (*la sixième*) through ninth grade (*la troisième*), *lycées* go from tenth grade (*la seconde*) to twelfth grade (*la terminale*). The last year of these schools is a period of specialized study in areas including philosophy, experimental sciences, mathematics, social sciences, etc. This year compares in difficulty with the second year of university work in the U.S. or Canada. The Baccalauréat examination completes this

program. It is a difficult examination, failed by 30 to 50 percent of the students. Most French universities admit students who have this degree.

28. Canivez, 87.

29. Ibid., 87–88.

30. Étienne Bonnotde Condillac, *Cours d'études pour l'instruction du prince de Parme,* VI. Extraits du cours d'histoire. Texte établi par Georges Le Roy. Corpus général des philosophes français, Auteurs modernes, tome XXXIII, Paris, PUF, 1948, 235. JD

31. Derrida's note, in bracket in original text.

32. Condillac, 235–236.

33. Ibid., 237.

34. Canivez, 90–91.

35. Letter from Napoleon to the rector of the University of Bologna (1805). Note on the *lycées.* In J. Christopher Herold, ed. and trans., *The Mind of Napoleon: A Selection from His Written and Spoken Words.* New York: Columbia University Press, 1955, 117–118.

Appendix

The Research Group on the Teaching of Philosophy (GREPH) was constituted during the first General Assembly on January 15, 1975. As early as the preceding year, preparatory meetings had taken place. During the session of April 16, 1974, a group of some thirty teachers and students had unanimously adopted the Preliminary Proposal presented below. This document, purposefully open to the largest consensus, was included with the invitation to the first constitutive assembly, addressed to the largest number of secondary students and teachers, and higher education teachers and students (philosophical or nonphilosophical disciplines, in Paris and the provinces).

Preliminary Proposal for the Constitution of a Research Group on the Teaching of Philosophy

Preliminary work has made it clear: today it is both possible and necessary to organize a set of research projects on what relates philosophy to its teaching. This research, which should have both a critical and a practical bearing, would attempt, initially, to respond to certain questions. We define these questions here, by virtue of an approximative anticipation, with reference to common notions to be discussed. The GREPH would be at least, first of all, a place which would make possible the coherent, long lasting, and pertinent organization of such a discussion.

1. What is the connection between philosophy and teaching in general?

What is teaching in general? What is teaching for philosophy? What is it to teach philosophy? In what respect would teaching (a category to be analyzed within the context of the pedagogical, the didactic, the doctrinal, the disciplinary, and so on) be essential to the philosophical operation? How did this essential indissociability of the didacto-philosophical get constituted and differentiated? Is it possible, and under what conditions, to propose a general, critical, and transformative history of this indissociability?

These questions are of great theoretical generality. Evidently, they demand elaboration. Such would precisely be the first task of the GREPH.

In opening up these questions, it would be possible—let us say only *for example* and in a very vaguely indicative way—to study *not only*:

a) models of didactic operations legible, with their rhetoric, their logic, their psychagogy, and so on, within *written* discourses (from Plato's dialogues for example, through Descartes's Meditations, Spinoza's Ethics, Hegel's Encyclopedia or Lectures, and so on, up to all the works of modernity one calls philosophical), but also

b) *pedagogical practices* administered according to rules in fixed places, in private or public *establishments* since the Sophists, for example, the Scholastic "quaestio" and "disputatio", and so on, up to the courses and other pedagogical activities instituted today in *collèges*, *lycées*, *écoles*,[1] universities, and so on. What are the forms and norms of these practices? What are their intended effects and the effects actually obtained? Things to be studied here would be, for example: the "dialogue," maieutics, the master-disciple relationship, the question, the interrogation, the test, the examination, the competitive selection, the inspection, the publication, the frames and programs of discourse, the dissertation, the presentation, the lesson, the thesis, the procedures of verification and examination, the repetition, and so on.

These different types of problematics should be articulated together as rigorously as possible.

2. How does the didacto-philosophical inscribe itself in the fields one calls instinctual, historical, political, social, economic?

How does it *inscribe itself there*, that is to say how does it operate and how does it itself represent to itself its inscription, and how is it *inscribed* in its very representation? What is the "general logic" and what are the specific modes of this inscription? Of its normalizing normativity and of its normalized normativity? For example, the Academy, the Lycée, the Sorbonne, preceptorships of all sorts, the universities or the royal, imperial, or republican schools of modern times all prescribe, according to determined and differentiated paths, not only a pedagogy which is indissociable from a philosophy, but also, at the same time, a moral and political system which forms at once both the object and the actualized structure of pedagogy. What about this pedagogical effect? How are we to theoretically and practically determine its limits?

Once again, these indicative questions remain too general. Mostly, by design, they are formulated according to common current representations, and therefore they need to be specified, differentiated, critiqued, transformed. Indeed, they could lead one to believe that the point is essentially, if not solely, to construct a sort of "critical theory of philosophical doctrinality or disciplinarity," or to reproduce the traditional debate which philosophy has regularly opened onto its "crisis." This "reproduction" will be, in and of itself, one of the objects of our research. In fact, the GREPH should mostly participate in the transforming analysis of the "present" situation, interrogating, analyzing, and displacing itself from that which, in this "situation," makes it possible and necessary. Therefore, the preceding questions should be continually worked over by these practical motivations. Also, without ever excluding the full importance of these problems outside of France, one would first massively insist on the conditions of philosophical teaching "here-and-now," in today's France. And in its concrete urgency, in the more or less dissimulated violence of its contradictions, the "here-and-now" would no longer be simply a philosophical object. This is not a restriction of the program, but the condition of a task of the GREPH on its own practical field and in relation to the following questions:

1. What are the past and present historical conditions of this system of education?

What about its power? What forces give it this power? What forces limit it? What about its legislation, its juridical code, and its traditional code? Its external and internal norms? Its social and political field? Its relation to other types of teachings (historical, literary, aesthetic, religious, scientific, for example), to other institutionalized discursive practices (psychoanalysis in general, psychoanalysis said to be didactic in particular—for example, and so on)? From these different viewpoints, what is the specificity of the didacto-philosophical operation? Can laws be produced, analyzed, tested on objects—but these are still only empirically accumulated indications—such as for example: the role of the Ideologues, or of one Victor Cousin, of their philosophy or of their political interventions in the French university; the constitution of the philosophy course; the evolution of the figure of the teacher-of-philosophy since the nineteenth century, in the lycée, in *khâgne*,[2] in the *écoles normales,* in the university, at the Collège de France; the place of the disciple, of the pupil, of the candidate; the history and the functioning of:

a) the programs to prepare for examinations and *concours,* the format of their tests (which authors are present and which are excluded, the organization of titles, themes and problems, and so on);

b) the examination committees, the general inspectors, the consultative committees, and so on;

c) the forms and norms of evaluations or of sanction (grading, ranking, comments, reports on competitive selections, examinations, theses, and so on);

d) the so-called research organisms (CNRS, Foundation Thiers,[3] and so on);

e) the research tools (libraries, selected texts, textbooks on the history of philosophy or general philosophy, their relations with the field of publishing on the one hand, and with the authorities responsible for public instruction or national education on the other);

f) the places of work (the topological structure of the classroom, the seminar, the lecture hall, and so on);

g) the recruiting of teachers and their professional hierarchy (the social background and political stances of the pupils, students, educators, and so on).

2. What is at stake in the struggles within and around the teaching of philosophy, today, in France?

The analysis of this conflictual field implies an interpretation of philosophy in general and, consequently, taking positions as well as an interpretation of the positions taken. Therefore it calls for actions.

Notes

1. The Grandes Écoles are fiercely selective higher education institutions separate from the university system. They are often simply called *écoles,* one example precisely being the École Normale Supérieure, referred to as l'École by tradition and in Derrida's text.

2. Two tiers called *hypokhâgne* and *khâgne* after the last year of high school and the *baccalauréat* prepare candidates for entrance examinations to the Grandes Écoles.

3. The Centre National de la Recherche Scientifique (CNRS) and the Foundation Thiers welcome permanent and part-time researchers whose responsibilities may or may not include teaching.

Peter Pericles Trifonas

TECHNOLOGIES OF REASON
Toward a Regrounding of Academic Responsibility

> Would it not be more "responsible" to try pondering the ground,
> in the history of the West, on which the juridico-egological values
> of responsibility were determined, attained, imposed? There is per-
> haps a fund here of "responsibility" that is at once "older" and—to
> the extent it is conceived anew, through what some would call a
> crisis of responsibility in its juridico-egological form and its ideal
> of decidability—is *yet to come,* or, if you prefer, "younger." Here,
> perhaps, would be a chance for the task of thinking what will have
> been, up to this point, the representation of university responsibil-
> ity, of what it is and might become, in the wake of upheavals no
> longer to be concealed from ourselves, even if we still have trouble
> analyzing them. Is a new type of university responsibility possible?
> —Jacques Derrida, "Mochlos;
> or, The Conflict of the Faculties"[1]

This chapter engages the range of the "dominant
metaphorical register"[2] of the Derridean call for the deconstruction of the institution—after the memorious professing of the pedagogical ends of the dialectical reason of Hegelianism—through its attending to the critical presuppositions of "a
certain architectural rhetoric"[3] of a post-Kantian type that retranslates the rational
ground of the systemic technologies of the classic interdisciplinarity of knowledge
constructions within the university as the basis for the possibility of the articulation
of a "new" ethics of academic responsibility. It presents a reading of "The Principle
of Reason: The University in the Eyes of its Pupils," the text of a public lecture
given by Jacques Derrida before an assembly at Cornell University in April of 1983.
Engaging the theme of the constation and performativity of academic responsibility, the chapter addresses the deconstruction of the metaphysical foundation of the

principle of reason. Or, what is the logic of the ground of the being of the modern university itself as the cultural product of the unification of philosophy and technology? The ramifications of the *idea of the principle of reason* are explored through an extended meditation on its pragmatic and hermeneutic consequences for the *instrumental and poietic aims of research*. The chapter finishes by way of a critical probing of some of the suggestions Derrida makes for "reawakening" or "resituating" the ethics of the responsibility of the *academic community-at-large*.

Reason Unbound

The Principle of Reason: The Institutional Ground of Modern Rationality

The analytic direction that I intend to follow hereafter takes its strategic cues from the *metareflexive* reverberations of a question Derrida asks during the discourse we have been reading closely, letting the critical timbre of its message resound noisily in the ear of the nameless, faceless Other within us : "Is the reason for reason rational?"[4] Coloring the post-metaphysical positionality of the attitude expressed therein, a modicum of ludic indiscretion enhances the deconstructive resonance of the appeal the philosopher makes for a reappraisal of the self-insulated myth of the innocuousness of the disarming logic of *"ratio sufficiens, ratio efficiens."*[5] Derrida, we will have glimpsed earlier, is strikingly clear about the peculiar *retrospectivity* of the lexico-conceptual lineage leading to the formulation of the principle of reason during the seventeenth century—the protracted time lag of its epistemic genealogy as it is played out from a *looking back on* the "Aristotelian requirements"[6] of all future science, "of metaphysics, of first philosophy, of the search for 'roots,' 'principles,' and 'causes'"[7]—that gave rise to the original *idea* and *ideal* of the University and its modern day reinstitution in the revisionist model constructed by Wilhelm von Humboldt:

> As far as I know, nobody has ever founded a university *against* reason. So we may reasonably suppose that the University's reason for being has always been reason itself, and some essential connection of reason to being. But what is called the principle of reason is not simply reason. We cannot for now plunge into the history of reason, its words and concepts, into the enigmatic scene of translation that has shifted *logos* to *ratio* to *reason, Grund, ground, Vernunft,* etc. What for three centuries now has been called the principle of reason was thought out and formulated, several times, by Leibniz. His most often quoted statement holds that "Nothing is without reason, no effect is without cause" (*"Nihil est sine ratione seu nullus effectus sine causa"*). According to Heidegger though, the only formulation Leibniz

himself considered authentic, authoritative, and rigorous is found in a late essay, *Specimen inventorum*: "There are two first principles in all reasoning, the principle of non-contradiction, of course . . . and the principle of rendering reason." (*"Duo sunt prima principia omnium ratiocinationum, principium nempe contradictionis . . . et principium reddendae rationis."*) The second principle says that for any truth—for any true proposition, that is—a reasoned account is possible. *"Omnis veritatis reddi ratio potest."* Or, to translate more literally, for any true proposition, *reason can be rendered.*[8]

There is a "cost" of economizing due the principle of reason that cannot be left unanalyzed or unheeded, especially if we do not wish to construe its "cardinal" and "secondary" mandates *solely* as aphorisms for the "rational faculty or power"[9]—the ability of mind and of speech—attributive of the sacred dignity of the human animal (*zoon logon ekhon*) by Aristotelian metaphysics. Doing so, Derrida warns, would be an unfortunate mistake: "The principle of reason installs its empire only to the extent that the abyssal question of the being (*l'être*) that is hiding within it remains hidden, and with it the question of the grounding of the ground itself, or of grounding as *gründen* (to ground, to give or take ground: *Boden-nehmen*), as *begründen* (to motivate, justify, authorize) or especially as *stiften* (to erect or institute, a meaning to which Heidegger [on whose analysis the interpretation given here relies] accords a certain preeminence)."[10] The *phoronomy*[11] of the *principium rationis* demands something more profound of the subject's thought and action than the self-aggrandizing hyperrelativism of the *doxa* of merely changing "opinion" emboldening itself on the excesses of itself. And that is an element of accountability (*Rechenschaft*) for the "truth-value" of the representation (*Vorstellung*) of judgments made about "an object [*Gegenstand*—"that-which-stands-over-against"] placed and positioned *before* a subject,"[12] an ego who, now more than ever, sure of its self, thinks "I" (*sum*). The justification (*Rechtfertigen*) of the certainty of such a self-grounding of the ground of knowledge yielded of the *cogitabilis* rests on the security of demonstrating the proof of the "evident correctness" of an explanation—or a reversal of the logic of the *percipio* as it is set back on the source of the response directed to language. Reason is sufficiently rendered, "given back,"[13] and *it has to be* for the determinacy of the *ens rationis* (intellect) to piece together an *idea of reality* in lieu of "esoteric" principle, only if and when a "representation that judges"[14] can display the "truth" of its propositional outcomes by redirecting the ground of the "connection" of subject and predicate—the "what" of "is"— back to a cogitating "I."[15] This structure of repetition orders the chain of consequence organizing the syntagm of language in the coming-back of its returning of presence to the "double effigy" of the sign/picture for concept (*Begriff*). It has the function of "holding" or "keeping" the world of beings firmly fixed (*fest-gestellt*) in the bright light of "objectivity" (*Gegenständlichkeit*)[16] over and against the underlying filter of the projecting self-consciousness of the "knowing self"[17] as *subjectum* or *hypokeimenon,* "that-which-lies-before" (*qua* prior). The firmament of the truth of experience depicted as such bears an anthropocentric foundation and the unmistakable mark of a *metaphysical humanism.*[18] For, as Derrida explains, "This relation of representation [between subject and object]—that in its whole extension is not merely a relation of knowing—has to be grounded, ensured, protected [by making the subject an object[19]]: that is what we are told by the principle of reason, the *Satz vom Grund.*"[20] To expand in a slightly different way, on the one hand, the productive reflexivity of a presuppositionless egoity sustains the "purity" of the ground of its reasoning by its "power-of-bringing-back-to-presence"[21] the self-presence of the *truth of representation* from within the abiding swells of an inwardly spectating imago of mind. But this is not enough. On the other, a collective form of the responsibility to *give an account of reason* (*logon didonai*) is coaffirmed outright by the *autopoietic* reflexivity of a self-consciousness of self and self*hood* disengaging of itself from empirical reality to set apart Sub-ject from Ob-ject, Self from Other, in its subordination of nature to a mortgaging of its foreclosure that is always ready to hand (*das Zuhanden*).[22] Taking these together, the sense of *ratio* understood in the affirmative form of the principle of reason, *Omnes ens habet rationem* (Every being has a reason), is interpretable as a reckoning to account *for* the calculability (*Berechenbarkeit*) of entities (*Seinden*).[23] Subjectivism thus precedes objectivism in and following the Cartesian age of modernity Derrida believes to be a portentous omen of philosophical innovation that prepares the way to the development of the University as we know it today.

Vouchsafing the ground of the predictable equationing of beings, the principle of reason convenes the primacy of calculation as the fate of Western thought. The *techne* of this amenability of the *ratio reddendae* we have outlined is the characterizing feature of the historicity of the evolution of "philosophy" to "science" that, after the epistemological trailblazing of the early Greeks (not the pre-Socratics), stimulates the ontogenesis of modern "Technoscience" without which there would be no contemporary university.[24] The method of its "Reason" as "the structure and closure of representation"[25] is not, nor could it ever be, outside the *scope of deconstruction,* but rather is a precursor of, and, moreover, integral to *the necessity for a critical questioning of the grounding of the foundation of the institutional frameworking of knowledge,* mainly because the metaphysical (logocentric) assumptions behind the objective setting of the value of truth are reductive, autarchical, and protective of the *practical ends of the task of thinking. Reason and the technologies of Reason are not without interest, not without ground or a grounded grounding that withdraws, refracts, is concealed.* And in this solicitation of a "crossing over" from *theoria* to *praxis,* where normative levels of the "optimal performance" of ideas have to be met to the utmost satisfaction of "rationality," there is hidden the *opening of the nonethical violence of the universal.*

"Beyond all those big philosophical words—reason, truth, principle—that generally command attention," Derrida tells us, "the principle of reason also holds that reason *must be rendered.*"[26] "Deconstruction"—and there cannot be just *one*—is not exempt from the responsibility of answering the obligation of thinking through this obdurate call to grounds *in full,* albeit in the profusive singularity of its own distinctive ways.[27] But the issue of the "properness" of response becomes more radical in conjunction with what has become a *post*modern "crisis of representation," a suspiciousness of reference and referentiality formed as a question of the *"Question of Reason"* and its "must." How are we then to comprehend the ramifications of the ethical aim of this modal behest unto being Derrida recognizes to be *nothing but essential,* convoking as it does, at the thematic fissures of its deepest openings toward education, the Socratic problem of the "(un)examined life" or *how one ought to live?* And therefrom, to unravel why "one cannot *think* the possibility of the modern university, the one that is restructured in the nineteenth century in all the Western countries, without inquiring into that event, the institution of the principle of reason."[28] The road we will take, to move on, with Derrida and after him (as we have endeavored to do from the start) will lead us from the metaphysical immanence of a ground of decidability to the deconstructive provenance of an abyss of undecidability; or from the rectitude of the technoscientific rationalism of (late) modernity to the amplitude of the limitless responsibility of deconstruction.

The "moralizing" disbursement of the rendering of reason—the practical objectives of its empirically conditioned "must" as the volitional basis of the causality of the freedom of being—Derrida says, "seems to cover the essence of our relationship to principle, it seems to mark out for us requirement, debt, duty, request, command, obligation, law, the imperative."[29] Who would want to deny this or be willing to reject it out of hand? Nihilism and anarchy would arguably be the negative forms of a plausible repercussion of "unschooled" reactions to opposing the welcoming of a responsibility to reason, given that, in all likelihood, the obscuration of intentionality or the meaninglessness of violence can irrevocably dampen the vitality of the human subject in the abject despairing of its *being-in-the-world.* But is not an uncritical servility to the principle of reason not also a denial of the liberating statute of its *law of right, the right of its law?* The regulated "objectiveness" of a prescriptive responsivity is of dubious integrity because it conflates the logic of the universal with that of the particular to override any justification of the heteronomous ground of subjective differences of judgment. Reason lays down the law (*Gesetz*). Yes. And the *principle* of reason must be "obeyed." No objection. Yet can we still respond with responsibility to reason without giving up the right to question to a not-so-automatically benign thought-less-ness?[30] And without duping the natural law of judgment—its capacity to exercize *uncompromising* discernment—by relinquishing the free will of conscience to the power (*Macht*) and authority of a violent means leading to what could be nothing else but unjust ends? Derrida asks: "Who is more faithful to reason's call, who hears it with a keener ear, who better sees the difference, the one who offers questions in return and tries to think through the possibility of that summons [of the principle of reason], or the one who does not want to hear any question about the reason of reason?"[31] The *irrationalism* of cleaving to hasty assumptions based on the self-deceiving conviction that we both completely know and agree on what the essence of the axiom is (for example, its *quiddity,* "whatness"[32]), or what it "wants to imply," along with what is expected of us, is brought out in the *irresponsibility* of a thought-less obedience to decree.[33] Although Derrida appropriates the deontological expressionism of a Kantian order of classifications to show how, by the categorical law of universalizability, "pure practical reason continually calls on the principle of reason, on its 'must,'"[34] the prelude to an aggressively deconstructive questioning of the teleology of the self-accounting ground of reason and of the being of the university the conclusion will later point to is seriously Heideggerian:

> A responsibility is involved here, however. We have to respond to the call of the principle of reason. In *Der Satz vom Grund* [*The Principle of Reason*], Heidegger names that call *Anspruch*: requirement, claim, request, demand, command, convocation; it always entails a certain addressing of speech. The word is not seen, it has to be heard and listened to, this apostrophe that enjoins us to respond to the principle of reason.
>
> A question of responsibility, to be sure. But is answering *to* the principle of reason the same act as answering *for* the principle of reason? Is the scene the same? Is the landscape the same? And where is the university located within this space?[35]

How are we to hear and grasp the ethical presumption of the invocation of the principle of reason? According to Heidegger, by way of the collected awareness of Being to the open realm of language (its "home," "abode," "in-dwelling"[36]) through which the fundamental difference of mind and body is united over time in the ecstatic broadening of hermeneutical countenance realized experientially—via the *circumspective immediacy* of meditative consciousness—as the "piety" of a "gathered hearkening"[37] that composes the authenticity of itself out of the giving of itself to a listening with a view to the "releasement" (*Gelassenheit*) of the originary thinking of being toward the mystery of the "letting be" of things.[38] A rejection of the epistemological opposition of "intelligible" and "sensory" knowing deeply undercuts the foundation of the self-legislating self-groundedness of subject centered reason and clears the way for the procreative resolve of effectuating a "new autochthony" [39] out of the past. It is this comportment of fused sensibilities directed to a *future-not-yet-realized* that carries with it the hope of building, through the *act of thought*, a better place to dwell (*Aufenthalten*).[40] This radical repositioning of thinking as *poiesis* (making or producing) and *praxis* (acting or doing) liberated from the stranglehold of a modernist theory of representation collapses the "noetic/somatic" duality of the Cartesian problematic of truth at the preontological ("lived") threshold of the *ego cogito* where the material ambiguities of the everyday play of "world" and "things" are brought together and borne apart. That said, these theoretical premises of Heidegger's that my rereading of the call of the principle of reason hinges on will capacitate Derrida in the discourse to play the *logic of rationality* against the *method of science* while reflecting on the ethics and politics of the work of research within the university[41]—as we shall see.

To provoke the philosophical imagination into judging the merits of reconstituting a fictional interchange between Charles Sanders Peirce and Heidegger on the tehnorational birth of the modern University from the self-accounting normativity of the principle of reason, Derrida cites a telling excerpt from the American proto-pragmatist, already having begun to refrain from initiating such a *tête-à-tête*:

> . . . discuss[ing] the purpose of [higher] education, without once alluding to the only motive [reason] that animates the genuine sceintific investigator. I am not guiltless in the matter myself, for in my youth I wrote some articles to uphold a doctrine called pragmatism, namely, that the meaning and essence of every conception lies in the application that is to be made of it. That is all very well, when properly understood. I do not intend to recant it. But the question arises, *what is* the ultimate application; and at the time I seem to have been inclined to subordinate the *conception* to the *act*, knowing to doing. Subsequent experience of life has taught me that the only thing that is really *desirable* without a reason for being so, is to render ideas and things reasonable. *One cannot well demand a reason for reasonableness itself.*[42]

At first blush, the leap of thought from "application" to "reason," grounded fully in the interest *of itself, for itself,* seems greatly at odds with the tenets of Peircean pragmaticism. However, as Christopher Norris has correctly noted, what distinguished Peirce from his philosophical contemporaries (John Dewey and William James) was the "belief that every intellectual discipline requires some ultimate cognitive faith, some idea (as Peirce expressed it) of 'truth at the end of inquiry.'"[43] Where one would expect an altogether oppositional stance toward the value of reason for the utility and "practicality" of research, it is an "epistemological lapse" that has left Richard Rorty a less-than-enthused advocate of pragmaticism.[44] And yet why does Derrida forego the chance of pursuing the matter of this dialogical intercourse of "pragmatism" and "phenomenological hermeneutics" any further in "The Principle of Reason"? To force arbitrarily (from the shards of what would be and are admittedly bracketed textual fragments) the sharp discordance of a theory of practice and a practice of theory separating Peirce and Heidegger. Is it simply because the sum and substance of the suppositious disquisition placed firmly in question could never *really* have happened anyway? There being, after all, no discernable compulsion for the one to "*speak to*" the other *in* these terms or *on* these terms of the *reasonable* ground of the University. The desiderata of this hypothetical repartee are obliquely displayed in "The Principle of Reason" by Derrida's strategic use of exemplarity that we have dealt with in the first part of this chapter to show how the discourse itself is a *praxeology of theory,* taking its philosophical inspiration, as it does, somewhat precipitously from the difference between Heidegger and Peirce. What is to be garnered from the suspension of this *all-but-chimerical agon,* it being, *in the last analysis,* very much under the *cull* and *sway* of a deconstructive (in)direction, if you will?

Well, for Derrida, "[t]o bring about such a dialogue between Peirce and Heidegger [around what he describes as 'the compound theme, indeed, of the university and the principle of reason'[45]], we would have to go *beyond* the conceptual oppositions between 'conception' and 'act,' between 'conception' and 'application,' theoretical view and praxis, theory and technique."[46] And this is what "The Principle of Reason," more or less, does, *works at,* achieves. But does not a fundamental irreconcilability continue to persist and so to inhibit a bridging together of the *aporias* of meditative reflection consuming the *unpracticable idea* with the apodicticity of habitual determination particularizing the *sensible event*?

The incommensurability between "thinking" and "doing," as such, accentuates *a fortiori* the methodological differences that both philosophers hold dearly to in the very heart of their dissatisfactions with the legislations of "pure reason" for the facilitating of educational aspirations.[47] Or, what is, *pace* Immanuel Kant, the ground proposition (*Grundsatz*) of the being of the university[48] where the ideal of a calculable rationality secures the *sine qua non* for a motive of a principle of (collective) action undergirding the law of its *practical essence*[49] and the viability of its autonomy as a public institution.[50] According to Derrida: "What Peirce only outlines," and willingly takes for granted by virtue of a theoretical impasse at work within the self-professed objectives of his own version of pragmatism that cancels out the fortuitous contingency of even a *rudimentary* examination of the vested interests of Reason's institution, "is the path where Heidegger feels the most to be at stake, especially in *Der Satz vom Grund* [*The Principle of Reason*]."[51] We have already begun in this journey and are on the way (*Unterwegs*) to "fleshing out" the labyrinth of its trails through the playfulness of a "poetic license" we might well be tempted to refer to here plainly enough as *a basic right of academic freedom.* But to return to a familiar crossroads, retreading it lightly, to go on in a different direction, we would have to ask here an important question: What warrants deconstruction to in-vade the space of the university as "an institutional practice for which the concept of institution remains a problem?"[52] Looking elswhere for an answer brings us to Heidegger who is—like Derrida was, in an earlier quotation—succinct: "The university is grounded on the principle of reason. How are we supposed to conceive this: the university grounded on a principle? May we venture such an assertion?"[53] We may and we must. For Derrida, and I am paraphrasing here, "*institutions are in deconstruction before deconstruction is in institutions.*" It is that simple and that complex.

We would have to forego then, as Derrida does, that the principle of reason lies positioned, rather awkwardly, between the "strange and necessary dialogue"[54] of Peirce and Heidegger on the epistemological foundations of an institution of higher education.[55] Each philosopher, in his own turn, gives testimony to strong convictions that cleave open the otherwise invisible contours of the chasm of Western thought, a most intractable void waiting to be filled by the "spirit" and "action" of philosophy, by extending the general realm of analysis across the continuum of a conceptual dichotomy pitting "interpretation" against "application." And like the paling chiaroscuro of a prophetic abyss, the *principium rationis* haunts the preoccupations of these, let us call them (for the sake of convenience), "*complementary figures*" within the epistemological ground (*Grund*) and non-ground (*Ab-grund*) of the history of metaphysics. Their propositions are—to differing degrees—expressive of the need for an assertive questioning of the rationalizing force (*Gewalt*) that authorizes the systemic organicity of the hierarchization of knowledge within the established composition of the modern University.[56] But in the sublimating of the immediately "given phenomena" of being (*Seiend*) to "abstract concepts" (*Verstand*) of ideas of Being (*Dasein*), these proclamations are overtures of nothing less than faithful judgments indicative of deeply divergent philosophical allegiances that have affected the university—fateful disclosures, consciously or unconsciously, ill at ease with the unforgiving dictates of the principle of reason. This is why the abrupt un-staging of this extraordinary confrontation (*Auseinandersetzung*) of Peirce and Heidegger that Derrida suggests *must* occur, but refrains from illuminating *stricto sensu*,[57] leaves "us" dangling precariously, at altogether loose ends, as it were, over a most contested philosophical divide, drifting freely along the interminable fluctuations of these oppositional limits of epistemic irresolution constructing the *khora* (literally the "'place,' 'location,' 'region,' 'country'"[58] or metaphorically the provisional movement and ephemeral stases[59]) of the truth of reason and the "untruth" of its other, *unreason,* within the institution. The *plus d'une langue*[60] of deconstruction, meanwhile, asserts itself amid the unlimited complexity of these tensions and repulsions that only appear to coalesce, however unhappily, toward the ambiguous mediality of a thin line separating "pure theory" from "pure practice" reproduced arbitrarily as the placeholder of technoscientific interests within the interdisciplinary model of the university;[61] that is, across the paradigmatic interspaces of this institutional struggle where the differential gamut of a range of "post-Kantian" philosophizing vies for the justifiable "right" to express a skepticism of the truthfulness of *a priori* knowledge claims[62]—between, *on the one hand,* an idea of "pure reason" from which the *compartmentality* synthesizing the form (*Bild*) of the programmatic structure of the university evolves[63] and, *on the other,* an idea of "pure practical reason" from which the *ethicity* orienting the employment of the first principles of a system of scientific knowledge surfaces. How can we assert this judgment? Because, as deconstruction has shown, there is no recourse to what would inevitably *have to be* the moderating code of a master language capable of bringing together the "inner world" of the *res cogitans* with the "outer world" of the *res extensa* to mercifully undermine, once and for all, the troubling diffraction of conflicting faculties of "reason"—a veritable "purveyor of truth" whose peremptory capacity for *semiotic reductionism* could clarify the interphenomenal terms of otherwise unpredictable pronouncements made from the ideolect of "sign-thing" correlations, namely, ideational constructions of a lifeworld (*Lebenswelt*) by and within the refracted self-consciousness of a decentered subject.

In this respect of the institutionalization of "interpretative finitude" or "hermeneutic universalism" Derridean deconstruction runs counter to, the elocution of the principle of reason codifies the obligation of thinking to the quasi-mystical eschatology of a Will to Truth by providing in itself the expletive outlet through which to achieve a consolidation of the *conditions of the possibility* of the course of Western knowledge and pedagogy after the ethical predisposition of that which Plato had specified through the so-called doctrine of Ideas as the quest for the good "beyond being" (*epekeina tes ousias*).[64] *By Law* and *by Right,* the performative dimension of the ("professional") field of human endeavours (philosophic-scientific-aesthetic) "*within*" and "*without*" the university is tied to the necessity of a theoretical justification of the decision supporting actions taken or abstained from. That is, a response or "even a nonresponse is charged *a priori* with responsibility"[65] to the principle of reason as a *fundamental principle of Being and beings,* and thence of *poiesis* and *praxis,* because the effects of the metaphysical exigency of "explain[ing] effects through their causes, rationally,"[66] are inescapable for *the living of the good life.* Here, in the wake of Heraclitus and the demise of the *logos*—from *legein* (to say), to which the Word is sent back to its roots in the *apophainesthai,* "to bring forward into appearance"—and with this, the shining of a light on Platonism, the first decisive steps are taken toward a calculable rationality that initiates the start of the modern epoch of "representational thinking."[67] What is the periodic culmination of an epistemological transmigration of philosophy and science away from a basic questioning of the ground of Being (*Seinsfrage*) *meta ta physika* and toward the intractable manipulation of ends through the mediation of technoscience?[68] The mantle of modernity rests on the directives of the principle of reason that pave the way—through Cartesian representationalism—for the instrumental logic of "purposive rationality" (*Zweckrational*) because the empire of metaphysics cannot abandon the "destinality" of being to the mystagogy of ill-calculation. There is no safety in the lack of a well-planned abode, the careful forging of a place for the in-stalling of *homo faber* to rule as undisputable master "of the totality of what is."[69] Even if—in the challenging forth (*Herausfordern*) of what is revealed of the raw materiality of the human world as "standing reserve" (*Bestand*), a resource always present at hand (*Vorhandenheit*) and ready to be used—the artificiality of a ready-made "techno-ecology" bringing nature and beings to the order of a stand still by the enframing (*Gestell*) of a world picture (*Weltbild*) contributes to feelings of alienation and homelessness (*Unheimlichkeit*).[70] A withdrawing from Being cast in the spectral emptiness of a "calculable and representable subjectivity"[71] allows us to see into the *oblivion of metaphysics*, not to dispense with its language or its stratagems, but to accept it for what it is, *a violence of light.*

My rereading of the "institution of modern technoscience that is the university *Stiftung* [foundation],"[72] like Derrida's, relies on the later philosophy of Heidegger after the infamous turn (*Kehre*). And the point is this: "[W]e can no longer dissociate the principle of reason from the very idea of technology in the realm of their modernity."[73] For the *self*-definition and *self*-presencing of the sovereign subject of "metaphysical humanism"[74] there is no other viable option than the commanding of the power of the Will to Will—and all that that means. When "Man" is the measure (*metron*) of the reason of the being of all things, metaphysics and technology, it stands, are largely equivalent terms—not the same but interconnected and intertwined in their refusal to think Being (*Dasein*).[75] Let us continue to deal with the question of the institutional retranscription of the principle of reason Derrida poses, to inquire further into the "the origin of that demand for grounds,"[76] while referring to the general problem of instrumentalism, a technologizing strand of metaphysics the text of our discourse will have only foreshadowed until now.

The significance of "end-oriented thinking" to the development of the modern university cannot be underestimated, justifying, as it does, the unity of the rationale for the organizational division of teaching and research among and within the disciplines. Inasmuch as the "verbal formulation" of the principle of reason "provides the impetus for a new era of purportedly 'modern' reason, metaphysics and technoscience,"[77] the objectification of its needs as universalizable goals to be achieved without fail comes to dominate the requirements for the "surety" of the "truths" that pervade the institution. For Derrida, questioning the neutrality of the epistemological foundation of claims to knowledge constrains but also opens up the larger purview of academic responsibility beyond the appeal to rationality. Once the "Originary Ethics" of the call of the principle of reason are entrenched within the representational ground of meaning so as to obligate a reproducing of the normative value of response, there is the problem of a conflict of self-interest that deconstruction *must* and *can* address:

> But to answer *for* the principle of reason, and thus for the university, to answer *for* this call, to raise questions about the origin or ground of this principle of foundation (*Satz vom Grund*), is not simply to obey it or to respond *in the face of* this principle. We do not listen the same way when we are responding to a summons as when we are questioning its meaning, its origin, its possibility, its goal, its limits. Are we obeying the principle of reason when we ask what grounds this principle that is itself a principle of grounding? We are not—which does not mean that we are disobeying it, either. Are we dealing here with a circle or an abyss? The circle would consist in seeking to account for reason by reason, to render reason to the principle of reason, in appealing to the principle in order to make it speak of itself at the very point where, according to Heidegger, the principle of reason says nothing about itself. The abyss, the hole, the *Abgrund,* the empty "gorge" would be the impossibility for a principle of grounding to ground itself. This very grounding, then, like the university, would have to hold itself suspended above a most peculiar void. Are we to use reason to account for the principle of reason?[78]

Up to this point, my own rereading of the "why" and "not-why" (the because) of the response demanded of being for a "proper" answering to the responsibility of the call to reason has turned on the lexico-hermeneutical axis of a Heideggerian *double-shifting* of the tonality common to the "popular" phrasing of the dictum, *nihil est sine ratione*—what Derrida briefly mentions, "given the limits of [his] talk."[79] Such a moving away from the "cognitive" phase of the principle that places the emphasis put on the first and third words of its abbreviated statement "*nothing* is *without* reason" in contradistinction to the modulated pitch of a newly conjugated register stressing "nothing *is* without *reason*" brings about the *perception* of an accord of Being (*Sein*) and ground (*Grund*).[80] Far-reaching conclusions follow from this.

The latter, "transposed," version of the principle of reason as a *principle of Being* seems to collide with the former as a *principle of beings.* There is no common denominator of logic or language that can relieve the tension of this ontico-ontological difference in the magical euphoria of a dialectical synthesis of opposing terms. *Leaving reason to account for the principle of reason obviates the problem of the essence of its ground.* For it reinforces the metaphysical presupposition of a conceptual unity—the redundant movement of a self-authorizing ascription—sealing the distance between *the proximity of being that has value and Being that has none.* Taking the argument one step further, for our purposes, a paradox ensues: *if the principle of reason must ground itself on the essence of itself (reason) to have any grounding at all, then it would seem to have no grounding given the tautological structure of the foundation.* What does this have to do with the University? Everything and nothing.

The University is founded on the principle of reason and on "what remains hidden in that principle,"[81] the "Other" of reason (not its opposite): an ungrounded grounding, the place and non-place of the abyss. This is very strange. One might even say that it reveals, already *in* metaphysics, a certain love of "irrationality." And yet, within the academic community of the institution, Derrida observes, "nowhere is th[e] [historicity of] this principle [or its 'instrumentality'] thought through, scrutinized, interrogated as to [the sources of] its origin."[82] Nothing could surprise us less. The University is a cultural artifact of the principle of reason that we will have *always already* existed in, ever since and even before the Academy of Plato or the Lyceum of Aristotle. A pleasing fiction—akin to how Kant described it[83]—of the philosophical anthropologism (read "humanism") of the West. Symbolizing the "place" where all knowledge and non-knowledge can be found or is housed, the *Panepistemion* is an enigmatic construct of both imaginary concord and very real resiliance indistinguishing of the difference between an appearance of totality and an idea of infinity. A flexibly self-correcting system of persistent re- and deorchestrations that have overcome the shortsighted density of human time.[84] As the *reason for its being* objectifies the valuation of an idealized vision of "*the good life*" that self-validates the autonomic "Right" of the institution through the *indispensable lie* of an intersubjective sharing of common interests among its collective rank and file,[85] the "archive of its archives"[86] remains haunted from the start by a specter of the past and a dream of the future—a daimon of multiple eyes and ears and hearts more at war than at peace with the *rational essence of the University,* or the "ethico-ideologico-philosophical" grounding of its knowledge politics and the technocratizing subdivisions of its interdisciplinarity. "The university is a (finished) product," Derrida has said elsewhere; "I would almost call it the child of an inseparable couple, metaphysics and technology."[87]

The Ethics of Science and/as Research

Deconstruction and the (Dis)Orientation of a New Responsibility

The principle of reason "as principle of grounding, foundation or institution"[88] tends to guide the *science of research* to techno-practical ends. The politics of academic work and the role "the ['modern'] university may play"[89] in helping to construct the arena experiencing the application of results or the "pay off"[90] of predirected outcomes of inquiry are fed by competing interests situated outside the rationale of the institution itself or the ideals of the "nation-state." The "orienta-tion" of research "programmed, focused, organized"[91] on the expectation of its future utilization, Derrida insists, is "centered instead on [the desires of] multina-tional military-industrial complexes of technoeconomic networks, or rather inter-national technomilitary networks that are apparently multi- or transnational in form."[92] Forces wielding the power of "investment"—not necessarily monetary—are always wanting to control the mechanisms of creative production to commodify knowledge. And with these "external" influences affecting and reflecting the pur-poses of the university that are found more and more in not obvious but strategic areas within the confines of the institution, thanks to the "channel of private foun-dations"[93] sustaining the direction of research through the irresistable lure of fund-ing and other incentives (power, status, career advancement, and so on), the "pragmatic" interests of an "applied science" are set adroitly in opposition to the "disinterestedness" of "fundamental" (basic) inquiry—a distinction of "real but lim-ited relevance"[94] given the deferred dividends of the "detours, delays and relays of 'orientation,' its more random aspects,"[95] that are either incalculable or go unrecog-nized until a suitable situation of advantageous use presents itself. For Derrida, it is naïve to believe there are some "basic disciplines ['philosophy,' 'theoretical physics,' and 'pure mathematics' are the examples he gives] shielded from power, inaccessible to programming by the pressures of the State or, under cover of the State, by civil society or capital interests."[96] That thought has now been unthinkable for some time since the dawning of the "postcritical" age of nuclear politics and the wake of the informativizing function of science as research "[a]t the service of war."[97] What is at stake concerning the "control" of knowledge pivots around the "higher-prior-ity" issue of protecting "national and international security"[98] interests, however heterogeneous the calculation of a plan of insurance or the lack of it is to the logic of "peace" or "democracy." The differentiation of the aims of research, Derrida con-tends, is not that discreet an indicator of its "use-value" so as to clearly distinguish between the profitability of application and the destructive effects of misappropria-tion, despite the usual "factoring in" of "reasonable" margins of error:

> . . . research programs have to [in the sense of *are made to*] encompass the entire field of information, the stockpiling of knowledge, the workings and thus also the essence of language and of all semiotic systems, translation, coding and decoding, the play of presence and absence, hermeneutics, se-mantics, structural and generative linguistics, pragmatics, rhetoric. I am ac-cumulating all these disciplines in a haphazard way, on purpose, but I shall end with literature, poetry, the arts, fiction in general: the theory that has all these disciplines as its object may be just as useful in ideological warfare as it

is in experimentation with variables in all-too-familiar perversions of the referential function. Such a theory may always be put to work in communications strategy, the theory of commands, the most refined military pragmatics of jussive utterances (by what token, for example, will it be clear that an utterance is to be taken as a command in the new technology of telecommunications? How are the new resources of simulation and simulacrum to be controlled? And so on. . . .) . . . Furthermore, when certain random consequences of research are taken into account, it is always possible to have in view some eventual benefit that may ensue from an apparently useless research project (in philosophy or the humanities, for example). The history of the sciences encourages researchers to integrate that margin of randomness into their centralized calculation. They then proceed to adjust the means at their disposal, the available financial support, and the distribution of credits. A State power or forces that it represents no longer need to prohibit research or to censor discourse, especially in the West. It is enough that they can limit the means, can regulate support for production, transmission, diffusion.[99]

Within the "concept of information or informatization"[100] the ethics and the politics of research take shape, as the conservative ideal of "science" the university stands on is overtaken by a sacrificing of the autonomy of its own self-regulating measures of knowledge advancement to the real-world pressures of securing a future for itself. And that is understandable, although it may not be acceptable to even those unquestioning defenders of the dominant (or onto-teleological) interpretation of the principle of reason and its "integrat[ing of] the basic to the oriented, the purely rational to the technical, thus bearing witness to that original intermingling of the metaphysical and the technical."[101]

The "responsibility" Derrida wishes to "awaken or resituate"[102] is "in the university or before (*devant*) the university, whether one belongs to it or not."[103] *Its double gesture bridges the ungrounded space of the conditions of possibility over which positions on ethics and responsibility, reason and rationality are thought out and taken.* Derrida begins to elaborate the difficulty of this "new responsibility" by opposing the "prohibiting limitations"[104] that "presses, [public and private] foundations, mass media,"[105] and other "interest groups" place on the act of research within the institution: "The unacceptability of a discourse, the noncertification of a research project, the illegitimacy of a course offering are declared by evaluative actions: studying such evaluations is, it seems to me [he emphasizes], one of the tasks most indispensable to the exercize of academic responsibility, most urgent for the maintenance of its dignity."[106] To intervene decisively in the business of the university is to appeal (to) reason, to ask for the concession of reasons out of which to judge judgments.

The medium in question that relates the obligation and responsibility of ethics to politics and the practices of the institution is language and two ways of thinking about the *value of language*. Derrida defines these in relation to the principle of reason as "instrumental" (informative) and "poetic" (creative) by associating their contrasting methods of semiological effect (for example, representation/undecidability) with research type, end-oriented and fundamental. And on the basis of the difference of values of finitude that must not proceed from knowledge but always head toward the possibility of its invention is grounded the deconstructive attempt to define a new academic responsibility "in the face of the university's total subjection to the technologies of informatization."[107] The cross-contamination between the "instrumental" and the "*poietic*" aims of research science is obvious "at the outer limits of the authority and power of the principle of reason"[108] where the specificity of goals or purposes is blurred by the shared logic of *praxis*. Derrida situates this antinomic responsibility—of "the experience and experiment of the *aporia*,"[109] more or less—within the general domain of a hypothetical "community of thought"[110] that is commited to the "sounding [of] a call to practice it."[111] The "*group-at-large*" refered to is not one "of research, of science, of philosophy, since these values [of 'professionalism' and 'disciplinarity,' no matter how 'radical,'] are most often subjected to the unquestioned authority of the principle of reason"[112] and can be absorbed into the homogeneous magma of intrainstitutional discourse (for example, the standardization of Marxism and psychoanalysis). Derrida has named this loosely gathered consortium a "community of the question," arising after the deaths of philosophy, a chance for safekeeping the possibility of the question of the *violence of metaphysics,* onto-theo-logical and proto-ethical. How would it function? Derrida explains as follows:

> Such a community would interrogate the essence of reason and of the principle of reason, the values of the basic, of the principial, of radicality, of the *arkhe* in general, and it would attempt to draw out all the possible consequences of this questioning. It is not certain that such a thinking can bring together a community or found an institution in the traditional sense of these words. What is meant by community and institution must be rethought. This thinking must also unmask—an infinite task—all the ruses of end-orienting reason, the paths by which apparently disinterested research can find itself indirectly reappropriated, reinvested by programs of all sorts. That does not mean that "orientation" is bad in itself and that it must be combatted, far from it. Rather, I am defining the necessity for a new way of educating students that will prepare them to undertake new analyses in order to evaluate these ends and choose, when possible, among them all.[113]

Less than a year after this lecture on the principle of reason, the Collège International de Philosophie (CIPH) would open its doors to students and scholars (during January of 1984), providing perhaps a much anticipated answer to the biding question of a "community of thought" and the suggestion of a rethinking of the institution of "higher" education.[114] Derrida was its first "acting director," to be followed by Jean-François Lyotard and others in a succession of one year appointments. The international makeup of the CIPH was and is reflected by the composition of the membership of its "governing bodies," the result of an open letter reprinted on the French Ministry of Research and Industry letterhead and circulated around the world in May 1982 to invite the participation of interested parties in its planning and operation.[115] There were more than 750 replies to the epistle Derrida drafted on behalf of the Socialist government of François Mitterand, who, on the eve of his election to office, had promised the GREPH to protect the discipline of philosophy within the organization of the public school and university curricula. All responses were evaluated, and the four members of the mission (Derrida, François Châtelet, Jean-Pierre Faye, and Dominique Lecourt) issued the lengthy *Rapport pour le Collège Internationale de Philosophie.*[116] The expressed intention or "regulating idea" of that document was to interrogate and displace "the ontological encyclopaedic model by which the philosophical concept of the *universitas* has been guided for the last two centuries,"[117] as was originally stated in the letter:

> The International College of Philosophy is to give (*doit donner*) priority to themes, problems, experiences that do not yet find a legitimate or sufficient place in other institutions, whether they concern philosophy or the relations between philosophy, sciences, techniques, and artistic productions. Beyond simple interdisciplinarity, it will be oriented toward new intersections and will work to open (*frayer*) other paths between constituted or compartmentalized disciplines (*savoirs*). In order to undo traditional isolations, the college will be broadly open, according to new modes, to exchanges from abroad.[118]

That the institution was to be a "College of Philosophy" is not incidental, secondary, or superfluous to the context of this lecture we are rereading on the principle of reason and the being of the university. The semiologico-symbolic interground of any and all potential articulations of academic responsibility is, for Derrida, an irreducible dimension of "thought" and "thinking" analogous with the poststructural metacriticality of deconstruction—an intellectual practice of grafting, confrontation, and productive interference that transgresses the fixed borders of "the arts" and "the sciences" for the transformative redistribution of knowledge values and the founding of new fields of research at the interspaces of philosophy and science. This is made explicit by Derrida's (quasi-)deconstruction of the interdisciplinary schematicism of the Kantian university model:

> One can no longer distinguish between technology on the one hand and theory, science and rationality on the other. . . . [A]n essential affinity ties together objective knowledge, the principle of reason, and a certain metaphysical determination of the relation to truth. . . . One can no longer maintain the boundary that Kant, for example, sought to establish between the schema that he called "technical" and the one he called "architectonic" in the systematic organization of knowledge—which was also to ground a systematic organization of the university. The architectonic is the art of systems. "Under the government of reason, our knowledge in general," Kant says, "should not form a rhapsody, but it must form a system in which alone it can support and favour the essential aims of reason." To that pure rationality of the architectonic, Kant opposes the scheme of the merely technical unity that is empirically oriented, according to views and ends that are incidental, not essential. It is thus a limit between two aims that Kant seeks to define, the essential and noble end of reason that gave rise to fundamental science versus the incidental and empirical ends that can be systematized only in terms of technical schemas and necessities.[119]

Kant had observed in *The Conflict of the Faculties* (*Der Streit der Fakultäten,* 1798)[120] that the University was created by the *enactment of an idea.* An objectivation of the Will to Reason as ceded, in principle, from what is *de jure* a metaphysical incipit *a priori* the inscription of being. Or a *fatum* of the time-less-ness of Being, the ground and abyss of its infinity—that is, the *principle of reason.* Kant, as only he could, attempted to re-theorize the insights and shortcomings of such a novel idea as the university in an architectonic division of intellectual labor, pure and practical—a uniform system of knowledge designations starting from "the idea of the whole field of what is presently teachable (*das ganze gegenwärtige Feld der Gelehrsamkeit*)."[121] But the irony is that, owing to the "artificiality" (*Künstliche*) of the institutional architecture, "one would [have to] treat knowledge a little like an industry (*gleichsam fabrikenmässig*)"[122] and be commited to reproducing the rigid partitions of unsurpassable limits of separation between disciplines. A development related to the themes of "profession," "professionalism" or "professionalization," Derrida views as "regulat[ing] university life [and research] according to the supply and demand of the marketplace [not excluding the institution itself] and according to a purely technical idea of competence."[123] Any "sociology or politology"[124] policing these border lines of the Academy—regardless of method (for example, "Marxist or neo-Marxist, Weberian or neo-Weberian, Mannheimian, some combination of these or something else entirely"[125])—in responding to the necessity of justifying the value of its own existence and acceptance to the structural logic of the organic whole, "never touches upon that which, in themselves, continues to be based on the principle of reason and thus on the essential foundation of the modern university."[126] Even the most underground thinking—"deconstruction"—can be rehabilitated or reappropriated to serve a "highly traditional politics of knowledge"[127] if the conditions of exposition ("historical, technoeconomic, politico-institutional, and linguistic"[128]) are not analyzed with a vigilant wariness, a radical suspicion. Rather than encouraging the open harmony of higher- and lower-level orders of theory and practice Kant envisions, wants, or presumes, the attempt to separate and compartmentalize interests is the source of the conflict of the faculties itself and an omen of the history of canonical battles among and within them for control over the charted and uncharted territory grounding the "economy and ecology"[129] of the institution.

Insofar as "no experience in the present allows for an adequate grasp of that present, presentable totality of doctrine, of teachable theory,"[130] Derrida, in rereading these idealist presuppositions of this seminal text on the straining interrelations of the disciplines, argues elsewhere that: "An institution—this is not merely a few walls or some outer structure surrounding, protecting, guaranteeing or restricting the freedom of out work; it is also and already the structure of our interpretation."[131] The ethics of the ground of that edifice of the university is what is being questioned here, in "The Principle of Reason," along with the responsibility to be taken for it—and who this "our" *does* or *can* refer to exactly. This is not to aver, as Kant would have it, that philosophy—the faculty from which the "Great Model of the University" acquires the academic legitimacy of its ideal autonomy—is completely "outside" and "above" any hierachization of knowledge due to a "higher" responsibility it claims to answer for/to Reason and Truth. There is another side to it.[132] Concurrently, philosophy (unlike other disciplines) would also need to be "inside" and "below" the structure of the institution, filling out the reason of the lower ground on which its being stands. But what of the originary violence of a *faculty of Right*? Is the "mystical foundation of its authority" as a legislator of "Reason" and "Truth" for the university assuaged by an inverted mirroring of its stature? Could it be?

Even if we choose to believe Kant, there is a minimal security, if any at all, to the tautological notion of "the essence of knowledge as knowledge of knowledge"[133]— the stolid (metaphilosophical) ground of university autonomy. It is "justified [Derrida stresses] by the axiom stating that scholars alone can judge other scholars."[134] But this still says nothing of academic responsibility. And by this we do not mean the obligation of the institution, a mere husk or shell, a clever figment of a living entity. It goes deeper. The responsibility we are speaking of is that of the teaching body (*le corps enseignant*), the soul of the university.

On both the personal (I/me) and the communal (us/we) planes of the ethico-juridical strata of the norms of responsibility epistemic or empirical subjectivity submit to, the *first* and *final* law of being is preserved by the ground of reason as the fundamental logic of an institution, *the right of its Right.* But the founding and conserving violence complicit with the historicity of the university does not *wholly* ensnare the inspirited bodies of "those who teach"[135] either. Derrida explains how an uncomplicated philosophy of language is the cause for the ambiguity Kant is blind to:

> Kant defines a university that is as much a safeguard for the most totalitarian of social forms as a place for the most intransigently liberal resistance to any abuse of power, resistance that can be judged in turns as most rigorous or most impotent. In effect, its power is confined to a power-to-think-and-judge, a power-to-say, though not necessarily to say *in public,* since this would involve an *action,* an executive power denied the university. How is the combination of such contradictory evaluations possible for a model of the university? What must be such a model, to lend itself thus to this? I can only sketch out an answer to this enormous question. Presuppositions in the Kantian delimitation could be glimpsed from the very start, but today they have become massively apparent. Kant needs, as he says, to trace between a responsibility concerning truth and a responsibility concerning action, a linear frontier, an indivisible and rigorously uncrossable line. To do so he has to submit language to a particular treatment. Language is an element common to both spheres of responsibility, and one that deprives us of any rigorous distinction between the two spaces that Kant at all costs wanted to dissociate. It is an element that opens a passage to all parasiting and simulacra.[136]

The radical breakdown of the architectonic system of the ethical reference of knowledge arising from within the Kantian conception of the Law and the Right of Reason's institution becomes perceptible when the philosophical endowment of the limit of its Truth is projected outside itself between language and something that is outside itself. That, for deconstruction, is but one measure of the injustice of the *universality of the university.* The inconsistency of the supplication of reason to its ground—the accounting of justification itself—surpasses the metaphysical fastidiousness of what Kant presents as an uncorrupted philosophy—of the Idea of Reason—always willing to aid the judgment of a subject "capable of deciding [as it] tries to limit the effects of confusion, simulacrum, parasiting, equivocality and undecidability produced by language."[137] Wanting to close off the University's inside from its outside (and what this means in a larger context) is a utopian flight of fancy, a fearful withdrawal from responsibility to the Other, as is the dream Kant had for a universal language of philosophy uncorrupted by a natural tongue—a wish to keep reason pure. But the freedom of decision to choose among manifold options of undecidable possibilities is not responsibility abdicated nor obligation ignored; it is responsibility multiplied, obligation intensified. Ethics is crystallized in the education of experience manifest of a subjective "trial of passage" wrought from the difficulty of knowledge. A decision without the possibility of choice, in this sense of achieving an informed optation spurring to performance, can be no decision at all. And that also implies a political dimension adducible of the laws of right and Right. For Derrida—like Kierkegaard before him—the ordeal of decision is an instant of madness, it "always risks the worst,"[138] especially, as concerns us here, in relation to the ungrounding of the preconditions of the violence of an existing foundation like the idea of the university's reason for being by defining a new educational problematics:

> It is not a matter simply of questions that one *formulates* while submitting oneself, as I am doing here [in the discourse], to the principle of reason, but also of preparing oneself thereby to transform the modes of writing, approaches to pedagogy, the procedures of academic exchange, the relation to languages, to other disciplines, to the institution in general, to its inside and its outside. Those who venture forth along this path, it seems to me, need not set themselves up in opposition to the principle of reason, nor give way to "irrationalism." They may continue to assusme *within* the university, along with its memory and and tradition, the imperative of professional rigour and competence.[139]

The metalogic of deconstruction—the double-sided responsibility of its "to" and "for" peripatetic—aims at a *Verwindung* of the principle of reason, a "going-beyond that is both an acceptance and a deepening,"[140] as Gianni Vattimo has argued of the postmodern experience, not to get over, overcome, or distort the principle by out-bidding it into submission, but to resign the compliance of thought to a rethinking of it, and thus to effectuate a change in the thinking of the being of the University. To avoid reproducing the classical architectonic of the Kantian institution, thereby entrenching it still further, Derrida asserts, "'Thought' requires *both* the principle of reason *and* what is beyond the principle of reason, the *arkhè* and an-archy"[141]—the creation of a chance for the future by keeping the memory of the past alive. It is at the interspaces of knowledge constructions, beyond the grasp of "meaning" or "reason," that risks are taken by endeavoring to put what may appear to be the grounded or static system of a multistratified and interlocking hierarchy of disciplinary subdivisions into motion, play, *kinesis*. The institutional meeting place of a deconstructive ethics and politics would be where the undecidability of interpretative links are forged between those faculties speaking a constative (theoretical) language of a Kantian type and others who make performative (interventive) statements of an Austinian type. Like a bridge across an abyss of reason.

A Doubled Closure

There is no ambivalence about the threat of resistance deconstruction poses to reason. For some, the analytical situation Derrida annotates, we could say "of deconstruction," is an equivocatory non-sense of self-cancellations, a being-on-both-sides of the issue betraying a lack of ethical or political resolve; for others, its complexity consigns the "*coups nouveau*" of a *post*modern responsivity to an ineffectual rejection of the totality of what has come before in the hopes of improving what will come after. Few concerned will have no appraisement to offer. The gamut of judgments arising from within the general distinctions of perspective I have made begs the question of the "Other of Reason" depicted as "irrationality" without classifiably reducing the content or the *mal*content of arguments under the qualitative dichotomy of a "good" versus "bad" opposition. That is because the open obligation of the academic reponsibility of deconstruction is of the order of rationality but not of the metaphysical standards of "critique." For as reason internalizes the difference of its Other within the *subjectivism* of itself, steadfastly determining the rules of its own activation, its delimitations, and its ends, we are, or at the least *we should be,* compelled to inquire about the ground of its *objectivism.* The immanent force of a deconstructive questioning succeeds in collapsing the oppositional logics of metaphysical self-substantiation that excludes, *sui generis,* the relative independence of the subalterned voice of an overlooked middle. And this is where the politics of ethics and ontology, of "first philosophy," lies. Submitting the principle of reason to the hermeneutical conundrum of its own *in-itself, for-itself* structurality so as to interrogate the grounds of its meaning, its origin, its possibility, its goal, its limits, yields tensions commanding neither an obeyance to its unforgiving precepts nor a rejection of them. And here we will give the last word to Derrida:

> The time of reflection is also the chance for turning back on the very conditions of reflection, in all the sense of that word, as if with the help of a new optical device one could finally see sight, could not only view the natural landscape, the city, the bridge and the abyss, but could view viewing. As if through an acoustical device one could hear hearing, in other words, seize the inaudible in a sort of poetic telephony. The time of reflection is also another time, it is heterogeneous with what it reflects and perhaps gives time for what calls for and is called thought.[142]

Notes

1. Parts of this chapter have appeared in *Educational Theory*, Volume 48, Summer, no. 4, 1998, pp. 395–410. Jacques Derrida, "Mochlos; or, The Conflict of the Faculties," in *Logomachia: The Conflict of the Faculties*, Richard Rand and Amy Wygant, trans., Richard Rand, ed. (Lincoln, NE: University of Nebraska Press, 1992), 11. (Original translation has been modified.).

2. Jacques Derrida, *Memoires for Paul de Man*, Cecilia Lindsay, Jonathan Culler, and Eduardo Cavava, trans. (New York: Columbia University Press, 1986), 72.

3. Ibid., 72.

4. Jacques Derrida, "The Principle of Reason: The University in the Eyes of Its Pupils," *Diacritics* 13, no. 3 (Fall 1983): 9.

5. John D. Caputo, *Radical Hermeneutics: Repetition, Deconstruction, and the Hermeneutic Project* (Bloomington, IN: Indiana University Press, 1987), 231.

6. Derrida, "The Principle of Reason," 8.

7. Ibid., 8.

8. Ibid., 7. (Translation has been modified.)

9. Ibid., 8.

10. Ibid., 10.

11. See Jacques Derrida, "Languages and Institutions of Philosophy," Sylvan Söderlin, Rebecca Comay, Barbara Havercroft, and Joseph Adamson, trans. *Recherches Semiotique/Semiotic Inquiry* 4, no. 2 (1984): 91–154. See also, Peter Pericles Trifonas, 2000, *The Ethics of Writing: Derrida, Deconstruction and Pedgogy* (Lanham, MD: Raunan & Littlefield Publishers).

12. Derrida, "The Principle of Reason," 10.

13. Ibid., 8.

14. Martin Heidegger, *The Principle of Reason*, Reginald Lilly, trans. (Bloomington, IN: Indiana University Press, 1991), 119.

15. See Jacques Derrida, "Sending: On Representation," Peter Caws and Mary Ann Caws, trans. *Social Research* 49, no. 2 (1982): 295–326.

16. See Martin Heidegger, *The Question Concerning Technology and Other Essays*, William Lovitt, trans. (New York: Harper & Row Publishers, 1977).

17. Derrida, "The Principle of Reason," 10.

18. See Martin Heidegger, *The Question Concerning Technology*.

19. Derrida, "The Principle of Reason," 10.

20. Ibid., 10. (Translation has been modified.)

21. Derrida, "Sending: On Representation," 307.

22. See Martin Heidegger, *The Principle of Reason*.

23. See ibid.

24. See Martin Heidegger, *The Question Concerning Technology*.

25. Derrida, "Sending: On Representation," 304.

26. Derrida, "The Principle of Reason," 8.

27. See Jacques Derrida, "Force of Law: The Mystical Foundation of Authority," in *Deconstruction and the Possibility of Justice,* Mary Quaintance, trans., Drucilla Cornell, Michael Rosenfeld, and David Carlson, eds. (New York: Routledge, 1992), 1–67, for the two "types" of deconstructive approaches—the one following the trails of an idea or concept, the other using a text as a springboard to reading and writing— and the "whole subjectal axiomatic of responsibility" (25).

28. Derrida, "The Principle of Reason," 8.

29. Ibid., 8.

30. See Martin Heidegger, *Discourse on Thinking,* John M. Anderson and E. Hans Freund, trans. (New York: Harper & Row Publishers, 1966).

31. Derrida, "The Principle of Reason," 9.

32. See Martin Heidegger, *The Question Concerning Technology.*

33. See Martin Heidegger, *Discourse on Thinking.*

34. Derrida, "The Principle of Reason," 8.

35. Ibid., 8.

36. See Martin Heidegger, *Poetry, Language, Thought,* Albert Hofstader, trans. (New York: Harper Colophon Book, 1971).

37. Heidegger, *Discourse on Thinking,* 65.

38. On this aspect of *Gelassenheit,* see Jacques Derrida, "Heidegger's Ear: Philopolemology (*Geschlecht* IV), in *Reading Heidegger: Commemorations,* John P. Leavey, Jr., trans., John Sallis, ed. (Bloomington, IN: Indiana University Press, 1993), 163–218.

39. Heidegger, *Discourse on Thinking,* 55.

40. See Martin Heidegger, *Poetry, Language, Thought.*

41. See Martin Heidegger, *The Question Concerning Technology.*

42. Cited in Derrida, "The Principle of Reason," 9.

43. Christopher Norris, *Derrida* (Great Britain: Fontana Press, 1987), 160.

44. The preference Richard Rorty has for John Dewey is stated in *The Consequences of Pragmatism* (Minneapolis: University of Minnesota Press, 1982): "To lump Dewey with Peirce, James, and Quine is to forget that he was swept off his feet, and into a new intellectual world, by Hegel's and Compte's visions of our past" (46).

45. Derrida, "The Principle of Reason," 9.

46. Ibid., 9.

47. See Jacques Derrida, "Force of Law."

48. See Jacques Derrid, "Mochlos."

49. See Immanuel Kant, *Critique of Practical Reason,* Lewis White Beck, trans. (New York: Macmillan Publishing Company, 1956) and Immanuel Kant, *The Conflict of the Faculties/Der Streit der Fakultäten,* Mary J. Gregor, trans. (New York: Abaris Books, 1979).

50. See Jacques Derrida "Mochlos."

51. Derrida, "The Principle of Reason," 9.

52. Derrida, *Du droit à la philosophie* (Paris: Galilée, 1990), 88. (Translation is my own.)

53. Heidegger, *The Principle of Reason,* 24. Also included in a slightly different translation in a footnote to Derrida's text.

54. Derrida, "The Principle of Reason," 9.

55. Derrida, "Languages and Institutions of Philosophy," 134.

56. See ibid.

57. See the comments on ghosts, specters, apparitions, and so forth. An on-running theme that appears in other texts such as *The Gift of Death,* "The Force of Law," *Specters of Marx: The State of the Debt, the Work of Mourning, and the New International,* Peggy Kamuf, trans. (New York: Routledge, 1994).

58. Jacques Derrida, *On the Name,* David Wood, John P. Leavey, Jr., and Ian McLeod, trans., Thomas Dutoit, ed. (Stanford CA: Stanford University Press, 1995), 93.

59. The semiotic facet of the *khora* as an aspect of the theory of poetic language and the psychoanalytic drives of the subject is found in Julia Kristeva, *Revolution in Poetic Language,* Margaret Waller, trans. (New York: Columbia University Press, 1978).

60. See the chapter entitled "Mnemosyne" in Jacques Derrida, *Memoires for Paul de Man.*

61. See Jacques Derrida, "Sendoffs," Thomas Pepper, trans. *Yale French Studies* 77 (1990): 7–43.

62. On guarding against the translation of skepticism to mystagogy see Jacques Derrida, "On a Newly Arisen Apocalytic Tone in Philosophy," in *Raising the Tone of Philosophy: Late Essays by Immanuel Kant, Transformative Critique by Jacques Derrida,* John P. Leavey, Jr., trans., Peter Fenves, ed. (Baltimore, MD: Johns Hopkins University Press, 1993), 117–171.

63. Derrida, "Languages and Institutions of Philosophy," 132.

64. See Jacques Derrida, *Dissemination,* Barbara Johnson, trans. (Chicago: University of Chicago Press, 1981).

65. Derrida, "Mochlos," 3. (Translation has been modifed, my emphasis.).

66. Derrida, "The Principle of Reason," 8.

67. See Jacques Derrida, "Sending."

68. And in fact we can follow a trail that leads from the transformation of the pre-Socratic notion of Being as *physis* and *aletheia* into the conception of Being as *eidos* and *idea* from Plato to Being as humanity's idea to technology.

69. Derrida, "The Principle of Reason," 10.

70. See Martin Heidegger, *The Question Concerning Technology* for the discussion of technology as a mode of *aletheuein,* revealing—the essence of technology being nothing "technological" but *poietic.*

71. Derrida, "Sending," 317.

72. Derrida, "The Principle of Reason," 10.

73. Ibid., 12.

74. Martin Heidegger, "Letter on Humanism," in *Basic Writings,* David Farrell Krell, ed. and trans. (New York: Harper Collins, 1977), 193–242.

75. See Martin Heidegger, *The Question Concerning Technology.*

76. Derrida, "The Principle of Reason," 10.

77. Ibid., 8.

78. Ibid., 8.

79. Ibid., 9.

80. See Martin Heidegger, *Principle or Reason.* Chapter 5, 6.

81. Derrida, "The Principle of Reason," 10.

82. Ibid., 10.

83. See Immanuel Kant, *The Conflict of the Faculties.*

84. See Jacques Derrida, *Du droit à la philosophie,* especially pages 99–100.

85. See Jürgen Habermas, "The Idea of the University—Learning Processes," John R. Blazek, trans. *New German Critique* 41 (Spring-Summer 1987): 3–22.

86. Derrida, "Mochlos," 3.

87. Ibid., 15.

88. Derrida, "The Principle of Reason," 11.

89. Ibid., 11.

90. Ibid., 12.

91. Ibid., 11.

92. Ibid., 11. "The Principle of Reason," we must remember, was written and presented in April of 1983. At the time—the peaking of the "Cold War"—this was a fair description of the homogeneous "conditionality" of the Western "nation-states"—most conspicuously exemplified by America and Russia—that, according to Derrida, were spending in total upwards of "two million dollars a minute" on the manufacture of armaments alone.

93. Ibid., 14.

94. Ibid., 12.

95. Ibid., 12.

96. Ibid., 12.

97. Ibid., 13.

98. Ibid., 13.

99. Ibid., 13.

100. Ibid., 14.

101. Ibid., 14.

102. Ibid., 14.

103. Ibid., 14.

104. Ibid., 13.

105. Ibid., 13.

106. Ibid., 13.

107. Ibid., 14.

108. Ibid., 14.

109. Jacques Derrida, *The Other Heading: Reflections of Today's Europe,* Pascale-Anne Brault and Michael Nass, trans. (Bloomington, IN: Indiana University Press, 1992), 41.

110. Derrida, "The Principle of Reason," 16.

111. Ibid., 16.

112. Ibid., 16.

113. Derrida, "The Principle of Reason," 16.

114. Two excellent discussions of the *Collège Internationale de Philosophie* are Vincent B. Leitch, "Research and Education at the Crossroads: A Report on the *Collège Internationale de Philosophie*," *Substance* 50 (1986): 101–114, and Steven Ungar, "Philosophy after Philosophy: Debate and Reform in France Since 1968," *Enclitic* 8, nos. 1–2 (1984): 13–26.

115. The open letter was published in the United States in *Substance* 35 (1982): 80–81.

116. Jacques Derrida, François Châtelet, Jean-Pierre Faye, and Dominique Lecourt, *Rapport pour le Collège Internationale de Philosophie* (Paris: Ministre de la Recherche et de l'Industrie, 1982).

117. Derrida, "Sendoffs," 13.

118. Cited in Leitch, "Research and Education at the Crossroads," 103–104.

119. Derrida, "The Principle of Reason," 12.

120. See Immanuel Kant, *The Conflict of the Faculties.*

121. Derrida, "The Principle of Reason," 6.

122. Derrida, "Mochlos," 5.

123. Derrida, "The Principle of Reason," 17.

124. Ibid., 16.

125. Ibid., 16.

126. Ibid., 16.

127. Ibid., 17.

128. Ibid., 17.

129. Ibid., 16.

130. Ibid., 6.

131. Derrida, "Mochlos," 22.

132. See Jacques Derrida, "Languages and Institutions of Philosophy."

133. Derrida, "Mochlos," 5.

134. Ibid., 5.

135. Derrida, "The Principle of Reason," 5.

136. Derrida, "Mochlos," 18.

137. Ibid.,18.

138. Derrida, "The Principle of Reason," 19.

139. Ibid., 17.

140. Gianni Vattimo, *The End of Modernity: Nihilism and Hermeneutics in Postodern Culture,* Jon R. Snyder, trans. (Baltimore: Johns Hopkins University Press, 1988), 172.

141. Derrida, "The Principle of Reason," 18–19.

142. Ibid., 19.

Peter McLaren

UNTHINKING WHITENESS
Rearticulating Diasporic Practice

Now, this is the road that White Men tread
When they go to clean a land—Iron underfoot and the vine overhead
And the deep on either hand.
We have trod that road—and a wet and windy road—
Our chosen star for guide.
Oh, well for the world when the White Men tread
Their highway side by side!
                    —Rudyard Kipling (cited in Said 1985, 226)

Who can deny that the use of gunpowder against pagans is the
burning of incense to our Lord.
                    —Oviedo, a governor of the settlement at
                        Hispaniola (cited in Todorov 1984, 151)

Introduction

In 1996, the following article appeared in
Crosscurrents:

It was not until March 2, 1996, that the mystery surrounding Ly's murder
ended. That day, police arrested Gunner Lindberg, age twenty-one, and Dominic Christopher, age seventeen, after discovering a letter that Lindberg
had written to a former prison inmate in New Mexico. The letter contained
graphic details about the murder, as well as the writer's apparent insolence
about the whole incident. Sandwiched between birthday plans, news about a

friend's baby, and talk about the need for a new tattoo was this boastful account of what happened the night of January 29:

"Oh, I killed a jap a while ago. I stabbed him to death at Tustin High School. I walked up to him; Dominic was with me and I seen this guy rollerblading and I had a knife. We walked in the tennis court where he was; I walked up to him. Dominic was right there; I walked right up to him and he was scared; I looked at him said, 'Oh I thought I knew you,' and he got happy that he wasn't gonna get jumped. Then I hit him. . . .

"I pulled the knife out, a butcher knife, and he said 'no,' then I put the knife to his throat and asked him, 'Do you have a car?' And he grabbed my hand that I had the knife in and looked at me, trying to get a description of me, so I stomped on his head 3 times and each time said, 'Stop looking at me,' then he was kinda knocked out, dazed, then I stabbed him in the side about 7 or 8 times; he rolled over a little, so I stabbed his back out 18 or 19 times, then he lay flat and I slit one side of his throat on his jugular vein. Oh, the sounds the guy was making were like, 'Uhhh.' Then Dominic said, 'do it again,' and I said, 'I already did, Dude. Ya, do it again,' so I cut his other jugular vein and Dominic said, 'Kill him, do it again' and I said 'he's already dead.' Dominic said, 'Stab him in the heart.' So I stabbed him about 20 or 21 times in the heart. . . .

"Then I wanted to go back and look, so we did and he was dying just then, taking in some bloody gasps of air so I nudged his face with my shoe a few times, then I told Dominic to kick him, so he kicked the f___ out of his face and he still has blood on his shoes all over . . . then I ditched the knife, after wiping it clean on the side of the 5 freeway . . . here's the clippings from the newspaper . . . we were on all the channels." ("Grisly Account of Ly Killing Believed Penned by Suspect," *Los Angeles Times* Orange County Edition, March 7, 1996)

Was there racial motivation behind the crime? White-supremacist paraphernalia were found at Lindberg's and Christopher's home (Mai Pham, "Former UCLA Student Leader Murdered in Hate Crime," *Crosscurrents* [Fall/Winter 1996], 11).

The concept of whiteness became lodged in the discursive crucible of colonial identity by the early 1860s. Whiteness at that time had become a marker for measuring inferior and superior races. Interestingly, Genghis Khan, Attila the Hun, and Confucius were at this time considered "white." Blackness was evaluated positively in European iconography from the twelfth to the fifteenth centuries, but after the seventeenth century and the rise of European colonialism, blackness became conveniently linked to inferiority (Cashmore 1996). For instance, during the sixteenth and seventeenth centuries, blood purity (*limpieza de sangre*) became raised to a metaphysical—perhaps even sacerdotal—status, as it became a principle used to peripheralize Indians, Moors, and Jews. Blackness was not immediately associated with slavery. In the United States, the humanistic image of Africans created by the abolitionist movement was soon countered by new types of racial signification in which white skin was identified with racial superiority. Poor Europeans were sometimes indentured and were in some sense *de facto* slaves. They occupied the same economic categories as African slaves and were held in equal contempt by the lords of the plantation and legislatures (Cashmore 1996). So poor Europeans were invited to align themselves with the plantocracy as "white" in order to avoid the most severe forms of bondage. This strategy helped plantation owners form a stronger social control apparatus; hegemony was achieved by offering "race privileges" to poor whites as acknowledgment of their loyalty to the colonial land (Cashmore 1996).

By the early twentieth century, European maritime empires controlled over half the world's land (72 million square kilometers) and a third of the world's population (560 million people). Seventy-five million Africans died during the centuries-long transatlantic slave trade. The logics of empire are still with us, bound to the fabric of our daily being-in the-world, woven into our posture toward others, connected to the muscles of our eyes, dipped in the chemical relations that excite and calm us, structured into the language of our perceptions. We cannot will our racist logics away. We need to work hard to eradicate them. We need to struggle with a formidable resolve in order to overcome what we are afraid to confirm exists, let alone to confront it, in the battleground of our souls.

Cornel West has identified three white supremacist logics: the Judeo-Christian racist logic, the scientific racist logic, and the psychosexual racist logic. The Judeo-Christian racist logic is reflected in the biblical story of Ham, son of Noah, who, in failing to cover Noah's nakedness, had his progeny blackened by God. In this logic, unruly behavior and catholic rebellion are linked to racist practices. The "scientific" racist logic is identified with the evaluation of physical bodies in light of Greco-Roman standards. Within this logic, racist practices are identified with physical ugliness, cultural deficiency, and intellectual inferiority. They psychosexual racist logic identifies black people with Western sexual discourses associated with sexual prowess, lust, dirt, and subordination. A serious question is raised by West's typology in relation to the construction of whiteness: What are the historically concrete and sociologically specific ways that white-supremacist discourses are guided by Western philosophies of identity and universality and capitalist relations of production and consumption? West has located racist practices in the commentaries by the Church Fathers on the Song of Solomon and the Ywain narratives from medieval Brittany, to name just a few historical sources. West has also observed that human bodies were classified according to skin color as early as 1684 (before the rise of modern capitalism) by French physician François Bernier. The famous eighteenth-century naturalist Carolus Linnaeus produced the first major written account of racial division in *Natural System* (1735). White supremacy is linked to the way culture is problematized and defined. As we have seen, theories of culture are themselves by-products of and symptoms of theorists' relation to an ongoing global struggle over issues of social class.

George Lipsitz (1995) argues that understanding the destructive quality of white identity requires what Walter Benjamin termed "presence of mind" or "an abstract of the future, and precise awareness of the present moment more decisive than foreknowledge of the most distant events" (370). Noting that "race" is not merely a "cultural construct" but a construct that has "sinister structural causes and consequences," Lipsitz argues that from colonial times to the present there have existed systematic efforts "to create a possessive investment in whiteness for European Americans" (371). Identifying what he calls a new form of racism embedded in "the putatively race-neutral liberal social democratic reforms of the past five decades" (371), Lipsitz asserts that the possessive investment in whiteness can be seen in legacies of socialization bequeathed to U.S. citizens by federal, state, and local policies toward African-Americans, Native Americans, Mexican-Americans, Asian-Americans, "and other groups designated by whites as 'racially other.'"

Lipsitz impressively covers a great deal of historical ground in his discussion of white privilege—from colonial legal systems and racialized chattel slavery to contemporary efforts at urban renewal and highway construction that victimize mainly minority neighborhoods. For instance, Lipsitz tells us that while blacks in Houston, Texas, make up a little more than one quarter of the local population, more than 75 percent of municipal garbage incinerators and 100 percent of city-owned garbage dumps are located in black neighborhoods. Lipsitz reports that in response to 1,177 toxic waste cases, the Environmental Protection Agency exacted penalties on polluters near the largest white populations that were 500 percent higher than penalties imposed on polluters in minority areas (income did not account for these differences). Not only were penalties for violating all federal environmental laws regarding air, water, and waste pollution in minority communities found to be 46 percent lower than in white communities, minority communities had to wait longer for cleanups, sometimes 42 percent longer than at white sites, and endure a 7 percent greater likelihood of "containment" (walling off a hazardous site) than cleanup. White sites enjoyed treatment and cleanup 22 percent more often than containment.

Urban renewal also favored the rich by constructing luxury housing units and cultural centers, rather than affordable housing for the poor, in order to help cities compete for corporate investment. After providing a long litany of policies and practices infused with institutionalized forms of racism that have persisted over decades—forms that included government subsidies to private sectors, tax breaks for the wealthy, tax increment redevelopment programs, industrial development bonds, tax reforms, and federal housing loan policies—Lipsitz goes on to argue that Americans produce largely cultural explanations for structural social problems. They do so, Lipsitz maintains, because they are "largely ignorant of even the recent history of the possessive investment in whiteness" (1995, 379). For instance, whites are often unaware that nationwide financial institutions receive more money in deposits from black neighborhoods than they invest in them in the form of home mortgage loans. Home lending has thus become a vehicle for the transfer of capital away from black savers and toward white investors. Disturbingly, some polls have revealed that whites believe blacks have the same opportunity to acquire a middle-class life as whites. At the same time, whites persist in viewing negatively blacks' abilities, work habits, and character.

Charles Gallagher (1994) has worked as a professor with working-class and middle-class white students at an urban U.S. university. He makes the important point that the efforts of the media and racial politics in general have made whiteness more distinct as a racial category and have prompted whites to see themselves other than "colorless or racially transparent" (166). Unlike other critics who maintain that whiteness is largely invisible to whites themselves, Gallagher maintains that the political and cultural mobilization of racially defined minorities has positioned whites to think about themselves in relation to other racial groups, and that the decline of ethnicity among late-generation whites has created an "identity vacuum" that has been, in part, replaced by a radicalized identity. In this milieu, right-wing factions are currently attempting to reconstruct being "white" as a nonracist cultural identity informed by decent citizens trying to preserve their white heritage and by white students trying to create an identity in ways "that do not demonize white as a racial category" (167).

Gallagher argues that "white reconstruction" is occurring "among a sizable part of the white population, particularly among young people" (1994, 168). White males especially feel under assault by nonwhites "even though the 47 percent of white males in the labor force account for almost 92 percent of corporate officers and 88 percent of corporate directors" (169). According to Gallagher, many white students view themselves as being victimized by black racists and used as targets because they are white. They feel further under attack by "university-sanctioned race-based curricula" and "social clubs" such as the NAACP and La Raza. But Gallagher believes that this is a construction of white students' "own racist projections about what blacks think about whites" (171). Feeling that their status is under siege, whites are now constructing their identities in reaction to what they feel to be the "politically correct" challenge to white privilege. Many whites, Gallagher notes, feel that being a minority is actually an asset and advantage in the job market and, furthermore, believe that "what is 'great' for minorities must be a handicap to whites" (176).

Many white students reportedly still "believe the United States is an egalitarian, colorblind society" and thus refuse to define themselves as oppressors or recipients of white privileges. Gallagher found that among college students a legitimate, positive narrative of one's own whiteness was often created by constructing an identity that negated white-oppressor accusations and framed whiteness as a liability. Not only do white students deny U.S. racial history but they believe that their skin color provides them with no benefits. Embracing a color-blind society permits white people to construct ideologies that help them to avoid the issue of racial inequality while simultaneously benefiting from it. The creation or invention of whiteness described by Gallagher suggests that the ways in which the white population "get raced" points to a process that needs to be better understood. White identity needs to be understood as "a reaction to the entrance of historically marginalized racial and ethnic groups into the political arena and the ensuing struggle over social resources" (1994, 183). It appears as if whiteness is beginning to be formed within the context of its own racial logics and essences. Gallagher explains:

> The explicit reinsertion of whiteness into politics is possible only by creating the illusion that being white is no different than belonging to any other racial group in the United States. If that illusion can be maintained, a white identity and white culture modeled on a Disney America theme park, with its purified historic revisionism, will allow whites to reinvent a cultural history that does not evoke such matters as the Ku Klux Klan or Japanese internment during World War II but instead is synonymous with egalitarianism, rugged individualism, and democracy. (184)

Within the legal system and within popular reasoning, there exists an assumption that whiteness is a property interest entitled to legal protection. Whiteness as property is essentially the reification in law of expectations of white privilege. This assumption has been supported not only by systematic white supremacy through the law of slavery and "Jim Crow" laws but also by recent decisions and rationales of the Supreme Court concerning affirmative action. Harris is correct in arguing that white racial identity provides the basis for allocating societal benefits in both public and private spheres. Whiteness as a property of status continues to assist in the reproduction of the existing system of racial classification and stratification that protects the socially entrenched white power elite. According to Harris, rejecting race-conscious remedial measures as unconstitutional under the equal-protection clause of the Fourteenth Amendment "is based on the Court's chronic refusal to dismantle the institutional protection of benefits for whites that have been based on white supremacy and maintained at the expense of Blacks" (1993, 1767).

Current legal definitions of race embrace the norm of color blindness and thus disconnect race from social identity and race consciousness. Within the discourse of color blindness, blackness and whiteness are seen as neutral and apolitical descriptions reflecting skin color and as unrelated to social conditions of domination and subordination and to social attributes such as class, culture, language, and education. In other words, color blindness is a concept that symmetrizes relations of power and privilege and flattens them out so that they appear symmetrical or equivalent. But blackness and whiteness exist symmetrically only as idealized oppositions; in the real world they exist as a dependent hierarchy, with whiteness constraining the social power of blackness by colonizing the definition of what is normal, by institutionalizing a greater allocation of resources for white constituencies, and by maintaining laws that favor whites. According to Harris:

> To define race reductively as simply color, and therefore meaningless, is as subordinating as defining race to be scientifically determinative of inherent deficiency. The old definition creates a false linkage between race and inferiority; the new definition denies the real linkage between race and oppression under systematic white supremacy. Distorting and denying reality, both definitions support race subordination. As Neil Gotanda has argued, colorblindness is a form of race subordination in that it denies the historical context of white domination and Black subordination. (1993, 1768)

Affirmation action needs to be understood not through privatizing social inequality through claims of bipolar corrective justice between black and white competitors but rather as an issue of distributive social justice and rights that focuses not on guilt or innocence but on entitlement and fairness.

Racism occurs when the characteristics that justify discrimination are held to be inherent in the oppressed group. This form of oppression is peculiar to capitalist societies; it arises in the circumstances surrounding industrial capitalism and the attempt to acquire a large labor force. Callinicos points out three main conditions for the existence of racism as outlined by Marx: economic competition among workers; the appeal of racist ideology to white workers; and efforts of the capitalist class to establish and maintain racial divisions among workers. Capital's constantly changing demands for different kinds of labor can be met only through immigration. Callinicos remarks that "racism offers for workers of the oppressing 'race' the imaginary compensation for the exploitation they suffer of belonging to the '*ruling* nation'" (1993, 39).

Callinicos notes how Marx grasped the fact that racial divisions between "native" and immigrant workers could weaken the working class. U.S. politicians take advantage of this division, which the capitalist class understands and manipulates only too well. George Bush, Jesse Helms, Pat Buchanan, Phil Gramm, David Duke, and Pete Wilson have effectively used racism to divide the working class.

At this point you might be asking yourselves: Doesn't racism predate capitalism? Here I agree with Callinicos that the heterophobia associated with precapitalist societies was not the same as modern racism. Precapitalist slave and feudal societies of classical Greece and Rome did not rely on racism to justify the use of slaves. The Greeks and Romans had no theories of white superiority. If they did, that must have been unsettling news to Septimus Severus, Roman emperor from A.D. 193 to 211, who was, many historians claim, a black man. Racism developed at a key turning point in capitalism during the seventeenth and eighteenth centuries in colonial plantations in the New World, where slave labor stolen from Africa was used to produce tobacco, sugar, and cotton for the global consumer market (Callinicos 1993). Callinicos cites Eric Williams, who remarks: "Slavery was not born of racism; rather, racism was the consequence of slavery" (cited in Callinicos 1993, 24). Racism emerged as the ideology of the plantocracy. It began with the class of sugar planters and slave merchants that dominated England's Caribbean colonies. Racism developed out of the "systemic slavery" of the New World. The "natural inferiority" of Africans was used by whites to justify enslaving them. According to Callinicos:

> Racism offers white workers the comfort of believing themselves part of the dominant group; it also provides, in times of crisis, a ready-made scapegoat, in the shape of the oppressed group. Racism thus gives white workers a particular identity, and one moreover which unites them with white capitalists. We have here, then, a case of the kind of "imagined community" discussed by Benedict Anderson in his influential analysis of nationalism. (1993, 38)

To abolish racism, we need to abolish global capitalism. Callinicos is very clear on this point. The educational left has largely failed to address the issue of whiteness and the insecurities that young whites harbor regarding their future during times of diminishing economic expectations. With their "racially coded and divisive rhetoric," neoconservatives may be able to enjoy tremendous success in helping insecure young white populations develop white identity along racist lines. Consider the comments by David Stowe:

> The only people nowadays who profess any kind of loyality to whiteness *qua* whiteness (as opposed to whiteness as an incidental feature of some

more specific identity) are Christian Identity types and Ayran Nation diehards. Anecdotal surveys reveal that few white Americans mention whiteness as a quality that they think much about or particularly value. In their day-to-day cultural preferences—food, music, clothing, sports, hair-styles—the great majority of American whites display no particular attachment to white things. There does seem to be a kind of emptiness at the core of whiteness. (1996, 74)

People do not discriminate against groups because they are different, but rather the act of discrimination constructs categories of difference that hierarchically locate people as "superior" or "inferior" and then universalize and naturalize such differences. When I refer to whiteness or to the cultural logics of whiteness, I need to qualify what I mean. Here I adopt Ruth Frankenberg's (1993) injunction that cultural practices considered to be white need to be seen as contingent, historically produced, and transformable. White culture is not monolithic, and its borders must be understood as malleable and porous. It is the historically specific confluence of economic, geopolitical, and ethnocultural processes. According to Alastair Bonnett (1996), whiteness is neither a discrete entity nor a fixed, asocial category. Rather, it is an "immutable social construction" (98). White identity is an ensemble of discourses, contrapuntal and contradictory. Whiteness—and the meanings attributed to it—are always in a state of flux and fibrillation. Bonnett notes that "even if one ignores the transgressive youth or ethnic borderlands of Western identities, and focuses on the 'center' or 'heartlands' of 'whiteness,' one will discover racialized subjectivities, that, far from being settled and confidant, exhibit a constantly reformulated panic over the meaning of 'whiteness' and the defining presence of 'non-whiteness' within it" (106). According to Frankenberg, white culture is a material and discursive space that "is inflected by nationhood, such that whiteness and Americanness, though by no means coterminous, are profoundly shaped by one another. . . . Similarly, whiteness, masculinity, and femininity are coproducers of one another, in ways that are, in their turn, crosscut by class and by the histories of racism and colonialism" (1993, 233).

Whiteness needs to be seen as *cultural*, as *processual*, and not ontologically different from processes that are nonwhite. It works, as Frankenberg notes, as "an unmarked marker of others' differentness—whiteness not so much void or formlessness as norm" (1993, 198). Whiteness functions through social practices of assimilation and cultural homogenization; whiteness is linked to the expansion of capitalism in the sense that "whiteness signifies the production and consumption of commodities under capitalism" (203). Yet capitalism in the United States needs to be understood as contingently white, since white people participate in maintaining the hegemony of institutions and practices of racial dominance in different ways and to greater or lesser degrees. Ruth Frankenberg identifies the key discursive repertoires of whiteness as follows:

> [First,] modes of naming culture and difference associated with west European colonial expansion; second, elements of "essentialist" racism . . . linked to European colonialism but also critical as rationale for Anglo settler colonialism and segregationism in what is now the USA; third, "assimilationist" or later "color- and power-evasive strategies for thinking through race first articulated in the early decades of this century; and, fourth, . . . "race-cognizant" repertoires that emerged in the latter half of the twentieth century and were linked both to U.S. liberation movements and to broader global struggles for decolonization. (239)

While an entire range of discursive repertoires may come into play, jostling against, superseding, and working in conjunction with each other, white identity is constructed in relation to an individual's personal history, geopolitical situatedness, contextually specific practices, and location in the materiality of the racialized social order. In other words, many factors determine which discursive configurations are at work and the operational modalities present.

Whiteness has no formal content. It works rhetorically by articulating itself out of the semiotic detritus of myths of European superiority. These are myths that are ontologically empty, epistemologically misleading, and morally pernicious in the way that they privilege descendants of Europeans as the truly civilized, in contrast to the quaint, exotic, or barbaric character of non-European cultures. Whiteness is a sociohistorical form of consciousness, given birth at the nexus of capitalism, colonial rule, and the emergent relationships among dominant and subordinate groups. Whiteness operates by means of its constitution as a universalizing authority by which the hegemonic, white, bourgeois subject appropriates the right to speak on behalf of everyone who is nonwhite while denying voice and agency to these others in the name of civilized humankind. Whiteness constitutes and demarcates ideas, feelings, knowledge, social practices, cultural formations, and systems of intelligibility that are identified with or attributed to white people and that are invested in by white people as "white." Whiteness is also a refusal to acknowledge how white people are implicated in certain social relations of privilege and relations of domination and subordination. Whiteness, then, can be considered as a form of social amnesia associated with modes of subjectivity within particular social sites considered to be normative. As a lived domain of meaning, whiteness represents particular social and historical formations that are reproduced through specific discursive and material processes and circuits of desire and power. Whiteness reflects a conflictual sociocultural, sociopolitical, and geopolitical process that animates commonsensical practical action in relationship to dominant social practices and normative ideological productions. Whiteness constitutes the selective tradition of dominant discourses about race, class, gender, and sexuality hegemonically reproduced. Whiteness has become the substance and limit of our common sense articulated as cultural consensus. As an ideological formation transformed into a principle of life, into an ensemble of social relations and practices, whiteness needs to be understood as conjunctural, as a composite social hieroglyph that shifts in denotative and connotative emphasis depending on how its elements are combined and on the contexts in which it operates.

Whiteness is not a pregiven, unified ideological formation but is a multifaceted collective phenomenon resulting from the relationship between the self and the ideological discourses, which are constructed out of the surrounding local and global cultural terrain. Whiteness is fundamentally Euro- or Western-centric in its episteme, as it is articulated in complicity with the pervasively imperializing logic of empire. Whiteness in the United States can be understood largely through the social consequences it provides for those who are considered to be nonwhite. Such consequences can be seen in the criminal justice system, in prisons, in schools, and in the boardrooms of corporations such as Texaco. It can be defined in relation to immigration practices and social policies and practices of sexism, racism, and nationalism. It can be seen historically in widespread acts of imperialism and genocide and can be linked to an erotic economy of "excess." Hatred of the other arises from the necessary hatred of one's own excess; ascribing this excess to the "degraded" other and indulging it—by imaging, incorporating, or impersonating the other—one conveniently and surreptitiously takes and disavows pleasure at one and the same time. This is the mixed erotic economy, what Homi Bhabha terms the "ambivalence," of American whiteness (1993, 482).

Whiteness is a type of articulatory practice that can be located in the convergence of colonialism, capitalism, and subject formation. It both fixes and sustains discursive regimes that represent self and Other; that is, whiteness represents a regime of differences that produces and racializes an abject Other. In other words, whiteness is a discursive regime that enables real effects to take place. Whiteness displaces blackness and brownness—specific forms of nonwhiteness—into signifiers of deviance and criminality within social, cultural, cognitive, and political contexts. White subjects discursively construct identity through producing, naming, "bounding," and marginalizing a range of others (Frankenberg 1993, 193).

Whiteness constitutes unmarked (Euro-American male) practices that have negative effects on and consequences for those who do not participate in them. Inflected by nationhood, whiteness can be considered an ensemble of discursive practices constantly in the process of being constructed, negotiated, and changed. Yet it functions to instantiate a structured exclusion of certain groups from social arenas of normativity.

Whiteness is not only mythopoetical in the sense that it constructs a totality of illusions formed around the ontological superiority of the Euro-American subject; it is also metastructural in that it connects whiteness across specific differences; it solders fugitive, breakaway discourses and rehegemonizes them. Consumer utopias and global capital flows rearticulate whiteness by means of relational differences.

Whiteness is dialectically reinitiated across epistemological fissures, contradictions, and oppositions through new regimes of desire that connect the consumption of goods to the everyday logic of Western democracy. The cultural encoding of the typography of whiteness is achieved by remapping Western European identity onto economic transactions, by recementing desire to capitalist flows, by concretizing personal history into collective memory linked to place, to a myth of origin. Whiteness offers a safe "home" for those imperiled by the flux of change.

Whiteness can be considered as a conscription of the process of positive self-identification into the service of domination through inscribing identity into an ontoepistemological framework of "us" against "them." For those who are non-white, the seduction of whiteness can produce a self-definition that disconnects the subject from his or her history of oppression and struggle, exiling identity into the unmoored, chaotic realm of abject otherness (while tacitly accepting the positioned superiority of the Western subject). Whiteness provides the Euro-American subject with a known boundary that places nothing "off limits" yet provides a fantasy of belongingness. It is not that whiteness signifies preferentially one pole of the white-nonwhite binarism. Rather, whiteness seduces the subject to accept the idea of polarity as the limit-text of identity, as the constitutive foundation of subjectivity.

In his important volume, *Psychoanalytic-Marxism*, Eugene Victor Wolfenstein describes the whiteness of domination as the "one fixed point" of America's many facisms. He argues that whiteness is a social designation and a "history disguised as biology" (1993, 331). Whiteness is also an attribute of language. Wolfenstein claims that "languages have skin colors. There are white nouns and verbs, white grammar and white syntax. In the absence of challenges to linguistic hegemony, indeed, language is white. If you don't speak white you will not be heard, just as when you don't look white you will not be seen" (331). Describing white racists as "virtuosos of denigration," Wolfenstein maintains that the language of white racism illustrates "a state of war" (333). Yet the battles are fought through lies and deceit. One such lie is the idea of "color-blindness."

Wolfenstein notes that color-blindness constitutes more than a matter of conscious deceit:

White racism is rather a mental disorder, an ocular disease, an opacity of the soul that is articulated with unintended irony in the idea of "color blindness." To be color blind is the highest form of racial false consciousness, a denial of both difference and domination. But one doesn't have to be color blind to be blinded by white racism. . . . Black people see themselves in white mirrors, white people see black people as their own photographic negatives. (1993, 334)

Wolfenstein suggests that two epistemological tasks be undertaken. Black people need to look away from the white mirror; white people need to attempt to see black people as they see themselves and to see themselves as they are seen by other black people. Wolfenstein links white racism to what he terms "epidermal fetishism." Epidermal fetishism reduces people to their skin color and renders them invisible. It is a type of social character that is formed within a process of exchange and circulation. As such, whiteness represents the superego (the standard of social value, self-worth, and morality). Since the ego is affirmatively reflected in the superego, it also must be white. What is therefore repressed is blackness, which "becomes identified with the unwanted or bad parts of the self" (1993, 336).

At the level of social character, white racism is self-limiting for white people, self-destructive for black people. White people alienate their sensuous potentialities from themselves. They are devitalized and sterilized. Blackness, officially devalued, comes to embody their estranged life and desire. They are able, however, to see themselves reflected in the mirrors of selfhood. But if black people have their selfhood structured by the whitened-out form of social character, they become fundamentally self-negating. Their blackness, hated and despised, must be hidden away. Hair straighteners and skin lighteners testify to the desire to go further and eradicate blackness altogether (1993, 336–337).

The incorporeal luminescence of whiteness is achieved, according to Wolfenstein, by the subsumption of blackness within whiteness. What cannot be subsumed and digested is excreted. White people both despise and lust after blackness. Wolfenstein describes some forms of interracial romantic heterosexual relationships as epidermally mediated erotic domination, as an epidermalized sexual rebellion against a repressive social morality, and as an epidermally mediated double violation of the Oedipal incest taboo. In order to resist epidermal fetishism, oppressed people need a language and a politics of their own.

It is important to recognize that white racism is neither purely systemic nor purely individual. Rather, it is a complex interplay of collective interests and desires. White racism in this instance "becomes a rational means to collective ends" (Wolfenstein 1993, 341) when viewed from the standpoint of ruling-class interests. Yet for the white working class it is irrational and a form of false consciousness.

White racism also circumscribes rational action for black people in that they are encouraged to act in terms of their racial rather than class interests. Whiteness offers coherency and stability in a world in which capital produces regimes of desire linked to commodity utopias where fantasies of omnipotence must find a stable home. Of course, the "them" is always located within the "us." The marginalized are always foundational to the stability of the central actors. The excluded in this case establish the condition of existence of the included. So we find that it is impossible to separate the identities of both oppressor and oppressed. They depend on each other. To resist whiteness means developing a politics of difference. Since we lack the full semantic availability to understand whiteness and to resist it, we need to rethink difference and identity outside of sets of binary oppositions. We need to view identity as coalitional, as collective, as processual, as grounded in the struggle for social justice.

Alastair Bonnett notes that the reified notion of whiteness "enables 'white' people to occupy a privileged location in antiracist debate; they are allowed the luxury of being passive observers, of being altruistically motivated, of knowing that their 'racial' identity might be reviled and lambasted but never actually made slippery, torn open, or, indeed, abolished" (1996, 98). Bonnett further notes: "To dismantle 'blackness' but leave the force it was founded to oppose unchallenged is to display both a political and theoretical naïveté. To subvert 'blackness' without subverting 'whiteness' reproduces and reinforces the 'racial' myths, and the 'racial' dominance, associated with the latter" (99).

Ian F. Haney López's book, *White by Law*, offers a view of white transparency and invisibility that is at odds with Gallagher's thesis that whites are growing more conscious of their whiteness. López cites an incident at a legal feminist conference in which participants were asked to pick two or three words to describe themselves. All of the women of color selected at least one racial term, but not one white woman selected a term referring to her race. This prompted Angela Harris to remark that only white people in this society have the luxury of having no color. An informal study conducted at Harvard Law School underscores Harris's remark. A student interviewer asked ten African-Americans and ten white Americans how they identified themselves. Unlike the African-Americans, most of the white Americans did not consciously factor in their "whiteness" as a crucial or even tangential part of their identity.

López argues that one is not born white but becomes white "by virtue of the social context in which one finds oneself, to be sure, but also by virtue of the choices one makes" (1996, 190). But how can one born into the culture of whiteness, one who is defined as white, undo that whiteness? López addresses this question in his formulation of whiteness. He locates whiteness in the overlapping of *chance* (for example, features and ancestry that we have no control over, morphology); *context*

(context-specific meanings that are attached to race, the social setting in which races are recognized, constructed, and contested); and *choice* (conscious choices with regard to the morphology and ancestries of social actors) in order to "alter the readability of their identity" (191).

In other words, López maintains that chance and context are not racially determinative. He notes:

> Racial choices must always be made from within specific contexts, where the context materially and ideologically circumscribes the range of available choices and also delimits the significance of the act. Nevertheless, these are racial choices, if sometimes only in their overtone or subtext, because they resonate in the complex of meanings associated with race. Given the thorough suffusion of race throughout society, in the daily dance of life we constantly make racially meaningful decisions. (1996, 193)

López's perspective offers real potential, it would seem, for abolishing racism, since it refuses to locate whiteness only as antiracism's Other. I agree with Bonnett when he remarks that "to continue to cast 'whites' as anti-racism's 'other,' as the eternally guilty and/or altruistic observers of 'race' equality work, is to maintain 'white' privilege and undermine the movement's intellectual and practical reach and utility" (1996, 107). In other words, whites need to ask themselves to what extent their identity is a function of their whiteness in the process of their ongoing daily lives and what choices they might make to escape whiteness. López outlines—productively in my view—three steps in dismantling whiteness. They are worth quoting in full:

> First, Whites must overcome the omnipresent effects of transparency and of the naturalization of race in order to recognize the many racial aspects of their identity, paying particular attention to the daily acts that draw upon and in turn confirm their whiteness. Second, they must recognize and accept the personal and social consequences of breaking out of a White identity. Third, they must embark on a daily process of choosing against Whiteness. (193)

Of course, the difficulty of taking such steps is partly due to the fact that, as López notes, the unconscious acceptance of a racialized identity is predicated upon a circular definition of the self. It is hard to step outside of whiteness if you are white because of all the social, cultural, and economic privileges that accompany whiteness. Yet whiteness must be dismantled if the United States is to overcome racism. Lipsitz remarks: "Those of us who are 'white' can only become part of the solution if we recognize the degree to which we are already part of the problem—not because of our race, but because of our possessive investment in it" (1995, 384).

The editorial in the book *Race Traitor* puts it thus: "The key to solving the social problems of our age is to abolish the white race. Until that task is accomplished, even partial reform will prove elusive, because white influence permeates every issue in U.S. society, whether domestic or foreign. . . . Race itself is a product of social discrimination; so long as the white race exists, all movements against racism are doomed to fail" (Ignatiev and Garvey 1996, 10).

While we lack the semantic availability to fully capture the meaning and function of whiteness, we can at least describe it as a discursive strategy, articulation, or modality; or we can refer to it perhaps as a form of discursive brokerage, a pattern of negotiation that takes place in conditions generated by specific discursive formations and social relations. Historically, whiteness can be seen as a tattered and bruised progeny of Western colonialism and imperialism.

Whiteness is crisscrossed by numerous social dynamics. It is produced through capitalist social relations or modes of domination. The marker "whiteness" serves as a discursive indicator or social hieroglyph (Cruz 1996)—an "effect" of systematic social relations of which those who are marked as "white" have little conscious understanding. Whiteness, therefore, is socially and historically embedded; it is a form of racialization of identity formation that carries with it a history of social, cultural, and economic relations. Whiteness is unfinalizable, but compared to other ethnic formations, its space for maneuvering in the racialized and genderized permutations of U.S. citizenship is infinitely more vast. The task here for critical educators is to denaturalize whiteness by breaking its codes and the social relations and privileging hierarchies that give such codes normative power. The codification of whiteness as a social hieroglyph associated with civility, rationality, and political advancement is part of inherited social and cultural formations, formations that were given birth after the early capitalist marriage of industrialism and militarism. Whiteness is linked in a fundamental—if not dramatic—way to the racialization of aggression. Inherited categories and classifications that made whiteness the privileged signifier over blackness is a theme I have addressed in "White Terror" (in McLaren 1995), and I will not rehearse that argument here.

I think that the relation between whiteness and privilege can be better understood by locating whiteness in the context of what Howard Winant (1994) calls "racial formation" and what David Theo Goldberg (1993) calls "racial modality." A racial modality refers to "a fragile structure of racist exclusions at a space-time conjuncture" that is sustained by the power of socioeconomic interests and the intersection of discursive fields and strategies of representation (Goldberg 1993, 210). Winant defines race as *"a concept that signifies and symbolizes sociopolitical conflicts and interests to different types of human bodies"* (1994, 115). This signals an understanding of race as an everyday phenomenon, one that is historically and socially constructed and is implicated in social structures, identities, and signification systems. The concept of racial formation also addresses the "*expansion and intensification of racial phenomena*" on a global basis (116). Further, it suggests "*a new conception of racial history and racial time*" (my italics, 116). Concerning the latter, then, whiteness can be seen as implicated in the progressive expansion of capitalism throughout the world and the genealogical racial time of European conquest, what Winant calls an "archetypal *longue durée*: a slow agony of inscription upon the human body, a murder mystery, if you will, but on a genocidal scale. The phenotypical signification of the world's body took place in and through conquest and enslavement, to be sure, but also as an enormous act of expression, of narration" (117).

Whiteness, of course, is also a product of historical time in terms of what Winant calls "contingency," or the contextual specificity of its hegemonic articulations. Whiteness is implicated on a global basis in the internationalization of capital, which is being accompanied by the internationalization of race. We are witnessing growing diasporic movements as former colonial subjects immigrate to the Western metropoles, challenging the majoritarian status of European groups. Winant remarks that we are also witnessing "the rise of 'diasporic' models of blackness, the creation of 'panethnic' communities of Latinos and Asians (in such countries as the United Kingdom and the United States), and the breakdown of borders in both Europe and North America all [which] seem to be hybridizing and racializing previously national policies, cultures and identities" (1994, 118).

I would follow Winant in maintaining that the focus of our investigation at this present juncture should be on the racial dimensions of capitalism and the mobilization of white racial antagonisms. Prior to World War II in the United States there existed a well-developed racial ideology, "a caste-based social structure developed to guarantee white workers their racial identity as a signifier of their 'freedom'" (125). White people represented the *Herrenvolk*—a democracy of white males. Winant observes that the *Herrenvolk*'s supremacy was seriously eroded during the Civil Rights era. Of course, the post–Civil Rights era is another matter altogether. As racial domination gave way to racial hegemony, the task was no longer to subdue the masses of disenfranchised minorities but to accommodate them. The caste-based logic of race was discarded by white folks in favor of an egalitarian politics underwritten by a culture of poverty thesis: People of color should pull themselves up out of the "underclass" through their own initiatives.

Consider the recent case in point of the University of California's dismantling of affirmative action, championed by Ward Connerly, a conservative African-American UC regent. When reports commissioned by the UC provost projected that the numbers of white and Asian UC undergraduates would markedly grow and numbers of underrepresented minority students would diminish, Connerly responded:

"This is the most tacit admission of the extent that we are using race for underrepresented students that one could ever find" (cited in Wallace 1996, 1, 18). Connerly's comment is underwritten by a belief that African American and Latino/a students, for instance, are being given an unfair advantage by affirmative action programs. This presumes that the playing field is now equal and that we have arrived at a point in our society where meritocracy actually exists. It ignores issues of culture, economics, and ideology and how these factors and others work in relation to public institutions and the (re)production of structural racism. Consequently, Connerly is unable to fathom how his position on affirmative action acts in the service of white privilege.

I do not believe in reverse racism, since I do not believe white people have transcended race; nor do I believe that Latino/as or African-Americans have acquired a systematic power to dominate whites. Yet, along with the editors of *Race Traitor*, I believe in reversing racism by systematically dismantling whiteness. Even so, I am acutely aware that people of color might find troubling the idea that white populations can simply reinvent themselves by making the simple choice of not being white. Of course, this is not what López and others appear to be saying. The choices one makes and the reinvention one aspires to as a race traitor are not "simple," nor are they easy choices for groups of whites to make. Yet from the perspective of some people of color, offering the choice to white people of opting out of their whiteness could seem to set up an easy path for those who do not want to assume responsibility for their privilege as white people.

Indeed, there is certainly cause for concern. David Roediger captures some of this when he remarks: "Whites cannot fully renounce whiteness even if they want to" (1994, 16). Whites are, after all, still accorded the privileges of being white even as they ideologically renounce their whiteness, often with the best of intentions. Yet the potential for nonwhiteness and antiwhite struggle is too important to ignore or dismiss as wishful thinking or to associate with a fashionable form of code-switching. Choosing not to be white is not an easy option for white people, not as simple as deciding to make a change in one's wardrobe. To understand the processes involved in the racialization of identity and consistently to choose nonwhiteness is a difficult act of apostasy, for it implies a heightened sense of social criticism and an unwavering commitment to social justice (Roediger 1994). Of course, the question needs to be asked: If we can choose to be nonwhite, then can we choose to be black or brown? Insofar as blackness is a social construction (often "parasitic" on whiteness), I would answer yes.

Theologian James H. Cone, author of *A Black Theology of Liberation*, urges white folks to free themselves from the shackles of their whiteness: "If whites expect to be able to say anything relevant to the self-determination of the black community, it will be necessary for them to destroy their whiteness by becoming members of an oppressed community. Whites will be free only when they become new persons—when their white being has passed away and they are created anew in black being. When this happens, they are no longer white but free" (1986, 97).

I want to be clear that I am not arguing for constructing a positive white identity where whiteness is defined with the best intentions as part of an antiracist and anti-imperialist ideology. I argue for a self-consciousness about one's whiteness in terms of recognizing the danger of its transparency, but I do not advocate celebrating whiteness in any form. Rather, I argue for the disassembly and destruction of whiteness and advocate its rearticulation as a form of critical agency dedicated to struggles in the interests of the oppressed. López notes that "because races are constructed diacritically, celebrating Whiteness arguably requires the denigration of Blackness. Celebrating Whiteness, even with the best of antiracist intentions, seems likely only to entrench the status quo of racial beliefs" (1996, 172). Since white identity is the antonym to the identity of nonwhites, as López maintains, it is a sobering acknowledgment to make that the only positive identification one can offer with respect to whiteness is to call for the disassembly of whiteness and for its eventual destruction. López remarks that "whiteness can only retain its positive meanings through the denial at every turn of the social injustices associated with the rise and persistence of this racial category" (185). The celebration of whiteness in any form is inseverably linked to the peripheralization and demonization of nonwhites. White identity serves implicitly as the positive mirror image to the explicit negative identities imposed on nonwhites (López 1996). Even in the case of white U.S. citizens who claim European American identity as a way of avoiding the white-versus-nonwhite opposition, such a move is actually based on the double negative of not being nonwhite (López 1996).

But again I would stress that becoming nonwhite is not a "mere" choice but a self-consciously political choice, a spiritual choice, and a critical choice. To choose blackness or brownness merely as a way to escape the stigma of whiteness and avoid responsibility for owning whiteness is still very much an act of whiteness. To choose blackness or brownness as a way of politically disidentifying with white privilege and instead identifying with and participating in the struggles of nonwhite peoples is an act of transgression, a traitorous act that reveals a fidelity to the struggle for justice. Lipsitz sums up the problems and the promise of the abolition of whiteness as follows:

Neither conservative "free market" policies nor liberal social democratic reforms can solve the "white problem" in America because both of them reinforce the possessive investment in whiteness. But an explicitly antiracist pan-ethnic movement that acknowledges the existence and power of whiteness might make some important changes. Pan-ethnic, antiracist coalitions have a long history in the United States—in the political activism of John Brown, Sojourner Truth, and the Magon brothers, among others—but we also have a rich cultural tradition of pan-ethnic antiracism connected to civil rights activism. . . . Efforts by whites to fight racism, not out of sympathy for someone else but out of a sense of self-respect and simple justice, have never completely disappeared; they remain available as models for the present. (1995, 384)

George Yúdice gives additional substance to Lipsitz's concerns related to coalition-building when he points out some of the limitations of current identity politics: "The very difficulty of imagining a new social order that speaks convincingly to over 70 percent of the population requires critics to go beyond pointing out the injustices and abuses and move on to an agenda that will be more effective in transforming structures. What good is it to fight against white supremacy unless whites themselves join the struggle?" (1995, 268). Stowe echoes a similar sentiment when he writes: "Race treason has its limits as a workable strategy. Consider the economistic language in which it is described. Whites are exhorted to renounce the wages of whiteness, to divest from their possessive investment in whiteness, to sabotage the exchange value of racial privilege. . . . How many social movements have gotten ahead through the renunciation of privilege, though?" (1996, 77).

Yúdice makes a lucid point when he criticizes *Race Traitor* for lacking a notion of political articulation. I agree with him that it is not enough to simply have faith in whites of goodwill to disidentify with their whiteness. He argues that change will not come suddenly as whites rise up against their whiteness. This position ignores that:

(1) we are living in a time of diminishing expectations and (2) what binds together a society is an overdetermined configuration or constellation of ideologemes: democracy, individuality, free enterprise, work ethic, upward mobility, and national security are articulated in complex ways that do not simply split apart when any one of them is challenged. Social formations tend to undergo processes of rearticulation, according to Ernesto Laclau, rather than the kind of upheaval that *Race Traitor* seeks. (Yúdice 1995, 271–272)

What is needed, argues Yúdice, is a multicultural politics that is capable of projecting "a new democratic vision that makes sense to the white middle and working classes" (273). Whites must be interpolated in rearticulating the whiteness of the dominant class. Whites need to "feel solidarity with those who have suffered deprivation as members of subordinated groups" (276). They must be offered more than a rationalized rights discourse. They need to struggle over the interpretation of needs through the proliferation of public spheres in which the struggle for democracy can take place. The key, Yúdice maintains, is to center the struggle for social justice around resource distribution rather than identity: "Shifting the focus of struggle from identity to resource distribution will also make it possible to engage such seemingly nonracial issues as the environment, the military, the military-industrial complex, foreign aid, and free-trade agreements as matters impacting local identities and thus requiring a global politics that works outside of the national frame." (280)

That whiteness was reproduced in the petri dish of European colonialism cannot be disputed, but it is wrong to think of whiteness as an incurable disease. Multiculturalists whose identities depend on whiteness being the static other to antiracist efforts will perhaps resist the abolition of whiteness even though its destruction is their stated aim. We need to transgress the external determinations of white identity, which has brought about the unique conjuncture I have labeled the social hieroglyphics of whiteness, an ensemble of discourses informed, in part, by a perceived lack of ethnicity and also by issues of race, sexual identification, religion, and nation. Since the meanings that suture whiteness to special options denied to other groups within the United States are socially and historically constituted through circuits of investment and exchange, such meanings are mutable and can be transformed, but certainly not by self-willed efforts at refashioning whiteness into a new liturgy of self-critique accompanied by a new white cultural etiquette. Not until the social relations of (re)production and consumption are recognized as class relations linked to whiteness and thus challenged and transformed can new ethnicities emerge capable of eliminating white privilege.

Euro-Americans still constitute the gatekeepers of the white racial order known as the United States. Its *Herrenvolk* democracy of white supremacy remains largely camouflaged under the logic of egalitarianism and meritocracy and the denial of the significance of race expressed by calls to abolish the "color line" through anti-affirmative-action measures. This "color line" is no longer bipolar—black versus white—but rather multipolar; Asians and Latino/as increase their pressure on white majoritarian constituencies in the larger struggle for racial democracy. Winant argues for the elimination of racial discrimination and inequality but emphasizes as well the liberation of racial identity itself. I agree with Winant that this will involve "a reenvisioning of racial politics and a transformation of racial difference" (1994, 169). This means making racial identity a matter of choice rather than an ascription of meaning to phenotype and skin color. Today the racist state still polices the "color line" as it did in the past, but this time by arguing that it is actually created by affirmative action.

The Struggle for Democracy

This final section will try to raise some of the concerns touched upon by Yúdice in the call for a radical vision of democratic practice. It is a vision which, in my view, is compatible with the struggle for a socialist democratic imaginary. Universal and particular rights will always be struggled over; they will never be fully compatible. For the critics of the universal there are no universal rights provided by the nation-state, only further exclusion and demonization as the "enemies of America." Paradoxically, if the universal and the particular ever achieve compatibility, then democracy will have disappeared and fascism will have taken its place. And while the practice of justice will always contain contradictions and ambiguities, critical educators still need to ask the tough question: How, for instance, do schools and other institutions restrict the universalisms of our shared political ideals only to privileged, white, Anglo groups? But in asking the tough questions, critical educators should not subsume the universal quest for liberty and equality into the particular. Rather, the spheres of the universal should be considerably widened and, as this widening occurs, the contents of this universality should be reformulated and proposed to include the voices of those already marginalized and excluded (Laclau 1992).

Etienne Balibar (1996) reflects a similar idea when he stresses the importance of understanding the social as well as the ideological conditions of democracy. He writes:

> If democracy as a system of living traditions finds its expression in both the representation of the governed and the control of those who govern—by a sufficient appropriateness of the representation of the population's interests and ideas and by a sufficient degree of popular control over the controllers themselves—it is never more than a fragile equilibrium between the functions of consensus and the functions of conflict. Ultimately democracy lies on the inverse excesses of these functions. In this way, democracy depends at least as much upon *fortuna* as upon *virtú*, as much upon favorable circumstances as upon the initiative of the ruling class, the parties, and the citizens. It is essential, if we want to understand history, that we not exaggerate the importance of consensus to the detriment of conflict. (370)

I want to argue that critical educators need to embrace what Nancy Fraser (1993) calls a "democratic socialist-feminist political imaginary" that entails, among other things, the following: expanding the vision of a fully social wage; defending the importance of public goods against commodities; challenging the technocratic discourses of the state that reduce citizens to clients and consumers; advocating for the importance of unwaged domestic work and the child-raising labor of women; enlarging the view of entitlement; criticizing "the hyperbolic mas-culinist-capitalist view that individual 'independence' is normal and desirable while 'dependence' is avoidable and deviant" (21); insisting on a view of public provision as a system of social rights; rejecting the idea of "personal responsibility" and "mu-tual responsibility" in favor of "social responsibility"; and promoting social solidar-ity through confronting racism, sexism, homophobia, and class exploitation. We need a sense of shared responsibility without necessarily having to depend upon a shared identity.

Broadly speaking, Bauman sees communitarian democracy as community with-out freedom, and liberal democracy as freedom without community. Bauman ar-gues that the liberal concept of difference is "external" to the individual and stands for "the profusion of choices between the ways of being human and living one's life" (1996, 81). For communitarians, however, difference is "internalized" and repre-sents "the refusal, or inability to consider other forms of life as options." Liberal dif-ference has to do with affirming individual freedom, while the difference spoken about by communitarians often has to do with the necessity of imposing limits on human freedom. In this latter view, freedom should be exercised in order to choose unfreedom. For communitarians, outcomes of choices need to be understood be-fore the actual choice is made. On the other hand, Bauman notes that liberal free-dom of choice "has become a major stratifying variable in our multi-dimensionally stratified society" (88). In postmodern/consumer society we are all fated to choose, but there exists a range of realistic choices because resources are needed to make those choices. While individual responsibility for choice is equally distributed, equality disappears, maintains Bauman, when we are considering the means to act on that responsibility. Bauman (1996) writes:

> What the liberal vision of the universal and equally awarded right to choose failed to take account of, is that "adding freedom of action to the fundamen-tal inequality of social condition will result in inequality yet deeper than be-fore." What liberal society offers with one hand, it tends to take back with the other; the duty of freedom without the resources that would permit a truly free choice is, for many affected, a recipe for life without dignity, filled instead with humiliation and self-deprecation. (88)

Scott Lash (1996) argues against some of Bauman's criticisms of communica-tion ethics, noting favorably that communitarian ethics has provided a "grounded-ness" necessary to promote an ethics linked to political collectivity and action. Lash offers some criticisms of the work of Levinas and his ethical imperative of uncondi-tional responsibility for the other. According to Levinas, totality must be decon-structed and infinitely embraced. Totality—referring to tradition and contractual individualism and institutions such as law, politics, and history—permits the judgment of the individual as a universal "I." However, Lash presciently observes that upon closer examination of Levinas's work, the concrete, particular "I" in its radical singularity and the Other appear both to be excluded in such an act of judgment. Lash criticizes Levinas for offering a choice only between a politics of institutions (totality) and a politics of radical difference (infinity) and consequently rejecting a "subinstitutional politics of practice" (94).

Lash maintains that in order for social transformation to take place, the singular "I" must be grounded in a set of political practices. According to Lash, Levinas might respond that such practices are necessarily "egotistical." Lash maintains that this is not necessarily the case, and on this point I agree with him. It is not mandatory that ethics be world-denying and focus solely on the "event" of the moral relationship between subjectivity and the Other (Lash 1996, 94). Levinas's "event" takes place at every instant of revelation that consciousness encounters its own singularity. Lash reports that the construction of meaning or the pretemporal event of revelation in which consciousness relates to the very act of saying is highly problematic in Levinas's conceptualization. For instance, the subject in this case is reduced to the signifier that brings about being in the event horizon of the word. Whereas a communitarian ethics would inhere in the world of social life and formations as regulative practices, for Levinas the ethical relation is constitutive, not regulative, and occurs only when subjectivity turns away from the messiness of social life and towards infinity and the voice of the Other (the excluded, the oppressed, the strangers among us, be recognized).

Lash does concede that a communitarian ethics cannot sufficiently address the singularity of the Other. Yet still Lash argues that a community-oriented ethics of practice is necessary and can be carefully fashioned so that a space is left open "for the inscrutability of the other's singularity" (98). Rather than conceiving of the stranger as the featureless Other (as in Levinas's work), Lash argues for an understanding of aspects of the horizon of the Other through dialogue. This dialogue would be grounded in diasporic understanding, that is, in communities of practice and the rhythms of shared languages and practices.

In Lash's view, a politics of difference should recognize the singularity of the other through a dialogical praxis, through the overlapping of horizons, and through an ethics of sociality. Levinas's space of infinity (where subjectivity confronts the face of the Other in an economy of being) must be made to extend beyond moral relationships in order to include dimensions of social relationships that exist exterior to totality and which embrace violence and death. Lash correctly points out that the ethical agent lives an infinite temporality that is not an empty eternity but, rather, one that is peopled and meaningful. He further observes—correctly in my view—that the concepts of patience and suffering in the work of Levinas do not open up to the world of flesh and body. In Levinas's ethical universe, pain takes place exterior to forms of social life. I should note, in passing, that Lash's position is reminiscent of my concept of enfleshment in which subjectivity is formed in the temporality of the flesh and the history of lived experience (see McLaren 1995).

According to Lash, Levinas gives us the polar opposite of the Third Reich's politics of spectacle, of the ethicization of aesthetics. We are offered an *éthique/esthétique* which begins with a subjectivity facing toward infinity. Yet, paradoxically, this Levinasian sublime does not mirror the Kantian sublime and the terror of aesthetic space but, rather, the ethical space of Kant's second critique, the realms of pure practical reason of *The Critique of Practical Reason*. Here, Levinas's figures of singular subjectivity encounter the face of the Other in the sphere of reason, where ethics becomes the primordial ground of knowledge and of truth. In this view we become our most moral selves when we are the furthest away from the constraints of time and space.

In arguing for an ethics grounded in dialogue, I also suggest examining the work of Bahktin. Bahktin's perspectives can also help to forge an ethics that can take us past some of the limit conditions of Levinas's position and in doing so bring us closer to a position compatible with that of the concept of "praxis" found in the work of the early Marx (Gardiner 1996, 138; See also the important book on Volosinov and bilingual education by Marcia Moraes 1996).

The materiality of ethics that is being discussed here, including Bahktin's notion of multivocality and dialogue, undergirds a concept of multiculturalism that I consider to be fundamental to a pedagogy of liberation.

The perspective on multiculturalism that I am advancing here I have referred to elsewhere as "critcial multiculturalism" (see McLaren 1995), and it bears a strong affinity to what Shohat and Stam (1994) refer to as "polycentric multiculturalism." Polycentric multiculturalism disidentifies with liberal pluralist multiculturalism premised on ethical universals; it is not simply about describing cultural history but about analyzing social power and transforming discourses, institutions, and social practices of privilege. It does not order cultures hierarchically against the invisible norm of whiteness in a liberal swirl of diversity, but rejects the idea of a preexisting center. That is, polycentric multiculturalism is articulated "from the margins" and views minoritarian communities "as active, generative participants at the very core of a shared, conflictual history" (48). It does not view identities as stable or fixed or essentialized but, rather, as unstable and historically situated. It is reciprocal and dialogical, and rejects narrow definitions of identity politics as simply the work of discrete, bounded communities. Accompanied by a strategy of political articulation, critical multiculturalism can be a crucial practice in cutting racism at the joints and working toward a vision of cultural democracy premised on social and economic justice.

Dear brothers and sisters in struggle, I have been slowly leading up to a conclusion. Let me summarize some of the more prescriptive points which follow from my previous discussions. It seems clear to me that we must steadfastly refuse to cut our ties to the lifeworld of our students and the communities in which they live. We must work together to try to help our students better understand both what is occurring at the global level of capitalist flows and transactions and how consumer culture within late capitalism is producing marketplace justice for the privileged and poverty for the rest. This means inviting our students to challenge the cultural logics of late capitalism and how they are not only turning individual subjects into servants of transnational regulatory banking institutions and corporations, but are also coordinating identities and subjectivities into a cybercitizenship which promotes character structures that respond to personal responsibility and the entrepreneurial spirit rather than to collective responsibility and equality and social justice. In other words, we need to provide for our students the conditions for critical consciousness and struggle not only for economic justice (although this is crucial) but also for justice in the political arenas of race, gender, and sexuality.

What can we say about critical pedagogy in light of the contexts I have discussed? Broadly speaking, critical pedagogy is about struggling at the level of the social relations of production for economic justice for all working people. It is also about re-creating culture and agency through the practice of criticism and a criticism of practice. I have tried to rescue in this article some undisputably Marxist foundations for critical pedagogy. Of course, much more work needs to be done in the area of pedagogy and class struggle, as unfashionable as this may seem in our current era of "post-Marxism."

"Is critical pedagogy about creating cultural heroes?" a student revolutionary once asked me following a lecture in Xalapa City, Mexico, a few years ago. Let me answer that question as a way of concluding my discussion. In my view, critical pedagogy is not mainly about struggling for cultural values (although values are certainly—fundamentally—important); it is, however, most emphatically about struggling with and for the oppressed. Critical citizenry is not about becoming a cultural hero by serving as a watchdog for family or civic values. Cultural heroes espouse certain values and may even die to defend them. They might even implore others to do the same (Bauman, 1992). While cultural heroes fight for cultural values, critical citizens, on the other hand, sacrifice themselves for disenfranchised others, and not necessarily for unpopular ideals. Life lived in service to others—rather than in service to abstract values—is one of the few measures that can give life within postmodern Gringolandia revolutionary meaning. Willingness to sacrifice ourselves for others is, as Emmanual Levinas, Mikhail Bakhtin, and Zygmunt Bauman argue, the only revolutionary way to live amidst the debris of existential uncertainty and alienation.

The Struggle for the Ethical Self

I am advocating here for the development of the ethical self as a way of living within the historical present of postmodern culture and transnational capitalism. Of the ethical self, Bauman writes:

> Only in the shape of the ethical self is humanity complete. Only in that shape does it attain the subtle blend and sought-for reconciliation of uniqueness and togetherness. Only when raised to the level of the ethical self, individuality does not mean loneliness, and togetherness does not mean oppression. "Concern for the other, up to the sacrifice, up to the possibility of dying for him; responsibility for the other"—this is, as Levinas insists, the "otherwise than being," the only exit from what otherwise would be self-enclosed, selfish, lonely, voiced (and ultimately meaningless) existence. (1992, 201)

I agree with Bauman when he explains that heroes traffic in ideas and die for them, whether these happen to be ideas about freedom, justice, race, class, or God. Ethical selves, unlike heroes, die for the dignity of other human beings and for their well-being, and in doing so they cannot justify any death or sacrifice but their own. Heroes often exhort others to die in the name of a cause (Bauman, 1992), whereas ethical selves cannot live at the expense of their responsibility to others.

As Bauman points out, "Death itself becomes a cause for the hero of a cause," whereas for the ethical self, life becomes the cause for those who are willing to die for the dignity and liberation of the other. As critical citizens we need to act as if the elimination of the needless suffering of all others depended upon the day-to-day choices that we make. We must refuse to allow postmodern culture to domesticate the people, to render them useless, and we must struggle to deny contemporary democracy the license to proclaim the people unworthy servants of the common good. That is what is meant by acting critically, and that is the power, promise, and sacrifice of critical pedagogy.

Acting critically also means acting with aesthetic sensibility, since in some fundamental ways aesthetic culture inevitably shapes political culture. Wolfgang Welsch (1996) suggests that relations of plurality, specificity, and partiality—as these operate within the realm of aesthetics—are structurally similar to the way in which they operate in everyday conditions of social life. Consequently, what is needed in contemporary formulations of critical pedagogy is an aesthetically reflexive awareness of difference in which social subjects are sensitized "for basic differences and for the peculiarity and irreducibility of different ways of life" (19). Welsch notes that aesthetically reflective awareness "perceives deviant principles, sees through imperialisms, is allergic to injustice and encourages one to intervene for the rights of the oppressed" (19). For example, Welsch claims that tolerance for difference without aesthetic sensibility is insufficient. He writes:

> The example of tolerance serves to make clear just how dependent political culture is on aesthetic culture. Tolerance without sensibility would be just a bare principle. One imagines a person who has made all of the maxims of tolerance their own, but who in day-to-day life lacks the sensitivity to even notice that the perceptions of others are different in principle and not just subject to some arbitrary lapse, that is, that it's a case not of a deficit as such, but of cultural difference. A person of this sort would never be embarrassed by so much as having to make use of his tolerance, but rather would incessantly practice imperialisms and oppression with the clearest of consciences and in the securest of beliefs that he's a tolerant person. Sensitivity for differences is then a real condition for tolerance but has little command of sensitivity. (1996, 19)

In fact, I would extend Welsch's example of tolerance by arguing that critical muliculturalism move beyond tolerance in order to embrace a politics of respect and affirmation. One way of extending Welsch's insights on aesthetic reflection— and a project that I do not have time to develop here—would be to follow Paul Trembath (1996) in utilizing Deleuze's work on "affective capacities" in conjunction with a revised Marxian theory of sensuous activity in ways that are compatable with poststructuralist theories of difference and cultural materialism's opposition to the idealization of sense. In other words, we need a new language and politics of the body (McLaren 1995).

The charge that I have leveled at U.S. democracy throughout this chapter is more than an arraignment of American civic-mindedness or national character, but speaks to deep-seated structural arrangements prohibitive of equality and social justice. I am drawing attention to the ominous historical moment of citizen abdication of democracy to the powers of capital and to the false prophets of the antigovernment Patriot movement. It is a time of capitulation of government to corporations and of the fundamental incompatibility of unbridled capitalism and democracy. In this historical moment we witness the marriage of dominant cultural life to *engabachamiento.*

I make this charge because the cause of liberation through schooling and other public spheres is too important to be left to narrow-minded educational researchers and pundits. The liberation of our schools is too vital a project to abandon to those who would domesticate critical pedagogy, such as some microethnographers who neutralize the social relations of production and consumption by either ignoring the larger context of capitalism or pretending that it does not exit, or to right-wing journalists, conservative talk show hosts, or conservative or liberal think tanks that seek democracy in our schools in only the most narrow functionalist or procedural sense. There are many arenas of struggle occupied by various groups offering strategies of hope: the EZLN in Chiapas; the EPR and PROCUP in Oaxaca, Guerrero, and Hidalgo; ecofeminists struggling in the southeast; educational activists trained at the Centro de Estudios sobre la Universidad UNAM in Mexico City; African-American urban activists in Detroit; student activists struggling to keep affirmative action in California; Puerto Rican students in Chicago politicizing their community; Chicano/a activists in Los Angeles fighting for *la raza*—the sites are multiple. Which arenas we are called to occupy will depend a great deal on the extent to which we can force democracy to provide for the basic needs of the people. Up to this point the situation is unequivocal: we have failed democracy and it has failed us.

What I am advocating is a postcolonial multiculturalism that moves beyond the ludic, metrocentric focus on identities as hybrid and hyphenated assemblages that exist alongside or outside of the larger social totality. Postcolonial multiculturalism, as I am articulating the term, takes as its condition of possibility the capitalist world system; it moves beyond a monoculturalist multiculturalism that fails to address identity-formation in a global context, and focuses instead on the idea that identities are shifting, changing, overlapping, and historically diverse (Shohat 1995). Multiculturalism is a politics of difference that is globally interdependent and raises questions about intercommunal alliances and coalitions. According to Ella Shohat, intercommunal coalitions are based on historically shaped affinities, and the multicultural theory that underwrites such a coalitionary politics needs "to avoid either falling into essentialist traps or being politically paralyzed by deconstructionist formulations" (1995, 177). Shohat articulates the challenge as follows:

> Rather than ask who can speak, then, we should ask how we can speak together, and more important, how we can move the dialogue forward. How can diverse communities speak in concert? How might we interweave our voices, whether in chorus, in antiphony, in call and response, or in polyphony? What are the modes of collective speech? In this sense, it might be worthwhile to focus less on identity as something one "has," than on identification as something one "does." (177)

Through critical pedagogy we can begin to ask questions about how we can live modernity's quest for emancipation within postmodern cultural climates without at the same time being deformed by its sufferings and practices of destruction. We can struggle to fathom how the goals of liberation can be won without dragooning less privileged groups into the service of our unacknowledged capitalist will to power.

We need to do more than simply invert relations of power because then the oppressed, newly freed from their bondage, would inevitably recuperate the logic of the oppressor so long as the same system of power informs their identities as emancipated agents. Consequently, we must define liberation from whiteness outside of the particular goals of such a struggle. We must invariably ask: From whiteness to where? Addressing such a question will play a crucial role in the struggle for social justice in the decades ahead. And this will be no small task in a world in which the theoretical pirouettes of the postmodern left have replaced a Marxian emphasis on concrete struggle and community activism; where a playful decentering of the signifier has replaced the struggle against oppression; and where the notion of oppression itself has been psychologized to mean anything that happens to be bothering you at the time, such as the condition of your front lawn. In this instance, resistance is co-opted and reduced to a variation of the monolithic theme of procedural democracy.

A revolutionary multiculturalism must engage what Enrique Dussel (1993) calls "the Reason of the Other." The debates over modernity and postmodernity have a different set of valences for *los olvidados,* for the peripheralized, for the marginalized, for the wrteched of the earth. Dussell writes about this distinction from his Latin American context:

> Unlike the postmodernists, we do not propose a critique of a violent, coercive, genocidal reason. We do not deny the rational kernel of the universalist rationalism of the Enlightenment, only its irrational moment as sacrificial myth. We do not negate reason in other words, but the irrationality of the violence generated by the myth of modernity. Against postmodernist irrationalism, we affirm the "Reason of Other."

I wish not to present critical pedagogy as a set of classroom teaching practices but rather to position it within a larger political problematic; here critical pedagogy is located as a politically informed disposition and commitment to marginalized others in the service of justice and freedom. Justice is conceptualized in this context from within the spirit of a transformative diasporic consciousness and encompassing issues of class, race, gender, and sexual orientation because all of these ongoing relations inform each other. A critical pedagogy grounded in a rearticulation of whiteness must seek to create a larger context in which it shares values with other struggles. We need, in other words, to fight for each other's differences and not just our own. This stipulates that we must identify a common ground of struggle in which a universality of rights and the common good passes into particular social struggles and then is reinitiated dialectically at a higher level of universality, and so on, without final closure. I am pointing to a nonabsolutist form of cultural politics, yet one that is never quite free from historically given languages, cultural codes,

positionings of time and space, and forms of memory and narration that make political articulation and expression possible in the first place (Rattansi 1994, 76).
The new political subject that will emerge will be constituted by de-essentializing
forms of agency and syncretic forms of political consciousness. An example of such
syncretic tactics in the realm of music can be seen in the work of Britain's Apache
Indian (Stephen Kuper), a Hindu Punjabi who was raised in a multiethnic area of
working-class Birmingham. Apache has been voted Best Newcomer at the British
Reggae Industry Awards and is popular among African-Caribbean and South Asian
disaporic communities, and his work topped the reggae and bhangra charts in 1991
(Bhachu, 1996). Similarly, the group PBN—Punjabi by Nature—is a Toronto-
based group of Canadian-born South Asians whose music has been influenced by
four continents, resulting in what Parminder Bhachu calls a "quadruple diasporic
consciousness" (1996, 286). George Lipsitz tells the story of an African man who
grew up believing that Pete Seeger was black because he knew Seeger was a Civil
Rights activist, sang freedom songs, and included Paul Robeson among his personal
friends. After coming to the U.S., the man got into an argument over Seeger's ethnicity and was shown a picture of Seeger that showed him to be white. Yet still the
man replied: "I know that Pete Seeger is Black . . . why should I change my mind
just because I see his face" (1996, 409).

Only through a multidimensional understanding of agency and a transformation of the human condition created by capitalism can we resist the the overwhelming power of transnational capital and truly live as liberated subjects of history.

Acknowledgments

This paper is based on several presentations which occurred at the University of California,
Berkeley, and Harvard University. They were developed on subsequent occasions into talks presented in Argentina, Mexico, Germany, Canada, Puerto Rico, and Japan.

References

Balibar, Etienne. 1996. "Is European Citizenship Possible?" *Public Culture* No. 19: 355–376.
Bauman, Zygmunt. 1992. *Mortality, Immortality, and Other Life Strategies.* Stanford, CA: Stan-
    ford University Press.
Bauman, Zygmunt. 1996. "On Communitarians and Human Freedom, or, How to Square the
    Circle." *Theory, Culture and Society* vol. 13, no. 2 (May): 79–90.
Bhachu, Parminder. 1996. "The Multiple Landscapes of Transnational Asian Women in the Dias-
    pora." In *Resituating Identities: The Politics of Race, Ethnicity and Culture.* Vered Amit-Talai

and Caroline Knowles, eds. Peterborough, Canada, and Essex, UK: Broadview Press, 283–303.

Bernstein, Sharon. 1996. "Storm Rises Over Ex-Klansman in Debate." *Los Angeles Times* (September 11): A3, A14.

Boggs, C. 1995. "The God Reborn: Pondering the Revival of Russian Communism." *Los Angeles View* 10, no. 20 (December 22–28): 8.

Bonnett, Alastair. 1996. "Anti-Racism and the Critique of White Identities." *New Community* 22(1): 97–110.

Bradlee Jr., B. 1996. "The Buchanan Role: GOP Protagonist." *Boston Sunday Globe* vol. 249, no. 63 (March 3):1 and 12.

Cashmore, Ellis. 1996. *Dictionary of Race and Ethnic Relations*. 4th ed. London and New York: Routledge.

Chomsky, Noam. 1996. *Class Warfare: Interviews with David Barsamian*. Monroe, ME: Common Courage Press.

Cone, James H. 1986. *A Black Theology of Liberation*. New York: Orbis Books.

Cruz, Jon. 1996. "From Farce to Tragedy: Reflections on the Reification of Race at Century's End." In *Mapping Multiculturalism*. Avery Gordon and Christopher Newfield, eds. Minneapolis and London: University of Minnesota Press, 19–39.

Dussell, Enrique. 1993. "Eurocentrism and Modernity." *Boundary 2* vol. 20, no. 3: 65–77.

Fanon, Frantz. 1967. *Black Skin, White Masks*. New York: Grove Press.

Frankenberg, Ruth. 1993. *The Social Construction of Whiteness: White Women, Race Matters*. Minneapolis, MN: University of Minnesota Press.

Fraser, Nancy. 1993. "Clintonism, Welfare, and the Antisocial Wage: The Emergence of a Neoliberal Political Imaginary." *Rethinking Marxism* vol. 6, no. 1: 9–23.

Gallagher, Charles A. 1994. "White Construction in the University." *Socialist Review* vol. 1 & 2: 165–187.

Gardiner, Michael. (1996). "Alterity and Ethics: A Dialogical Perspective." *Theory, Culture and Society* vol. 13, no. 2 (May): 121–144.

Goldberg, David Theo. 1993. *Racist Culture: Philosophy and the Politics of Meaning*. Cambridge, MA, and Oxford, UK: Blackwell Publishers.

Gutierrez, Ramón. 1996. "The Erotic Zone Sexual Transgression on the U.S.-Mexican Border." In *Mapping Multiculturalism*. Avery Gordon and Christopher Newfield, eds. Minneapolis, MN: University of Minnesota Press.

Holston, James, and Appadurai, Arjun. 1996. "Cities and Citizenship." *Public Culture* No. 19: 187–204.

Ignatiev, Noel, and Garvey, John. 1996. *Race Traitor*. New York and London: Routledge.

Laclau, Ernesto. 1992. "Universalism, Particularism, and the Question of Identity," *October* vol. 61 (Summer): 83–90.

Lash, Scott. 1996. "Postmodern Ethics: The Missing Ground." *Theory, Culture and Society* vol. 13, no. 2 (May): 91–104.

Lipsitz, George. 1995. "The Possessive Investment in Whiteness: Racialized Social Democracy and the 'White' Problem in American Studies." *American Quarterly* vol. 47, no. 3: 369–387.

Lipsitz, George. 1996. "'It's All Wrong, but It's All Right': Creative Misunderstandings in Intercultural Communication." In *Mapping Multiculturalism*. Avery Gordon and Christopher Newfield, eds. Minneapolis and London: University of Minnesota Press, 403–412.

López, Ian F. Haney. 1996. *White by Law*. New York and London: New York University Press.

Macedo, Donald, and Bartolome, Lilia. 1998. "Dancing with Bigotry: The Poisoning of Racial and Ethnic Identities." In *Ethnic Identity and Power*. Enrique Torres Trueba and Yali Zou, eds. Albany, NY: State University of New York Press.

McLaren, Peter. 1995. *Critical Pedagogy and Predatory Culture*. London and New York: Routledge.

Moraes, Marcia. 1996. *Bilingual Education: A Dialogue with the Bakhtin Circle*. Albany, NY: SUNY Press.

Novik, Michael. 1995. *White Lies, White Power: The Fight against White Supremacy and Reactionary Violence*. Monroe, ME: Common Courage Press.

O'Brien, Conor Cruise. 1996. "Thomas Jefferson: Radical and Racist." *Atlantic Monthly* (October), 53–74.

Perea, Juan, F. 1995. "Los Olvidados: On the Making of Unvisible People." *New York University Law Review* vol. 70, no. 4: 965–991.

Rattansi, Ali. 1994. "'Western' Racisms, Ethnicities and Identities in a 'Postmodern' Frame." In *Racism, Modernity and Identity on the Western Front*. Ali Rattansi and Sallie Westwood, eds. Cambridge and Oxford: Polity Press, 403–412.

Roediger, David. 1994. *Towards the Abolition of Whiteness*. London and New York: Verso.

Said, Edward. 1985. *Orientalism*. London: Penguin.

Shohat, Ella. 1995. "The Struggle Over Representation: Casting, Coalitions, and the Politics of Indentification." In *Late Imperial Culture*. Román de la Campa, E. Ann Kaplan, and Michael Sprinker, eds. London and New York: Verso, 166–178.

Shohat, Ella, and Stam, Robert. 1994. *Unthinking Eurocentrism: Multiculturalism and the Media*. New York and London: Routledge.

Simon, S. 1996. "Job Hunt's Wild Side in Russia." *Los Angeles Times* (January 2): 1, 9.

Stowe, David W. 1996. "Uncolored People: The Rise of Whiteness Studies." *Lingua Franca* vol. 6, no. 6: 68–77.

Southern Poverty Law Center. 1996. *False Patriots: The Threat of Antigovernment Extremists*. Montgomery, AL: SPLC.

Time. 1995. "Banker to Mexico: 'Go get 'em.'" vol. 145, no. 7 (February 20), 9.

Todorov, Tzvetan. 1984. *The Conquest of America: The Question of the Other*. New York: Harper and Row.

Trembath, Paul. 1996. "Aesthetics without Art or Culture: Toward an Alternative Sense of Materialist Agency." *Strategies* vol. 9/10: 122–151.

Wallace, Amy. 1996. "Less Diversity Seen as UC Preferences End." *Los Angeles Times* (October 2): A1, 18.

Welsch, Wolfgang. 1996. "Aestheticization Processes: Phenomena, Distinctions and Prospects." *Theory, Culture and Society* 13, no. 2: 1–24.

Winant, Howard. 1994. *Racial Conditions: Politics, Theory, Comparisons.* Minneapolis and London: University of Minnesota Press.

Wolfenstein, Eugene Victor. 1993. *Psychoanalytic-Marxism; Groundwork.* New York and London: Guilford Press.

Wood, Ellen Meiskins. 1995. *Democracy against Capitalism: Renewing Historical Materialism.* Cambridge and New York: Cambridge University Press.

Wray, Matt, and Newitz, Annalee, eds. 1997. *White Trash: Race and Class in America.* New York: Routledge.

Yúdice, George. 1995. "Neither Impugning nor Disavowing Whiteness Does a Viable Politics Make: The Limits of Identity Politics." In *After Political Correctness: The Humanities and Society in the 1990s.* Christopher Newfield and Ronald Strickland, eds. Boulder, CO: Westview Press, 255–285.

Zamichow, N. 1996. "Captains Courageous Enough Not to Fight." *Los Angeles Times* (January 23): 1, 9–10.

Zinn, Howard. 1970). *The Politics of History.* Boston: Beacon Press.

Henry A. Giroux

POSTMODERN EDUCATION AND DISPOSABLE YOUTH

Introduction

The "postmodern debate" has spawned little consensus and a great deal of confusion and animosity. The themes are, by now, well known: master narratives and traditions of knowledge grounded in first principles are spurned; philosophical principles of canonicity and the notion of the sacred have become suspect; epistemic certainty and the fixed boundaries of academic knowledge have been challenged by a "war on totality" and a disavowal of all-encompassing, single, worldviews; the rigid distinctions between high and low culture have been rejected by the insistence that the products of the so-called mass culture and popular and folk art forms are proper objects of study; the Enlightenment correspondence between history and progress and the modernist faith in rationality, science, and freedom have incurred a deep-rooted skepticism; the fixed and unified identity of the humanist subject has been replaced by a call for narrative space that is pluralized and fluid; and, finally, though far from complete, history is spurned as a unilinear process that moves the West progressively toward a final realization of freedom.[1]

While these and other issues have become central to the postmodern debate, they are connected through the challenges and provocations they provide to modernity's conception of history, agency, representation, culture, and the responsibility of intellectuals. The postmodern challenge not only constitutes a diverse body of cultural criticism, it must also be seen as a contextual discourse that has challenged specific disciplinary boundaries in such fields as literary studies, geography, education, architecture, feminism, performance art, anthropology, sociology, and many other areas.[2] Given its broad theoretical reach, its political anarchism, and its challenge to "legislating" intellectuals, it is not surprising that there has been a growing movement on the part of diverse critics to distance themselves from postmodernism.

While postmodernism may have been elevated to the height of fashion hype in both academic journals and the popular press in North America during the last twenty years, it is clear that a more sinister and reactionary mood has emerged which constitutes something of a backlash. Of course, postmodernism did become something of a fashion trend, but such events are short-lived and rarely take any subject seriously. The power of fashion and commodification should not be underestimated in terms of how such practices bestow on an issue a cloudy residue of irrelevance and misunderstanding, but there is more at stake in the recent debates on postmodernism than the effects of fashion and commodification; in fact, the often essentialized terms in which critiques of postmodernism have been framed suggest something more onerous. In the excessive rhetorical flourishes that dismiss postmodernism as reactionary nihilism, fad, or simply a new form of consumerism, there appears a deep-seated anti-intellectualism, one that lends credence to the notion that theory is an academic luxury and has little to do with concrete political practice. Anti-intellectualism aside, the postmodern backlash also points to a crisis in the way in which the project of modernity attempts to appropriate, prescribe, and accommodate issues of difference and indeterminacy.

Much of the criticism that now so blithely dismisses postmodernism appears trapped in what Zygmunt Bauman (1992) refers to as modernist "utopias that served as beacons for the long march to the rule of reason [which] visualized a world without margins, leftovers, the unaccounted for—without dissidents and rebels" (xi). Against the indeterminacy, fragmentation, and skepticism of the postmodern era, the master narratives of modernism, particularly Marxism and liberalism, have been undermined as oppositional discourses. One consequence is that "a whole generation of postwar intellectuals have experienced an identity crisis. What results is a mood of mourning and melancholia" (Mercer 1992, 424).

The legacy of essentialism and orthodoxy seems to be reasserting itself on the part of left intellectuals who reject postmodernism as a style of cultural criticism and knowledge production. It can also be seen in the refusal on the part of intellectuals to acknowledge the wide-ranging processes of social and cultural transformation taken up in postmodern discourses that are appropriate to grasping the contemporary experiences of youth and the wide-ranging proliferation of forms of diversity within an age of declining authority, economic uncertainty, the proliferation of electronically mediated technologies, and the extension of what I call consumer pedagogy into almost every aspect of youth culture.

In what follows, I want to shift the terms of the debate in which postmodernism is usually engaged, especially by its more recent critics. In doing so, I want to argue that postmodernism, as a site of "conflicting forces and divergent tendencies" (Patton 1988, 89), becomes useful pedagogically when it provides elements of an oppositional discourse for understanding and responding to the changing cultural and educational shift affecting youth in North America. A resistant or political postmodernism seems invaluable to me in helping educators and others address the changing conditions of knowledge production in the context of emerging mass electronic media and the role these new technologies are playing as critical socializing agencies in redefining both the locations and the meaning of pedagogy.

My concern with expanding the way in which educators and cultural workers understand the political reach and power of pedagogy as it positions youth within a postmodern culture suggests that postmodernism is to be neither romanticized nor casually dismissed. On the contrary, I believe that it is a fundamentally important discourse that needs to be mined critically in order to help educators understand the modernist nature of public schooling in North America.[3] It is also useful for educators to comprehend the changing conditions of identity-formation within electronically mediated cultures and how they are producing a new generation of youth who exists between the borders of a modernist world of certainty and order, informed by the culture of the West and its technology of print, and a postmodern world of hybridized identities, electronic technologies, local cultural practices, and pluralized public spaces. A critical and politically charged postmodernism is crucial for educators to address the performative role and promise that education and schooling offer in educating youth(s) to understand and, where necessary, strategically engage and transform a world lodged within and between modernist past and a modernist/postmodernist present and future.

In what follows, I want to illuminate and then analyze some of the tensions between schools as modernist institutions and the fractured conditions a postmodern culture of youth along with the problems they pose for critical educators. First, there is the challenge of understanding the modernist nature of existing schooling and its refusal to relinquish a view of knowledge, culture, and order that undermines the possibility for constructing a radical democratic project in which a shared conception of citizenship simultaneously challenges growing regimes of oppression and struggles for the conditions needed to construct a multiracial and multicultural democracy. Second, there is a need for cultural workers to address the emergence of a new generation of youth who are increasingly constructed within postmodern economic and cultural conditions that are almost entirely ignored by the schools. Third, there is the need critically to appropriate those elements of a postmodern pedagogy that might be useful in educating youth to be the subjects of history in a world that is increasingly diminishing the possibilities for radical democracy and global peace.

Modernist Schools and Postmodern Conditions

Wedded to the language of order, certainty, and mastery, public schools are facing a veritable sea change in the demographic, social, and cultural composition of the United States for which they are radically unprepared. As thoroughly modernist institutions, public schools have long relied upon moral, political, and social technologies that legitimate an abiding faith in the Cartesian tradition of rationality, progress, and history. The consequences are well known. Knowledge and authority in the school curricula are organized not to eliminate differences but to regulate them through cultural and social divisions of labor. Class, racial, and gender differences are either ignored in school curricula or subordinated to the imperatives of a history and culture that is linear and uniform.

Within the discourse of modernism, knowledge draws its boundaries almost exclusively from a European model of culture and civilization and connects learning to the mastery of autonomous and specialized bodies of knowledge. Informed by modernist traditions, schooling becomes an agent of those political and intellectual technologies associated with what Ian Hunter (1988) terms the "governmentalizing" of the social order.

The result is a pedagogical apparatus regulated by a practice of ordering that views "contingency as an enemy and order as a task"(Bauman 1992, xi). The practice of ordering, licensing, and regulating that structures public schooling is predicated on a fear of difference and indeterminacy. The effects reach deep into the structure of public schooling, and include an epistemic arrogance and faith in certainty that sanctions pedagogical practices and public spheres in which cultural differences are viewed as threatening; knowledge becomes positioned in the curricula as an object of mastery and control; the individual student is privileged as a unique source of agency irrespective of iniquitous relations of power; the technology and culture of the book are treated as the embodiment of modernist high learning and the only legitimate object of pedagogy.

While the logic of public schooling may be utterly modernist, it is neither monolithic nor homogeneous. But at the same time, the dominant features of public schooling as we enter the new millennium are characterized by a modernist project that has increasingly come to rely upon instrumental reason and the standardization of curricula. In part, this can be seen in the regulation of class, racial, and gender differences through rigid forms of testing, sorting, and tracking. Teaching within this logic is subordinated to the mastery of test skills, and educational outcomes are predicted on the narrow success of test scores. Within this discourse, the concept of education as training dominates schooling, and the overriding purpose of schooling is, in large part, to prepare students "to take their place in the corporate order" (Aronowitz 1998, 4). The Western rule of reason reveals its racially coded cultural legacy in a highly centered curricula that, more often than not, privileges the histories, experiences, and cultural capital of largely white, middle-class students. Moreover, the modernist nature of public schooling is evident in the refusal of educators to incorporate popular culture into the curricula or to take account of the new electronically mediated, informational systems in the postmodern age that are generating massively new socializing contexts for contemporary youth.

The emerging conditions of indeterminacy and hybridity that the public schools face but continue to ignore can be seen in a number of elements that characterize what I loosely call postmodern culture. First, the United States is experiencing a new wave of immigration which, by the end of this century, may exceed, in volume and importance, the last wave at the turn of the twentieth century. In key geographic areas within the country—chiefly large metropolitan regions of the Northeast and Southwest, including California—major public institutions, especially those of social welfare and education, are grappling with entirely new populations that bring with them new needs. In 1940, 70 percent of immigrants came from Europe, but in 1992 only 15 percent came from Europe while 44% came from Latin America and 37 percent came from Asia. National identity can no longer be written through the lens of cultural uniformity or enforced through the discourse of assimilation. A new postmodern culture has emerged, marked by specificity, difference, plurality, and multiple narratives.

Second, the sense of possibility that has informed the American Dream of material well-being and social mobility is no longer matched by an economy that can sustain such dreams. In the last two decades, the American economy has entered a prolonged era of stagnation punctuated by short-term growth spurts. In the midst of an ongoing recession and declining real incomes for low- and middle-income groups, the prospects for economic growth over the next period of U.S. history appear extremely limited. The result has been the expansion of service-industry jobs and an increase in the number of companies that are downsizing and cutting labor costs in order to meet global competition. Not only are full-time jobs drying up, but there has also been an surge in the "number of Americans—perhaps as many as 37 million—[who] are employed in something other than full-time permanent positions" (Jost 1993, 633). These so called "contingent workers" are "paid less than full-time workers and often get no health benefits, no pensions and no paid holidays, sick days or vacations" (628). Massive unemployment and diminishing expectations have become a way of life for youth all over North America. *MacLean's* magazine reports that in Canada "People ages 15 to 24 are currently facing unemployment rates of more than 20 percent, well above the national average of 10.8 percent" (Blythe 1993, 35). For most contemporary youth, the promise of eco-

nomic and social mobility no longer warrants the legitimating claims it held for earlier generations of young people. The signs of despair among this generation are
everywhere. Surveys strongly suggest that contemporary youth from diverse classes,
races, ethnicities, and cultures "believe it will be much harder for them to get ahead
than it was for their parents—and are overwhelmingly pessimistic about the long-
term fate of their generation and nation" (Howe and Strauss 1993, 16).

Clinging to the modernist script that technological growth necessitates progress,
educators refuse to give up the long-held assumption that school credentials provide the best route to economic security and class mobility. While such a truth may
have been relevant to the industrializing era, it is no longer sustainable within the
post-Fordist economy of the West. New economic conditions call into question the
efficacy of mass schooling in providing the "well-trained" labor force that employ-
ers required in the past. In light of these shifts, it seems imperative that educators
and other cultural workers reexamine the mission of the schools (Aronowitz and
Difazio, 1994).

Rather than accepting the modernist assumption that schools should train students for specific labor tasks, it makes more sense in the present historical moment
to educate students to theorize differently about the meaning of work in a postmodern world. Indeterminacy rather than order should become the guiding principle of a pedagogy in which multiple views, possibilities, and differences are opened
up as part of an attempt to read the future contingently rather than from the perspective of a master narrative that assumes rather than problematizes specific notions of work, progress, and agency. Under such circumstances, schools need to
redefine curricula within a postmodern conception of culture linked to the diverse
and changing global conditions that necessitate new forms of literacy, a vastly expanded understanding of how power works within cultural apparatuses, and keener
sense of how the existing generation of youth are being produced within a society in
which mass media play a decisive if not unparalleled role in constructing multiple
and diverse social identities.

As Stanley Aronowitz and I (1993) have pointed out elsewhere:

> Few efforts are being made to rethink the *entire* curriculum in the light of
> the new migration and immigration, much less develop entirely different
> pedagogies. In secondary schools and community colleges for example,
> students still study "subjects"—social studies, math, science, English and
> "foreign" languages. Some schools have "added" courses in the history and
> culture of Asian, Latin American and Caribbean societies, but have little
> thought of transforming the entire humanities and social studies curricula
> in the light of the cultural transformations of the school. Nor are serious
> efforts being made to integrate the sciences with social studies and the

humanities; hence, science and math are still being deployed as sorting devices in most schools rather than seen as crucial markers of a genuinely innovative approach to learning. (6)

As modernist institutions, public schools have been unable to open up the possibility of thinking through the indeterminate character of the economy, knowledge, culture, and identity. Hence it has become difficult, if not impossible, for such institutions to understand how social identities are fashioned and struggled over within political and technological conditions that have produced a crisis in the ways in which culture is organized in the West.

Border Youth and Postmodern Culture

The programmed instability and transitoriness characteristically widespread among a generation of 18-to-25-year-old border youth are inextricably rooted in a larger set of postmodern cultural conditions informed by the following assumptions: a general loss of faith in the modernist narratives of work and emancipation; the recognition that the indeterminacy of the future warrants confronting and living in the immediacy of experience; an acknowledgment that homelessness as a condition of randomness has replaced the security, if not misrepresentation, of home as a source of comfort and security; an experience of time and space as compressed and fragmented within a world of images that increasingly undermine the dialectic of authenticity and universalism. For border youth, plurality and contingency, whether mediated through the media or through the dislocations spurned by the economic system, the rise of new social movements, or the crisis of representation, have resulted in a world with few secure psychological, economic, or intellectual markers. This is a world in which one is condemned to wander across, within, and between multiple borders and spaces marked by excess, otherness, difference, and a dislocating notion of meaning and attention. The modernist world of certainty and order has given way to a planet in which hip-hop and rap condense time and space into what Paul Virilio (1991) calls "speed space." No longer belonging to any one place or location, youth increasingly inhabit shifting cultural and social spheres marked by a plurality of languages and cultures.

Communities have been refigured, as space and time mutate into multiple and overlapping cyberspace networks. Youth talk to each other over electronic bulletin boards in coffeehouses in North Beach, California. Cafes and other public salons, once refuges of beatniks, hippies, and other cultural radicals, have given way to members of the hacker culture. They reorder their imaginations through connections to virtual reality technologies and lose themselves in images that wage a war on traditional meaning by reducing all forms of understanding to random access spectacles.

This is not meant to endorse a Frankfurt School dismissal of mass or popular culture in the postmodern age. On the contrary, I believe that the new electronic technologies, with their proliferation of multiple stories and open-ended forms of interaction, have altered not only the context for the production of subjectivities but also how people "take in information and entertainment" (Parkes 1994, 54). Values no longer emerge from the modernist pedagogy of foundationalism and universal truths, nor from traditional narratives based on fixed identities and with their requisite structure of closure. For many youths, meaning is in rout, media has become a substitute for experience, and what constitutes understanding is grounded in a decentered and diasporic world of difference, displacement, and exchanges.

I want to take up the concept of border youth through a general analysis of some recent films that have attempted to portray the plight of young people within the conditions of a postmodern culture. I will focus on four films: *River's Edge* (1986), *My Own Private Idaho* (1991), *Slackers* (1991), and *187* (1997). All of these films point to some of the economic, racial, and social conditions at work in the formation of dominant perceptions of youth. And they often do so within a narrative that combines a politics of despair with a fairly sophisticated depiction of the sensibilities of a generation of youth pressured by an adult population that has become increasingly hostile to them.

The challenge for critical educators is to question how a transformative pedagogy might be employed to cancel out the worst dimensions of postmodern cultural criticism while appropriating some of its more radical aspects. At the same time, there is the issue of how a politics and project of pedagogy might be constructed to create the conditions for social agency and institutionalized change among existing generations of postmodern youth.

For many postmodern youth, showing up for adulthood at the *fin de siècle* means pulling back on hope and trying to put off the future, rather than taking up the modernist challenge of trying to shape it. Postmodern cultural criticism has captured much of the ennui among youth and has made clear that "[w]hat used to be the pessimism of a radical fringe is now the shared assumption of a generation" (Anshaw 1992, 27). Postmodern cultural criticism has helped to alert educators and others to the fault lines marking a generation, regardless of race or class, whose members seem neither motivated by nostalgia for some lost conservative vision of America nor at home in the New World Order paved with the promises of the expanding electronic information highway. For most commentators, youth have become "strange," "alien," and disconnected from the real world.

For instance, in Gus Van Sant's film, *My Own Private Idaho*, the main character, Mike, who hustles his sexual wares for money, is a dreamer lost in fractured memories of a mother who deserted him as a child. Caught between flashbacks of Mom shown in 8mm color and the video world of motley street hustlers and their clients, Mike moves through his existence by falling asleep in times of stress, only to awake in different geographic and spatial locations. What holds Mike's psychic and geographic travels together are the metaphor of sleep, the dream of escape, and the ultimate realization that even memories cannot fuel hope for the future. Mike becomes a metaphor for an entire generation forced to sell themselves in a world with no hope, a generation that aspires to nothing, works at degrading McJobs, and lives in a world in which chance and randomness, rather than struggle, community, and solidarity, drive their fate.

A more disturbing picture of youth can be found in *River's Edge*. Teenage anomie and drugged apathy are given painful expression in the depiction of a group of working-class youth who are casually told by John, one of their friends, that he has strangled his girlfriend, another of the group's members, and left her nude body on the riverbank. The group at different times visit the site to view and probe the dead body of the girl. Seemingly unable to grasp the significance of the event, the youths initially hold off in informing anyone of the murder and with different degrees of concern initially try to protect John, the teenage sociopath, from being caught by the police. The youths in *River's Edge* drift through a world of broken families, blaring rock music, schooling marked by dead time, and a general indifference to life in general. Decentered and fragmented, they view death, like life itself, as merely a spectacle, a matter of style rather than substance. In one sense, these youth share the quality of being "asleep" that is depicted in *My Own Private Idaho*. But what is more disturbing in *River's Edge* is that lost innocence gives way not merely to teenage myopia but to a culture in which human life is experienced as a voyeuristic seduction, a video game, good for passing time and diverting oneself from the pain of the moment. Despair and indifference cancel out the language of ethical discriminations and social responsibility while elevating the immediacy of pleasure to the defining moment of agency.

In *River's Edge*, history as social memory is reassembled through vignettes of 1960s types portrayed as either burned-out bikers or as the ex-radical turned teacher whose moralizing relegates politics simply to cheap opportunism. Exchanges among the young people in *River's Edge* appear like projections of a generation waiting either to fall asleep or to commit suicide. After talking about how he murdered his girlfriend, John blurts out, "You do shit, it's done, and then you die." Pleasure, violence, and death, in this case, reassert how a generation of youth takes seriously the dictum that life imitates art, or how life is shaped within a violent culture of images in which, as another character states, "It might be easier being dead," to which her boyfriend, a *Wayne's World* type replies, "Bullshit, you couldn't get stoned anymore." *River's Edge* and *My Own Private Idaho* reveal the seamy and dark side of a youth culture while employing the Hollywood mixture of fascination and horror to titillate the audiences drawn to these films. Employing the postmodern aesthetic of revulsion, locality, randomness, and senselessness, youth in these films appear to be constructed outside a broader cultural and economic landscape. Instead, they become visible only through visceral expressions of psychotic behavior or the brooding experience of a self-imposed comatose alienation.

One of the more celebrated youth films of the 1990s is Richard Linklater's *Slacker*. A decidedly low-budget film, *Slacker* attempts in both form and content to capture the sentiments of a twenty-something generation of white youth who reject most of the values of the Reagan/Bush era but have a difficult time imagining what an alternative might look like. Distinctly nonlinear in its format, *Slacker* takes place in a twenty-four-hour time frame in the college town of Austin, Texas. Borrowing its antinarrative structure from films such as Luis Bunuel's *Phantom of Liberty* and Max Ophlus's *La Ronde, Slacker* is loosely organized around brief episodes in the lives of a variety of characters, none of whom are connected to each other except that each provides the pretext to lead the audience to the next character in the film. Sweeping through bookstores, coffee shops, auto-parts yards, bedrooms, and night-clubs, *Slacker* focuses on a disparate group of young people who possess little hope in the future and drift from job to job speaking a hybrid argot of bohemian intensities and New Age–pop cult babble.

The film portrays a host of young people who randomly move from one place to the next, border crossers with no sense of where they have come from or where they are going. In this world of multiple realities, "schizophrenia emerges as the psychic norm of late capitalism" (Hebdige 1988, 88). Characters work in bands with names such as "Ultimate Loser" and talk about being forcibly put in hospitals by their parents: one neopunker attempts to sell a Madonna Pap smear to two acquaintances she meets in the street. "Check it out, I know it's kind of disgusting, but it's like sort of getting down to the real Madonna." This is a world in which language is wedded to an odd mix of nostalgia, popcorn philosophy, and MTV babble. Talk is organized around comments like: "I don't know . . . I've traveled . . . and when you get back you can't tell whether it really happened to you or if you just saw it on TV." Alienation is driven inward and emerges in comments like "I feel stuck." Irony slightly overshadows a refusal to imagine any kind of collective struggle. Reality seems too despairing to care about. This is humorously captured in one instance by a young man who suggests: "You know how the slogan goes, workers of the world, unite? We say workers of the world, relax." People talk but appear disconnected from themselves and each other; lives traverse each other with no sense of community or connection.

There is a pronounced sense in *Slacker* of youth caught in the throes of new information technologies that contain their aspirations while at the same time holding out the promise of some sense of agency. At rare moments in the film, the political paralysis of solipsistic refusal is offset by instances in which some characters recognize the importance of the image as a vehicle for cultural production, as a representational apparatus that not only can make certain experiences available but can also be used to produce alternative realities and social practices. The power of the image is present in the way the camera follows characters throughout the film, at once stalking them and confining them to a gaze that is both constraining and incidental.

In one scene, a young man appears in a video apartment surrounded by televisions that he claims he has had on for years. He points out that he has invented a game called a "Video Virus" in which, through the use of a special technology, he can push a button and insert himself onto any screen and perform any one of a number of actions. When asked by another character what this is about, he answers: "Well, we all know the psychic powers of the televised image. But we need to capitalize on it and make it work for us instead of working for it." This theme is taken up in two other scenes. In one short clip, a history graduate student films the video camera he is using to film himself, indicating a self-consciousness about the power of the image and the ability to control it at the same time. In another scene, with which the film concludes, a carload of people, each equipped with their super 8 cameras, drive up to a large hill and throw their cameras into a canyon. The film ends with the images being recorded by the cameras as they cascade to the bottom of the cliff in what suggests a moment of release and liberation.

One of the most disturbing depictions of youth in the postmodern age is *187*. Unlike the films discussed above, this film embodies a postmodern notion of youth not simply as Other but as dangerous and disposable, outside the pale of the modernist concept of civilized, worthy, and educated. Directed by Kevin Reynolds and written by Scott Yagemann, a former schoolteacher, *187* narrates the story of Trevor Garfield (Samuel L. Jackson), a science teacher who rides to school on a bike in order to teach at a high school in Bedford-Stuyvesant. Garfield is portrayed as an idealistic teacher who is trying against all odds to make his classes interesting and do his best to battle daily against the ignorance, chaos, and indifference that characterize the urban public school in the Hollywood imagination. But the film quickly turns away from a call for educational reform and a defense of those teachers who face a Sisyphean task in trying to improve the lives of urban youth, and quickly degenerates into a rationale for abandoning urban public schools and the black and brown students who inhabit their hallways and classrooms.

In the film's opening scenes, students move through metal detectors under the watchful eyes of security guards—props that have become all too familiar to urban high school settings. Clearly, the students in *187* are far removed from the squeaky-clean, high-tech classrooms of white suburbia. On the contrary, the school looks more like a prison, and the students, with their rap music blaring in the background, look more like inmates being herded into their cells. The threat of violence is palpable in this school, and Garfield confronts it as soon as he enters his classroom and picks up his textbook, which has the figure "187" scrawled all over it. Recognizing that the number is the police code for homicide, Garfield goes to the principal to report what he believes is a threat on his life. The principal tells Garfield he is overreacting, dismissing him with, "You know what your problem is? On the one hand, you think someone is going to kill you, and on the other hand, you actually think kids are paying attention in your class."

But before Garfield leaves, the principal confirms his worse fears by revealing that he has told a student in Garfield's class that he has flunked the course. Not only has the principal violated Garfield's privacy, but the student he has flunked is on probation and, as a result of the failing grade, will now be sent back to prison. The threat of violence and administrative ineptitude set the stage for a hazardous series of confrontations between Garfield and the public school system. Garfield leaves the principal's office terrified and walks back to his classroom. Each black male student he now sees appears menacing and poised to attack. Shot in slow motion, the scene is genuinely disturbing. And before Garfield reaches his classroom, he is viciously and repeatedly stabbed with a nine-inch nail in the hallway by the black male student he has flunked.

Fifteen months later, Garfield has relocated and finds a job as a substitute teacher at John Quincy Adams High School in Los Angeles. The students in this school are mostly Latino. They wear oversized pants and torn shirts, carry boom boxes blaring rap music, and appear as menacing as the African-American students Garfield taught in Brooklyn. As the camera pans their bodies and expressions, it becomes clear that what unites these inner-city students of color is a culture that is dangerous, crime-ridden, and violent. Assigned to teach his class in a bungalow, Garfield's first day is a nightmare, as students taunt him, throw paper wads at him, and call him "bitch." Garfield has moved from New York to California only to find himself in a public high school setting that has the look and feel of hell. Images of heat rising from the pavement, pulsating rap music, shots of graffiti, and oversized shadows of gang members playing basketball filtering through the classroom window paint an ominous picture of a what Garfield is about to experience.

But Garfield has to face more than dangerous students. His new principal prides himself on never having been a teacher, refers to students as clients, and makes it clear that his primary concern is to avoid potential lawsuits. Hollywood's message in this case is clear: public schools are filled with administrators who would rather cater to a liberal discourse about the civil rights of students—who clearly do not deserve any—than protect the welfare of teachers who face the threat of daily violence.

Garfield's fellow teachers are no better. The first teacher he meets, Dave Childress

(John Heard), is an alcoholic burnout who stashes a .357 magnum in his desk drawer, thoroughly hates his students, and, we later learn, has had sexual relations with a very young, emotionally shaken Latina student. Hanging on for the paycheck, Childress serves as a reminder of what such schools do to teachers. Robbed of his passion, Childress regards every kid as a social menace or macho punk waiting to kill or be killed. Garfield does strike up a friendship and romance with Ellen Henry (Kelly Rowan), a perky, blonde computer science teacher, but it soon turns sour as the bleak and dangerous environment in which they find themselves eventually pushes Garfield over the edge. Ellen tries to draw close to Garfield, but he is too battered and isolated, telling Ellen at one point that when he was assaulted in New York, it robbed him of his "passion, my spark, my unguarded self—I miss them."

Garfield's descent into madness begins when his bungalow is completely trashed by the gang members in his class. He becomes edgy, living in a shadow of fear heightened by his past. Ellen then tells Garfield that Benny, a particularly vicious gang member in his class, has threatened to hurt her, and indicates to Garfield that she does not know what to do. Soon afterwards Benny disappears, but her troubles are not over, as Benny's sidekick, Cesar, and his friends kill her dog. As a result, Cesar becomes the object of vigilante justice. Roaming drunk near the LA freeway, he is stalked, shot with a spiked arrow, and while unconscious his finger is cut off. The tension mounts as Ellen finds Benny's rosary beads in Garfield's apartment and confronts him with the evidence that he might be the killer. Garfield is immune to the reproach, arguing that someone has to take responsibility, because the system will not protect "us" from "them." Ellen tells Garfield she does not know him anymore, and Garfield replies, "I am a teacher just like you."

As the word circulates that Garfield may be the vigilante killer and assailant, the principal moves fast to protect the school from a lawsuit and fires him. Garfield, now completely broken, goes home and is soon visited by Cesar and his gang, who, inspired by the film *The Deer Hunter*, force Garfield into a game of Russian roulette. With little to lose, Garfield tells Cesar he is not really a man, and ups the stakes of the game by taking Cesar's turn. Garfield pulls the trigger and kills himself. Forced into questioning his own manhood, Cesar decides to take his turn, puts the gun to his head, and fatally shoots himself as well. In the final scene of the film, a student is reading a graduation speech about how teachers rarely get any respect; the shot switches to Ellen, who is in her classroom. Ellen takes her framed teaching certificate off the wall, throws it into the wastebasket, and walks out of the school.

Films such as *187* cash in on the prevailing racially coded popular "wisdom" that public schools are out of control, largely inhabited by illiterate, unmotivated, and violent urban youth who are economically and racially marginalized. This increasingly familiar script suggests a correlation between urban public space and rampant drug use, daily assaults, broken teachers, and schools that do nothing more than contain deviants who are a threat to themselves and everybody else. *187* is a recent addition to this genre, but it takes the pathologizing of poor, urban students of color to extremes that go so far beyond existing cinematic conventions that it stands out as a public testimony to broader social and cultural formations within American society that makes the very existence of this blatantly racist film possible.

Within the postmodern culture depicted in these films, there are no master narratives at work, no epic modernist dreams, nor is there any element of social agency that accompanies the individualized sense of dropping out, of self-consciously courting chaos and uncertainty. In many respects, these movies present a culture of youth who appear overwhelmed by "the danger and wonder of future technologies, the banality of consumption, the thrill of brand names, [and] the difficulty of sex in alienated relationships" (Kopkind 1992, 183). The significance of these films rests, in part, in their attempt to capture the sense of powerlessness that increasingly cuts across race, class, and generations. But what is missing from these films, along with the various books, articles, and reportage concerning what is often called the Nowhere Generation, Generation X, 13thGen, or Slackers, is any sense of the larger political and social conditions in which youth are being framed. What in fact should be seen as a social commentary about "dead-end capitalism" and racism emerges simply as a celebration of refusal dressed up in a rhetoric of aesthetics, realism, style, fashion, and solipsistic protests. Within this type of commentary, postmodern criticism is useful but limited because of its often theoretical inability to take up the relationship between identity and power, biography and the commodification of everyday life, or the limits of agency in a racialized, post-Fordist economy as part of a broader project of possibility linked to issues of history, struggle, and transformation. In what follows, I want briefly to comment on how pedagogy might be used to think at the limits of postmodern criticism by both appropriating and going beyond the boundaries of its discourse as regards issues of politics, power, and race. I will then return to a more positive assessment of the pedagogical value of postmodern discourses for critical educators.

Engaging the potential discursive effects of films such as *187* might mean discussing the implication of this Hollywood film appropriating the name of the controversial California proposition to deny mostly nonwhite students access to public schools. It might mean engaging how *187* contributes to a public discourse that rationalizes both the demonization of minority youth and the defunding of public and higher education at a time when, in states such as California, "approximately 22,555 African Americans attend a four-year public university . . . while 44,792 (almost twice as many) African Americans are in prison [and] this figure does not include all the African Americans who are in county jails or the California Youth authority or those on probation or parole" (Criminal Justice Policy Report 1996, 2).[4]

Hollywood films such as *187* must be addressed and understood within a broader set of policy debates about education and crime which often serve to legitimate policies that disempower poor and racially marginalized youth. For example, nationwide state spending for corrections has increased by 95 percent over the last decade, while spending on higher education decreased by 6 percent. Similarly, "over a ten year period, the number of correctional officers increased [at] four times the rate of public higher education faculty." Again, it is not surprising that the chosen setting for *187* is primarily California, a state that now "spends more on corrections (9.4% of the General Fund) than on higher education."[5] While it would be absurd to suggest to students that films such as *187* are responsible for recent government spending allocations, they do take part in a public pedagogy and representational politics that cannot be separated from a growing racial panic and fear over minorities, the urban poor, and immigrants.

As a public discourse, *187*, like most Hollywood films about youth, fails to rupture the racial stereotypes that support harsh, discriminatory crime policies and growing incidents of police brutality, such as the highly publicized torture of Abner Louima by Brooklyn patrolmen or the recent shooting death of Amadou Diallo by four New York City plainclothes policemen who riddled his body and an apartment building vestibule with forty-one bullets, in spite of the fact that Diallo was unarmed.

What is unique about *187* is that it explores cinematically what the logical conclusion might be in dealing with urban youth for whom reform is no longer on the national agenda, for which containment or the militarization of school space seem both inadequate and too compromising. Carried to the extreme, *187* flirts with the ultimate white-supremacist logic—that is, extermination and genocide of those Others deemed beyond the pale of social reform, inhuman, and despicable. *187* capitalizes on the popular conception reported endlessly in the media that public education is not safe for white, middle-class children, that racial violence is rampant in the public schools, that minority students have turned classroom discipline into a joke, that administrators are paralyzed by insensitive bureaucracies, and that the only thing that teachers and students share is the desire to survive the day. But the implications of cultural texts such as *187* become meaningful not just as strategies of understanding and critical engagement that raise questions about related discourses, texts, and social issues, but also in probing what it might mean to move beyond the sutured institutional space of the classroom to address social issues in related spheres marked by racial injustices and unequal relations of power.

The pedagogical challenge represented by the emergence of a postmodern generation of youth suggests that educators need to address both the conditions through which they teach and what it means to learn from a generation that is experiencing life in a way that is vastly different from the representations offered in modernist versions of schooling. The emergence of the electronic media coupled with a diminishing faith in the power of human agency has undermined the traditional visions of schooling and the meaning of pedagogy. The language of lesson plans and upward mobility and the forms of teacher authority on which it was based have been radically delegitimated by the recognition that culture and power are central to the authority/knowledge relationship. Modernism's faith in the past has given way to a future for which traditional markers no longer make sense.

Postmodern Education

In this section, I want to develop the thesis that postmodern discourses offer the promise, but not the solution, for alerting educators to a new generation of border youth. Indications of the conditions and characteristics that define such youth are far from uniform or agreed upon. But the daunting fear of essentializing the category of youth should not deter educators and cultural critics from addressing the effects on a current generation of young people who appear hostage to the vicissitudes of a changing economic order, with its legacy of diminished hopes, on the one hand, and a world of schizoid images, proliferating public spaces, and an increasing fragmentation, uncertainty, and randomness that structure postmodern daily life, on the other. Central to this issue is whether educators are dealing with a new kind of student forged within organizing principles shaped by the intersection of the electronic image, popular culture, and a dire sense of indeterminacy. Differences aside, the concept of border youth represents less a distinct class, membership, or social group than a referent for naming and understanding the emergence of set of conditions, translations, border crossings, attitudes, and dystopian sensibilities among youth that cuts across race and class and represents a fairly new phenomenon. In this scenario, the experiences of contemporary Western youth in the late modern world are being ordered around coordinates that structure the experience of everyday life outside the unified principles and maps of certainty that offered up comfortable and secure representations to previous generations. Youth increasingly rely less on the maps of modernism to construct and affirm their identities; instead, they are faced with the task of finding their way through a decentered cultural landscape no longer caught in the grip of a technology of print, closed narrative structures, or the certitude of a secure economic future. The new emerging technologies which construct and position youth represent interactive terrains that cut across "language and culture, without narrative requirements, without character complexities. . . . Narrative complexity [has given] way to design complexity; story [has given] way to a sensory environment" (Parkes 1994, 50).

A postmodern pedagogy must address the shifting attitudes, representations, and desires of this new generation of youth being produced within the current historical, economic, and cultural juncture. For example, the terms of identity and the production of new maps of meaning must be understood within new hybridized cultural practices inscribed in relations of power that intersect differently with race, class, gender, and sexual orientation. But such differences must be understood not only in terms of the context of their struggles but also through a shared language of resistance that points to a project of hope and possibility. This is where the legacy of a critical modernism becomes valuable, in that it reminds us of the importance of the language of public life, democratic struggle, and the imperatives of liberty, equality, and justice.

Educators need to understand how different identities among youth are being produced in spheres generally ignored by schools. Included here would be an analysis of how pedagogy works to produce, circulate, and confirm particular forms of knowledge and desires in those diverse public and popular spheres where sounds, images, print, and electronic culture attempt to harness meaning for and against the possibility of expanding social justice and human dignity. Shopping malls, street communities, video halls, coffee shops, television culture, and other elements of popular culture must become serious objects of school knowledge. But more is at stake here than an ethnography of those public spheres where individual and social identities are constructed and struggled over. More important is the need to fashion a language of ethics and politics that serves to discriminate between relations that do violence and those that promote diverse and democratic public cultures through which youth and others can understand their problems and concerns as part of a larger effort to interrogate and disrupt the dominant narratives of national identity, economic privilege, and individual empowerment.

Pedagogy must redefine its relationship to modernist forms of culture, privilege, and canonicity, and serve as a vehicle of translation and cross-fertilization. Pedagogy as a critical cultural practice needs to open up new institutional spaces in which students can experience and define what it means to be cultural producers capable of both reading different texts and producing them, of moving in and out of theoretical discourses but never losing sight of the need to theorize for themselves. Moreover, if critical educators are to move beyond the postmodern prophets of hyperreality, politics must not be exclusively fashioned to plugging into the new electronically mediated community. The struggle for power is not merely about expanding the range of texts that constitute the politics of representation; it is also about struggling within and against those institutions that wield economic, cultural, and economic power.

It is becoming increasingly fashionable to argue for a postmodern pedagogy in which it is important to recognize that "[o]ne chief effect of electronic hypertext lies in the way it challenges now conventional assumptions about teachers, learners, and the institutions they inhabit" (Landow 1992,120). As important as this concern is for refiguring the nature of the relationship between authority and knowledge and the pedagogical conditions necessary for decentering the curriculum and opening up new pedagogical spaces, it does not go far enough and runs the risk of degenerating into another hyped-up methodological fix.

Postmodern pedagogy must be more sensitive to how teachers and students negotiate both texts and identities, but it must do so through a political project that articulates its own authority within a critical understanding of how the self recognizes others as subjects rather than as objects of history. In other words, postmodern pedagogy must address how power is written on, within, and between different groups as part of a broader effort to reimagine schools as democratic public spheres. Authority in this instance is linked to autocritique and becomes a political and ethical practice through which students become accountable to themselves and others. By making the political project of schooling primary, educators can define and debate the parameters through which communities of difference, defined by relations of representation and reception within overlapping and transnational systems of information, exchange, and distribution, can address what it means to be educated as a practice of empowerment. In this instance, schools can be rethought as public spheres, as "borderlands of crossing," actively engaged in producing new forms of democratic community organized as sites of translation, negotiation, and resistance.

What is also needed by postmodern educators is a more specific understanding of how affect and ideology mutually construct the knowledge, resistances, and sense of identity that students negotiate as they work through dominant and rupturing narratives, attempting in different ways to secure particular forms of authority. Fabienne Worth (1993) is right in castigating postmodern educators for undervaluing the problematic nature of the relationship between "desire and the critical enterprise" (8). A postmodern pedagogy needs to address how the issue of authority can be linked to democratic processes in the classroom that do not promote pedagogical terrorism and yet still offer representations, histories, and experiences that allow students critically to address the construction of their own subjectivities as they simultaneously engage in an ongoing "process of negotiation between the self and other" (Worth 1993, 26).

The conditions and problems of contemporary border youth may be postmodern, but they will have to be engaged through a willingness to interrogate the world of public politics while at the same time recognizing the limits of postmodernism's more useful insights. In part, this means rendering postmodernism more political by appropriating modernity's call for a better world while abandoning its linear narratives of Western history, unified culture, disciplinary order, and technological progress. In this case, the pedagogical importance of uncertainty and indeterminacy can be rethought through a modernist notion of the dreamworld in which youth and others can shape, without the benefit of master narratives, the conditions for producing new ways of learning, engaging, and positing the possibilities for social struggle and solidarity. Radical educators can subscribe neither to an apocalyptic emptiness nor to a politics of refusal that celebrates the immediacy of experience over the more profound dynamic of social memory and moral outrage forged within and against conditions of exploitation, oppression, and the abuse of power. Postmodern pedagogy needs to confront history as more than simulacrum and ethics as something other than the casualty of incommensurable language games. Postmodern educators need to take a stand without standing still, to engage their own politics as public intellectuals without essentializing the ethical referents to address human suffering.

A postmodern pedagogy needs to go beyond a call for refiguring the curriculum to include new informational technologies; instead, it needs to assert a politics that makes the relationship among authority, ethics, and power central to a pedagogy that expands rather than closes down the possibilities of a radical democratic society. Within this discourse, images do not dissolve reality into simply another text; on the contrary, representations become central to revealing the structures of power relations at work in the public, schools, society, and the larger global order. Difference does not succumb to fashion in this logic (another touch of ethnicity); instead, difference becomes a marker of struggle in an ongoing movement toward a shared conception of justice and a radicalization of the social order.

Notes

1. For a particularly succinct examination of postmodernism's challenge to a modernist conception of history, see Vattimo 1992, especially Chap.1.

2. Several excellent readers have appeared that provide readings in postmodernism that cut across a variety of fields. Some of the more recent examples include: Jencks 1992; Natioli and Hutcheon 1993; Docherty 1993; Nicholson and Seidman 1995. Also see Lemert 1997.

3. I have taken this issue up in great detail in Giroux (1988, 1992, 1986, 1997).

4. Figures cited in The Justice Policy Institute/Center on Juvenile and Criminal Justice Policy Report, 1996, 2.

5. Cited in *From Classrooms to Cell Blocks: A National Perspective*. The Justice Policy Institute (February 1997), 2.

References

Anderson, Perry. 1984. "Modernity and Revolution." *New Left Review* 144: 96–113.
Anshaw, Carol. 1992. "Days of Whine and Poses." *Village Voice* 10 (November): 25–27.

Aronowitz, Stanley. 1998. "Introduction." In Paulo Freire, *Pedagogy of Freedom*. Lanham, MD: Rowman and Littlefield.

Aronowitz, Stanley, and William Defazio. 1994. *The Jobless Future*. Minneapolis, MN: University of Minnesota Press.

Aronowitz, Stanley, and Henry A. Giroux. 1991. *Postmodern Education*. Minneapolis, MN: University of Minnesota Press.

Aronowitz, Stanley, and Henry A. Giroux. 1993. *Education Still Under Siege*. 2nd ed. Westport, CT: Bergin and Garvey.

Atkinson, Michael. 1997. "Skateboard Jungle." *Village Voice* 37 (September): 64–67.

Bauman, Zygmunt. 1992. *Intimations of Postmodernity*. New York: Routledge.

Bell, Daniel. 1976. *The Cultural Contradictions of Capitalism*. New York: Basic Books.

Bérubé, Michael. 1992/1993. "Exigencies of Value." *The Minnesota Review* 39: 63–87.

Best, Stephen, and Douglas Kellner. 1990. *Postmodern Theory*. New York: Guilford Press.

Bishop, Katherine. 1992. "The Electronic Coffeehouse." *New York Times* (2 August): Section: The Street, 3.

Blythe, Scott. 1993. "Generation Xed." *Maclean's* (August): 35.

Bordo, Susan. 1993. *Unbearable Weight: Feminism, Western Culture, and the Body*. Berkeley, CA: University of California Press.

Butler, Judith. 1991. "Contingent Foundations: Feminism and the Question of Postmodernism." In *Feminists Theorize the Political*. Judith Butler and Joan Scott, eds. New York: Routledge, 3–21.

Chambers, Iain. 1990. *Border Dialogues*. New York: Routledge.

Clarke, John. 1991. *New Times and Old Enemies*. New York: Harper Collins.

Collins, Jim. 1989. *Uncommon Cultures*. New York: Routledge.

Connor, Steven. 1989. *Postmodernist Culture*. Cambridge, MA: Blackwell.

Criminal Justice Policy Report. 1996. *From Classrooms to Cell Blocks: How Prison Building Affects Higher Education and African American Enrollment in California*. San Francisco, CA: October, 1–35.

Denzin, Norman. 1991. *Images of a Postmodern Society*. Newbury Park, CA: Sage.

Docherty, Thomas, ed. 1993. *Postmodernism: A Reader*. New York: Columbia University Press.

Eagleton, Terry. 1996. *The Illusions of Postmodernism*. Oxford: Basil Blackwell Publishers.

Ebert, Teresa. 1991. "Writing in the Political: Resistance(Post)modernism." *Legal Studies Forum* 15, no. 4: 291–303.

Foster, Hal, ed. 1985. *Postmodern Culture*. London: Pluto Press.

Fraser, Nancy. 1997. *Justice Interruptus: Critical Reflections on the 'Postsocialist' Condition*. New York: Routledge.

Giroux, Henry. 1988. *Schooling and the Struggle for Public Life*. Minneapolis, MN: University of Minnesota Press.

Giroux, Henry. 1992. *Border Crossings*. New York: Routledge.

Giroux, Henry. 1994. *Disturbing Pleasures: Learning Popular Culture*. New York: Routledge.

Giroux, Henry. 1996. *Fugitive Cultures*. New York: Routledge.

Giroux, Henry. 1997. *Channel Surfing: Race Talk and the Destruction of Today's Youth*. New York: St. Martin's Press.

Green, Bill, and Chris Bigum. Forthcoming. "Aliens in the Classroom." *Australian Journal of Education*.

Habermas, Jurgen. 1978. *The Philosophical Discourse of Modernity*. Cambridge, MA: MIT Press, 1978.

Harvey, David. 1989. *The Conditions of Postmodernity*. Cambridge, UK: Basil Blackwell, 1989.

Hebdige, Dick. 1988. *Hiding in the Light*. New York: Routledge.

Hollingsworth, Pierce. 1993. "The New Generation Gaps: Graying Boomers, Golden Agers, and Generation X." *Food Technology* 47, no. 10 (October): 30.

Howe, Neil, and Bill Strauss. 1993. *13th Gen: Abort, Retry, Ignore, Fail?* New York: Vantage Books.

Hunter, Ian. 1988. *Culture and Government: The Emergence of Literary Education*. London: Macmillan.

Hutcheon, Linda. 1988. *The Poetics of Postmodernism*. New York: Routledge.

Jencks, Charles. 1992. "The Postmodern Agenda." In *The Postmodern Reader*. Charles Jencks, ed. New York: St. Martin's Press.

Jost, Kenneth. 1993. "Downward Mobility." *Congressional Quarterly Researcher* 3, no. 27 (July 23): 627–644.

Kopkind, Andrew. 1992. "Slacking Toward Bethlehem." *Grand Street* 44: 177–188.

Landow, George. 1992. *Hypertext: The Convergence of Contemporary Critical Theory and Technology*. Baltimore, MD: The Johns Hopkins University Press.

Lasch, Scott. 1990. *Sociology of Postmodernism*. New York: Routledge.

Lemert, Charles. 1997. *Postmodernism Is Not What You Think*. Lanham, MD: Rowman and Littlefield.

MacCannell, Dean. 1992. *Empty Meeting*. New York: Routledge.

Mercer, Kobena. 1992. "'1968': Periodizing Politics and Identity." In *Cultural Studies*. Lawrence Grossberg, Cary Nelson, and Paula Treichler, eds. New York: Routledge.

Natioli, Joseph, and Linda Hutcheon, eds. 1993. *A Postmodern Reader*. Albany, NY: SUNY Press.

Nicholson, Linda, ed. 1990. *Feminism/Postmodernism*. New York: Routledge.

Nicholson, Linda, and Steven Seidman, eds. 1995. *Social Postmodernism*. New York: Routledge.

Owens, Craig. 1992. *Beyond Recognition: Representation, Power, and Culture*. Scott Bryson et al., eds. Berkeley, CA: University of California Press.

Parkes, Walter. 1994. "Random Access, Remote Control: the Evolution of Story Telling." *Omni* (January): 48–54, 90–91.

Patton, Paul. 1988. "Giving up the Ghost: Postmodernism and Anti-Nihilism." In *It's a Sin*, Lawrence Grossberg, ed. Sydney: Power Publications, 88–95.

Ross, Andrew, ed. 1988. *Universal Abandon? The Politics of Postmodernism*. Minneapolis, MN: University of Minnesota Press.

Smart, Barry. 1991. "Theory and Analysis After Foucault." *Culture and Society* 8: 144–145.

Smart, Barry. 1992. *Modern Conditions, Postmodern Controversies.* New York: Routledge.

Tomlinson, John. 1991. *Cultural Imperialism.* Baltimore, MD: Johns Hopkins University Press.

Vattimo, Gianni. 1992. *The Transparent Society.* Baltimore, MD: Johns Hopkins University Press.

Virilio, Paul. 1991. *Lost Dimension.* Daniel Moshenberg, trans. New York: Semiotext(e).

Willinsky, John. 1991. "Postmodern Literacy: A Primer." *Interchange* 22, no. 4: 56–76.

Worth, Fabienne. 1993. "Postmodern Pedagogy in the Multicultural Classroom: For Inappropriate Teachers and Imperfect Strangers." *Cultural Critique* 25 (Fall): 5–32.

DOUGLAS KELLNER

MULTIPLE LITERACIES AND CRITICAL PEDAGOGIES
New Paradigms

We are in the midst of one of the most dramatic technological revolutions in history, which is changing everything from the ways that we work, to the ways that we communicate with each other, to how we spend our leisure time. The technological revolution centers on information technology, is often interpreted as the beginnings of a knowledge society, and therefore ascribes to education a central role in every aspect of life. This Great Transformation poses tremendous challenges to educators to rethink their basic tenets, to deploy the new technologies in creative and productive ways, and to restructure schooling to respond productively and progressively to the technological and social changes that we are now experiencing.

Consequently, transformations in pedagogy must be as radical as the technological transformations that are taking place. Critical pedagogy must thus rethink the concepts of literacy and the very nature of education in a high-tech and rapidly evolving society. For at the same time that we are undergoing a technological revolution, important demographic and sociopolitical changes are occurring in the United States and throughout the world. Emigration patterns have brought an explosion of new peoples into the U.S. in recent decades, and the country is now more racially and ethnically diverse, more multicultural, than ever before. This creates the challenge of providing people from diverse races, classes, and backgrounds with the tools to enable them to succeed and participate in an ever more complex and changing world.

In this chapter, I argue that we need multiple literacies for our multicultural society, that we need to develop new literacies to meet the challenge of the new technologies, and that literacies of diverse sorts—including an even more fundamental importance for print literacy—are of crucial importance in restructuring education for a high-tech and multicultural society. "Literacy" in my conception comprises gaining competencies involved in effectively using socially constructed forms of communication and representation. Learning literacies involves attaining competencies in practices in contexts that are governed by rules and conventions. Literacies are socially constructed in educational, governmental, and cultural practices involved in various institutional discourses and practices. Literacies evolve and shift in response to social and cultural change and the interests of elites who control hegemonic institutions.

My argument is that we are in a period of dramatic technological and social change and that education today needs to foster a variety of new types of multiple literacies to empower students and to make education relevant to the demands of the present and future. My assumption is that new technologies are altering every aspect of our society and that we need to comprehend and make use of them to both understand and transform our worlds. My goal would be to introduce new literacies to empower individuals and groups traditionally excluded, and thus to reconstruct education to make it more responsive to the challenges of a democratic and multicultural society.

Even traditionalists would agree that education and literacy are intimately connected. Literacy involves gaining the skills and knowledge to read and interpret the text of the world and to navigate and negotiate successfully its challenges, conflicts, and crises. Reading and writing, media literacy, computer literacy, and multimedia literacies provide basic skills but require supplementation by multiple social and cultural literacies, ranging from ecoliteracy, economic and financial literacy to a variety of other competencies that enable us to live well in our social worlds. Schooling, at its best, provides the symbolic and cultural capital that empowers people to survive and prosper in an increasingly complex and changing world and the resources to produce a more cooperative, democratic, egalitarian, and just society. As the world changes, so too must education, which will be part of the problem or part of the solution as we enter a new millennium.

In advancing my reconstructive pedagogical agenda, I discuss how critical pedagogy can promote multicultural education and sensitivity to cultural difference. To begin, I focus on the importance of developing media literacy to engage critically the wealth of media materials that currently immerse us. Critical pedagogy considers how education can provide individuals with the tools to better themselves and strengthen democracy, to create a more egalitarian and just society, and thus to deploy education in a process of progressive social change. Media literacy involves teaching the skills that will empower citizens and students to become sensitive to the politics of representations of race, ethnicity, gender, sexuality, class, and other cultural differences in order to foster critical thinking and enhance democratization. Critical media literacy aims to make viewers and readers more critical and discriminating readers and producers of texts. Critical media pedagogy provides students and citizens with the tools to analyze critically how texts are constructed and in turn construct and position viewers and readers. It provides tools so that individuals can dissect the instruments of cultural domination, transform themselves from objects to subjects, from passive to active. Thus critical media literacy is empowering, enabling students to become critical producers of meanings and texts, able to resist manipulation and domination.

In addition, I discuss a wide range of multiple literacies needed to deal with the exigencies of the cultural and technological revolution that we are currently involved in, ranging from computer literacy to multimedia literacy to new forms of cultural literacy. The challenges from new technologies, I will argue, force us to rethink literacy, pedagogy, and curricula to make education viable and relevant for the next century. Such concerns are part of a critical pedagogy which summons educators, students, and citizens to rethink established curricula and teaching strategies in order to meet the challenge of empowering individuals to participate democratically in our increasingly multicultural and technological society.

Media Literacy, Critical Pedagogy, and the Challenges of Contemporary Education

Cultural studies and critical pedagogy have begun to teach us to recognize the ubiquity of media culture in contemporary society, the growing trends toward multicultural education, and the need for media literacy that addresses the issue of multicultural and social difference.[1] There is expanding recognition that media representations help construct our images and understanding of the world and that education must meet the dual challenges of teaching media literacy in a multicultural society and sensitizing students and publics to the inequities and injustices of a society based on gender, race, and class inequalities and discrimination. Recent critical studies see the role of mainstream media in exacerbating or diminishing these inequalities and the ways that media education and the production of alternative media can help create a healthy multiculturalism of diversity and more robust democracy. They thus confront some of the most serious difficulties and problems that face us as educators and citizens as we move toward the twenty-first century.

Multicultural education is in part a response to deal creatively with growing diversity, which facilitates "strategies for sharing, understanding, and enjoying" our proliferating cultural hybridities and differences (Carson and Friedman 1995, x). Progressive educators have thus been urging the development of pedagogic practices that will promote multicultural understanding, that will empower students, and that will help reconstruct education. Postmodern theory has alerted us to the importance of perceiving and accepting differences and to the ways that hierarchies of difference are socially constructed. Since cultural differences are constructed in part at the level of meaning and signification through the mediation of media and cultural representations, students and citizens must become aware of the ways that culture constructs a system of social differences, with hierarchies, exclusions, defamations, and sometimes legitimation of the dominant social groups' power and domination. A critical multicultural education will thus make teachers and students sensitive to the politics of representation, to how media audiences' images of race, gender, sexuality, and cultural differences are in part generated by cultural representations, how negative stereotyping presents harmful cultural images, and the need for a diversity of representations to capture the cultural wealth of contemporary postmodern and global societies.

But the media can also be used to teach positively multicultural understanding and education. Through cultivating the skills of media literacy, teachers can discover how to use media to advance multicultural education and to use this material to teach media literacy as well. If multicultural education is to champion genuine diversity and expand the curriculum, it is important both for groups excluded from mainstream education to learn about their own heritage and for dominant groups to explore the experiences and voices of minority and excluded groups. Moreover, as Carson and Friedman (1995) stress, while it is important and useful to study cultures and voices excluded from traditional canons, dead white European male authors may have as much of importance to teach all students as excluded representatives of minority groups whom multiculturalists want, often with good reason, to include in the curriculum. Thus Friedman convincingly argues that: "Western culture, despite its myriad faults, remains a crucial influence on American political, intellectual and social thought and, as such, should play an important role in classrooms" (Carson and Friedman 1995, 3).

In reality, few advocates of multicultural education call for jettisoning the traditional canon and altogether replacing the classics with new multicultural fare. Genuine multicultural education requires expanding, not contracting, the curricula, broadening and enriching it, not impoverishing it. It also involves, as Friedman stresses, including white ethnic groups in the multicultural spectrum and searching out those common values and ideals that cut across racial and cultural boundaries. Thus multicultural education can both help us understand our history and culture and can move toward producing a more diverse and inclusive democratic society.

Media materials such as films, TV shows, or documentaries can provide dramatic and accessible materials that enable individuals to experience the joys and tragedies, the specificities and commonalties of a multiplicity of cultures. Thus media materials can be used positively to enable individuals to enter the lifeworlds of people who live in different cultures and societies and to appreciate their lives and cultures. While print media may provide useful contextualizing and explanatory information, it is also helpful to see the embodiment and concretizing of different cultures and societies in images, scenes of everyday life, dramatic narratives, or illuminating documentaries that enable audiences to emphasize and involve themselves in different cultures and lifeworlds.

On the other hand, media culture constructs models of multicultural difference, privileging some groups while denigrating others. Grasping the construction of difference and hierarchy in media texts requires learning how they are constructed, how they communicate and metacommunicate, and how they influence their audiences. Textual and semiotic analysis of media artifacts helps to reveal their codes and conventions, their values and ideologies, and thus their meanings and messages (see Kellner 1995a and 1995b). In particular, critical cultural studies should analyze representations of class, gender, race, ethnicity, sexual preference, and other identity markers in the texts of media culture, as well as attending to national, regional, and other cultural differences, how they are articulated in cultural representations, and how these differences among audiences create different readings and receptions of cultural texts.

The argument for developing media literacy as part of standard educational training is that the media themselves are a form of cultural pedagogy and thus must be countered by a critical media pedagogy that dissects how media communicate and affect their audiences and how students and citizens can gain skills to analyze the media critically. The media are an important form of socialization and pedagogy that teach proper and improper behavior, gender roles, values, and knowledge of the world. One is often not aware that one is being educated and constructed by media culture; thus its pedagogy is often invisible and subliminal, requiring critical approaches that make us aware of how media construct meanings, influence and educate audiences, and impose their messages and values.

Consequently, key books in the emerging field of media literacy over the past decade start from the premise of the ubiquity of media culture in contemporary society and produce a more general argument for critical media literacy as a response to media pedagogy. Media literacy thus involves knowledge of how media work, how they construct meanings, how they serve as a form of cultural pedagogy, and how they function in everyday life. A media literate person is skillful in analyzing media codes and conventions, able to criticize media stereotypes, values, and ideologies, and thus literate in reading media critically. Media literacy thus empowers people to use media intelligently, to discriminate and evaluate media content, to dissect media forms critically, and to investigate media effects and uses.

Media literacy thus enables us to see how media culture creates differences, hierarchies, and negative or positive representations of different groups, and how it constitutes a sort of cultural pedagogy. A critical cultural studies and media pedagogy helps to enable individuals to see how the media position, construct, and manipulate identities. Media pedagogy provides tools so that individuals can dissect the instruments of cultural domination, transform themselves from objects to subjects, from passive to active. It also shows how individuals can come to create their own identities from the resources of their cultures and is thus doubling empowering, freeing individuals from media manipulation and domination and enabling self-construction and the creation of more cooperative and democratic social relations and institutions.

Critical media literacy engages a multiplicity of methods to sensitize students to the diversity of ways in which the artifacts of media culture communicate and construct meanings. Genre analysis analyzes the major types and forms of the conventions of media culture; narrative analysis dissects how media stories are constructed and communicate; semiotic analysis analyzes both the formal codes of meaning and the social codes and conventions reproduced in media texts; hermeneutical analysis helps unpack the layers of meaning in a text; and critical methods such as feminism, Marxism, critical race theory, psychoanalysis, and other methods help analyze the social construction of gender, class, race, and sexuality in media culture. Critical discourse analysis notes how institutions, discourses, and texts construct and position people in different ways. Media texts, public speeches and spectacles, classroom pedagogies and practices all position their audiences as objects to be shaped, molded, and influenced. Critical discourse analysis sees how texts specifically address and position spectators and deconstructs the ways that meanings and messages are constructed and communicated in media artifacts.

Critical media literacy thus provides students and citizens with the tools to analyze critically how texts are constructed and in turn construct and position viewers and readers. Critical media pedagogy therefore helps to make viewers and readers more critical and discriminating readers of texts. A critical media literacy is necessary to develop educated students and citizens, since media culture strongly influences our view of the world, imparting knowledge of geography, of technology and the environment, of political and social events, of how the economy works, of what is currently going on in our society and the world at large. It is crucially important to see how media entertainment is a form of cultural pedagogy, teaching dominant values, ways of thought and behavior, style, and fashion and providing resources for constituting individual identities (Kellner 1995a). The media are both crucial sources of knowledge and information and sources of entertainment and leisure activity. They are our storytellers and entertainers and are especially influential because we are often not aware that media narratives and spectacles are themselves a form of education, imparting cultural knowledge and values and shaping how we see and live our social worlds.

Consequently, media literacy is an important part of multicultural education, since many people's conceptions of gender, sexuality, race, ethnicity, and class are constituted in part by the media, which are often important in determining how people view social groups and reality, conceive of gender roles of masculinity and femininity, and distinguish between good and bad and right and wrong attitudes and behavior. Since the media also provide role models, conceptions of proper and improper conduct, and crucial cultural and political information, they are an important form of pedagogy and socialization. A media-literate person is thus able to read, understand, evaluate, discriminate among, and criticize media materials and, ultimately, produce media artifacts in order to use media as means of expression and communication.[2]

Thus a critical media pedagogy also provides the skills that can help individuals to produce their own print, audiovisual, and multimedia texts. Insight into how texts are constructed helps individuals not only to dissect texts critically, but to acquire the skills both to produce more effectively their own interpretations and to create media artifacts themselves. Indeed, entry into media production is a carrot that often motivates students to take more seriously the work of learning critical media literacy, although fascination with the popular materials that constitute their lived culture usually provides sufficient motivation to engage students in the task of learning critical media literacy.

Sometimes "the media" are lumped into one homogeneous category, but it is important to discern that there are many media of communication and forms of cultural pedagogy, ranging from print media, such as books, newspapers, and magazines, to film, radio, television, popular music, photography, advertising, and many other multimedia cultural forms, including video games, computer culture, CD-ROMs, the Internet, and the like. Media literacy thus requires traditional print literacy skills as well as visual literacy, aural literacy, and the ability to analyze narratives, spectacles, and a wide range of cultural forms. Media literacy involves reading images critically, interpreting sounds, and seeing how media texts produce meaning in a multiplicity of ways (Kellner 1989c, 1995a). Since media are a central part of our cultural experience from childhood to the grave, training in media literacy should begin early in life and continue into adulthood, as new technologies are constantly creating new media, and new genres, technical innovations, aesthetic forms, and conventions are constantly emerging.

The challenge to education and educators is to devise strategies to teach media literacy while using media materials to contribute to the advance of multicultural education. For, against McLuhan, who claims that the younger generation is naturally media-literate (1964), I would argue that developing critical media literacy requires cultivating explicit strategies of cultural pedagogy and models of media education. Media literacy involves making unconscious and prereflective understanding conscious and reflective, drawing on people's learned abilities to interact with media. All people in a media culture such as ours are media-literate to a certain extent—they are able to read and interpret the multitude of cultural forms with which they daily interact, but their media literacy is often unconscious and unreflective, requiring the cultivation of cognitive skills of analysis, interpretation, and critique. Moreover, as many students and teachers of media literacy have discovered, most individuals who cultivate media literacy competencies actually reach new levels of media enjoyment due to their abilities to apply critical skills which disclose new dimensions, connections, and meanings.

Yet within educational circles, there is a debate over what constitutes the field of media pedagogy, with different agendas and programs. A traditionalist, "protectionist" approach would attempt to "inoculate" young people against the effects of media addiction and manipulation by cultivating a taste for book literacy, high culture, and the values of truth, beauty, and justice and by denigrating all forms of media and computer culture. Neil Postman, in his books *Amusing Ourselves to Death* (1985) and *Technopolis* (1992), exemplifies this approach. A "media literacy" movement, by contrast, attempts to teach students to read, analyze, and decode media texts, in a fashion parallel to the cultivation of print literacy. Media arts education, in turn, teaches students to appreciate the aesthetic qualities of media and to use various media technologies as tools of self-expression and creation. Critical media literacy, as I would advocate it, builds on these approaches, analyzing media cultures as products of social production and struggle and teaching students to be critical of media representations and discourses, but also stressing the importance of learning to use the media as modes of self-expression and social activism.

Critical media literacy not only teaches students to learn from media, to resist media manipulation, and to empower themselves *vis-à-vis* the media, but is concerned with developing skills that will empower citizens and that will make them more motivated and competent participants in social life. Critical media literacy is thus tied to the project of radical democracy and is concerned to develop skills that will enhance democratization and participation. Critical media literacy takes a comprehensive approach that would teach critical skills and how to use media as instruments of social change. The technologies of communication are becoming more and more accessible to young people and average citizens, and they should be used to promote education, democratic self-expression, and social progress. Thus technologies that could help produce the end of participatory democracy by transforming politics into media spectacles and the battle of images, and by turning spectators into cultural zombies, could also be used to help invigorate democratic debate and participation (Kellner 1995a, 1995c).

Indeed, teaching critical media literacy should be a participatory, collaborative project. Students are often more media-savvy, knowledgeable, and immersed in media culture than their teachers and thus can contribute to the educational process through sharing their ideas, perceptions, and insights. On the other hand, critical discussion, debate, and analysis should be encouraged, with teachers bringing to bear their critical perspectives on student readings of media material. Since media culture is often part and parcel of students' identities and most powerful cultural experience, teachers must be sensitive in criticizing artifacts and perceptions that students hold dear, yet an atmosphere of critical respect for difference *and* inquiry into the nature and effects of media culture should be encouraged.

A major challenge in developing critical media pedagogy results from the fact that it is not a pedagogy in the traditional sense, with firmly established principles, a canon of texts, and tried-and-true teaching procedures. Critical media pedagogy is in its infancy; it is just beginning to produce results and is thus more open and experimental than established print-oriented pedagogy. Moreover, the material of media culture is so polymorphous, multivalent, and polysemic that it requires sensitivity to different readings, interpretations, and perceptions of the complex images, scenes, narratives, meanings, and messages of media culture which in their own ways are as complex and challenging to decipher critically as are those of book culture.

Unfortunately, there is considerable hostility toward media education and the media themselves in educational circles. Educational traditionalists conceive of literacy in more limited print-media paradigms and, as I suggested above, often adopt a "protectionist" approach when they address the issue of the media at all, warning students against corruption or urging that they limit media use to "educational" materials. Yet many teachers at all levels, from kindergarten to the university, have discovered that media material, judiciously used, can be valuable in a variety of instructional tasks, helping to make complex subject matter accessible and engaging. Obviously, media cannot substitute for print material and classroom teaching and should be seen as supplements to traditional materials rather than as a magic panacea for the failures of traditional education. Moreover, as I argue in the next section, traditional print literacy and competencies are more important than ever in our new high-tech societies.

It is also highly instructive, I would argue, to teach students at all levels to engage *popular* media materials critically, including the most familiar film, television, music, and other forms of media culture. Yet here one needs to avoid an uncritical media populism of the sort that is emerging within certain sectors of British and North American cultural studies. In a review of *Rethinking Media Literacy* (McLaren, Hammer, Sholle, and Reilly 1995), for instance, Jon Lewis attacked what he saw as the overly critical postures of the contributors to this volume, arguing: "If the point of a critical media literacy is to meet students halfway—to begin to take seriously what *they* take seriously, to read what *they* read, to watch what *they* watch—teachers *must* learn to love pop culture" (1996, 26). Note the authoritarian injunction that "teachers *must* learn to love popular culture" (italics are Lewis's), followed by an attack on more critical approaches to media literacy.

Teaching critical media literacy, however, involves occupation of a site above the dichotomy of fandom and censor. One can teach how media culture provides significant statements or insights about the social world, positive visions of gender, race, and class, or complex aesthetic structures and practices, thus putting a positive spin on how it can provide significant contributions to education. Yet one should also indicate how media culture can advance sexism, racism, ethnocentrism, homophobia, and other forms of prejudice, as well as misinformation, problematic ideologies, and questionable values. A more dialectical approach to media literacy engages students' interests and concerns and should, as I suggested above, involve a collaborative approach between teachers and students since students are deeply absorbed in media culture and may know more about some of its artifacts and domains than their teachers do. Consequently, they should be encouraged to speak, discuss, and intervene in the teaching/learning process. This is not to say, however, that media literacy training should romanticize student views that may be superficial, mistaken, uniformed, and full of various problematical biases. Yet exercises in media literacy can often productively involve intense student participation in a mutual learning process where both teachers and students together learn media literacy skills and competencies.

It is also probably a mistake to attempt to institute a top-down program of media literacy imposed from above on teachers, with fixed texts, curricula, and prescribed materials. Diverse teachers and students will have very different interests and concerns and will naturally emphasize different subject matter and choose examples relevant to their own and their students' interests. Courses in critical media literacy should thus be flexible enough to enable teachers and students and to address their own interests to constitute their own curricula to engage material and topics of current concern. Moreover, and crucially, educators should discern that we are in the midst of one of the most intense technological revolutions in history and must learn to adapt new computer technologies to education, as I suggest in the following section, and this requires the development of new multiple literacies.

New Technologies, Multiliteracies, and Postmodern Pedagogy: The New Frontier

Many of the studies on multicultural education and critical media literacy that I have examined so far neglect to interrogate computer culture and the ways that the Internet and new computer technologies and cultural forms are dramatically transforming the circulation of information, images, and various modes of culture. And so in this section, which is looking toward education in the next century, I want to argue that students should learn new forms of computer literacy that involve both how to use computer culture to do research and gather information, as well as learning to perceive the computer as a cultural terrain which contains texts, spectacles, games, and new interactive multimedia requiring new modes of literacy. Moreover, computer culture is a discursive and political location in which students, teachers, and citizens can all intervene, engaging in discussion groups and collaborative research projects, creating their own Web sites, producing new multimedia for cultural dissemination, and engaging in new modes of social interaction and learning. Computer culture enables individuals actively to participate in the production of culture ranging from discussion of public issues to creation of their own cultural forms. However, to take part in this culture requires not only accelerated forms of traditional modes of print literacy, which are often restricted to the growing elite of students who are privileged to attend adequate and superior public and private schools, but new forms of literacy as well, thus posing significant challenges to education.

It is indeed a salient fact of the present age that computer culture is proliferating, and so we have to begin teaching computer literacy from an early age. Computer literacy, however, itself needs to be theorized. Often the term is synonymous with technical ability to use computers, master existing programs, and maybe engage in some programming oneself. I want, however, to suggest expanding the conception of computer literacy from using computer programs and hardware to a broader concept of information literacy and of developing, in addition, more sophisticated abilities in traditional reading and writing, as well as the capability to dissect critically cultural forms taught as part of critical media literacy and new forms of multiple literacy. Information literacy involves both the accessing and processing of diverse sorts of information proliferating in our infotainment society.[3] It encompasses learning to find sources of information ranging from traditional sites like libraries and print media to new Internet Web sites and search engines.

Thus, on this conception, genuine computer literacy involves not just technical knowledge and skills, but refined reading, writing, research, and communicating ability that involves heightened capacities for critically accessing, analyzing, interpreting, and processing print, image, sound, and multimedia material. Computer literacy involves the ability to discover and access information and intensified abilities to read, to scan texts, computer databases, and Web sites, and to download or print the information in a form appropriate for further information processing. Utilizing information accessed in an educational context further requires putting it together in meaningful patterns and mosaics to construct meanings and interpretations, to contextualize and evaluate, and to discuss and articulate one's own views.

Within computer culture, visual literacy takes on increased importance. On the whole, computer screens are more graphic, visual, and interactive than conventional print fields, which disconcerted many of us when first confronted with the new environments. Icons, windows, mouses, and the various clicking, linking, and interaction required by computer-mediated hypertext require new competencies and a dramatic expansion of literacy. Visuality is obviously crucial, requiring one to scan visual fields quickly, perceive and interact with icons and graphics, and use technical devices such as the mouse to access the desired material and field. One must also learn the navigational skills to proceed from one field and screen to another, to search for information on the Internet and computer databases, and to move from one program to another if one operates, as most now do, in a Windows-based computer environment.

The new multimedia environments require, in fact, a diversity of multisemiotic and multimodal interactions, involving interfacing with words and print material and often with images, graphics, and new audio and video material. The New London Group has produced the concept of "multiliteracy" to describe the types of literacy required to engage new multimedia technology, while the concept of "intermediality" calls attention to the need to generate literacies that allow interaction between various media and new multimedia and that promote interdisciplinary and interactive education in an attempt to create education that promotes democratic social change. In a similar vein, individuals involved in the University of California at Los Angeles and San Diego with the *la classa magica* project are using new computer and multimedia technology to teach basic reading and writing skills, as well as new computer and multimedia literacy and forms of social cooperation and interaction.[4]

As technological convergence develops apace, one needs to combine the skills of critical media literacy with traditional print literacy and new forms of multiliteracy to access the new multimedia hypertext environments.[5] Literacy, in my conception, involves socially constructed forms of communication and representation and the corresponding competencies involved in effectively using them. Thus reading and interpreting print was the appropriate mode of literacy for books, while critical media literacy requires reading and interpreting discourse, images, spectacle, narratives, and the forms and genres of media culture. Forms of multimedia communication involve print, speech, visuality, and audio in a hybrid field which combines these forms, all of which involve skills of interpreting and critique.

Obviously, here the key root is the multiple, the proliferation of media and forms that require a multiplicity of competencies and skills and abilities to navigate and construct a new semiotic terrain—hence the term "multiliteracy" and the notion of multiple literacies that I develop in the next section. Multiliteracies involve reading across multiple and hybrid semiotic fields and being able critically and hermeneutically to process print, graphics, images, and perhaps moving images and sounds. The term "hybridity" suggests the combination and interaction of diverse media and the need to synthesize the various forms in an active process of the construction of meaning. Reading a music video, for instance, involves processing images, music, spectacle, and sometimes narrative in a multisemiotic process that simultaneously draws on diverse aesthetic forms. Interacting with a Web site or CD-ROM involves scanning text, graphics, and often moving images and clicking onto the fields that one seeks to peruse and appropriate. This might involve combining video, audio, print, and graphics in new interactive learning or entertainment environments.

While traditional literacies involve practices in contexts that are governed by rules and conventions, the conventions and rules of multiliteracies are currently evolving, so their pedagogies are a new although quite bustling and competitive field. Multimedia fields are not entirely new, however. Multisemiotic textuality was first evident in newspapers (consider the difference between the *New York Times* and *USA Today* in terms of image, text, color graphics, design, and content) and is now evident in textbooks that are much more visual, graphic, and multimodal than the previously linear and discursive texts of old. But CD-ROMs, Web sites, and new multimedia are the most distinctively multimodal and multisemiotic forms. These sites are the new frontier of learning and literacy, the great challenge to education for the millennium. As we proceed into the next century, we need to theorize the literacies necessary to navigate and interact in these new multimedia environments and to gain the skills that will enable us to learn, work, and create in new cultural spaces and domains.

Parenthetically, I might note that we are soon going to have to rethink SATs and standard tests in relation to the new technologies; having the literacy and skills successfully to navigate, communicate, work, and create within computer and multimedia cultures is quite different from reading and writing in the mode of print literacy, and while this mode of literacy continues to be of utmost importance, it is sublated within multiliteracy, so eventually an entirely different sort of test is going to need to be devised to register individuals' multiliteracy competency and to predict success in a new technological and educational environment.[6]

Thus, in my expanded conception, computer literacy involves technical abilities concerning developing basic typing skills, mastering computer programs, accessing information, and using computer technologies for a variety of purposes ranging from verbal communication to artistic expression to political debate. There are ever more hybrid implosions between media and computer culture as audio and video material becomes part of the Internet, as CD-ROMs and multimedia develop, and as new technologies become part and parcel of the home, school, and workplace. Therefore the skills of decoding images, sounds, and spectacle learned in critical media literacy training can also be valuable as part of computer literacy as well. Furthermore, print literacy takes on increasing importance in the computer world, as one needs critically to scrutinize and scroll tremendous amounts of information, putting new emphasis on developing reading and writing abilities. In fact, Internet discussion groups, chat rooms, e-mail, and various forums require writing skills in which a new emphasis on the importance of clarity and precision is emerging as communications proliferate. In this context of information saturation, it becomes an ethical imperative not to contribute to cultural and information overload and to communicate one's thoughts and feelings concisely.

In a certain sense, computers are becoming the technological equivalent of Hegel's Absolute Idea, able to absorb everything into their form and medium. Computers are now not only repositories of text and print-based data, but also contain a wealth of images, multimedia sights and sounds, and interactive environments that, like the media, are themselves a form of education that require a critical pedagogy of electronic, digitized culture and communication. From this conception, computer literacy is something like a Hegelian synthesis of print and visual literacy, technical skills, and media literacies brought together at a new and higher stage. While Postman and others produce a simplistic Manichean dichotomy between print and visual literacy, we need to learn to think dialectically, to read together text and image, to decipher sight and sound, and to develop forms of computer and multimedia literacy adequate to meet the exigencies of an increasingly high tech society.

Thus a postmodern pedagogy requires developing critical forms of print, media, computer, and multiliteracy, all of which are of crucial importance in the new technoculture of the present and fast-approaching future.[7] Whereas modern pedagogy tended to be specialized, fragmented, and differentiated and was focused on print culture, a postmodern pedagogy involves developing multiple literacies and critically analyzing, dissecting, and engaging a multiplicity of cultural forms, some of which are the products of new technologies and require developing new literacies to engage the new cultural forms and media. In fact, contemporary culture is marked by a proliferation of cultural machines which generate a panoply of diverse aesthetic artifacts within which we wander, trying to make our way through this forest of symbols. New multimedia literacies require the ability to scan, interact with, traverse, organize, and create new multimedia educational environments. Multimedia literacy thus involves not just reading, but interacting: clicking to move from one field to another if one is involved in a hypertext environment such as one finds on Web sites or CD-ROMs; capturing, saving, downloading, and perhaps printing material relevant to one's own projects; and maybe responding verbally or adding one's own material if it is a site that invites genuinely interactive participation.

In addition to the linear cognitive skills needed for traditional reading of print material, multimedia literacy thus requires a multisemiotic ability to read hypertexts that are often multidimensional, requiring the connecting of images, graphics, texts, and sometimes audio-video material. It also involves new forms of intertextuality and contextualizing multimedia material. Multimedia thus involves making connections between the complex and multilayered cyberworld and its connection with the real world. As Carmen Luke reminds us: "Since all meaning is situated relationally—that is, connected and cross-referenced to other media and genres, and to related meanings in other cultural contexts—a critical literacy relies on broad-based notions of intertextuality" (1997a, 10). Intertextuality draws attention to the complex ways that language, image, and types of texts are related to various genres, forms, narratives, and modes of meaning such as visual design.

Thus, on the one hand, one must learn to read multimedia forms that are themselves overlapping and interrelated, switching from text to graphics to video to audio, decoding in turn sight, sound, and text. In a global information environment, this may also involve switching from sites from one country to another requiring contextual understanding and literacy that is able to read and interact with people and sites from different cultures. As Carmen Luke puts it:

> [N]ew [forms of] virtual communication are emerging, which require an intertextual understanding of how meanings shift across media, genres, and cultural frames of reference. Whether one "visits" the Louvre on-line, joins an international newsgroup of parents of Downs Syndrome children, or visits the www site of an agricultural college in Kenya, cross-cultural understanding and "netiquette" is increasingly crucial for participating effectively in global communications. (Luke 1997a, 10)

Crucially, multimedia literacy should be contextual. It requires thematizing the background and power relations of cultural forms (that is, including analysis of the political economy of the media and technology, of how corporate organizations control production and dissemination, and how oppositional and alternative media and uses are possible; see Kellner 1995a), as well as the context and power relations of the specific media use in question (that is, the differences between television-watching in the classroom, at home with one's family, with one's friends, or alone; or the differences between computer use for research, data organization, e-mail, or playing games, and so on). Multimedia literacy also envisages new modes of collaborative work on research projects or Web sites, new forms of student/teacher participation and interaction, and new pedagogical uses for the new technologies which may often appear exotic in the present, but which will become increasingly commonplace in the future and will force a rethinking of education.

Finally, multiliteracy must become critical, and in response to excessive hype concerning new technologies and education, it is necessary to maintain the critical dimension. Rather than following such modern logic of either/or, we need to pursue the logic of both/and, seeing design and critique, deconstruction and reconstruction, as complementary and supplementary rather than as antithetical choices. Certainly, we need to design new technologies, pedagogies, and curricula for the future, and we should attempt to design new social and pedagogical relations as well, but we need to criticize misuse, inappropriate use, overinflated claims, and exclusions and oppressions involved in the introduction of new technologies into education. The critical dimension is needed more than ever; as we attempt to develop *new* teaching strategies and pedagogy, as we design new technologies and curricula, we must be constantly critical, practicing critique and self-criticism, putting in question our assumptions, discourses, and practices as we experimentally develop new literacies and pedagogy.

In such an experimental program, critique is obviously of fundamental importance. From the Deweyan perspective, progressive education involves experiment and the experimental method, which involves critique of limitations, failures, and flawed design. In discussing new technologies and multiliteracy, one also needs constantly to raise the questions: Whose interests are these new technologies and pedagogies serving? Are they serving all social groups and individuals? Who is being excluded, and why? We also need to raise the questions about whether new technologies and literacies are preparing students and citizens for the present and future and producing conditions for a more vibrant democratic society or simply reproducing existing inequalities and inequity.

Multiculturalism and Multiple Literacies: Some Concluding Remarks

And so we need to begin learning how to read and deploy these new multimedia environments and interact with these fascinating and seductive cultural forms whose massive impact on our lives we have only begun to understand. Surely education should attend to the new multimedia culture and teach how to read and interact with new computer and multimedia environments as part of new forms of multiple literacy. Such an effort would be part of a new critical pedagogy that attempts to empower individuals critically so that they can analyze and criticize the emerging technoculture as well as participate in its cultural forums and sites.

Thus, in addition to the critical media literacy, print literacy, computer and information literacy, and multimedia literacies discussed above, *multiple literacies* involve a multiplicity of literacies which enable us to understand and interact within our increasingly complex cultural and social worlds, as well as to better understand our bodies and natural environment. While *multiliteracy* involves cultivating the abilities to navigate multimedia and the multisemiotic and multimodal hybrid cultural fields of the new technologies, which I discussed in the last section, *multiple literacies* involve gaining skills in interpreting and acting within one's culture and society, and thus encompasses development of capacities for cultural literacy, social literacy, ecoliteracy, and the like, encompassing the fields of the natural and social sciences.

Since a multicultural society is the context of education in the contemporary moment, new forms of social interaction and cultural awareness are needed that appreciate differences, multiplicity, and diversity. Therefore, expanded social and cultural literacy is needed that appreciates the cultural heritage, histories, and contributions of a diversity of groups. Thus, whereas one can agree with E.D. Hirsch (1987) that we need to be literate in our shared cultural heritage, we also need to become culturally literate in cultures that have been hitherto invisible, as Henry Louis Gates and his colleagues have been arguing in their proposals for a multicultural education (1996).

Social literacy should also be taught throughout the educational systems, ranging from how to relate and get along with a variety of individuals, how to negotiate differences, and how to resolve conflicts, to how to communicate and socially interact in a diversity of situations. Social literacy also involves ethical training in values and norms, delineating proper and improper individual and social values. It also requires knowledge of contemporary societies and thus overlaps with social and natural science training. In fact, given the tremendous role of science and technology in the contemporary world, given the threats to the environment and the need to preserve and enhance the natural as well as social and cultural worlds, it is scandalous how illiterate the entire society is concerning science, nature, and even our own bodies. An ecoliteracy should thus appropriately teach competency in interpreting and interacting with our natural environment, ranging from our own bodies to natural habitats such as forests and deserts.

The challenge for education today is thus to develop multiple literacies to empower students and citizens to use the new technologies to enhance their lives and to create a better culture and society based on respect for multicultural difference and aimed at fuller democratic participation of individuals and groups largely excluded from wealth and power in the previous modern society. A positive postmodernity would thus involve creation of a more egalitarian and democratic society in which more individuals and groups were empowered to participate. The great danger facing us, of course, is that the new technologies will increase the current inequalities based on class, gender, and racial divisions. So far, the privileged groups have had more direct and immediate access to the new technologies. It is therefore a challenge of education today to provide access to the new technologies, and to the literacies needed for competence, to excluded or oppressed individuals and groups in order to overcome some of the divisions and inequalities that have plagued contemporary societies during the entire modern age.

What I am trying to do in this paper, and my work as a whole, is to connect the phenomena of the new technologies and technological revolution with the multicultural explosion and drama of conflicting ethnicities, classes, genders, and so on, so that differences can create diversity, tolerance, and an enhanced and strengthened democracy and society, and not conflict, intolerance, division, and violence. So it is not just a question of talking about media literacy, computer literacy, multiliteracy and so forth from a technological viewpoint, but of thinking together new technologies and multiculturalism with technological and social transformation. Thus I am interested in how the new technologies and literacies can serve the interests of multiculturalism, making teachers, students, and citizens aware of how the new technologies are transforming everything from education to work to war, the challenges involved, the new literacies needed, and the opportunities for educational reform and social reconstruction.

To be sure, legitimate concerns have been raised in regard to the possibilities that new technologies will increase the regnant inequalities in relation to privileged class, gender, and racial groupings. As is well known, the original computer culture was largely inhabited by white, male middle- to upper-class "geeks," or "nerds"; the culture tended to exclude women, people of color, and members of classes without access to computer technologies. As new technologies become a more central aspect of schooling, work, and everyday life, however, more and more women and members of groups previously excluded from computer culture are now becoming participants as they gain access to computers and new technologies in schools, at the workplace, and at home. Of course, the question of access to new technologies becomes increasingly important, as work, education, and every other aspect of social life are undergoing transformation, making multiliteracy essential to work, cultural, educational, and political exigencies of the future. If the previously disadvantaged and marginalized groups will not gain access to the new technologies, class, gender, race, and other divisions will exponentially grow, creating ever more virulent divisions and the prospects of social upheaval and turbulence.

Yet there are aspects of the forms of literacy being spawned by new technologies and multimedia culture that are potentially democratizing and empowering for individuals and groups previously on the bottom end of prevailing configurations of class, gender, and racial power. The increased informality, closeness to speech patterns, and spontaneity of e-mail composition, participation in chat rooms, and computer-mediated communications and forums provide access to individuals and groups whose literacies and modes of writing were deemed inferior or deficient from more standard classical print-media perspectives. Indeed, the openness of many forums of computer-mediated communication, the possibility of ever more individuals being able to produce their own Web sites, and access to volumes of information previously limited to those who had access to elite libraries potentially democratize education, cultural production, and participation in cultural and political dialogue.

Thus issues of access and exclusion in relation to new technologies and new literacies are crucial to realizing the promises of democracy. Yet there are potential threats in the new technologies. There is the danger that youth will become totally immersed in a new world of high-tech experience and lose their social connectedness and ability to communicate interpersonally and relate concretely to other people. Statistics suggest that more and more sectors of youth are able to access cyberspace and that college students with Internet accounts are spending as much as four hours a day in the new realm of technological experience.[8] Moreover, the media have been generating a moral panic concerning allegedly growing dangers in cyberspace, with lurid stories of young boys and girls lured into dangerous sex or running away from home, endless accounts of how pornography on the Internet is proliferating, and the publicizing of calls for increasing control, censorship, and surveillance of communication—usually by politicians or others who are computer-illiterate. The solution, however, is not to ban access to new technologies, but to teach students and citizens how to use these technologies so that they can be employed for productive and creative rather than problematical ends.

To be sure, there are dangers in cyberspace as well as elsewhere, but the threats to adolescents are significantly higher from family violence and abuse than from seduction by strangers on the Internet. And while there is a flourishing trade in pornography on the Internet, this material has become increasingly available in a variety of venues, from the local video shop to the newspaper stand, so it seems unfair to demonize the Internet. Thus attempts at Internet censorship are part of the attack on youth which would circumscribe their rights to obtain entertainment and information and create their own subcultures.[9] Consequently, devices such as the V-chip, which would exclude sex and violence on television, or means to block computer access to objectionable material are more an expression of adult hysteria and moral panic than responses to genuine dangers faced by youth—such dangers certainly exist, but much more strikingly in the real world than in the sphere of hyperreality.

Throughout this century, there has been a demonization of new media and forms of media culture ranging from comic books to film to popular music to television and now to the Internet. As Jenkins argues (1997), this demonization is supported by an assumption of the innocence of childhood, that children are merely passive receptacles, easily seduced by cultural images, and in need of protection from nefarious and harmful cultural content. But as Jenkins contends (1997, 30ff), the myth of "childhood innocence" strips children of active agency, of being capable of any thoughts of their own, of having the ability to decode and process media materials themselves. Of course, children need media education, they need to be involved in an active learning process concerning their culture, but censorship and vilification of media do not help young people become active critics and participants in their culture.

Accordingly, Jon Katz (1996) has argued for children's "cyber-rights," arguing that our youth's access to Internet cyberculture and media culture in general is necessary for their participation in the larger culture and their own education and development. Mastery of the culture can be the difference between economic success and hardship, and the Internet in particular allows participation in many dimensions of social and cultural life as well as the cultivation of technical skills that can help children in later life.

Therefore, it is necessary to divest ourselves of myths of childhood innocence and the passivity of children's media consumption, positing instead the possibility of active and creative use of media material in which media education is seen as part of youth's self-development and constitution. Accordingly, Henry Jenkins proposes

> a new kind of radical media education based on the assumption that children are active participants within popular culture rather than passive victims. We need to help our children become more critically reflective about the media they use and the popular culture they embrace, yet we can only achieve this by recognizing and respecting their existing investments, skills, and knowledge as media users. In the end, our goals must be not to protect our children but to empower them. (1997, 31)

Thus, rather than demonizing and rejecting new technologies out of hand, we should criticize their misuse but also see how they can be used constructively for positive ends. In studying the kaleidoscopic array of discourses which characterize the new technologies, I am rather bemused by the extent to which either they expose a technophilic discourse which presents new technologies as our salvation, that will solve all our problems, or they embody a technophobic discourse that sees technology as our damnation, demonizing it as the major source of all our problems. It appears that similarly one-sided and contrasting discourses greeted the introduction of other new technologies this century, often hysterically. It is indeed curious that whenever a new technology is introduced, a polarized response emerges in relation to its novelty and differences from previous technologies. New technologies seem to attract both advocates and champions and critics and detractors. This was historically the case with film, radio, TV, and is now the case with computers.

Film, for instance, was celebrated by early theorists as providing new documentary depiction of reality, even redemption of reality, a new art form, new modes of mass education and entertainment—as well as demonized for promoting sexual promiscuity, juvenile delinquency and crime, violence, and copious other forms of immorality and evils. Its demonization led in the United States to a Production Code that rigorously regulated the content of Hollywood film from 1934 until the 1950s and 1960s—no open-mouthed kissing was permitted, crime could not pay, drug use or attacks on religion could not be portrayed, and a censorship office rigorously surveyed all films to make sure that no subversive or illicit content emerged (Kellner 1997).

Similar extreme hopes and fears were projected onto radio and television. It appears whenever there are new technologies, people project all sorts of fantasies, fears, hopes, and dreams onto them, and I believe that this is now happening with computers and new multimedia technologies. It is indeed striking that if one looks at the literature on new technologies—and especially computers—it is either highly celebatory and technophilic or sharply derogatory and technophobic. A critical theory of technology, however, and critical pedagogy should avoid either demonizing or deifying the new technologies and should instead develop pedagogies that will help us use the technologies to enhance education and life and to criticize the limitations and false promises made on behalf of new technologies.

Certainly there is no doubt that the cyberspace of computer worlds contains as much banality and stupidity as real life, and one can waste much time in useless activity. But compared to the bleak and violent urban worlds portrayed in rap music and youth films like *Kids* (1995), the technological worlds are havens of information, entertainment, interaction, and connection where youth can gain valuable skills, knowledge, and power necessary to survive the postmodern adventure. Youth can create new, more multiple and flexible selves in cyberspace, as well as new subcultures and communities. Indeed, it is exciting to cruise the Internet and to discover how many interesting Web sites young people and others have established, often containing valuable educational and political material. There is, of course, the danger that corporate and commercial interests will come to colonize the Internet, but it is likely that there will continue to be spaces where individuals can empower themselves and create their own communities and identities. A main challenge for youth (and others) is to learn to use the Internet for positive cultural and political projects, rather than just for entertainment and passive consumption.

Reflecting on the growing social importance of computers and new technologies makes it clear that it is of essential importance for youth today to gain various kinds of literacy to empower themselves for the emerging new cybersociety (this is true of teachers and adults as well). To survive in a postmodern world, individuals of all ages need to gain skills of media and computer literacy to enable ourselves to negotiate the overload of media images and spectacles; we all need to learn technological skills to use the new media and computer technologies to subsist in the new high-tech economy and to form our own cultures and communities; and youth especially need street smarts and survival skills to cope with the drugs, violence, and uncertainty in today's predatory culture (McLaren 1995), as well as new forms of multiple literacy.

It is therefore extremely important for the future of democracy to make sure that youth of all classes, races, genders, and regions gain access to new technology, receiving training in media and computer literacy skills in order to provide the opportunities to enter the high-tech job market and society of the future and to prevent an exacerbation of class, gender, and race inequalities. And while multiple forms of new literacies will be necessary, traditional print literacy skills are all the more important in a cyber-age of word processing, information gathering, and Internet communication. Moreover, what I am calling multiple literacy involves training in philosophy, ethics, value thinking, and the humanities, which I would argue is necessary now more then ever. In fact, *how* the Internet and new technologies will be used depends on the overall education of youth and the skills and interests they bring to the new technologies, which can be used to access educational and valuable cultural and political material or pornography and the banal wares of cybershopping malls.

Thus, the concept of multiple literacies and the postmodern pedagogy that I envisage would argue that it is not a question of either/or—for instance, either print literacy or multimedia literacy, either the classical curriculum or a new curriculum—but, rather, a question of both/and that preserves the best from classical education, that enhances emphasis on print literacy, but that also develops new literacies to engage the new technologies. Obviously, cyberlife is just one dimension of experience, and one still needs to learn to interact in a "real world" of school, jobs, relationships, politics, and other people. Youth—indeed, all of us!—need to learn to interact in many dimensions of social reality and to gain a multiplicity of forms of literacy and skills that will enable us to create identities, relationships, and communities that will nurture and develop our full spectrum of potentialities and satisfy a wide array of needs. Our lives are more multidimensional than ever, and part of the postmodern adventure is learning to live in a variety of social spaces and to adapt to intense change and transformation. Education, too, must meet these challenges and utilize new technologies to both improve education and devise pedagogical strategies in which those new technologies can be deployed to create a more democratic and egalitarian multicultural society.

Acknowledgments

An earlier and different version of this study appeared in *Educational Theory*, vol. 48, no. 1 Winter, 1998, pp. 103–122, and I am grateful to its editor Nicholas Burbules for discussion that helped develop my ideas. Another version was presented at UCLA in February 26, 1998, at my Kneller Chair Inaugural Lecture, and I am grateful to members of the audience for discussion of the issues in this chapter. For ongoing discussions of the issues in this chapter, I am especially grateful to Rhonda Hammer and Allan and Carmen Luke.

Notes

1. Carson and Friedman 1995 contains studies dealing with the use of media to deal with multicultural education. Examples of teaching media literacy which I draw on include Masterman 1989; Schwoch, White, and Reilly 1992; Fleming 1993; Giroux 1994 and 1996; Sholle and Densky 1994; McLaren, Hammer, Sholle, and Reilly 1995; McLaren 1995; Kellner 1995a; Luke 1997a and 1997b. See also the work of Barry Duncan and the Canadian Association for Media Literacy (website: http://www.nald. ca/province/que/litcent/media.htm).

2. See Hammer (1995), who indicates how student video projects can empower students to learn the conventions and techniques of media production and use the media to engage in self-development and the creation of counterhegemonic culture. Whereas film production involves heavy capital investment and expensive technology, and thus restricts access, video production is more accessible to students, easier to use, and enables a broad spectrum of students actually to produce media texts, providing alternative modes of expression and communication. Video technology thus provides access to a large number of voices excluded from cultural production and expression, materializing the multicultural dream of democratic culture as a dialogue of a rainbow of voices, visions, ideas, and experiences.

3. In 1991, the Association of Supervision and Curriculum Development (ASCD) concluded: "Information literacy equips individuals to take advantage of the opportunities inherent in the global information society. Information literacy should be a part of every student's educational experience. ASCD urges schools, colleges, and universities to integrate information literacy programs into learning programs for all students." The project has been taken up by the National Forum on Information Literacy (NFIL). Building on these projects, it is important to see that computer literacy involves developing a wide range of information literacies and that the latter also involve developing multiliteracies that access and interpret images, media spectacles, narratives, and new cultural sites in an expanded concept of information that resists its reduction to print paradigms alone.

4. For other recent conceptions of multimedia literacy, see the discussions of literacies needed for reading hypertext in Burbules and Callister 1996; Luke 1997a; and the concept of hyperreading in Burbules, 1997.

5. There are two major modes and concepts of hypertext; one that is primarily literary and involves new literary/writing strategies and practices, and one that is more multimedia, multisemiotic, and multimodal. Hypertext was initially seen as an innovative and exciting new mode of communication that increased potentials for writers to explore new modes of textuality and expression and to expand the field of writing. As multimedia hypertext developed, it was soon theorized as a multisemiotic and multimodal form of communication. Yet some early advocates of

hypertext attacked the emergence of the World Wide Web as a debased medium which brought back into play the field of earlier media, such as television, forcing the word to renegotiate its power with the image and spectacles of sight and sound, once again decentering the written word.

6. While I have not myself researched the policy literature on this issue, in the many discussions of SAT tests and their biases which I have read, I have not encountered critiques that indicate the obsolescence of many standardized tests in a new technological environment and the need to come up with new testing procedures based on the new cultural and social fields that we are increasingly immersed in. I would predict that proposals for devising such tests will emerge and that this issue will be hotly debated and contested in the future.

7. For my take on postmodern theory, see Kellner 1989b and 1989c; Best and Kellner 1991, 1997, and forthcoming; and my Web site: http://ccwf.cc.utexas.edu/~kellner/pm/pm.html. For an earlier sketch of postmodern pedagogy, see Kellner 1989c.

8. *Wired* magazine is a good source for statistics and data concerning growing computer and Internet use among all sectors of youth and documents the vicissitudes of cyberculture. Studies of Internet addiction are starting to emerge. The *Chronicle of Higher Education* has reported that "Students are unusually vulnerable to Internet addiction according to a new quarterly journal called *Cyberpsychology and Behavior*" (February 6, 1998, A25). The study indicated that students from 18–22 are especially at risk and points to a correlation between high Internet use and a dropout rate that more than doubled among heavy users. Accordingly, the University of Washington has limited the amount of Internet time available to students to cut down on overuse, and several other colleges have set up support groups for Internet addiction. But such studies do not record the benefits of heavy Internet use or indicate potentially higher productive uses than, say, watching television, drinking, or engaging in traditional forms of collegiate socializing.

9. On the attack on youth in contemporary society and culture, see Giroux 1996 and 1997; Manes 1996; and Best and Kellner, forthcoming.

References

Appiah, K. Anthony. 1997. "The Multiculturalist Misunderstanding." *New York Review of Books* (October 9): 30–36.

Best, Steven, and Kellner, Douglas. 1991. *Postmodern Theory: Critical Interrogations*. London and New York: MacMillan and Guilford Press.

Best, Steven, and Kellner, Douglas. 1997. *The Postmodern Turn*. New York: Guilford Press.

Best, Steven, and Kellner, Douglas. Forthcoming. *The Postmodern Adventure*. New York: Guilford Press.

Burbules, Nicholas C. 1997. "Rhetorics of the Web: Hyperreading and Critical Literacy in Page to Screen." In *Taking Literacy into the Electronic Era*. Ilana Snyder, ed. New South Wales: Allen and Unwin, 102–122.

Burbules, Nicholas C., and Callister, Thomas. 1996. "Knowledge at the Crossroads: Some Alternative Futures of Hypertext Learning Environments." *Educational Theory* 46, no. 1 (Winter): 23–50.

Carson, Diane, and Lester D. Friedman. 1995. *Shared Differences. Multicultural Media and Practical Pedagogy*. Urbana and Chicago: University of Illinois Press.

Cazden, Courtney, Cope, Bill, Fairclough, Norman, Gee, James, Kalantzis, Mary, Kress, Gunter, Luke, Allan, Luke, Carmen, Michaels, Sarah, and Nakata, Martin. 1996. "A Pedagogy of Multiliteracies: Designing Social Futures." *Harvard Educational Review* 66: 60–92.

Dines, Gail, and Jean Humez, eds. 1995. *Gender, Race, and Class in Media*. Thousand Oaks, CA, and London: Sage.

Fiske, John. 1993. *Power Plays. Power Works*. New York and London: Verso.

Fiske, John. 1994. *Media Matters*. Minneapolis, MN: University of Minnesota Press.

Fleming, Dan. 1993. *Media Teaching*. Oxford: Basil Blackwell.

Gates, Henry Louis, Jr. 1996. *Loose Canons: Notes on the Culture Wars*. New York: Oxford University Press.

Giroux, Henry. 1992. *Border Crossing*. New York: Routledge.

Giroux, Henry. 1993. *Living Dangerously. Multiculturalism and the Politics of Difference*. New York: Peter Lang.

Giroux, Henry. 1994. *Disturbing Pleasures*. New York: Routledge.

Giroux, Henry. 1996. *Fugitive Cultures: Race, Violence, and Youth*. New York: Routledge.

Giroux, Henry. 1997. *Channel Surfing: Race Talk and the Destruction of Today's Youth*. New York: St. Martin's Press.

Giroux, Henry, and Peter McLaren, eds. 1994. *Between Borders. Pedagogy and the Politics of Cultural Studies*. New York: Routledge.

Giroux, Henry, and Shannon, Patrick. 1997. *Education and Cultural Studies*. London and New York: Routledge.

Grossberg, Lawrence. 1992. *We Gotta Get Out of This Place*. New York and London: Routledge.

Grossberg, Lawrence, Nelson, Cary, and Treichler, Paula, eds. 1992. *Cultural Studies*. New York: Routledge.

Hammer, Rhonda. 1995. "Strategies for Media Literacy." In *Rethinking Media Literacy. A Critical Pedagogy of Representation*. Peter McLaren, Rhonda Hammer, David Sholle, and Susan Reilly, eds. New York: Peter Lang, 225–235.

Hirsch, E.D. 1987. *Cultural Literacy*. New York: Random House.

Innes, Harold. 1951. *The Bias of Communication*. Toronto: University of Toronto Press.

Jenkins, Henry. 1997. "Empowering Children in the Digital Age: Towards a Radical Media Pedagogy." *Radical Teacher* 50: 30–35.

Katz, Jon. 1996. "The Rights of Kids in the Digital Age." *Wired* (July 1996): 120ff.

Kellner, Douglas. 1989a. *Jean Baudrillard: From Marxism to Postmodernism and Beyond*. Cambridge, UK, and Palo Alto, CA: Polity Press and Stanford University Press.

Kellner, Douglas, ed. 1989b. *Postmodernism/Jameson/Critique*. Washington, DC: Maisonneuve Press.

Kellner, Douglas. 1989c. "Reading Images Critically: Toward a Postmodern Pedagogy." *Journal of Education* vol. 170, no. 3: 31–52.

Kellner, Douglas. 1990. *Television and the Crisis of Democracy.* Boulder, CO: Westview.

Kellner, Douglas. 1992. *The Persian Gulf TV War.* Boulder, CO: Westview.

Kellner, Douglas. 1995a. *Media Culture.* London and New York: Routledge.

Kellner, Douglas. 1995b. "Cultural Studies, Multiculturalism, and Media Culture." In *Gender, Race, and Class in Media.* Gail Dines and Jean Humez, eds. Thousand Oaks, CA, and London: Sage, 5–17.

Kellner, Douglas. 1995c. "Intellectuals and New Technologies." *Media, Culture, and Society* vol. 17: 201–217.

Kellner, Douglas. 1997. "Hollywood and Society: Critical Perspectives." In *Oxford Encyclopaedia of Film.* John Hill, ed. Oxford: Oxford University Press.

Kellner, Douglas, and Michael Ryan. 1988. *Camera Politica: The Politics and Ideology of Contemporary Hollywood Film.* Bloomington, IN: Indiana University Press.

Lewis, Jon. 1996. "Practice What You Preach." *Afterimage* (Summer 1996): 25–26.

Luke, Carmen. 1996. "Reading Gender and Culture in Media Discourses and Texts." In *The Literacy Lexicon.* G. Bull and M. Anstey, eds. New York and Sydney: Prentice-Hall.

Luke, Carmen. 1997a. *Technological Literacy.* Melbourne: National Languages and Literacy Institute, Adult Literacy Network.

Luke, Carmen. 1997b. "Media Literacy and Cultural Studies." In *Constructing Critical Literacies.* Sandy Muspratt, Allan Luke, and Peter Freebody, eds. Cresskill, NY: Hampton Press, 19–50.

Manes, Mike A. 1996. *The Scapegoat Generation. America's War on Adolescents.* Monroe, ME: Common Courage Press.

Masterman, Len. 1989 [1985]. *Teaching the Media.* London and New York: Routledge.

McLaren, Peter. 1995. *Critical Pedagogy and Predatory Culture.* London and New York: Routledge.

McLaren, Peter. 1996. *Revolutionary Multiculturalism.* London and New York: Routledge.

McLaren, Peter, Hammer, Rhonda, Sholle, David, and Reilly, Susan. 1995. *Rethinking Media Literacy. A Critical Pedagogy of Representation.* New York: Peter Lang.

McLuhan, Marshall. 1964. *Understanding Media: The Extensions of Man.* New York: Signet Books.

Postman, Neil. 1985. *Amusing Ourselves to Death.* New York: Viking-Penguin.

Postman, Neil. 1992. *Technopoly: The Surrender of Culture to Technology.* New York: Random House.

Schwoch, James, White, Mimi, and Reilly, Susan. 1992. *Media Knowledge.* Albany, NY: SUNY Press.

Sholle, David, and Denski, Stan. 1994. *Media Education and the (Re)Production of Culture.* Westport, CN: Bergin & Garvey.

III THE DISCOURSE OF THEORY

Michael W. Apple

THE SHOCK OF THE REAL
Critical Pedagogies and Rightist Reconstructions

Gritty Materialities

Much of the literature on "critical pedagogies" has been politically and theoretically important and has helped us make a number of gains. However, too often it has not been sufficiently connected to the ways in which the current conservative restoration both has altered common sense and has transformed the material and ideological conditions surrounding schooling. It thereby sometimes becomes a form of what may best be called "romantic possibilitarian" rhetoric (Whitty 1974), in which the language of possibility substitutes for a consistent tactical analysis of what the balance of forces actually is and what is necessary to change it.

In this chapter, I examine the ways in which the social and cultural terrain of educational policy and discourse has been altered "on the ground" so to speak. I argue that we need to make closer connections between our theoretical and critical discourses, on the one hand, and the real transformations that are currently shifting educational policies and practices in fundamentally rightist directions, on the other. Thus part of my discussion will need to be conceptual, but part of it will appropriately need to be empirical in order for me to pull together what is known about the real and material effects of the shift to the right in education.

My focus on the "gritty materialities" of these effects is not meant to dismiss the importance of theoretical interventions. Nor is it meant to suggest that dominant discourses should not be constantly interrupted by the creative gains that have emerged from various neo-Marxist, postmodern, poststructural, postcolonial, queer, and other communities. Indeed, critical and revolutionary pedagogies *require* the fundamental interruption of common sense. However, while the construction of new theories and utopian visions is important, it is equally crucial to base these theories and visions in an unromantic appraisal of the material and discursive terrain that now exists. Common sense is already being radically altered, but not in directions that any of us on the left would find comforting. Without an analysis of such transformations and of the balance of forces that have created such discomforting alterations, without an analysis of the tensions, differential relations of power, and contradictions within it, we are left with increasingly elegant new theoretical formulations, but with a less-than-elegant understanding of the field of social power (Bourdieu 1994) on which they operate.

Right Turn

In his influential history of curriculum debates, Herbert Kliebard has documented that educational issues have consistently involved major conflicts and compromises among groups with competing visions of "legitimate" knowledge, what counts as "good" teaching and learning, and what is a "just" society (Kliebard 1986). That such conflicts have deep roots in conflicting views of racial, class, and gender justice in education and the larger society is ratified in even more critical recent work as well (Selden forthcoming). While I believe neither that these competing visions have ever had equal holds on the imagination of educators or the general citizenry nor that they have ever had equal power to effect their visions, it is still clear that no analysis of education can be fully serious without placing at its very core a sensitivity to the ongoing struggles that constantly shape the terrain on which education operates.

Today is no different from in the past. A "new" set of compromises has been found and a new alliance or power bloc has been formed that has increasing influence in education and all things social. This power bloc combines multiple fractions of capital that are committed to neoliberal marketized solutions to educational problems, neoconservative intellectuals who want a "return" to higher standards and a "common culture," authoritarian, populist, religious fundamentalists who are deeply worried about secularity and the preservation of their own traditions, and particular fractions of the professionally oriented new middle class who are committed to the ideology and techniques of accountability, measurement, and "management." While there are clear tensions and conflicts within this alliance, in general its overall aims are in providing the educational conditions believed necessary both for increasing international competitiveness, profit, and discipline and for returning us to a romanticized past of the "ideal" home, family, and school (Apple 1993, 1996).

In essence, the new alliance has integrated education into a wider set of ideological commitments. The objectives in education are the same as those which guide its economic and social welfare goals. They include the dramatic expansion of that eloquent fiction, the free market; the drastic reduction of government responsibility for social needs; the reinforcement of intensely competitive structures of mobility both inside and outside the school; the lowering of people's expectations for economic security; the "disciplining" of culture and the body; and the popularization of what is clearly a form of social-Darwinist thinking, as the recent popularity of *The Bell Curve* (Herrnstein and Murray 1994; see also Kincheloe and Steinberg 1996) so obviously and distressingly indicates.

The seemingly contradictory discourses of competition, markets, and choice, on the one hand, and accountability, performance objectives, standards, national testing, and national curriculum, on the other, have created such a din that it is hard to hear anything else. As I have shown in *Cultural Politics and Education* (Apple 1996), these tendencies actually oddly reinforce each other and help cement conservative educational positions into our daily lives.

While lamentable, the changes that are occurring present an exceptional opportunity for serious critical reflection. Here I am not speaking of merely the accumulation of studies to promote the academic careers of researchers, although the accumulation of serious studies is not unimportant. Rather, I am suggesting that in a time of radical social and educational change it is crucial to document the processes and effects of the various and sometimes contradictory elements of the conservative restoration and of the ways in which they are mediated, compromised with, accepted, used in different ways by different groups for their own purposes, and/or struggled over in the policies and practices of people's daily educational lives (Ransom 1995, 427). I want to give a sense in this chapter of how this might be happening in current "reforms" such as marketization and national curricula and national testing. For those interested in critical educational policies and practices, not to do this means that we act without understanding the shifting relations of power that are constructing and reconstructing the social field of power. While Gramsci's saying, "Pessimism of the intellect, optimism of the will," has a powerful resonance to it and is useful for mobilization and for not losing hope, it would be foolish to substitute rhetorical slogans for the fuller analysis that is undoubtedly required if we are to be successful.

New Markets, Old Traditions

Behind a good deal of the New Right's emerging discursive ensemble was a position that emphasized "a culturalist construction of the nation as a (threatened) haven for white (Christian) traditions and values" (Gillborn 1997a, 2). This involved the construction of an imagined national past that is at least partly mythologized, and then employing it to castigate the present. Gary McCulloch argues that the nature of the historical images of schooling has changed. Dominant imagery of education as being "safe, domesticated, and progressive" (that is, as leading toward progress and social/personal improvement) has shifted to become "threatening, estranged, and regressive" (McCulloch 1997, 80). The past is no longer the source of stability but a mark of failure, disappointment, and loss. This is seen most vividly in the attacks on the "progressive orthodoxy" that supposedly now reigns supreme in classrooms in many nations (Hirsch 1996).

For example, in Britain—though much the same is echoed in the United States, Australia, and elsewhere—Michael Jones, the political editor of the *Sunday Times,* recalls the primary school of his day.

> Primary school was a happy time for me. About 40 of us sat at fixed wooden desks with ink wells and moved from them only with grudging permission. Teacher sat in a higher desk in front of us and moved only to the blackboard. She smelled of scent and inspired awe. (Quoted in McCulloch 1997, 78)

The mix of metaphors invoking discipline, scent (visceral and almost "natural"), and awe is fascinating. But he goes on, lamenting the past thirty years of "reform" that transformed primary schools. Speaking of his own children's experience, Jones says:

> My children spent their primary years in a showplace school where they were allowed to wander around at will, develop their real individuality and dodge the 3Rs. It was all for the best, we were assured. But it was not. (Quoted in McCulloch 1997, 78)

For Jones, the "dogmatic orthodoxy" of progressive education "had led directly to educational and social decline." Only the rightist reforms instituted in the 1980s and 1990s could halt and then reverse this decline (McCulloch 1997, 78). Only then could the imagined past return.

Much the same is being said on this side of the Atlantic. These sentiments are echoed in the public pronouncements of such figures as William Bennett, E.D. Hirsch, Jr., and others, all of whom seem to believe that progressivism is now in the dominant position in educational policy and practice and has destroyed a valued past. All of them believe that only by tightening control over curriculum and teaching (and students, of course), restoring "our" lost traditions, making education more disciplined and competitive, as they are certain it was in the past—only then can we have effective schools. These figures are joined by others who have similar criticisms, but who instead turn to a different past for a different future. Their past is less that of scent and awe and authority, but one of market "freedom." For them, nothing can be accomplished—even the restoration of awe and authority—without setting the market loose on schools so as to ensure that only "good" ones survive.

We should understand that these policies are radical transformations. If they had come from the other side of the political spectrum, they would have been ridiculed in many ways, given the ideological tendencies in our nations. Further, not only are these policies based on a romanticized pastoral past; these reforms have not been notable for their grounding in research findings. Indeed, when research has been used, it has often either served as a rhetoric of justification for preconceived beliefs about the supposed efficacy of markets or regimes of tight accountability or has been based—as in the case of Chubb's and Moe's much publicized work on marketization (Chubb and Moe 1990)—on quite flawed research (see, for example, Whitty 1997).

Yet, no matter how radical some of these proposed "reforms" are and no matter how weak the empirical basis of their support, they have now redefined the terrain of debate of all things educational. After years of conservative attacks and mobilizations, it has become clear that "ideas that were once deemed fanciful, unworkable—or just plain extreme" are now increasingly being seen as commonsensical (Gillborn 1997b, 357).

Tactically, the reconstruction of common sense that has been accomplished has proven to be extremely effective. For example, there are clear discursive strategies being employed here, ones that are characterized by "plain speaking" and speaking in a language that "everyone can understand." (I do not wish to be wholly negative about this. The importance of these things is something many "progressive" educators, including many writers on critical pedagogy, have yet to understand [Apple 1988].) These strategies also involve not only presenting one's own position as "common sense," but also usually tacitly implying that there is something of a conspiracy among one's opponents to deny the truth or to say only that which is "fashionable" (Gillborn 1997b, 353). As Gillborn notes:

> This is a powerful technique. First, it assumes that there are no *genuine* arguments against the chosen position; any opposing views are thereby positioned as false, insincere or self-serving. Second, the technique presents the speaker as someone brave or honest enough to speak the (previously) unspeakable. Hence, the moral high ground is assumed and opponents are further denigrated. (Gillborn 1997b, 353)

It is hard to miss these characteristics in some of the conservative literature, such as Herrnstein and Murray's (1994) publicizing of the unthinkable "truth" about genetics and intelligence or E.D. Hirsch's (1996) latest "tough" discussion of the destruction of "serious" schooling by progressive educators.

Markets and Performance

Let us take as an example of the ways in which all this operates one element of the conservative restoration—the neoliberal claim that the invisible hand of the market will inexorably lead to better schools. As Roger Dale reminds us, "the market" acts as a metaphor rather than an explicit guide for action. It is not denotative but connotative. Thus it must itself be "marketed" to those who will exist in it and live with its effects (Roger Dale, quoted in Menter et al. 1997, 27). Markets are marketed, are made legitimate, by a depoliticizing strategy. They are said to be natural and neutral and governed by effort and merit. And those opposed to them are, by definition, hence also opposed to effort and merit. Markets, as well, are supposedly less subject to political interference and the weight of bureaucratic procedures. Plus they are grounded in the rational choices of individual actors (Menter et al. 1997, 27). Thus markets and the guarantee of rewards for effort and merit are to be coupled together to produce "neutral," yet positive, results. Mechanisms hence must be put into place that give evidence of entrepreneurial efficiency and effectiveness. This coupling of markets and mechanisms for the generation of evidence of performance is exactly what has occurred. Whether it works is open to question.

In what is perhaps the most comprehensive critical review of all of the evidence on marketization, Geoff Whitty cautions us not to mistake rhetoric for reality. After examining research from a number of countries, Whitty argues that while advocates of marketized "choice" plans assume that competition will enhance the efficiency and responsiveness of schools as well as give disadvantaged children opportunities that they currently do not have, this may be a false hope (Whitty 1997, 58). These hopes are not now being realized and are unlikely to be realized in the future "in the context of broader policies that do nothing to challenge deeper social and cultural inequalities" (Whitty 1997, 58). As he goes on to say, "Atomized decision-making in a highly stratified society may appear to give everyone equal opportunities, but transforming responsibility for decision-making from the public to the private sphere can actually reduce the scope of collective action to improve the quality of education for all" (58). When this is connected to the fact that, as I shall show shortly, in practice neoliberal policies involving market "solutions" may actually serve to reproduce—not subvert—traditional hierarchies of class and race, this should give us reason to pause (Whitty 1997; Whitty, Edwards, and Gewirt 1993; Apple 1996).

Thus, rather than taking neoliberal claims at face value, we should want to ask about their hidden effects that are too often invisible in the rhetoric and metaphors of their proponents. Given the limitations of what one can say in a chapter of this length, I shall select a few issues that have been given less attention than they deserve but on which there is now significant research.

The British experience is apposite here, especially since proponents of the market, such as Chubb and Moe (1990), rely so heavily on it and because that is where the tendencies I analyze are most advanced. In Britain, the 1993 Education Act documents the state's commitment to marketization. Governing bodies of local educational authorities (LEAs) are now mandated formally to consider "going GM" (that is, opting out of the local school system's control and entering into the competitive market) every year (Power, Halpin, and Fitz 1994, 27). Thus the weight of the state stands behind the press toward neoliberal reforms there.[1] Yet, rather than leading to curriculum responsiveness and diversification, the competitive market has not created much that is different from the traditional models so firmly entrenched in schools today (Power, Halpin, and Fitz 1994, 39). Nor has it radically altered the relations of inequality that characterize schooling.

In their own extensive analyses of the effects of marketized reforms "on the ground," Ball and his colleagues point to some of the reasons why we need to be quite cautious here. As they document, in these situations educational principles and values are often compromised such that commercial issues become more important in curriculum design and resource allocation (Ball, Bowe, and Gewirtz 1994, 19). For instance, the coupling of markets with the demand for and publication of performance indicators such as "examination league tables" in Britain has meant that schools are increasingly looking for ways to attract "motivated" parents with "able" children. In this way, schools are able to enhance their relative position in local systems of competition. This represents a subtle but crucial shift in emphasis—one that is not openly discussed as often as it should be—from student needs to student performance and from what the school does for the student to what the student does for the school. This is also accompanied too uncomfortably often by a shift of resources away from students who are labelled as having special needs or learning difficulties, with some of these needed resources now being shifted to marketing and public relations. "Special needs" students are not only expensive, but deflate test scores on those all-important league tables.

Not only does this make it difficult to "manage public impressions," but it also makes it difficult to attract the "best" and most academically talented teachers (Ball, Bowe, and Gewirtz 1994, 17–19). The entire enterprise does, however, establish a new metric and a new set of goals based on a constant striving to win the market game. What this means is of considerable import, not only in terms of its effects on daily school life but in the ways all of this signifies a transformation of what counts as a good society and a responsible citizen. Let me say something about this generally.

I noted earlier that behind all educational proposals are visions of a just society and a good student. The neoliberal reforms I have been discussing construct this in a particular way. While the defining characteristic of neoliberalism is largely based on the central tenets of classical liberalism, in particular classic economic liberalism, there are crucial differences between classical liberalism and neoliberalism. These differences are absolutely essential in understanding the politics of education and the transformations education is currently undergoing. Mark Olssen clearly details these differences in the following passage. It is worth quoting in its entirety.

> Whereas classical liberalism represents a negative conception of state power in that the individual was to be taken as an object to be freed from the interventions of the state, neo-liberalism has come to represent a positive conception of the state's role in creating the appropriate market by providing the conditions, laws and institutions necessary for its operation. In classical liberalism, the individual is characterized as having an autonomous human nature and can practice freedom. In neo-liberalism the state seeks to create an individual who is an enterprising and competitive entrepreneur. In the classical model the theoretical aim of the state was to limit and minimize its role based on postulates which included universal egoism (the self-interested individual); invisible hand theory which dictated that the interests of the individual were also the interests of the society as a whole; and the political maxim of laissez-faire. In the shift from classical liberalism to neo-liberalism, then, there is a further element added, for such a shift involves a change in subject position from "homo economicus," who naturally behaves out of self-interest and is relatively detached from the state, to "manipulatable man," who is created by the state and who is continually encouraged to be "perpetually responsive." It is not that the conception of the self-interested subject is replaced or done away with by the new ideals of "neo-liberalism," but that in an age of universal welfare, the perceived possibilities of slothful indolence create necessities for new forms of vigilance, surveillance, "performance appraisal" and of forms of control generally. In this model the state has taken it upon itself to keep us all up to the mark. The state will see to it that each one makes a "continual enterprise of ourselves". . . in what seems to be a process of "governing without governing." (Olssen 1996, 340)

The results of Ball's and his colleagues' research document how the state does indeed do this, enhancing that odd combination of marketized individualism and control through constant and comparative public assessment. Widely publicized league tables determine one's relative value in the educational marketplace. Only those schools with rising performance indicators are worthy. And only those students who can "make a continual enterprise of themselves" can keep such schools going in the "correct" direction. Yet while these issues are important, they fail to illuminate fully some of the other mechanisms through which *differential* effects are produced by neoliberal reforms. Here class issues come to the fore in ways that Ball, Bowe, and Gewirtz (1994) make clear.

Middle-class parents are clearly the most advantaged in this kind of cultural assemblage, and not only because, as we saw, schools seek them out. Middle-class parents have become quite skilled, in general, in exploiting market mechanisms in education and in bringing their social, economic, and cultural capital to bear on them. "Middle class parents are more likely to have the knowledge, skills and contacts to decode and manipulate what are increasingly complex and deregulated systems of choice and recruitment. The more deregulation, the more possibility of informal procedures being employed. The middle class also, on the whole, are more able to move their children around the system" (Ball, Bowe, and Gewirtz 1994, 19). That class and race intersect and interact in complex ways means that—even though we need to be clear that marketized systems in education often *expressly* have their conscious and unconscious *raison d'être* in a fear of the Other and often are hidden expressions of a racialization of educational policy—the differential results will "naturally" be decidedly raced as well as classed.[2]

Economic and social capital can be converted into cultural capital in various ways. In marketized plans, more affluent parents often have more flexible hours and can visit multiple schools. They have cars—often more than one—and can *afford* to drive their children across town to attend a "better" school. They can also provide the hidden cultural resources such as camps and after-school programs (dance, music, computer classes, and so on) that give their children an "ease," a "style," that seems "natural" and acts as a set of cultural resources. Their previous stock of social and cultural capital—who they know, their "comfort" in social encounters with educational officials—is an unseen but powerful storehouse of resources. Thus more affluent parents are more likely to have the informal knowledge and skill—what Bourdieu would call the *habitus* (Bourdieu 1984)—to be able to decode and use marketized forms to their own benefit. This sense of what might be called "confidence"—which is itself the result of past choices that tacitly but no less powerfully depend on the economic resources actually to have had the ability to make economic choices—is the unseen capital that underpins their ability to negotiate marketized forms and "work the system" through sets of informal cultural rules (Ball, Bowe, and Gewirtz 1994, 20–22).

Of course, it needs to be said that working-class, poor, and/or immigrant parents are not skill-less in this regard, by any means. (After all, it requires an immense amount of skill, courage, and social and cultural resources to survive under exploitative and depressing material conditions. Thus collective bonds, informal networks and contacts, and an ability to work the system are developed in quite nuanced, intelligent, and often impressive ways here.) However, the match between the historically grounded habitus expected in schools and in its actors and those of more affluent parents, combined with the material resources available to more affluent parents, usually leads to a successful conversion of economic and social capital into cultural capital (see Bourdieu 1996; Swartz 1997). And this is exactly what is happening in Britain.

These claims both about what is happening inside of schools and about larger sets of power relations are supported by even more recent synthetic analyses of the overall results of marketized models. This research on the effects of the tense but still effective combination of neoliberal and neoconservative policies examines the tendencies internationally by comparing what has happened in a number of nations—for example, the United States, Britain, Australia, and New Zealand—where this combination has been increasingly powerful. The results confirm the arguments I have made here. Let me rehearse some of the most significant and disturbing findings of such research.

It is unfortunately all too usual that the most widely used measures of the "success" of school reforms are the results of standardized achievement tests. This simply will not do. We need constantly to ask what reforms do to schools as a whole and to each of their participants, including teachers, students, administrators, community members, local activists, and so on. To take one set of examples, as marketized "self-managing" schools grow in many nations, the role of the school principal is radically transformed. More, not less, power is actually consolidated within an administrative structure. More time and energy are spent on maintaining or enhancing a public image of a "good school" and less time and energy are spent on pedagogic and curricular substance. At the same time, teachers seem to be experiencing not increased autonomy and professionalism but intensification (Apple 1988, 1993). And oddly, as noted before, schools themselves become more *similar* and more committed to standard, traditional, whole-class methods of teaching and a standard and traditional (and often monocultural) curriculum. Directing our attention only to test scores would cause us to miss some truly profound transformations, many of which we may find disquieting.

One of the reasons these broader effects are so often produced is that in all too many countries, neoliberal visions of quasi-markets are usually accompanied by neoconservative pressure to regulate content and behavior through such things as national curricula, national standards, and national systems of assessment. The combination is historically contingent; that is, it is not absolutely necessary that the two emphases are combined. But there are characteristics of neoliberalism that make it more likely that an emphasis on the weak state and a faith in markets will cohere with an emphasis on the strong state and a commitment to regulating knowledge, values, and the body.

This is partly the case because of the increasing power of the "evaluative state." This signifies what initially may seem to be contradictory tendencies. At the same time as the state appears to be devolving power to individuals and autonomous institutions which are themselves increasingly competing in a market, the state remains strong in key areas. As I claimed earlier, one of the key differences between classical liberalism, with its faith in "enterprising individuals" in a market, and current forms of neoliberalism is the latter's commitment to a regulatory state. Neoliberalism does indeed demand the constant production of evidence that one is in fact "making an enterprise of oneself" (Olssen 1996). Thus under these conditions not only does education become a marketable commodity like bread and cars, in which the values, procedures, and metaphors of business dominate, but its results must be reducible to standardized "performance indicators." This is ideally suited to the task of providing a mechanism for the neoconservative attempts to specify what knowledge, values, and behaviors should be standardized and officially defined as "legitimate," a point I shall expand upon in the next section of this chapter.

In essence, we are witnessing a process in which the state shifts the blame for the very evident inequalities in access and outcome it has promised to reduce from itself onto individual schools, parents, and children. This is, of course, also part of a larger process in which dominant economic groups shift the blame for the massive and unequal effects of their own misguided decisions from themselves onto the state. The state is then faced with a very real crisis in legitimacy. Given this, we should not be at all surprised that the state will then seek to export this crisis outside itself (Apple 1995).

Of course, the state is not only classed, but is inherently *sex/gendered* and *raced* as well. This is evident in Whitty, Power, and Halpin's arguments. They point to the gendered nature of the ways in which the management of schools is thought about as "masculinist" business models become increasingly dominant (Whitty, Power, and Halpin 1998, 60–62). While there is a danger of these claims degenerating into reductive and essentializing arguments, there is a good deal of insight here. They do cohere with the work of other scholars inside and outside education who recognize that the ways in which our very definitions of public and private, of what knowledge is of most worth, and of how institutions should be thought about and run are fully implicated in the gendered nature of this society. These broad ideological effects—for example, enabling a coalition between neoliberals and neoconservatives to be formed, the masculinization of theories, policies, and management talk—are of considerable import and make it harder to change common sense in more critical directions.

Other, more proximate, effects inside schools are equally striking. Because of the intensification that I mentioned before, both principals and teachers experience considerably heavier workloads and ever escalating demands for accountability, a never ending schedule of meetings, and in many cases a growing scarcity of resources both emotional and physical (Whitty, Power, and Halpin 1998, 67–68).

Further, as in the research in Britain, in nearly all of the countries studied the market did *not* encourage diversity in curriculum, pedagogy, organization, clientele, or even image. It instead consistently devalued alternatives and increased the power of dominant models. Of equal significance, it also consistently exacerbated differences in access and outcome based on race, ethnicity, and class.

The return to "traditionalism" led to a number of things. It *delegitimated* more critical models of teaching and learning, a point that is crucial to recognize in any attempt to think through the possibilities of cultural struggles and critical pedagogies in schools. It both reintroduced restratification within the school and lessened the possibility that detracking would occur. More emphasis was given to "gifted" children and "fast track" classes, while students who were seen as less academically able were therefore "less attractive." In Britain, the extent of this was nowhere more visible than in the alarming rate of students being excluded from schools. Much of this was caused by the intense pressure to constantly demonstrate higher achievement rates. This was especially powerful in marketized contexts in which there was an intensified commercial emphasis.

In their own analysis of these worrisome and more hidden results, Whitty, Power, and Halpin (1998) demonstrate that among the dangerous effects of quasi-markets are the ways in which schools that wish to maintain or enhance their market position engage in "cream-skimming," ensuring that *particular* kinds of students with particular characteristics are accepted and particular kinds of students are found wanting. For some schools, stereotypes were reproduced in that girls were seen a more valuable, as were students from some Asian communities. Afro-Caribbean children were often clear losers in this situation.

Some of these data come largely from schools outside the United States, although they should make us stop dead in our tracks and give some very serious thought to whether we want to proceed with similar policies here. Yet the United States still sits at the center of much of the discussion in this literature. For example, charter schools and their equivalents in the U.S. and Britain are also put under critical scrutiny. In both places, they tend to attract parents who live and work in relatively privileged communities. Here too, "it would appear that any new opportunities are being colonized by the already advantaged, rather than the 'losers' identified by Chubb and Moe" (Whitty, Power, and Halpin 1998, 98).

In the process, this critical research suggests that there are hidden similarities between advocates of school effectiveness research and those committed to neoliberal "reforms." Both tend to ignore the fact that external characteristics of schools such as poverty, political and economic power, and so on consistently account for much more of the variation in school performance than things like organizational features or those characteristics that supposedly guarantee an "effective school" (Whitty, Power, and Halpin 1998, 112–113).

The overall conclusions are clear. "[In] current circumstances choice is as likely to reinforce hierarchies as to improve educational opportunities and the overall quality of schooling" (Whitty, Power, and Halpin 1998, 14). As Whitty, Power, and Halpin put it in their arguments against those who believe that what we are witnessing in the emergence of "choice" programs is the postmodern celebration of difference:

> There is a growing body of empirical evidence that, rather than benefitting the disadvantaged, the emphasis on parental choice and school autonomy is further disadvantaging those least able to compete in the market. . . . For most disadvantaged groups, as opposed to the few individuals who escape from schools at the bottom of the status hierarchy, the new arrangements seem to be just a more sophisticated way of reproducing traditional distinctions between different types of school and the people who attend them. (Whitty, Power, and Halpin 1998, 42)

All of this gives us ample reason to agree with Henig's insightful argument that "the sad irony of the current education-reform movement is that, through over-identification with school-choice proposals rooted in market-based ideas, the healthy impulse to consider radical reforms to address social problems may be channeled into initiatives that further erode the potential for collective deliberation and collective response" (Henig 1994, 222).

This is not to dismiss either the possibility or the necessity of school reform. However, we need to take seriously the probability that only by focusing on the exogenous socioeconomic features, not simply the organizational features, of "successful" schools can all schools succeed. Eliminating poverty through greater income parity, establishing effective and much more equal health and housing programs, and positively refusing to continue the hidden and not-so-hidden politics of racial exclusion and degradation that so clearly still characterize daily life in many nations (and in which marketized plans need to be seen as partly a structure to avoid the body and culture of the Other)—only by tackling these issues together can substantive progress be made. Unless discussions of critical pedagogy are themselves grounded in a recognition of these realities, they too may fall into the trap of assuming that schools can do it alone.

These empirical findings are made more understandable in terms of Pierre Bourdieu's analysis of the relative weight given to cultural capital as part of mobility strategies today (Bourdieu 1996). The rise in importance of cultural capital infiltrates all institutions in such a way that there is a relative movement away from the *direct* reproduction of class privilege (where power is transmitted largely within families through economic property) to *school-mediated* forms of class privilege. Here, "the bequeathal of privilege is simultaneously effectuated and transfigured by the intercession of educational institutions" (Wacquant 1996, xiii). This is *not* a conspiracy; it is not "conscious" in the ways we normally use that concept. Rather it is the result of a long chain of relatively autonomous connections between differentially accumulated economic, social, and cultural capital operating at the level of daily events as we make our respective ways in the world, including, as we saw, in the world of school choice.

Thus, while not taking an unyieldingly determinist position, Bourdieu argues that a class habitus tends to reproduce the conditions of its own reproduction "unconsciously." It does this by producing a relatively coherent and systematically *characteristic* set of seemingly natural and unconscious strategies—in essence, ways of understanding and acting on the world that act as forms of cultural capital that can be and are employed to protect and enhance one's status in a social field of power. He aptly compares this similarity of habitus across class actors to handwriting:

> Just as the acquired disposition we call "handwriting," that is a particular way of forming letters, always produces the same "writing"—that is, graphic lines that despite differences in size, matter, and color related to writing surface (sheet of paper or blackboard) and implement (pencil, pen, or chalk), that is despite differences in vehicles for the action, have an immediately recognizable affinity of style or a family resemblance—the practices of a single agent, or, more broadly, the practices of all agents endowed with similar habitus, owe the affinity of style that makes each a metaphor for the others to the fact that they are the products of the implementation in different fields of the same schemata of perception, thought, and action. (Bourdieu 1996, 273)

This very connection of habitus across fields of power—the ease of bringing one's economic, social, and cultural resources to bear on "markets"—enables a comfort between markets and self that characterizes the middle-class actor here. This constantly *produces* differential effects. These effects are not neutral, no matter what the advocates of neoliberalism suggest. Rather, they are themselves the results of a particular kind of morality. Unlike the conditions of what might best be called "thick morality," where principles of the common good are the ethical basis for adjudicating policies and practices, markets are grounded in aggregative principles. They are constituted out of the sum of individual goods and choices. "Founded on individual and property rights that enable citizens to address problems of interdependence via exchange," they offer a prime example of "thin morality" by generating both hierarchy and division based on competitive individualism (Ball, Bowe, and Gewirtz 1994, 24). And in this competition, the general outline of the winners and losers *has* been identified empirically.

National Curriculum and National Testing

I showed in the previous section that there are connections between at least two dynamics operating in neoliberal reforms, "free" markets and increased surveillance. This can be seen in the fact that in many contexts, marketization has been accompanied by a set of particular policies for "producers," for those professionals working within education. These policies have been strongly regulatory and have been quite instrumental in reconstituting common sense. As in the case of the linkage between national tests and performance indicators published as league tables, they have been organized around a concern for external supervision, regulation, and external judgment of performance (Menter et al. 1997, 8) and have increasingly been colonized by parents who possess what is seen as "appropriate" economic, social, and cultural capital. This concern for external supervision and regulation is not only connected with a strong mistrust of "producers" (that is, teachers) and with the need for ensuring that people continually make enterprises out of themselves. It is also clearly linked both to the neoconservative sense of a need to "return" to a lost past of high standards, discipline, awe, and "real" knowledge and to the professional middle class's own ability to carve out a sphere of authority within the state for its own commitment to management techniques and efficiency. The focus on efficient management plays a prime role here, one that many neoliberals and neoconservatives alike find useful.

There has been a shift in the relationship between the state and "professionals." In essence, the move toward a small, strong state that is increasingly guided by market needs seems inevitably to bring with it reduced professional power and status (Menter et al. 1997, 57). Managerialism takes center stage here. Managerialism is largely charged with "bringing about the cultural transformation that shifts professional identities in order to make them more responsive to client demand and external judgment" (Menter et al. 1997, 9). It aims to justify and to have people internalize fundamental alterations in professional practices. It both harnesses energy and discourages dissent (Menter et al. 1997, 9).

There is no necessary contradiction between a general set of marketizing and deregulating interests and processes—such as voucher and choice plans—and a set of enhanced regulatory processes—such as plans for national curricula and national testing. "The regulatory form permits the state to maintain 'steerage' over the aims and processes of education from within the market mechanism" (Menter et al. 1997, 24). Such steerage has often been vested in such things as national standards, national curricula, and national testing. Forms of all of these are being pushed for in the United States currently and are the subject of considerable controversy, some of which cuts across ideological lines and shows some of the tensions within the different elements contained under the umbrella of the conservative restoration.

I have argued that, paradoxically, a national curriculum and especially a national testing program are the first and most essential steps toward increased marketization. They actually provide the mechanisms for comparative data that "consumers" need to make markets work as markets (Apple 1996). Absent these mechanisms, there is no comparative base of information for "choice." Yet we do not have to argue about these regulatory forms in a vacuum. Like the neoliberal markets I discussed in the previous section, they too have been instituted in Britain; and, once again, there is important research available that can and must make us duly cautious in going down this path.

One might want to claim that a set of national standards, national curricula, and national tests would provide the conditions for "thick morality." After all, such regulatory reforms are supposedly based on shared values and common sentiments that also create social spaces in which common issues of concern can be debated and made subject to moral interrogation (Ball, Bowe, and Gewirtz 1994, 23). Yet, what counts as the "common," and how and by whom it is actually determined, is rather more thin than thick.

It is the case that while the national curriculum now so solidly in place in England and Wales is clearly prescriptive, it has not always proven to be the kind of straightjacket it has often been made out to be. As a number of researchers have documented, it is not only possible that policies and legislative mandates are interpreted and adapted, but it seems inevitable. Thus the national curriculum is "not so much being 'implemented' in schools as being 'recreated,' not so much 'reproduced,' as 'produced'" (Power, Halpin, and Fitz 1994, 38).

In general, it is nearly a truism that there is no simplistic linear model of policy formation, distribution, and implementation. There are always complex mediations at each level of the process. There is a complex politics that goes on within each group and between these groups and external forces in the formulation of policy, in its being written up as a legislative mandate, in its distribution, and in its reception at the level of practice (Ransom 1995, 436). Thus the state may legislate changes in curriculum, evaluation, or policy (which is itself produced through conflict, compromise, and political maneuvering), but policy writers and curriculum writers may be unable to control the meanings and implementations of their texts. All texts are "leaky" documents. They are subject to "recontextualization" at every stage of the process (Ransom 1995, 436).

However, this general principle may be just a bit too romantic. None of this occurs on a level playing field. As with market plans, there are very real differences in power in one's ability to influence, mediate, transform, or reject a policy or a regulatory process. Granted, it is important to recognize that a "state control model"—with its assumption of top-down linearity—is much too simplistic and that the possibility of human agency and influence is always there. However, having said this, this should not imply that such agency and influence will be powerful (Ransom 1995, 437).

The case of national curriculum and national testing in England and Wales documents the tensions in these two accounts. It was the case that the national curriculum that was first legislated and then imposed there was indeed struggled over. It was originally too detailed and too specific, and hence was subject to major transformations at the national, community, school, and then classroom levels. However, even though the national curriculum was subject to conflict, mediation, and some transformation of its content, organization, and its invasive and immensely time-consuming forms of evaluation, its utter power is demonstrated in its radical reconfiguration of the very process of knowledge selection, organization, and assessment. It has changed the entire terrain of education radically. Its subject divisions "provide more constraint than scope for discretion"; the "standard attainment targets" that have been mandated cement these constraints in place; "[t]he imposition of national testing locks the national curriculum in place as the dominant framework of teachers' work whatever opportunities teachers may take to evade or reshape it" (Richard Hatcher and Barry Troyna, quoted in Ransom 1995, 438).

Thus it is not sufficient to state that the world of education is complex and has multiple influences. The purpose of any serious analysis is to go beyond such overly broad conclusions. Rather, we need to "discriminate degrees of influence in the world," to weigh the relative efficacy of the factors involved. Hence, although it is clear that while the national curriculum and national tests that now exist in England and Wales have come about because of a complex interplay of forces and influences, it is equally clear that "state control has the upper hand" (Ransom 1995, 438).

The national curricula and national tests *did* generate conflict about issues. They did partly lead to the creation of social spaces for moral questions to get asked. (Of course, these moral questions had been asked all along by dispossessed groups.) Thus it was clear to many people that the creation of mandatory and reductive tests that emphasized memory and decontextualized abstraction pulled the national curriculum in a particular direction—that of encouraging a selective educational market in which elite students and elite schools with a wide range of resources would be well (if narrowly) served (O'Hear 1994, 66). Diverse groups of people argued that such reductive, detailed, and simplistic paper-and-pencil tests "had the potential to do enormous damage," a situation that was made even worse because the tests were so onerous in terms of time and record keeping (O'Hear 1994, 55–56). Teachers had a good deal of support when as a group they decided to boycott the administration of the test in a remarkable act of public protest. This also led to serious questioning of the arbitrary, inflexible, and overly prescriptive national curriculum. While the curriculum is still inherently problematic and the assessment system does still contain numerous dangerous and onerous elements within it, organized activity against them did have an impact (O'Hear 1994, 56–57).

Yet, unfortunately, the story does not end there. By the mid-1990s, even with the government's partial retreat on such regulatory forms as its program of constant and reductive testing, it had become clearer by the year that the development of testing and the specification of content had been "hijacked" by those who were ideologically committed to traditional pedagogies and to the idea of more rigorous selection (O'Hear 1994, 68). The residual effects are both material and ideological. They include a continuing emphasis on trying to provide the "rigor [that is] missing in the practice of most teachers, . . . judging progress solely by what is testable in tests of this kind" and the development of a "very hostile view of the accountability of teachers" that was seen as "part of a wider thrust of policy to take away professional control of public services and establish so called consumer control through a market structure" (O'Hear 1994, 65–66).

The authors of an extremely thorough review of recent assessment programs instituted in England and Wales provide a summary of what has happened. Gipps and Murphy argue that it has become increasingly obvious that the national assessment program attached to the national curriculum is more and more dominated by traditional models of testing and the assumptions about teaching and learning that lie behind them. At the same time, equity issues are becoming much less visible (Gipps and Murphy 1994, 209). In the calculus of values now in place in the regulatory state, efficiency, speed, and cost control replace more substantive concerns about social and educational justice. The pressure to get tests in place rapidly has meant that "the speed of test development is so great, and the curriculum and assessment changes so regular, that [there is] little time to carry out detailed analyses and trialing to ensure that the tests are as fair as possible to all groups" (Gipps and Murphy 1994, 209). The conditions for "thin morality"—in which the competitive individual of the market dominates and social justice will somehow take care of itself—are reproduced here. The combination of the neoliberal market and the regulatory state, then, does indeed "work." However, it works in ways in which the metaphors of free market, merit, and effort hide the differential reality that is produced. While, on the one hand, this makes a socially and culturally critical pedagogy even more essential, it also makes it much more difficult actually to accomplish.

Basil Bernstein's discussion of the general principles by which knowledge and policies ("texts") move from one arena to another is useful in understanding this. As Bernstein reminds us, when talking about educational change there are three fields with which we must be concerned. Each field has its own rules of access, regulation, privilege, and special interests: (1) the field of "production," where new knowledge is constructed; (2) the field of "reproduction," where pedagogy and curriculum are actually enacted in schools; and, between these other two, (3) the "recontextual-izing" field where discourses from the field of production are appropriated and then transformed into pedagogic discourse and recommendations (Bernstein 1990; Bernstein 1996; Apple 1993). This appropriation and recontextualization of knowledge for educational purposes is itself governed by two sets of principles. The first—delocation—implies that there is always a *selective* appropriation of knowl-edge and discourse from the field of production. The second—relocation—points to the fact that when knowledge and discourse from the field of production are pulled within the recontextualizing field, the field is subject to ideological transfor-mations due to the various specialized and/or political interests whose conflicts structure the recontextualizing field (Evans and Penney 1995).

A good example of this, one that confirms Gipps's and Murphy's analysis of the dynamics of national curricula and national testing during their more recent itera-tions, is found in the process by which the content and organization of the man-dated national curriculum in physical education were struggled over and ultimately formed in Britain. In this instance, a working group of academics both within and outside the field of physical education, headmasters of private and state-supported schools, well-known athletes, and business leaders (but *no* teachers) was formed.

The original curriculum policies that arose from the groups were relatively mixed educationally and ideologically, taking account of the field of production of knowledge within physical education. That is, they contained both critical and pro-gressive elements and elements of the conservative restoration, as well as academic perspectives within the specialized fields from the university. However, as these made their way from report to recommendations and then from recommendations to action, they steadily came closer to restorational principles. An emphasis on effi-ciency, basic skills, and performance testing, on the social control of the body, and on competitive norms ultimately won out. Like the middle-class capturing of the market discussed earlier, this too was not a conspiracy. Rather, it was the result of a process of "overdetermination." That is, it was due not to an imposition of these norms but to a combination of interests in the recontextualizing field—an eco-nomic context in which public spending was under severe scrutiny and cost savings had to be sought everywhere, government officials were opposed to "frills" and con-sistently intervened to institute only a selection of the recommendations (preferably conservative ones that did *not* come from "professional academics"), ideological at-tacks on critical, progressive, or child-centered approaches to physical education, and a predominant discourse of "being pragmatic." These came together in the re-contextualizing field and helped ensure in practice that conservative principles would be reinscribed in policies and mandates and that critical forms were seen as too ideological, too costly, or too impractical (Evans and Penney 1995, 41–42). "Standards" were upheld; critical voices were heard, but ultimately to little effect; the norms of competitive performance were made central and employed as regulatory devices. Regulatory devices served to privilege specific groups in much the same way as did markets. Thus goeth democracy in education.

Thinking Strategically

So far in this chapter, I have raised serious questions about current educational "reform" efforts now under way in a number of nations. I have used research largely, but not solely, on the British experience(s) to document some of the hidden differential effects of two connected strategies—neoliberal-inspired market proposals and neoliberal, neoconservative, and middle-class managerial-inspired regulatory proposals. Taking a key from Herbert Kliebard's (1986) historical analysis, I have described how different interests with different educational and social visions compete for dominion in the social field of power surrounding educational policy and practice. In the process, I have documented some of the complexities and imbalances in this field of power. These complexities and imbalances result in "thin" rather than "thick" morality and in the reproduction of both dominant pedagogical and curricular forms and ideologies and the social privileges that accompany them. I have suggested that the rhetorical flourishes of the discourses of critical pedagogy need to come to grips with these changing material and ideological conditions. Critical pedagogy cannot and will not occur in a vacuum. Unless we honestly face these profound rightist transformations and think tactically about them, we will have little effect either on the creation of a counterhegemonic common sense or on the building of a counterhegemonic alliance. The growth of that odd combination of marketization and regulatory state, the move toward pedagogic similarity and "traditional" academic curricula and teaching, the ability of dominant groups to exert leadership in the struggle over this, and the accompanying shifts in common sense—all this cannot be wished away. Instead it needs to be confronted honestly and self-critically.

Having said this, however, I want to point to a hidden paradox in what I have done. Even though much of my own and others' research recently has been on the conservative restoration, there are dangers in such a focus of which we should be aware. Research on the history, politics, and practices of rightist social and educational movements and "reforms" has enabled us to show the contradictions and unequal effects of such policies and practices. It has enabled the rearticulation of claims to social justice on the basis of solid evidence. This is all to the good. However, in the process, one of the latent effects has been the gradual framing of educational issues largely in terms of the conservative agenda. The very categories themselves—markets, choice, national curricula, national testing, standards—bring the debate onto the terrain established by neoliberals and neoconservatives. The analysis of "what is" has led to a neglect of "what might be." Thus, there has been a withering of substantive large scale discussions of feasible alternatives to neoliberal and neoconservative visions, policies, and practices, ones that would move well beyond them (Seddon 1997, 165–166).

Because of this, at least part of our task may be politically and conceptually complex, but it can be said simply. In the long term, we need to "develop a political project that is both local yet generalizable, systematic without making Eurocentric, masculinist claims to essential and universal truths about human subjects" (Luke 1995, vi–vii). Another part of our task, though, must be and is more proximate, more appropriately educational. Defensible, articulate, and fully fleshed out alternative critical and progressive policies and practices in curriculum, teaching, and evaluation need to be developed and made widely available. But this, too, must be done with due recognition of the changing nature of the social field of power and the importance of thinking tactically and strategically. Let me specific here.

For example, in the United States the increasingly popular journal *Rethinking Schools* has provided an important forum for social and educational criticism and for descriptions of critical educational practices in schools and communities. At times influenced directly by the work of Paulo Freire and by educators who have themselves elaborated and extended it, and at other times coming out of diverse indigenous, radical, educational traditions specific to the U.S., *Rethinking Schools* and emerging national organizations such as the National Coalition of Educational Activists have jointly constructed spaces for critical educators, cultural and political activists, radical scholars, and others to teach each other, to provide supportive criticism of each other's work, and to build a collective set of responses to the destructive educational and social polices coming from the conservative restoration.[3]

In using the phrase "collective set of responses," however, I need to stress that this phrase does not signify anything like "democratic centrism" in which a small group or a party cadre speaks for the majority and establishes the "appropriate" position. Given the fact that there are diverse emancipatory movements whose voices are heard in publications like *Rethinking Schools* and in organizations such as the National Coalition of Educational Activists—antiracist and postcolonial positions, radical forms of multiculturalism, gays and lesbians, multiple feminist voices, neo-Marxists and democratic socialists, "greens," and so on—a more appropriate way of looking at what is happening is to call it a *decentered unity*. Multiple progressive projects, multiple "critical pedagogies," are articulated. Like Freire, each of them is related to real struggles in real institutions in real communities. We of course should not be romantic about this. There are very real differences—political, epistemological, and/or educational—in these varied voices. Yet they are united in their opposition to the forces involved in the new conservative hegemonic alliance. There *are* tensions, but the decentered unity has remained strong enough for each constituent group to support the struggles of the others.

This is not all. At the same time as these critical movements are being built, critical educators are also attempting to occupy the spaces provided by existing "mainstream" publication outlets to publish books that provide *critical* answers to teachers' questions about "What do I do on Monday?" during a conservative era. This space has too long been ignored by many theorists of critical pedagogy. Some of these attempts have been remarkably successful. Let me give one example. One very large "professional" organization in the United States—the Association for Supervision and Curriculum Development (ASCD)—publishes books that are distributed each year to its more than 150,000 members, most of whom are teachers or administrators in elementary, middle, or secondary schools. ASCD has not been a very progressive organization, preferring to publish largely technicist and overtly depoliticized material. Yet it has been concerned that its publications have not sufficiently represented socially and culturally critical educators. It, thus, has been looking for ways to increase its legitimacy to a wider range of educators. Because of this legitimacy problem and because of its large membership, it became clear to a number of people who were part of the critical educational traditions in the United States that it might be possible to convince ASCD to publish and widely circulate material that would demonstrate the actual practical *successes* of critical models of curriculum, teaching, and evaluation in solving real problems in schools and communities, especially with working class and poor children and children of color.

After intense negotiations that guaranteed an absence of censorship, a colleague of mine and I agreed to publish a book—*Democratic Schools* (Apple and Beane 1995)—with ASCD that provided clear practical examples of the power of Freirean and similar critical approaches at work in classrooms and communities. *Democratic Schools* not only was distributed to all 150,000 members of the organization, but has gone on to sell an additional 100,000 copies. Thus nearly 250,000 copies of a volume that tells the practical stories of the largely successful struggles of critically oriented educators in real schools are now in the hands of educators who daily face similar problems.[4] This is an important intervention. While there is no guarantee that teachers will always be progressive (nor is there any guarantee that those who are progressive around class and union issues will be equally progressive around issues of gender, sexuality, and race), many teachers do have socially and pedagogically critical intuitions. However, they often do not have ways of putting into these intuitions into practice because they cannot picture them in action in daily situations. Due to this, critical theoretical and political insights, then, have nowhere to go in terms of their embodiment in concrete pedagogical situations where the politics of curriculum and teaching must be *enacted*. This is a tragic absence, and strategically filling it is absolutely essential. Thus we need to use and expand the spaces in which critical pedagogical "stories" are made available so that these positions do not remain only on the theoretical or rhetorical level. The publication and widespread distribution of *Democratic Schools* provide one instance of using and expanding such spaces in ways that make Freirean and similar critical educational positions seem actually doable in "ordinary" institutions such as schools and local communities.

Although crucial, it is, then, not enough to deconstruct restorational policies in education. The right has shown how important changes in common sense are in the struggle for education. It is our task to help collectively rebuild it by reestablishing a sense that "thick" morality, and a "thick" democracy, are truly possible today.

This cannot be done without paying considerably more attention to two things. The first—the material and ideological transformations that the right has effected—has been a key topic of this chapter. Yet there is another element that needs to be stressed—the building of large-scale counterhegemonic movements that connect educational struggles to those in other sites and also assist both in creating new struggles and defending existing ones within educational institutions themselves. In the current conservative context, there are characteristics of some of the material on critical pedagogy that make this an even more difficult act, however.

In the past, I have warned that the stylistic politics of some of our most "advanced" work forces the reader to do all of the work (Apple 1988). Neologism after neologism reign supreme. The discourse of critical pedagogy in its Freirean and feminist forms has increasingly been influenced by postmodern theories. While this has proven to be very useful in reconceptualizing the field and its politics, it has also opened up the discourse to the criticism that it has become too theoretical, abstract, esoteric, and out of touch with the conflicts and struggles that teachers, students, and activists act on. Henry Giroux and others have defended these discourses as necessary in critical pedagogy, since to reconstruct the world one must first learn to speak a new language. This is undoubtedly correct. Indeed, such a position is one I self-consciously took when I first intruduced Gramscian and Habermasian theories into education in the early 1970s.

Yet, having said this, given the very real success of the strategy of "plain speaking" by neoliberals and neoconservatives, some of the criticisms of material on critical pedagogy do have power. Even though a good deal of it is rich and provocative, some of it *is* conceptually and politically confused and confusing. Some of it *is* disconnected from the gritty materialities of daily economic, political, and educational/cultural struggles. Some of it *does* romanticize the cultural at the expense of equally powerful traditions of analysis based in political economy and the state.

And some of it *does* place so much emphasis on "post-" that it forgets the structural realities that set limits on real people in real institutions in everyday life.

Much more effort must be given to ground the discourse of critical pedagogy in the concrete struggles of multiple and identifiable groups. Much of it needs to be considerably less dismissive of previous critical traditions that—rightly—continue to influence educational and cultural activists. Just as important and as I've just noted, what critical pedagogies actually look like when put into practice—not only their theoretical elaborations—needs to made much more visible than we have been apt to do. Unfortunately, when rightist mobilizations have had no small measure of success in creating a reactionary common sense about education (and even among many educators), the linguistic styles of all too much critical work get labeled as "arrogant" (sometimes appropriately) and cut themselves off from many of the radical teachers and activists they want to support.

It is *hard* work not to be sloppy. It is hard work to write in such a way that theoretical and political nuance are not sacrificed on the altar of common sense, but also in a way that the hard work of reading can actually pay off for the reader her- or himself. And it is hard and time-consuming work to write at multiple levels. But if we do not, neoliberals and neoconservatives will. And we will be much the worse for it. In this time of conservative restoration, the multiple projects of critical education are indeed crucial. A good dose of reality will do no harm, and I believe, will actually make them more effective in the long run.

Notes

1. Whether there will be significant changes in this regard given the victory by "New Labour" over the Conservatives in the last election remains to be seen. Certain aspects of neoliberal and neoconservative policies have already been accepted by the Labour Party, such as the acceptance of stringent cost controls on spending put in place by the previous Conservative government and an aggressive focus on "raising standards" in association with strict performance indicators.

2. See the discussion of the racial state in Omi and Winant (1994) and the analyses of race and representation in McCarthy and Crichlow (1994) and McCarthy (1998).

3. *Rethinking Schools* is one of the best examples of the ways critical academics, elementary/middle/high school teachers, students, and community activists can work together in nonelitist ways. Information is available from *Rethinking Schools*, 1001 E. Keefe Avenue, Milwaukee, Wisconsin 53212, U.S. For faxes, the number is 414-964-7220. The e-mail adress is: rethink@execpc.com.

4. Translations of this volume have been or are due to be published in Japan, Spain, Argentina, Brazil, Spain, Portugal, and elsewhere. Thus it is clear that providing critical answers to the pressing issues of "What do I do on Monday?" is seen as crucial in a number of nations.

References

Apple, M.W. 1988. *Teachers and Texts*. New York: Routledge.

Apple, M.W. 1993. *Official Knowledge*. New York: Routledge.

Apple, M.W. 1996. *Cultural Politics and Education*. New York: Teachers College Press.

Apple, M.W., and J.A. Beane. 1995. *Democratic Schools*. Washington, DC: Association for Supervision and Curriculum Development.

Ball, S., R. Bowe, and S. Gewirtz. 1994. "Market Forces and Parental Choice." In *Educational Reform and Its Consequences*. S. Tomlinson, ed. London: IPPR/Rivers Oram Press.

Bernstein, B. 1990. *The Structuring of Pedagogic Discourse*. New York: Routledge.

Bernstein, B. 1996. *Pedagogy, Symbolic Control, and Identity*. Bristol, PA: Taylor and Francis.

Bourdieu, P. 1994. *Distinction*. Cambridge, MA: Harvard University Press.

Bourdieu, P. 1996. *The State Nobility*. Stanford, CA: Stanford University Press.

Chubb, J., and T. Moe. 1990. *Politics, Markets, and America's Schools*. Washington, DC: Brookings Institution.

Evans, J., and D. Penney. 1995. "The Politics of Pedagogy." *Journal of Education Policy* 10: 27–44.

Gillborn, D. 1997a. "Race, Nation, and Education." Unpublished paper, Institute of Education, University of London.

Gillborn, D. 1997b. "Racism and Reform." *British Educational Research Journal* 23: 345–360.

Gipps, C., and P. Murphy. 1994. *A Fair Test?* Philadelphia: Open University Press.

Herrnstein, R., and C. Murray. 1994. *The Bell Curve*. New York: Free Press.

Kincheloe, J., and S. Steinberg, eds. 1996. *Measured Lies*. New York: St. Martin's Press.

Kliebard, H. 1986. *The Struggle for the American Curriculum*. New York: Routledge.

Luke, A. 1995. "Series Editor's Introduction." In J.L. Lemke, *Textual Politics*. Bristol, PA: Taylor and Francis.

McCarthy, C. 1998. *The Uses of Culture*. New York: Routledge.

McCarthy, C., and W. Crichlow, eds. 1994. *Race, Identity, and Representation in Education*. New York: Routledge.

McCulloch, G. 1997. "Privatizing the Past?" *British Journal of Educational Studies* 45: 69–82.

Menter, I., P. Muschamp, P. Nicholls, J. Ozga, with A. Pollard. 1997. *Work and Identity in the Primary School*. Philadelphia, PA: Open University Press.

O'Hear, P. 1994. "An Alternative National Curriculum." In *Educational Reform and Its Consequences*. S. Tomlinson, ed. London: IPPR/Rivers Oram Press.

Olssen, M. 1996. "In Defence of the Welfare State and Publicly Provided Education." *Journal of Education Policy* 11: 337–362.

Omi, M., and H. Winant. 1994. *Racial Formation in the United States*. New York: Routledge.

Power, S., D. Halpin, and J. Fitz. 1994. "Underpinning Choice and Diversity?" In *Educational Reform and Its Consequences*. S. Tomlinson, ed. London: IPPR/Rivers Oram Press.

Ransom, S. 1995. "Theorizing Educational Policy." *Journal of Education Policy* 10: 427–448.

Seddon, T. 1997. "Markets and the English." *British Journal of Sociology of Education* 18: 165–185.

Selden, S. Forthcoming. *Ethnic Diversity, Race Betterment and Education: A History of Eugenics in Education 1903–1948*. New York: Teachers College Press.

Swartz, D. 1997. *Culture and Power*. Chicago: University of Chicago Press.

Wacquant, L. 1996. "Foreword." In P. Bourdieu, *The State Nobility*. Stanford, CA: Stanford University Press.

Whitty, G. 1974. "Sociology and the Problem of Radical Educational Change." In *Educability, Schools and Ideology*. M. Flude and J. Ahier, eds. London: Halstead.

Whitty, G. 1997. "Creating Quasi-Markets in Education." In *Review of Research in Education*. Vol. 22. M.W. Apple, ed. Washington, DC: American Educational Research Association.

Whitty, G., T. Edwards, and S. Gewirtz. 1993. *Specialization and Choice in Urban Education*. New York: Routledge.

Whitty, G., S. Power, and D. Halpin. 1998. *Devolution and Choice in Education*. Buchingham, UK: Open University Press.

Nicholas C. Burbules

THE LIMITS OF DIALOGUE AS A CRITICAL PEDAGOGY

Introduction

It seems that hardly anyone has a bad word to say against dialogue. A broad range of political orientations hold out the aim of "fostering dialogue" as a potential resolution to social conflict and as a basis for rational public deliberation. A range of pedagogical approaches, from constructivist scaffolding to Socratic instruction to Freirean liberatory pedagogy, all proclaim the virtues of an interactive engagement of questions and answers in the shared pursuit of knowledge and understanding. Philosophical accounts of dialogue from Plato to the present employ the dialogical form as a literary genre that represents the external expression of an internal, dialectical thought process of back-and-forth ratiocination. Dialogue constitutes a point of opportunity at which these three interests—political, pedagogical, and philosophical—come together. It is widely assumed that the aim of teaching with and through dialogue serves democracy, promotes communication across difference, and enables the active coconstruction of new knowledge and understandings.[1]

Nevertheless, the ideal of dialogue has received withering criticism, particularly from poststructural feminist theorists in education and from those for whom "difference" is a lived experience of marginalization and not just a demographic category of identification. For these critics, "dialogue" has exerted a kind of hegemonic dominance that belies its emancipatory rhetoric, its apparent openness to difference, and its stress on equality and reciprocity within the dialogical relation. The way in which dialogue has become almost synonymous with critical pedagogy has tended to submerge the voices and concerns of groups who feel themselves closed out of dialogue or compelled to join it only at the cost of restricting their self-expression into acceptable channels of communication. Finally, an idealized, prescriptive conception of dialogue has abstracted the situated historicity of specific practices of communicative engagement from their consequences for people and groups who encounter the invitation to dialogue in difficult circumstances of conflict.

In light of such reactions, the claims made on behalf of dialogue as an inherently liberatory pedagogy need to be reassessed. The insistence that dialogue is somehow self-corrective, that if there are unresolved power differentials or unexamined silences and omissions within a dialogue, simply persisting with the same forms of dialogical exchange can bring them to light, seems not only counterproductive but itself a form of hegemony: if dialogue fails, the solution to the problem is more of the same.

Yet it also remains true that the ideal of "dialogue" expresses hope for the possibility of open, respectful, critical engagements from which we can learn about others, about the world, and about ourselves. Is there a space between the exaggerated claims made on behalf of dialogue entirely as an inherently liberatory pedagogy and the rejection of dialogue as an ideal? Can dialogue continue in good faith while acknowledging the inherent limits to (and dangers arising from) its aspirations toward understanding across differences? Or must such aspirations toward understanding and communication be abandoned entirely? These are the questions animating this essay.

The Fetishization of Dialogue

We seem to be living in an era in which, for many, "dialogue" has become the foundation of last resort in an antifoundational world. The thoroughgoing proceduralism of placing trust in processes of interpersonal communication has proven to be compatible with a wide range of otherwise quite different social and political stances. Dialogue represents, to one view or another, a way of reconciling differences; a means of promoting empathy and understanding for others; a mode of collaborative inquiry; a method of critically comparing and testing alternative hypotheses; a form of constructivist teaching and learning; a forum for deliberation and negotiation about public policy differences; a therapeutic engagement of self- and Other-exploration; and a basis for shaping uncoerced social and political consensus.[2] I will briefly review six dominant traditions that have centrally invoked the concept of dialogue, particularly in relation to the aims and methods of education.

(1) For liberal views of dialogue, such as those of John Dewey or Benjamin Barber, dialogue is the fulcrum around which the imperatives of democracy can be reconciled with the facts of diversity and conflict. For exponents of "deliberative democracy" it is in public, communicative engagements that democracy works its will, and a chief aim of democratic education must be to foster in learners the capabilities and dispositions to participate in such deliberations. An implication of this

stance, however, is that those who do not, who cannot, or who choose not to develop or exercise these capabilities suffer an attenuated relation, at best, to the democratic public sphere, if not an actual exclusion from it: "Proponents of liberal
dialogue are not sensitive enough to the fact that a theory of conversational restraint may be damaging precisely to the interests of those groups that have not
been traditional actors in the public space of liberalism—like women, nonwhite
peoples, and sometimes nonpropertied males."[3] Public education is supposed to be
an arena of training for engagement in the rough and tumble of public deliberation;
but the very avenues of opportunity for access to deliberation *on these terms* can be
seen from a different vantage point as barriers of exclusion.

(2) Some versions of feminism, by contrast, tend to reject the agonistic features
of dialogue in this sense and to promote a more receptive, caring stance in the dialogical relation. Deborah Tannen's recent popular book, *The Argument Culture:
Moving from Debate to Dialogue*, is an extended paean to this nonconfrontational
view.[4] More detailed and modulated treatments of this theme can be found in Mary
Belenky and colleagues, Carol Gilligan, and Nel Noddings.[5] What relates all of
these accounts is a linkage between a competitive, adversarial approach to public or
private disagreements and the stereotypical norms of masculine behavior, and the
association of "dialogue" with the more open, receptive, inclusive spirit of women's
values. Educational and social deliberation that privileges the more adversarial
mode of interaction and discourages or dismisses the more tentative and cooperative spirit of dialogue, in this view, discriminates against females in schools and in
the public sphere generally. These authors are always careful to insist that this more
receptive stance does not preclude vigorous disagreement and self-assertion, but it is
not difficult to see why these views have come to be labeled by other feminists as
"good girl" feminism.[6] Without intruding myself into this particular disagreement,
I think it is clear why the mode of dialogue proposed under this view of feminism
has not been seen as adequate for the more confrontational politics favored by certain other feminists and by the aggrieved members of other groups.

(3) Platonic views of dialogue stress the role of communicative interchange as a
proving ground for inquiries into truth: while in his dialogues the protagonist
Socrates distinguishes "disputatious" and "friendly" forms of dialogue (paralleling
in some ways the distinction just explored under point 2), in both forms the joint
endeavor is to propose and oppose, to formulate arguments and to put forth coun-
terexamples and counterarguments, as the mechanism by which truth is ascer-
tained. It is an intriguing feature of this view, reflected later in a different context in
the work of Freire and others, that this philosophical conception of dialogue coin-
cides with a preferred pedagogy, for, in Plato's view, the way in which knowledge
claims are adjudicated and tested is also the way to teach. Dialogue is a way of
drawing forth latent, unformed understandings and facilitating the discovery of

truths by the learner for himself or herself—hence the ubiquity of teachers from law schools to kindergartens to adult literacy programs ascribing their teaching to "*the* Socratic method" (though this method never comprised only one style of teaching[7]). But the Platonic view of dialogue rested upon a view of knowledge as absolute, unchanging, and humanly attainable through recollection—an epistemological stance that almost no one would feel comfortable with today. I suspect that few contemporary advocates of the Socratic method as a pedagogy would want to be held to the underpinnings by which Plato advocated and justified it.

(4) Hermeneutic views of dialogue tend to emphasize dialogue as a condition of intersubjective understanding: what Hans-Georg Gadamer calls "the fusing of horizons." A precursor of this view can be found in the existential theology of Martin Buber's I-Thou relation. Hermeneutic dialogue emphasizes the relational, to-and-fro movement of question and answer as an avenue toward understanding and agreement. This intersubjective confirmation stands in direct contrast to the objectivist view of convergence around the truth that we find in Platonic views of dialogue. But critics of this hermeneutic view of dialogue have tended to question its limited capacity for critique and for engaging issues of power and inequality that stand outside the dialogical relation; these contexts need to be problematized in terms that go beyond their impact on interpersonal understanding. Moreover, some have questioned the aim of understanding itself as insufficiently attuned to cultural differences and as dangerously naive in supposing that when "fusing" occurs, it occurs on neutral ground:

> By communicative dialogue, I mean a controlled process of interaction that seeks successful communication, defined as the moment of full understanding. For those who advocate it in education, communicative dialogue drives toward mutual understanding as a pedagogical ideal. . . . What kind of knowledge does dialogue proffer? What techniques does it use to regulate knowledge and the relationship of the teacher and student within the dialogue to knowledge and truth? I'm persuaded that dialogue . . . is not just a neutral conduit of insights, discoveries, understandings, agreements, or disagreements. It has a constitutive force. It is a tool, it is *for* something. . . . [It] tries to accurately represent the world through the conventions and politics of realism.[8]

(5) Most contemporary critical views of dialogue, especially those in education, invariably refer to the important work of Paulo Freire. Indeed, for an entire generation of critical educators, his writings and life's work stand as an inspiring model of committed pedagogy, and he has had a primary impact on the work of widely read North American authors including Henry Giroux, Peter McLaren, and Ira Shor. Yet

it must be said that this very popularity and loyalty have interfered at times with the selective, critical appropriation and reinterpretation of his ideas. Freire's distinctions of monological versus dialogical pedagogies, his critique of "banking" forms of education as the mere "depositing" of information in the minds of students, his conception of *conscientization* as the overcoming of what he calls "intransitive consciousness" are all virtually canonical. Freirean pedagogy is sometimes taken as simply synonymous with critical pedagogy or radical pedagogy, forcing feminists and others to find different ways of describing alternative critical educational theories and practices.[9] Yet, as the roots of Freire's pedagogy have come to be more clearly identified in specifically Hegelian, Marxist, and Catholic assumptions, it has become necessary to ask whether this particular constellation of theories is the best or only basis for a radical theory and practice of pedagogy. In some accounts, Freirean dialogue is regarded as a practice with *intrinsic* critical and emancipatory potential; but many authors, notably some feminists, do not find space within it for critique and emancipation on their terms.[10]

(6) Finally, there are what might be termed postliberal views of dialogue, especially the work of Jürgen Habermas.[11] Perhaps no contemporary theorist has gone further in proposing a model of communicative dialogue as the nonfoundational foundation for epistemological, political, and moral adjudication. For Habermas, all claims are filtered through the medium of discourse, but it is a medium with evaluative standards built in: communicative claims rest upon implicit norms that can be, and should be, critically questioned and redeemed. The grounding of truth and value claims lies in the uncoerced consensus that such deliberations can achieve—including, significantly, critical reflection on the conditions under which that agreement is obtained. These conditions—uncoerced consensus and the implicit norms (discursively redeemed) that regulate communicative interactions—give the outcomes of such deliberation a generalizability not based upon absolute claims of truth or rightness, but secured on the nonrelative criterion of valid agreement among those parties concerned.

Critics of Habermas, including Seyla Benhabib, have complained that this account of communication assumes a commonality in modes of communication and a kind of impersonality toward the way in which participants in deliberation are identified: the emphasis is on the conditions under which consensus is obtained, not the specific choices and identities of those party to it. While sharing the basic idea of discursive justification, Benhabib wants to situate this process in the actual identities, positions, and differences among participants. She calls this "interactive universalism":

Interactive universalism acknowledges the plurality of modes of being human, and differences among humans, without endorsing all these pluralities and differences as morally and politically valid. While agreeing that normative disputes can be settled rationally, and that fairness, reciprocity, and some procedure of universalizability are constituents, that is necessary conditions of the moral standpoint, interactive universalism regards difference as a starting point for reflection and action. In this sense, "universality" is a regulative ideal that does not deny our embodied and embedded identity, but aims at developing moral attitudes and encouraging political transformations that can yield a point of view acceptable to all. Universality is not the ideal consensus of fictitiously defined selves, but the concrete process in politics and morals of the struggle of concrete, embodied selves, striving for autonomy.[12]

Benhabib's move, emphasizing the actual difference, embodiment, and situatedness of communicative participants, and her shift from rational agreement *per se* to the ongoing conditions (social and interpersonal) that can support sustained deliberation among contesting points of view, make the Habermasian model both more concrete and more responsive to the fact of cultural diversity.

Nevertheless, even this account has been challenged, for example by Judith Butler, as insufficiently sensitive to difference and as essentially normalizing, that is, tending to discipline the acceptable forms of communication in terms of dominant norms.[13] For Butler and other poststructural critics, the process of relentlessly problematizing conventional norms and categories proceeds through the interrogation of the silences, gaps, and paradoxes of inclusion/exclusion that bedevil even the most "participatory" models of public deliberation—including the disciplinary regimes that suggest (however invitingly): "we fully welcome your participation *on these terms.*" The subtle workings-out of asymmetries of power and access often belie the open and reasonable self-conception of the Habermasian (or even the Benhabibian) models of communication, making even their sincerely invitational gestures a kind of false seduction into conformity. For Butler, Ellsworth, Lather, and other critics, the response is to resist the "good behavior" that is made a condition of participation in favor of what Anderson calls "performative subversion," pointedly refusing to valorize such conditions.[14]

These six conceptions of dialogue comprise almost the entire range of discussion about the topic within the field of education. I have briefly reviewed them, and some of the prominent criticisms against them, not to engage each of these debates in detail, but to draw the background against which current disputes over dialogue are situated. While these six views are quite different from one another, and indeed disagree among themselves over many issues, they have certain crucial features in common. They all place primary emphasis on dialogue as the adjudicative basis for social and political discussion and disagreement. They all privilege dialogue as the basis for arriving at valid intersubjective understanding or knowledge. And they all, in the educational domain, recommend dialogue as the mode of pedagogical engagement best able to promote learning, autonomy, and an understanding of one's self in relation to others. The prominence of these six views, particularly among educational theorists and practitioners of what might be called broadly the "progressivist" stripe, has meant that *dialogue* is the topic of the day and that promoting dialogue and the conditions which can support it is taken as a central educational task. But the critics of dialogue raise issues that cannot easily be swept aside; and, in my view, some of these criticisms have raised deep problems for that approach.

Dialogue, Diversity, and Difference

As noted, one major point of criticism that has been raised against some accounts of dialogue is whether it is sufficiently sensitive to conditions of diversity, that is, the different forms of cultural communication, the different aims and values held by members of different groups, and the serious conflicts and histories of oppression and harm that have excluded marginalized groups from public and educational conversations in the past. Certainly, many accounts of dialogue have tried to respond positively to such criticisms.[15] Yet even these attempts to respond have pointed up serious limitations in the standard accounts of dialogue.

What seems to recommend dialogue as a pedagogy is its capacity for active participation by all parties; its room for the coconstruction of understanding or knowledge that can be negotiated between the perspectives of different members; its critical potential, which allows for not only questioning "within" the dialogue, but questioning its very terms and assumptions; and its open-endedness, its capacity for continuing and expanding the conversation to include multiple voices and perspectives—indeed, for many purposes, actively seeking them out. These are not trivial advantages, especially compared against many of the pedagogical practices currently in favor in education at all levels of schooling. Yet, as noted earlier, there is something self-confirming about this model: that its capacity to be self-corrective, in certain instances, is taken as proof that there is no legitimate "outside" to its procedures. One could call this "the hegemony of reasonableness": that precisely because dialogue seems to hold out the hand of inclusiveness and respect for all points of view, it makes those suspicious of its tacit rules of engagement, its "modes of address," as Ellsworth calls them, its scope of what is and is not up for discussion, appear as if *they* are at fault for remaining outside the conversation.

Dialogue runs up against difficulty in encounters with diversity. Not everyone speaks the same language. Whose language will be used? Are the ground rules for participation, however thinly procedural they might appear, actually substantive restrictions on what can be talked about, on how things can be talked about, and so upon who can or will be part of the conversation? What are the limits of reflexivity within dialogue? Is the invitation to participate already a kind of co-optation of *radical* critique and rejectionism? Are the dialogical aims of consensus, provisional agreement, and even understanding (across unresolved differences) based upon ideals of harmony and community that are always on *somebody's* terms, and so threaten the maintenance of separate, self-determined identities? Finally, are there some differences that are simply unbridgeable in dialogue, gaps of understanding or belief that cannot be bridged—but which, in the attempt to bridge them, put some people more at risk more than others?

There are three broad ways that different models of dialogue have tried to address such issues of diversity. To an extent, these cut across the six traditions described above, although some are more amenable to certain approaches than others. None of them adequately addresses, in my view, the criticisms of radical diversity just discussed. The first, *pluralism*, or the "melting pot" ideal, regards social and cultural diversity as a positive resource for the exchange of beliefs, values, and experiences that can inform and invigorate dialogue, but with the specific aims of reconciling these differences in agreements or compromises that combine the best elements from each perspective or form new, common understandings with which all parties can identify. In many instances, however, pluralism in this sense simply comes to the end of assimilating diverse groups into predominantly mainstream beliefs and values (though, to a much lesser extent, dominant or mainstream views may be modified over time as well). This asymmetry of change threatens, in the long run, to erase significant cultural difference or to relegate it entirely to the private, not public, sphere.

The second approach to diversity, *multiculturalism*, perhaps the most widely held view in education today, emphasizes respecting (or celebrating) differences, not for the sake of assimilating them into dominant cultural forms but to preserve them, both out of respect for the integrity of diverse cultural traditions and out of an appreciation of cultural variety for its own sake. However, this inclusive or celebratory attitude can also have the effect of exoticizing differences, rendering them quaint or interesting as artifacts and not as critical points of reference against which to view one's self. The framework within which multiculturalism often takes shape, a broad (and sometimes patronizing) "tolerance" for difference, leaves dominant beliefs and values largely unquestioned—indeed even insulated from challenge and change—because they are shielded within the comforting self-conception of openness and inclusivity. But as Cameron McCarthy has noted, multiculturalism means little if it is only Other-regarding and does not become an occasion for questioning the dominant cultural orientation as itself one of many, unprivileged, and just as quaint or strange (needing to be "tolerated") when viewed from the outside. Where cultural dominance comes from, and how it settles into a taken-for-grantedness that makes its own specificity invisible, is a question rarely explored within the multicultural framework.[16]

A third view, *cosmopolitanism*, of growing interest recently, emphasizes the unreconciled coexistence of diverse cultures and groups.[17] Informed to some extent by a global perspective that recognizes not only the radical diversity of cultural difference but also the attenuated circumstances that bring these cultures in contact with one another, this view of diversity (while often sharing many features with multiculturalism) acknowledges the limits of assimilation, agreement, or even understanding across certain cultural divides, and concludes that in many cases there must simply be an end to talk that seeks to bridge or minimize differences. Where such conversations exacerbate or heighten the awareness of disagreements or conflicting interests, continuing them may weaken rather than strengthen the prospects for a minimally harmonious condition in which each agrees to allow (and not necessarily respect or approve) the cultural domain and prerogatives of the other. The problem with this view, however, is that it abrogates—and sometimes prejudges and rejects out of hand—the value of engagement, excluding both the possibility of mutual accommodation and the possibility of a critical questioning of one view from a radically different other.

Because of the currency of debates over these three views, the question of the possibility and prospects for dialogue in contexts of diversity has become one of the central, if not *the* central, issues in contemporary educational theory and practice (to say nothing of larger social and political debates). The conventional view is that such dialogue is always a worthy effort and learning opportunity, even if in some cases it may unfortunately fall short of its ideals.

The problem here is that dialogue is variously viewed from these positions as a means of bridging differences, reconciling differences, coordinating action despite differences, or achieving understanding, respect, or tolerance in the face of differences. These objectives are clearly desirable under many circumstances, including educational circumstances; but these dynamics cannot be viewed symmetrically from all points of view. While some may view dialogue as a benefit, or a potential benefit, others may regard it as a threat, and others as an impossibility. The rejection of dialogue, or the refusal to submit one's views to questioning, compromise, or renegotiation, is not always a mark of irrationality. The very aim of dialogue to speak and understand across differences is not an unalloyed benefit to all potential parties to such dialogue. Moreover, "difference" here is constituted as a dimension of *diversity*—categorical differentiation according to demographic, cultural, or identity categories. Dialogue tends to construct differences as instances of diverse values and points of view along continuums where middle grounds may exist, where commonalties may be found, or where translations across gulfs of misunderstanding may be achieved. Sometimes these are realistic prospects. Sometimes they are not; and where they are not, the reasonable gestures of inclusion made within dialogue can actually constitute co-opting or even coercive moves that put upon those with strong differences the burden of justifying why they will not participate.

In some of my earlier work, I suggested that dialogue could yield a range of outcomes, ranging from *agreement*; to a *consensus* (or in Rawlsian terms an "overlapping consensus") that falls short of full agreement; to an *understanding* that falls short of agreement or consensus; to a respectful *tolerance* that falls short of full understanding. Each of these, I suggested, can have fruitful educational benefits. My main point was that dialogue does not have to achieve agreement, consensus, or even understanding to be educationally (or socially and politically) worthwhile. Theoretically, this represented my departure from Habermasian or Gadamerian views of dialogue. I now think that this view suffered from three serious limitations. One is that these outcomes cannot be placed easily along a single continuum, like railroad stations at which a train may stop; that they are actually quite discontinuous sorts of paths, often entailing very different sorts of dialogical interactions— and so one cannot simply say that dialogue moves along a single "track" and gets as far along it as possible, aiming toward agreement or consensus, perhaps, but being satisfied with something less than that if full "success" cannot be achieved. Instead, assumptions at the start concerning which of several ends is possible or desirable have a determinative effect upon the form and tone of the *type* of dialogue in which one is engaged (and into which one is inviting others).[18] *This* determination ("What type of dialogue are we having?") is one in which unilateral judgment and cultural dominance often play a central role.

The second failing was to underestimate the role of misunderstanding, and even incommensurability, as potentially necessary and even educationally beneficial ends under certain circumstances. I regarded them as failures of dialogue, or a sign that dialogue had not proceeded long enough. I stressed that one should never presume the outcome of incommensurability and suggested that one should always approach dialogue "as if" it need not end up that way. This was a mistake. There are instances in which the very encounter with a radically different, unreconciled, and unreconcilable point of view, value, voice, or belief can serve important educational purposes: to cause us to question the horizons of our own assumptions, to explore within ourselves (and not only within the other) the causes of why dialogue "fails," and to consider the possibility of a radically different way of approaching the world. Dialogue in the mode of resolving or dissolving differences provides no tools for coping with such encounters or deriving meaning from them; it regards them as failures or breakdowns, and not as limitations within the model of dialogue itself.

The third failing was to conceive difference solely in the sense of categorical diversity. As Homi Bhabha and others argue, cultural difference can be taken in a different way: as a less stable, noncategorical dimension that is a feature of lived experience and identity.[19] From this standpoint, differences are enacted. They change over time. They take shape differently in varied contexts. They surpass our attempts to classify or define them. Ellsworth puts it well, that the purpose of dialogue is not just speaking across given positions of difference, but a relation in which those very positions can be (need to be) questioned. Difference, then, is more than a matter of multicultural diversity, of speaking within and across stable identities; it is a challenge to these in three ways, which I have sketched in more recent work as *differences within*, *differences beyond*, and *differences against*.[20] Respectively, these three phrases refer to the ways in which: (1) difference stands not only as an external feature of the "other," but as an unexplored and unrecognized dimension of one's self (for example, in the ways by which heterosexuality is defined and defended implicitly as *not-homosexual*, thereby invoking its "opposite" as a part of its own self-conception); (2) difference exceeds categories of understanding, challenging these in ways that confound conventional vocabularies and assumptions (for example, when racial categories such as "black" and "white" become denaturalized and subject to all sorts of redefinitions, including those of skin color themselves [no one actually has black or white skin], the conflating of racial with national or ethnic differences, the emphasis on hybrid, creole, or border identities, and so on); and (3) difference is defined by its resistance, defined against dominant norms, and its persistent refusal to allow itself to be characterized from dominant, conventional points of view. In each of these three ways difference poses a fundamental challenge to views of dialogue oriented around achieving understanding or agreement—each, in its own way, is a repudiation of convergent models of discourse generally, and each, in its own way, resists the categorical characterization of diversity—no category can possibly contain these sorts of difference.

It is possible to put the point even more strongly: that the effect of traditional views of dialogue has been to "domesticate" difference: to make it safe and comprehensible by regarding all differences as elements of mere variation (diversity), and hence as starting points of potential reconciliation. This is not a neutral standpoint, even as it represents itself as such; it misses deeper, more radical conceptions of difference.

Dialogue as Decontextualized Pedagogy

The crucial shift in perspective outlined here is from a prescriptive model of dialogue as a neutral communicative process, a procedure in which all participants are treated equally, concerned only with the search for knowledge, understanding, and perhaps agreement, to dialogue as a situated practice, one implicated by the particulars of who, when, where, and how the dialogue takes place. The elevation of dialogue as a general pedagogical method abstracts its operations from those particulars and, as noted earlier, treats deviations from that ideal as either illegitimate violations of its rules or as unfortunate shortcomings that can be remedied through the application of more of the same—continuing with dialogue until these failures of understanding or agreement can be remedied. Radical difference, difference that *resists* accommodation or assimilation, is rendered inexplicable or perverse. But when one examines the who, when, where, and how of dialogue, such characterizations become much more difficult to defend.[21]

WHO. The first issue begins with the growing diversity of classrooms (at all levels of education) and the increasing awareness of the margins or borders of common school culture as it interacts with the very different values and orientations that students bring to the classroom. The conditions of globalization and mobility have promoted both direct forms of migration across national/cultural categories and (especially with the rise of new communication and information technologies) an increasing proximity and interaction of multiple lines of national/cultural influence. In this context, the central assumptions of common schooling—of a canon of texts, of a shared historical tradition, of a common language—are thrown into question, since even where such elements might be defended, their value and significance are going to be regarded differently from different positions as teachers and students. In some cases they will be directly challenged. The shift to a dialogical approach, in itself, does not remedy these conflicts; and when more radical conceptions of difference are at stake, the very notion of "remedying" such conflicts and disagreements becomes deeply problematic.

A dialogue is not an engagement of two (or more) abstract persons, but of people with characteristics, styles, values, and assumptions that shape the particular ways in which they engage in discourse. Any prescriptive conception of dialogue must confront the challenge of acknowledging persons who do not engage in communication through those forms and who might in fact be excluded or disadvantaged by them. Conversely, an account of dialogue that acknowledges the enormous multiplicity of forms in which people from different cultures do enact pedagogical communicative relations (let alone communicative relations generally) needs to address the question of why some versions are rewarded with the prescriptive label "dialogue" and others are not.

Aside from the multiplicity of communicative forms, there is also a multiplicity of communicative purposes in dialogue. In many contexts, for example, the formation and negotiation of identity may constitute the primary purpose in mind for some participants in a dialogical relation, supplanting more overt teaching-learning goals. Such dynamics may be only partly intended or conscious (and hence only partly susceptible to reflection or change). Participation in dialogue, even at the microlevel of apparent personal "choice," is not *simply* a matter of choice. The utterances that comprise an ongoing dialogue are already made (or not made) in the context of an awareness of the reactions—real, anticipated, or imagined—of other participants. The more that one pushes this sort of analysis, the more the achievement, or suppression, of dialogical possibilities comes to be seen as an expression of a group interdynamic, and not something resulting simply from the choices and actions of individuals.

WHEN. We do not just use language; language uses us. As Bakhtin argued, the nature of discourse is that the language we encounter already has a history; the words that we speak have been spoken by others before us (he calls this "the internal dialogism of the word").[22] As a result, what we speak always means more than we mean to say; the language that we use carries with it implications, connotations, and consequences that we can only partly intend. The words that others hear from us, how they understand them, and what they say in response are beyond our unilateral control. The multivalence of discourse situates specific speech acts or relations in a web of potential significations that is indeterminate, nonlinear, and highly susceptible to the effects of context and cultural difference.

A dialogue is not simply a momentary engagement between two or more people; it is a discursive relation situated against the background of previous relations involving them and the relation of what they are speaking today to the history of those words spoken before them. These background conditions are also not simply matters of choice, and they impinge upon the dialogical relation in ways that may shape or limit the possibilities of communication and understanding. Often these relations are expressed as forms of power or privilege, because the relative positions of people place asymmetrical constraints on who can speak, who can be heard, and who has a stake in maintaining a particular dialogue or in challenging it. The prescriptive model of dialogue has reinforced a view of dialogue as a finite and bounded engagement, often described with little or no context and with scant consideration given to what might have transpired before or may transpire after the dialogue at hand. This has tended to support the idea of a dialogue as a unitary, goal-oriented conversation with a discrete purpose and a beginning, middle, and end, not as a slice of an ongoing communicative relation, as it nearly always is in educational settings.

WHERE. Recent years have seen a growth of interest in such problems as situated cognition, group learning, the relation of expert and novice understandings, real-world problem solving, distributed intelligence, and a whole range of similar notions that address in different ways the actual means by which the learning of individuals occurs in the contexts of existing social relations and practice.

These concerns apply directly to the matter of dialogue. The situatedness of dialogue, considered as a discursive practice, means that the dialogical relation depends not only upon what people are saying to each other, but the context in which they come together (the classroom or the cafeteria, for example), where they are positioned in relation to each other (standing, sitting, or communicating on-line), and what other gestures or activities work with or against the grain of the interaction. Dialogue has a materiality, which means paying attention to both facilitating and inhibitive characteristics in the circumstances under which it takes place. Nor is it simply a matter of the present context at hand but also of other contexts—including anticipated future contexts of need or use—that shape the understanding of purposes that guide or direct a dialogical engagement. For example, interactions at home, in the playground or lunchroom, or on the street before or after school may constitute contexts of teaching and learning that are at least as important for certain participants as the interaction in the classroom; and relative importance aside, they certainly impinge upon the thoughts, feelings, and motivations participants bring to the classroom.

HOW. Another aspect of this situatedness, or materiality, is that the texts and objects of representation that mediate classroom discourse can have distinctive effects on what can be said and how it can be understood. Where interaction takes place in an immediate, face-to-face circumstance, these "texts" include not only the words themselves, but facial expressions, gestures, and similar representational forms. Yet dialogue often also takes place in mediated forms: a dialogue between a book's reader and its author; a dialogue between correspondents writing to one another; a dialogue over a telephone; a dialogue through e-mail; and so on. The tendency of previous accounts of dialogue has been to ignore such factors or, if they are considered at all, to relegate them to trivial significance compared to what the words themselves express. Yet substantial research across a range of fields has highlighted the ways in which the circumstances of form and medium are *not* trivial but can influence what is said and how it is understood and the ways in which these media are signifying elements themselves.[23]

In these four ways, then, the prescriptive account of dialogue has been impeded by the formal, idealized models through which it has been characterized: impeded because these models have often not taken account of the situated, relational, material circumstances in which such discursive practices actually take place. Attending to the social dynamics and contexts of classroom discourse heightens the awareness of the complexities and difficulties of changing specific elements within larger communities of practice. These communities may be the primary shapers of teaching and learning processes, but not always in ways that serve intended or ideal educational objectives; other purposes, such as identity-formation or negotiating relations of group solidarity, may predominate. The power of such social processes may restrict lines of inquiry, distort dialogical interactions, and silence perspectives in ways that conflict with the explicit purposes of education.

Rethinking dialogue along these lines holds promise for developing theoretical accounts of dialogue that are richer, more complex, and better attuned to the material circumstances of pedagogical practice. Dialogue, from this standpoint, cannot be viewed simply as a form of question and answer, but as a relation constituted in a web of relations among multiple forms of communication, human practices, and mediating objects or texts.

Criticizing the Decontextualized, Prescriptive Model of Dialogue

The major contemporary critic of the prescriptive model of dialogue and its virtually unquestioned role in critical pedagogy is Elizabeth Ellsworth. Her current critique focuses on considering dialogue as a "mode of address," one that positions teacher and learner in a determinate relation (even one that is ostensibly egalitarian) and, in so doing, constrains the possibilities of communicative exchange, no matter how "open" it aspires to be. Instead, Ellsworth calls for "pedagogical modes of address that aren't founded on striving for and desiring certainty, continuity, and control" and "pedagogical modes of address that *multiply* and *set in motion* the positions from which they can be 'met' and responded to."[24] Referring in part directly to some of my own earlier work, she writes,

> By communicative dialogue, I mean a controlled process of interaction that seeks successful communication, defined as the moment of full understanding. For those who advocate it in education, communicative dialogue drives toward mutual understanding as a pedagogical ideal. . . . In other words, what must come first in communicative dialogue is understanding—that is, a supposedly innocent, disinterested reading of the other's message. *Then* disagreement is allowed. . . . What communicative dialogue cannot tolerate, what it *must* exclude, is the one who says, "Our differences are such that you cannot understand me, and I cannot understand you.". . . Communicative dialogue works only when we act as if its mode of address is a neutral conduit of reality, and not itself a rhetoric—not itself a mediation of knowledge and of its participants' relations to knowledge.[25]

I think that this criticism is basically correct: a conception of dialogue based on the idea that "successful communication" can only mean "full understanding," and the idea that dialogue is, or can be, a "neutral conduit of reality," itself proof from question, is entirely inadequate—even damaging. There are many cases in which the striving for understanding (or agreement) at all costs will run roughshod over individual or group differences that cannot be bridged easily or reconciled with dominant understandings. It must be seen that dialogue can be "successful" just in the sense of bringing to light the experience and perspectives of others quite different from ourselves (and this can be a kind of success even when we cannot entirely understand, let along agree, with them). Ellsworth is right that the ideal of "dialogue" can become an actual impediment to human freedom, diversity, and coexistence. Moreover, Ellsworth is also right that, if the implicit communicative rules and aims of a dialogical engagement cannot themselves be questioned or challenged, reflexively, from within the dialogue, then not only will certain voices or perspectives be excluded from possible participation, but the medium of dialogue itself becomes a way of structuring interpersonal knowledge and understanding, in a decidedly nonneutral way, without recourse to considering alternative frames that might be possible.

What puzzles me about Ellsworth's criticisms of "communicative dialogue" is, first of all, to wonder where she finds such a caricatured view of dialogue in my own work (where I have repeatedly said that knowledge, agreement, and understanding are only some of the potential outcomes of dialogue; that dialogue sometimes encounters differences that surpass our ability to understand them and lead to unreconciled disagreement; and that these, too, can foster important educational benefits and learning opportunities).[26] But of greater concern to me is whether Ellsworth thinks that, having disposed of "communicative dialogue," in the sense she describes it, one has refuted somehow the idea of dialogue itself. Sometimes she has written as if she thinks that she has.[27] But in her latest work, in fact, she actually defends an alternative ideal of dialogue, which she terms (following psychoanalytic theory) "analytic dialogue":

> What gets "analyzed". . . is the route of a reading. How did you *arrive* at this interpretation, without knowing it—maybe even without desiring it? How have your/our passages through history, power, desire, and language on the way to this interpretation become integral parts of the very structure of the interpretation—of our knowledge?[28]

I believe that Ellsworth is exploring here a crucial sense in which any communicative form, including "dialogue," needs to be subject to question itself. No medium is neutral, no utterance or observation can claim an entirely disinterested or nonpositioned vantage point. Whenever any pedagogical practice or relation becomes "naturalized" and comes to be seen as the only possibility, the best possibility, or the most "politically correct" possibility, it becomes (ironically) an impediment to human freedom, diversity, exploration, and—therefore—the possibilities of learning and discovery. As I have noted, in many accounts of dialogue and pedagogy the "fetishization" of dialogue has obscured some of its real limitations and contradictions. Moreover, the proclamation of any particular dialogical genre as *the* instrument of human emancipation (such as the Socratic method, Freirean pedagogy, or a Habermasian search for consensus) will inevitably exclude, silence, or normalize others from radically different subject positions. I and other theorists working on these topics owe appreciation to Ellsworth, Patti Lather, Mary Leach, Alison Jones, and other feminist poststructural critics for pressing this issue so strongly.

Engaging the Criticisms: From Prescriptivism to the Practice of Dialogue

I would like to think that I am open to criticism and try to learn from my mistakes. Still, I persist in thinking that some of these very criticisms reinforce the value of "dialogue" in some sense, if in a very different sense from its conventional uses (and, as I have noted, even Ellsworth wants to defend a conception of "dialogue"). I believe that this alternative view of dialogue begins by questioning two elements in most conventional views of dialogue: *prescriptivism* and *proceduralism*.[29] Questioning prescriptivism entails reflecting on the ways in which "dialogue" has become a kind of unquestioned ideal, a norm, and a rhetorical device. To invite others into dialogue is seen as an unassailable gesture of good will. Who could criticize or reject such a gesture, except the ill-willed, the alienated, the recalcitrant? Such a stance, however, ignores the many ways in which this invitation may *not* be open-ended or neutral, or not experienced as such by others, even when it is intended to be. To enter into a conversation is to accept a set of tacit communicative norms; it is to run the (often asymmetrical) risks of disclosure; it is to undertake to explain one's self, perhaps justify one's self, under questioning; it is to submit to a set of assumptions about what "the subject" of the dialogue is about and what it is not. The point here is not that these commitments are *never* fair expectations to have of participants to a dialogue; it is to acknowledge that for many parties, under specific circumstances, they represent a kind of entrapment, a kind of co-optation, in which some persons have more to lose than do others. From this standpoint the humanistic ideal of "engaging in dialogue" comes to be seen as subtly coercive, even threatening. And for theorists, such as myself, who have tended to favor persistence and "keeping the dialogue going" as prescriptive norms, this criticism provides a much-needed rebuke.

Alison Jones provides a fascinating analysis of this problem in practice. Juxtaposing the ideal versions of dialogical pedagogy with the realities of conversation in a class where she brings together Maori (native, minority culture) and Pakeha (European, dominant-culture) students in New Zealand, she notes that "an ideal dialogical model for the classroom asserts that stories and meanings of less powerful as well as more powerful groups will intermingle and 'be heard' in mutual communication and progressive understanding. . . . [It] assumes that the opportunity for subordinate groups to express themselves in the critical classroom becomes an opportunity for 'empowerment.'" But Jones shows how in practice even this apparently benevolent, receptive stance by those in relative positions of power can in fact reinscribe their privileges and advantages: "Border-crossing and 'recognitions of difference' turns out to be *access for dominant groups to the thoughts, cultures, lives of others.*" She even terms this a "cannibal desire to 'know the other,'" a further sort of exploitation, which the Maori students understandably resist:

> In the midst of all this mess and discomfort, I wonder what is the pleasure in (ethnic) difference for the dominant group in education? Why do we repeat the phrase in our theories and writing, at this fashionable moment of respect for, if not celebration of, difference? Apart from a certain voyeurism, is it not that "we" (the liberal/radical dominant) can be reassured . . . by the other-who-now-speaks that we are part of the scene of redemption; that we are not the unfashionable colonizer/oppressor whose despised description fills our textbooks, and from whom we . . . are usually pleasingly distanced? . . . [*We*] seek liberation, through "your" dialogue with us. Touched by your attention, *we are included with you*, and therefore cleaned from the taint of colonization and power which *excludes*.[30]

The second, related issue is the proceduralism of most accounts of dialogue: the characterization of dialogue in terms of a particular set of communicative norms and the response, when conflict or friction arises, that the resolution of these can (and should) take place through a reinvigorated application *of those same norms*. It is clear from Ellsworth's critique that this shields from questioning or criticism those norms themselves. Yet here we encounter a paradox (the first of several to follow), one that begins to turn the discussion of dialogue into a different, more productive theoretical vein. For if questioning the restrictive norms of dialogue is regarded as a good thing, is it not at least in part so that a fuller, fairer, more inclusive dialogue might be made *possible*? If persons choose to withdraw from a dialogue with those who do not or cannot understand them, is it not in part so that they are able to enter a dialogue with others who *can* understand them? If "analytic dialogue" seeks (rightly, I would say) to uncover the nonneutral, historically specific conditions under which its own interpretations proceed, is this not so that others might *come to share the same understanding, at least in part, about these conditions*? It seems strange indeed to imagine a dialogue in which *every* understanding emerges as entirely idiosyncratic and separate from every other or one that is so persistently pulling up the roots of its own genealogy that the participants never talk *about* the topic at hand.

One of the most admirable elements in Ellsworth's book is her honesty about some of the paradoxes of her own pedagogical practice.[31] She writes, "At the same time, as an educator, I can't pretend that my own teaching practices haven't been troubled by the paradoxes and impossibilities of communicative dialogue, of democracy, and of teaching itself."[32] The tone of confession in such passages is striking, as if she is trying to reform, but keeps backsliding into disreputable misconduct. I would want to reframe the issue in a different way: our teaching practices remain troubled by the paradoxes and impossibilities of "communicative dialogue" because there is no way to engage in teaching *without* encountering them. A fuller, less dyadic, understanding of dialogue must recognize multiple moments within it, some inevitably "communicative," others perhaps "analytic" (in Ellsworth's senses); some convergent toward agreement and understanding, others transgressive and dispersive (Bakhtin referees to these as the centrifugal and centripetal forces within any dialogical engagement); some "friendly" and others "disputatious"; and so on. Indeed, once one starts thinking of dialogue in such terms, the more difficult it is to maintain the dyadic character of these either/ors. For in any ongoing dialogue, all of these moments may recur, with no one of them defining "dialogue" as such. [33] Such a view of diverse forms, purposes, and relations is partly a corrective to what I have called the "fetishization" of dialogue, or the reification of any particular form (even including the "analytic").

In short, the criticisms posed against dialogue by Ellsworth and others have had a tremendously constructive benefit in unsettling the prescriptive account that has predominated in educational discussions. Her challenges to the silences, exclusions, and coercive or co-opting elements in dialogue, which challenge its self-conception as something open, neutral, and inviting to all, need to be addressed directly. What these criticisms have done is to refocus attention on the *practice* of dialogue, with its tensions, paradoxes, and material effects on those who are not willing or able to participate in educational discussions *in that manner*. Engaging in this practice requires awareness of these difficulties and dilemmas and an acknowledgment that particular forms of dialogue *cannot* serve the very aims that they avow.[34]

Yet these criticisms, in turn, confront some of their own difficulties. The first of these is that the elevation of difference, while an invaluable corrective to those views of "communicative dialogue" that emphasize the pursuit of agreement, consensus, or understanding as the only legitimate outcomes of dialogue, cannot stand as an absolute principle in its stead. Agreement, consensus, or understanding (which, as I have discussed, are very different sorts of outcomes) may sometimes be unobtainable in dialogue, and—even where attainable—they may be problematic, provisional, and properly subject to questions concerning *how* and *on whose terms* they have been obtained. Fair enough. But Ellsworth often writes as if these were inherently undesirable outcomes, never justifiable as voluntary and intersubjective. This cannot be true, both as a matter of experience and of history, where such outcomes—even in the face of deep difference and conflict—have been satisfactorily arrived at, and as a matter of social and political principle, where there are occasions in which the pursuit of such outcomes, with all their risks of difficulty and failure, is the sole alternative to violent adjudications of conflict. What the theory of dialogue needs is a modulated account of where and when such outcomes can be secured and how to be suspicious of them *while also* recognizing their value for different groups' purposes. If asymmetrical and unequal power were always conditions that abrogated the value of human engagement (including communicative engagement), then there would be no legitimate engagements at all, because power is never entirely asymmetrical and unequal. And, as I tried to show earlier, alternatives such as "analytic dialogue" believe in the value of understanding and agreement too.

Second, and building upon this point, the corrective elevation of radical difference sometimes segues into the presumption of incommensurability. I have addressed this issue in other writings. In the face of radical difference, misunderstanding or nonunderstanding are certainly possibilities. Sometimes dialogue reaches an impasse. But this account, taken on its own, is an oversimplification. For one thing, misunderstanding is not an all-or-nothing state; in real, situated contexts, degrees of misunderstanding are mixed with degrees of understanding, and the practical question at hand is where and for what purposes (and for whom) the degree of understanding is sufficient for the purposes—including the educational purposes—at hand. Too much rhetorical ink has been spilled, in my view, drawing the false alternatives of a realist, objectivist view of dialogue centered on a single "Truth," and a radically incommensurable alternative in which all knowledge is politically contested and culturally idiosyncratic. We need to get beyond these useless alternatives, especially if we are to speak in any constructive way about *educational* interactions. The paradoxical challenge here is to recognize the excess of meaning, the *differend*, as Lyotard calls it, that may be beyond translation or comprehension in many, even most, communicative encounters and to realize that sometimes this excess may be of crucial import in adjudicating, or failing to adjudicate, a serious difference of belief or value, while at the same time recognizing the practical need to pursue the degrees of understanding appropriate to particular purposes, including educational purposes. Sometimes, indeed, this endeavor fails—and, as noted earlier, this failure can have crucial educational import in alerting us to the horizons of our own assumptions, to our own culpability in why the dialogue "failed," and to the possibility of considering a radically different way of approaching the world. But if one believed truly that such encounters always fail, it is unclear what meaning "education" could ever have.

Third, and finally, the juxtaposition of what I have called the *prescriptive* perspective (represented by formal, idealized models) and the *practical* perspective (represented by situated, politically critical analysis) on dialogue itself draws an overly sharp distinction. For reasons that cannot be developed fully here, social practices always entail at least implicitly prescriptive norms, and in this sense *always* run the risk of being impositional, normalizing, and exploitative of relatively powerless persons or groups. Alternative social practices may avoid *those* failings, but replace them with others. Critical dialogue, communicative dialogue, analytical dialogue, and every other educational approach entail their own latent prescriptions—even apart from those they try to make explicit and open to question—and so inevitably encounter a limit to their capacities to be self-reflexive and self-problematizing. Some communicative relations, such as Habermas's acceptance of the legitimacy of "validity claims" and challenges within a discursive context or Ellsworth's advocacy of "modes of address that *multiply* and *set in motion* the positions from which they can be 'met' and responded to," bring these possibilities of reflexivity more to the surface; other communicative relations tend to be more oblivious or even resistant to such reflexivity. But paradoxically, again, it may actually be that those very communicative relations that try to be most open about their implicit commitments and prescriptions may be *for that very reason* more difficult to diagnose in terms of their blind spots and, hence, more difficult to resist. Or, to put this a different way, those modes of dialogue that put the greatest emphasis on criticality and inclusivity may also be the most subtly co-opting and normalizing. Such a recognition unsettles critical pedagogies of all sorts, whether feminist or Freirean, rationalist or deconstructionist.[35]

Notes

1. This point has been defended by the present author, among others: Nicholas C. Burbules, *Dialogue in Teaching: Theory and Practice* (New York: Teachers College Press, 1993); Nicholas C. Burbules and Suzanne Rice, "Dialogue across Differences: Continuing the Conversation," *Harvard Educational Review*, vol. 61, no. 4 (1991): 393–416.

2. For an overview of research on dialogue in teaching, see Nicholas C. Burbules and Bertram C. Bruce, "Theory and Research on Teaching as Dialogue," *Handbook of Research on Teaching*, 4th ed., Virginia Richardson, ed. (Washington, DC: American Educational Research Association, forthcoming).

3. Seyla Benhabib, "Liberal Dialogue versus a Critical Theatre of Discursive Communication," in *Liberalism and the Moral Life,* Nancy L. Rosenblum, ed. (Cambridge, MA: Harvard University Press, 1989), 154.

4. Deborah Tannen, *The Argument Culture: Moving from Debate to Dialogue* (New York: Random House, 1998).

5. Belenky, M.F., Clinchy, B.M., Goldberger, N.R., and Tarule, J.M., *Women's Ways of Knowing: The Development of Self, Voice, and Mind (*New York: Basic Books, 1986); Gilligan, C., *In a Different Voice: Psychological Theory and Women's Development* (Cambridge, MA: Harvard

University Press, 1982); Nel Noddings, *Caring: A Feminine Approach to Ethics and Moral Education* (Berkeley: University of California Press, 1984); Carol Witherell and Nel Noddings, eds., *Stories Lives Tell: Narrative and Dialogue in Education* (New York: Teachers College Press, 1991).

6. See Mary Leach, "Can We Talk? A Response to Burbules and Rice," *Harvard Educational Review*, vol. 62, no. 2 (1992): 257–263. See also Patti Lather, "Critical Pedagogy and Its Complicities: A Pedagogy of Stuck Places," *Educational Theory*, vol. 48, no. 4 (1998): 487–497.

7. See Burbules, *Dialogue in Teaching*, for an extended argument on this point.

8. Elizabeth Ellsworth, *Teaching Positions: Difference, Pedagogy, and the Power of Address* (New York: Teachers College Press, 1997), 15–16.

9. Jennifer Gore, *The Struggle for Pedagogies: Critical and Feminist Discourses as Regimes of Truth* (New York: Routledge, 1993).

10. A point certainly made by Elizabeth Ellsworth, repeatedly, as well as by Jennifer Gore; Jennifer Gore, "On the Limits to Empowerment through Critical and Feminist Pedagogies," in *Critical Theory in Unsettling Times*, Dennis Carlson and Michael Apple, eds. (Minneapolis: University of Minnesota Press, forthcoming).

11. Jürgen Habermas, *The Theory of Communicative Action*, Vol. 1 (Boston: Beacon Press, 1981); and *Between Facts and Norms* (Cambridge, MA: MIT Press, 1996).

12. Benhabib, "Liberal Dialogue," 153.

13. An excellent analysis of the Benhabib/Butler debate can be found in Amanda Anderson, "Debatable Performances: Restaging Contentious Feminisms," *Social Text*, vol. 16, no. 1 (1998): 1–24.

14. Anderson, "Debatable Performances," 11.

15. See Burbules and Rice, "Dialogue across Differences."

16. Cameron McCarthy, "Multicultural Discourses and Curriculum Reform: A Critical Perspective," *Educational Theory*, vol. 44, no. 1 (1994): 81–98.

17. Cosmopolitanism covers a broad range of views. For example, see Martha Nussbaum, "Citizens of the World," in Martha C. Nussbaum, *Cultivating Humanity: A Classical Defense of Reform in Liberal Education* (Cambridge, MA: Harvard University Press, 1997), 50–84. For a very different vision of cosmopolitanism, see Iris Marion Young, *Justice and the Politics of Difference* (Princeton, NJ: Princeton University Press, 1990), especially Chap. 8. Young directly challenges the ideal of cosmopolitanism conceived as a form of "universal citizenship": see "Polity and Group Difference," in *Throwing Like a Girl and Other Essays in Feminist Philosophical and Social Theory* (Bloomington, IN: Indiana University Press, 1990), 114–137.

18. In *Dialogue in Teaching*, I argue that there are at least four discrete types of dialogue: conversation, inquiry, instruction, and debate. Each exhibits characteristic forms of communicative interaction, each pursues distinct sorts of outcomes, and each has a different quality of tone or feel in relation.

19. Homi K. Bhabha, "Cultural Diversity and Cultural Difference," in *The Post-Colonial Studies Reader*, Bill Ashcroft, Gareth Griffiths, and Helen Tiffin, eds. (New York: Routledge, 1995), 206.

20. Nicholas C. Burbules, "A Grammar of Difference: Some Ways of Rethinking Difference and Diversity as Educational Topics," *Australian Education Researcher*, vol. 24, no. 1 (1997): 97–116.

21. Some of this material is adapted from Burbules and Bruce, "Theory and Research on Teaching as Dialogue."

22. Bakhtin, M.M., *The Dialogic Imagination,* M. Holquist, ed. (Austin, TX: University of Texas Press, 1981).

23. Nicholas C. Burbules, "Technology and Changing Educational Communities." *Educational Foundations*, vol. 10, no. 4 (1996): 21–32.

24. Ellsworth, *Teaching Positions*, 9.

25. Ellsworth, *Teaching Positions*, 15, 93, 107, 82.

26. See Burbules, *Dialogue in Teaching;* and Burbules and Rice, "Dialogue across Differences."

27. Ellsworth, E., "Why Doesn't This Feel Empowering? Working through the Repressive Myths of Critical Pedagogy," *Harvard Educational Review,* 59 (1989): 297–324.

28. Ellsworth, *Teaching Positions*, 125.

29. Some of this material is adapted from Nicholas C. Burbules, "Dialogue," in *Power/Knowledge and the Politics of Educational Meaning*, David Gabbard, ed. (New York: Erlbaum, forthcoming).

30. Alison Jones, "Pedagogical Desires at the Border: Absolution and Difference in the University Classroom," in *Educational Theory* (forthcoming, emphasis in the original).

31. Ellsworth, *Teaching Positions*, 17.

32. Ellsworth, *Teaching Positions*, 113.

33. Burbules, *Dialogue in Teaching*.

34. Nicholas C. Burbules, "Teaching and the Tragic Sense of Education," in *Teaching and Its Predicaments*, Nicholas C. Burbules and David Hansen, eds. (Boulder, CO: Westview Press, 1997), 65–77.

35. For more on this issue, see Nicholas C. Burbules and Rupert Berk, "Critical Thinking and Critical Pedagogy: Relations, Differences, and Limits," in *Critical Theory in Educational Discourse*, Thomas S. Popkewitz and Lynn Fendler, eds. (New York: Routledge, forthcoming).

John Willinsky

THE SOCIAL SCIENCES AS INFORMATION TECHNOLOGY
A Political Economy of Practice

The social sciences, no less than literary study or nuclear physics, can often seem divided between those who do research and those who do theory. Those who do empirical research in the social sciences typically imagine that they study real people to answer real questions for real people, while those who do theory are likely to think themselves alone in understanding the reason why researchers believe that. There are, of course, many ways of casting the divide between theory and practice, and yet more than a few of us in the social sciences, having worked both sides of the divide, now realize that the best way may be simply to stop casting it as a division. After all, it is easy enough to establish that theory is itself an effective form of practice and that practice is theory-riddled to its very core.

In an effort to do something more than demonstrate analytical finesse in dissolving conceptual boundaries, however, I take up the theory of practice here with an eye to pursuing the particular politics of theory that can be said to prevail in social science research. I do so as part of a project that would improve the public value of this research, as if the various forms of inquiry had something more to teach and learn, extending beyond the professional interests of social scientists. The revolutionary pedagogy at issue here is not about teaching. It is about learning. It is about the social sciences learning how to turn their accumulating knowledge into a public resource. It is thus about the ends of education, insofar as it is about how this knowledge can better serve the determination of people's lives.

For such purposes, I treat the social sciences as practicing a *political economy* through which they garner public and private support by deploying a variety of techniques for generating information about social structures and human dynamics. Insofar as the social sciences develop sophisticated techniques for generating and warranting forms of information, they represent an information technology, one that is torn in this political economy in ways that can pit the professional status of the researcher against the public interests in this knowledge. The political ineffectiveness of this unwieldy beast known as social science research is among the more troubling aspects of this political economy. Is this just a matter of working out the bugs in this information technology, with upgrades to follow, or is it endemic to the social sciences' political economy? This is the theory of practice that I am trying to force into the open within the scope of a larger project on public knowledge and the social sciences.[1]

I am using "political" to focus on the relationships of responsibility that occur between university researchers and the constituencies which the researchers presume to serve and which support the work. I take those constituencies to include in large measure, judging by the social sciences' own claims, the public, whose welfare this research is dedicated to improving. This service to the public also works indirectly, as the social sciences inform the related helping professions, such as education, law, health, and so on.

To treat social science research as a form of information technology may seem unfair to my colleagues, undermining as it does the field's sense of intellectual accomplishment. However, I do not use technology here to suggest that the research is merely the mechanical acquisition and transfer of information. The operating concept of technology I am employing here encompasses the methods and habits of mind, the techniques, that not only formulate the approach to the problem to be investigated, but determine and, in a sense, certify the quality of the information produced. It encompasses the social scientist's manner of asking questions, of seeking people's opinion; it includes the peer review process and the distribution and storage of the results on a global basis. The social sciences offer an information technology of protocols, platforms, channels, networks, and content. Whether the social sciences generate a model of children's cognitive development aimed at assisting their academic performance or assess the effectiveness of affirmative action programs, these research activities can be said to be directed at feeding information into political and social processes.

Social science research has always steered a wide variety of paths through political and economic processes, advising on institutional structures for governments and citizens as well as on retail packaging for manufacturers and consumers. The point of my review of its current political economy is how this information technology could better serve the public good in a more direct and responsive manner. For what is most troubling about the current state of this political economy is how poorly the social sciences fulfill their political promise of public service. And while I use information technology somewhat metaphorically in the case of the social sciences, I mean "political promise" in a literal, if not legal, sense.

As a general rule, social scientists promise, on grant applications and elsewhere, that their work is devoted to improving the quality of people's lives. The granting agencies, in turn, like to frame their research support as an investment in public good. I am continuing that tradition—with a difference. I am asking that the knowledge resulting from research, the very power of knowing, be made to contribute more directly to extending the democratic and self-determined direction of people's lives. That is, I want to hold the social sciences far more responsible for making this knowledge publicly available, turning it into a public resource that people can draw on in political, legal, and other public processes.

Now, it is true that the social sciences, as a field of inquiry, are torn between their public-spirited do-goodism, rooted in the last century, and their contemporary claims to the highest academic respectability. There are social *scientists* who believe that what keeps their practice honest, pure, and free of politics is how little it owes to the world, at least to the world outside the academic discipline's structure. But even then, they tend to hold that this is precisely what increases the value of the their work. The politics of theory, in this case, is all about negotiating between these themes of professional service and academic autonomy.

As it now stands, the social sciences' public service is often a font of frustration for both public and researchers. The public frequently feels it cannot get a straight answer from social scientists on how best to educate the young, create a social safety net, or administer a justice system. At the same time, social scientists grow tired of the public's impatient interest in sound-bite answers and the frequent distortion of hard-won ideas. The flow from social science research into public knowledge is by no means straightforward or easily achieved. Yet this immense effort to assemble a body of knowledge—although I use a word suggesting the coherence of a *body* reservedly—appears to be hardly deterred in the least by the countless indications that this accumulating knowledge is making only the most limited of contributions to the realm of public knowledge.

I have come to ask myself whether there is not some way, amid this new wave of information technologies, to improve how we manage this knowledge so that it might deliver far more public good than it has been able to up to this point. There are close to a hundred new studies being published each day, judging by the Social Science Index, all of them in the name of public interest, all of them financed in some fashion from public and private support. Given this level of production, we need to ask what it is within this political economy, within the theories of practice, that so constrains the ability of this carefully and thoughtfully constructed knowledge to do more to help with existing problems and challenges in health, education, justice, governance, or any of the other areas of inquiry within the social sciences. It would appear that the social sciences are not sufficiently governed in the public interest. This information technology appears flawed as a system of techniques organized around the coordination, management, and delivery of ideas that live up to their claimed value, as sources of understanding that hold the potential of guiding action.

After all, the public might reasonably expect that the social sciences could shed some light on issues such as bilingual education, breast cancer prevention techniques, reading programs, and IQ, to take examples I work with in the larger project from which this essay is drawn. For each of these issues, there is no shortage of publicly funded studies. The resulting research, however, has left a chaotic undertow of info-fragments in its wake, marked by incompatible, sometimes incompetent, research methods producing an array of contradictory findings. Now, the social sciences have proven decisive sources of helpful knowledge on occasion, most noticeably, perhaps, in turning the tide against smoking by providing evidence, when strictly biological explanations were not available, of its association with fatal diseases, just as the social sciences produced effective evidence on gender inequalities in wages and other areas. How this comes about, between social issues that are left in tatters and others for which we have a useful body of knowledge, reflects the politics of social sciences theory, a politics that seems geared to trickle-down benefits for the public.

As we press ahead with—and feel the professional press for—more studies and publications as measures of productivity in and of themselves, I am asking the social sciences to devote some part of their energy and resources to thinking through what I have termed a "corporation for public knowledge work." It would see new ways of coordinating research results—from design to dissemination—so as to limit the increasing fragmentation of knowledge. It would experiment with ways of creating a public space for this knowledge that fosters an appreciation for the diversity of research methods and for the inevitable discrepancies among findings. Having succeeded in the social sciences in creating a culture of academic professionalism—which is, after all, very much about specialization and autonomous authority—now may be the time to return to the original aims of public service by offering people greater access to these forms of knowledge intended to improve the quality of life.[2]

It must seem perverse, at this historical juncture, to ask what the social sciences could gain through central planning or engineering models for coordinating the analysis of social dilemmas. I can appreciate how implausible it must seem to propose that a corporation for public knowledge might assume responsibility for ensuring that the social sciences offer greater public value to individuals and organizations. I am inspired to such wild considerations, however, by our apparent inability to produce a coherent body of information with which to inform public and private decisions on increasingly complex social problems. I pose it because the political economy of the social sciences suggests a very poor rate of public return on the work of, perhaps, 100,000 professors of social science in the U.S., along with a small number of private research enterprises such as the RAND Corporation and

Public Interest. Outside of the work done through contract research, the social sciences have established an information technology that can be said effectively to serve social scientists, largely by enabling them to fill and cite some 1,700 social science journals on a regular basis.

The problem is not, I should point out, that the social sciences fail to recommend or predict the single best program or policy in any given setting. The problem is ensuring that coherent and comprehensible forms of knowledge—even in its diversity of methods and findings—are available for parents, educators, legislators, and the public at large, as well as for model builders and theorists analyzing the system as a whole. I may be wrong about how we should go about it, but not to do everything in our power to offer a useful if various body of knowledge is, I fear, to open ourselves to charges of engaging in this research enterprise in bad faith. The social sciences' theory of practice can be seen to amount to a politics of public disengagement, one that is not necessarily covered by traditional claims to academic freedom, which I address in the final section of this chapter.

But first I want to make clear two related dimensions of this political economy, namely the social sciences' social contract and research ethos. These two should make it apparent why I think that we should be doing something more about the quality of our contribution to the known world, something more than limiting the value of our work to little more than professional mechanisms such as peer review. This is about the most fundamental sort of politics of practice; it is about the leadership and accountability which fall within the scope of, as I discuss for the remainder of this chapter, the social contract between the social sciences and the public, the research ethos and ethics that guide our practices, and the claims of academic freedom that protect the integrity of our work.

The Social Contract

To understand the current relationship between the social sciences and the public, one does well to turn to where the money changes hands, to the literal point of contact and contract between public and researchers. In the United States, the principal federal funding agency for the social sciences is the Social, Behavioral, Economic (SBE) Sciences division of the National Science Foundation (NSF). It defines its research mission as seeking "to improve understanding of human beings, their many activities, and the organizations they create." In this expression of intention, which I do want hold the social sciences to, there is a slight ambiguity that falls between improving the understanding of human beings and improving humanity's understanding. By offering humanity this improved understanding of its activities and organizations, the social sciences contribute to the democratic project

of an informed and self-governing citizenry. This understanding is the particular return on the public investment in the social sciences, and it contrasts as a public
good with the implied economic benefits of the sciences and engineering that are
highlighted in the NSF's claim that "there is consensus among economists and policy researchers that public investments in science and engineering yield very high
annual rates of return to society."[3]

If the value of the social sciences is unlikely to produce a consensus among
economists and policy researchers, it only places greater emphasis on the social contract underwriting this knowledge domain. If social scientists are to see through the
NSF's "investment" in bolstering "the nation's quality of life and standard of living"
in good faith, they need to do more to ensure that this information technology
does, in fact, improve the state of public knowledge.[4] This investment in 1996 represented $81 million in research contracts for the SBE divisions of the NSF. This
may seem little enough of the NSF's total budget of roughly $2.5 billion, but it
needs to be seen in association with the far wider range of activity within the social
sciences that falls within the scope of this social contract.[5]

Others, as it turns out, are also seeking to improve the public value of the social
science research conducted within the scope of this social contract. I would hold up
the example of the President's Committee of Advisers on Science and Technology
proposal in 1997 for the spending of $1.5 billion dollars in the years ahead on edu-
cational technology research, a proposal which has been met by calls from Senator
Jeff Bingaman and others to form a national consortium of business concerns,
higher education, research institutes, and government that will be devoted to coordinating the research done on content, software development, and Internet use.[6]
Bingaman is asking for another layer of bureaucracy, but he is also trying to improve the public value of the research through participation and coordination. He is
speaking to the sense of just so many more studies that do not seem to add up or
even speak to each other, at least not in a manner that helps educators decide how
to achieve what matters most to them. As offensive as this sort of interference may
be to social scientists, the social contract works only if these issues are addressed.
The new initiatives around the use of technology in education, which currently
have considerable political and public support, certainly afford an opportunity to
explore new ways of organizing research so that it may be able to do more people
more good than it has in assessing educational programs up to this point.

The social contract represented by various forms of public and foundation
funding needs to be seen by all who participate in it as honoring a faith in the
power of knowledge to lead the way forward for good government and economic
prosperity. Two centuries ago, in early America, the Northwest Ordinance of 1787
was composed, even as the Founding Fathers were still drafting what would become
the American constitution; it included a clear affirmation that "knowledge, being

necessary to good government and the happiness of mankind, schools and means of education, shall forever be encouraged."[7] I am asking that the social sciences see it as part of their social contract to improve how well the research produced by the social sciences serves as a form of public education and, thus, of good government. As it now stands, however, the sense of this contract with the public—to serve as a source of improved understanding and a means of education—appears to be missing a serious part within the research ethos and ethics of the social sciences.

Research Ethos and Ethics

The insularity of social sciences, in which research is principally produced for other researchers and those whom they teach, stands for me as a breach of the social contract. Or at least, I think social scientists have an obligation to consider whether more could be done to improve the public value of their work. Despite grant-winning prose from social scientists to the contrary, the profession appears to rely on trickle-down infomatics to carry some part of its work down from the great scholarly journals into the public domain. What goes missing is consideration of public access rights or whether the information is in a readily comprehensible form.

Lest you think my judgment of social science research ethos and ethics extreme, let me offer evidence from two research guides. My first exhibit is one of the profession's more substantial how-to books. *Research Methods in the Social Sciences* by Chava Frankfort-Nachmias and David Nachmias, of the University of Wisconsin, Madison, now into its fifth edition, is written for students and experienced researchers alike, with the intent of introducing them to the folkways and formal practices of their trade.[8] The two issues of interest here are finding a topic and setting the parameters of research ethics. The book's approach to choosing a topic illustrates how the social sciences could do far more to secure the connections between public and research interests. The relevant chapter opens this way: "In the beginning is the problem." Time and the world begin, it might seem, with the problem in hand. Failing that, the authors allow, "the best source for stimulating the statement of problems and hypothesis is the professional literature."[9]

On the other hand, I am arguing that this implied social contract requires that social science research is a way of improving our knowledge in ways that will serve the public, both by what it adds to the overall coherence of existing knowledge and by how it speaks to current understandings.[10] This means addressing in the design of the research, for example, the continuing fragmentation of knowledge within the social sciences that results from measures that cannot be properly compared, case studies that cannot be related, discrepancies among results that are not explained, and a host of other issues that reflect a lack of concern with how the studies fit together, including those that challenge existing work or public stances. Now, this is not about discovering the true unity of knowledge or a single-mindedness of research approaches. It is simply about assuming responsibility for improving how research, in all of its diverse ways of knowing, works together to afford a far more useful public resource. Otherwise, the continuing proliferation of research is doomed to reduce the overall value of this inquiry. None of this is currently seen in *Research Methods in the Social Sciences* as part of determining "the problem" behind one's study, and as such, its failure to address this political economy, which apparently only the theory of practice is worried about, ensures that each study contributes to what I am portraying as the real *problem* of research.

It is true that some researchers do develop their projects in collaboration with the public or professional communities, which in itself is a two-way educational process concerned with establishing just what social sciences can contribute to public discourse. There is currently a body of "outreach scholarship" that has developed around this collaborative service theme, but there can clearly be varying degrees of community participation and consultation.[11] I should add that that there is nothing within this model of research-as-public-service that precludes critical and disruptive work that addresses head-on what the community refuses or denies. Such initiatives are no less driven by the need to augment public knowledge. But then I would also allow that my project is not intended to encompass all that is done in the name of social science scholarship but only that part of it which claims to be in the public interest.

Let me draw some support, at this point, from another social scientist making a similar call for greater accountability in the social sciences. Political scientist Rogers Smith, at Yale, would temper the free and rigorous pursuit of all matters political by calling for "special attention to those [topics or problems] that are predictably neglected, for both intellectual and political reasons, by governmental and private-sector analysts, politicians, and the media."[12] Smith exhorts the profession to pursue questions that people care about, to work with what people "experience as problems" but lack the skills (and I would add the privileged position of professorial work) to explore. He makes no bones about the importance of going after the hard and sometimes "impolitic" questions that arise from pursuing public concerns: "I cannot think of a different sense of disciplinary purpose that would be as likely to contribute important knowledge about politics that people would not get elsewhere, at least not in as careful or rigorous a form." This is, for Smith, "about as scientific and as serviceable to democracy as we can honestly get."[13] Although he pays little enough attention to how best to make this knowledge public, he at least observes how the technical specialization of political science—with its talk of strategically rational goal-maximizing behaviors within institutional matrices—can lead citizens to "to decide that politics *is* beyond them."[14] This is to name the antipedagogy of the research process and the social sciences' break with the social contract. It speaks to how research can become not simply irrelevant to democratic determination of our lives but an impediment to it.

Now, the one area in which social scientists have demonstrated an impressive concern for public rights is in their carefully defined policies governing research ethics. For Frankfort-Nachmias and Nachmias, in *Research Methods in the Social Sciences*, "ethical issues arise from the kinds of problems social scientists investigate and the methods used to obtain valid and reliable data." Their list of ethical challenges does an excellent job of setting out the current ethical boundaries of research in the social sciences:

> [Ethical issues] may be evoked by the research problem itself (e.g., genetic engineering, determinants of intelligence, program evaluation), the setting in which the research takes place (hospitals, prisons, public schools, government agencies), the procedures required by the research design (exposure of the experimental group to conditions that might have effects on the participants), the method of data collection (covert participant observation), the kinds of persons serving as research participants (the poor, children, people with AIDS, politicians), and the type of data collected (personal information, recruitment practices in public agencies).[15]

What is judged to be an ethical issue is the immediate impact of the research on the research subject or program rather than on a larger ethics of what responsibilities are entailed in seeking knowledge in the name of some greater public good. Even the genetic engineering reference, which is a caution over the impact of the research on the world, carries no greater social obligation than to take into account the damage that might be done if things go awry.

The Frankfort-Nachmias and Nachmias chapter also includes "A Code of Ethics for Social Scientists," complied by Paul Davidson Reynolds on the basis of twenty-four codes he assembled from various universities. Reynolds's list does specify that research reports should be made freely available, along with their sources of funding. But for me the ethical question also falls between what is freely available and what is publicly intelligible or adds to the coherence of the research venture, in all of its diversity. The list does not mention ethical concerns with the research's contribution to public or practitioner.[16] Reynolds's code also has no place for an ethics of intention or effectiveness. Missing is the sense of the larger public sponsorship and trust that might be entailed in this social contract between researcher and society.

Given that there are no comparable codes or policies (or overseeing committees, outside of peer reviews) devoted to protecting public interests in the knowledge so rigorously pursued, it might seem that the adoption of a very strong program of research ethics over the last few decades has taken care of any issues around public accountability and responsibility, reducing them all to informed consent letters and elaborate measures to protect the anonymity of the research project. The research community might then seem quit of any further *ethical* responsibilities for this knowledge once those who have donated some aspect of their lives to its creation have been treated fairly and squarely.

What is left to drive this quest for knowledge is the researcher's autonomy as a professional, in an ethics of self-interest that is most commonly suggested by how often researchers will phrase their work in terms of: "what interests me is. . . . " In their handbook, Frankfort-Nachmias and Nachmias can comfortably speak of "the responsibility of the scientist" without addressing what the research process and the knowledge it affords owe to others. I am not suggesting that the research lacks accountability. It is, of course, peer-reviewed at every stage, from the acceptance of the grant proposal to the selection of its final report for publication. My concern is with how those blind and disinterested peers share an ethos that may be too little concerned with the larger public value of the work, too little aware of a political economy that sustains this work while ensuring that its full public impact is blunted by all that undermines ready public access to it.

If this seems the case in a handbook for researchers, it is no less apparent in the thirty-seven "moral imperatives" offered to social scientists by sociologist Gary Marx while he was a Fellow at the Woodrow Wilson International Center for Scholars in Washington, D.C.[17] His prescription of "methods and manners" was inspired by a desire to prevent "many a mid-life crisis" by sharing what had worked for him.[18] He rightly admonishes social scientists to write clearly and think critically. He questionably advises them to write books, rather than read them. He is more suggestive in asking that research be problem-focused and that it speak truth to power. He asks that researchers recognize when they are "operating as a scientist" and when as "a more explicit political actor."[19] Marx playfully admonishes his colleagues to have fun and a sense of humor, which I would welcome, too, and yet I am less comfortable with his strictures to "have a fresh argument" and "write everywhere, all the time, on everything." This absence of purpose, beyond the production of more writing and argument, may be more telling of the profession than Marx realizes, with its image of social scientists simply seeking to fill up the spaces, hoping against odds that something will come of it all. Is there not some greater purpose or urgency to this calling, one wants to ask? The question leads one to Marx's final and most substantial moral imperative.

It begins elliptically with "Keep the faith! . . . " and goes on to define that faith as a belief "that empirical and scientific knowledge about human and social conditions can result in the improvement of those conditions."[20] How is it that this "improvement" is taken as an act of faith, rather than the very reasoned focus on our efforts? Taking it on faith seems to me an inadequate basis for building a research enterprise. The project I am describing here and elsewhere is about keeping faith with the social contract between the social sciences and the public; it is about doing all that we can to test the potential of research to contribute to improved human conditions and understanding. It calls for an expanded research ethics and ethos, with the social sciences far more attuned to how knowledge can serve as a public resource. Having said that, I cannot put off any longer the question of whether this will so unduly compromise academic freedom that our very hopes for knowledge will be dashed.

Academic Freedom

When it comes to discussions of academic freedom, scholars are quick to reach for John Stuart Mill's credo that the truth emerges from an unimpeded and free marketplace of ideas. The economic analogy, however, has become a little shopworn. The university proves a highly subsidized marketplace, with ideas circulating largely among producers in a cycle of supply without demand. Meanwhile government and private granting agencies exert their own market pressure through special funding initiatives and other sorts of targeted programs. But then I suppose the literal marketplace, on which this metaphor is based, has become increasingly focused on mergers and acquisitions intended to limit and impede the market.

Still, it is certainly reasonable to ask whether the political theory of practice I am trying to develop will run roughshod over academic freedom and right into the arms of anti-intellectualism. As I understand and appreciate it, academic freedom protects one's work from undue outside interference; it ensures that it need not pass a popularity contest or popular vote except from within the profession, which has the expertise to judge the quality of the work. The balloting of a peer-review process is, of course, far from perfect. Consider the instructive example of feminist literary critics, who initially ran afoul and continue to run afoul of their peers in their pursuit of a scholarship in which they felt compelled to addresses the decidedly public problem of patriarchal structures. Academic freedom failed them a number of times then and now, and the problem was not public interference but their colleagues. Still, the efforts I would promote to achieve greater coordination and coherence, to improve the public intelligibility of the research enterprise, still assume that the social sciences remain in the hands of social scientists, if now inspired by something of a Hippocratic oath that asks that the research contribute to the health of public knowledge, rather than otherwise. Such a stance on academic freedom would not have disturbed the obviously concerned Herbert London, professor of Humanities at New York University, when he recently called for redefining academic freedom so that: "propagandizing on behalf of one's favorite cause [apart from, say, academic freedom] should be discouraged unless it can be demonstrated that such an appeal is consistent with the canons of scholarship."[21]

In 1915, the then recently formed American Association of University Professors addressed this relationship between public and profession by holding up the university as an "intellectual experiment station" that offered an "inviolable refuge" against the forces of public opinion and political authority. At the same time, the association identified that "the responsibility of the university teacher is to the public itself, and to the judgment of his [sic] own profession."[22] The knowledge that comes from this experimental station can be cast as both a service and a force on the public. At this point, however, academic knowledge reaches the public most often through talking-head sound bites, as Professor X comments on distressing situation Y only to be countered by Professor Z. These brief media spots hardly do justice to the craft and contribution which research might otherwise bring to bear for those among the public who really wanted to see what the social sciences have assembled in the name of knowledge.

Among contemporary discussions of academic freedom, I would hold with Richard Rorty's way of framing the discussion within the "good which these universities do, to their role in keeping democratic government and liberal institutions alive and functioning."[23] Rorty would move the argument from traditional concerns with "an epistemological justification for academic freedom" toward the forms of knowledge which can help the institution play that vital political role. After all, Rorty insists, "neither philosophers nor anyone else can offer us nice sharp distinctions between appropriate social utility and inappropriate politicization." And the debate around the necessarily fuzzy sense of knowledge's value, he insists, is the very work of the university, if it is to remain "healthy and free."[24] As for the social sciences, Rorty proposes that "sociologists and psychologists might stop asking themselves whether they are following rigorous scientific procedures and start asking themselves whether they have any suggestions to make to their fellow citizens about how our lives, or our institutions, should be changed."[25]

Rorty ultimately turns to John Dewey's pragmatic sense of a truth which "clears up difficulties," as Dewey writes, and "removes obscurities, puts individuals into more experimental, less dogmatic, and less arbitrarily skeptical relation to life."[26] As it now stands, the social sciences have it within their reach, if not completely within their ethos, to do a far better job of clearing up difficulties and obscurities rather than contributing to them. This newfound concern with improving the coherence of research programs and the systematic coverage of pressing issues might diminish people's skepticism not only about the world around them but also about what the social sciences have to offer the world. Although Rorty tends to favor poets and novelists over social scientists or philosophers as inspirations for social advancement, he is clearly an inspirational figure for projects such as mine.

This call for greater public accountability in the social sciences may seem to play into the hands of conservative and commercial demands that the universities operate more like businesses and provide better service and support for the private sector. I would counter that these interests in improving public access to social science research are all about strengthening the state of public knowledge and defending the play of ideas and information within the public sector. This project is about ensuring that the university plays a vital role in the democratic processes, enabling people to marshal and test arguments, to challenge and question programs and policies, to contribute to a public process of experimentation and investigation. This places the social sciences within a political economy of knowledge of far greater public value. It makes research practices dependent on a theory of how knowledge exists by virtue of its public engagement and how that calls for a rethinking of those practices from the very formulation of the "problem" through to how the results are made to fit within the larger arena of public knowledge.

The revolutionary *pedagogy* at play here is not about teaching, at least not in any direct sense. It is about *learning*. It is about the social sciences learning new ways of producing a more engaging and productive intellectual resource, a resource that stays true to the differences that mark the knowledge that it fosters, differences in its assumptions, methods, and conclusions. It is about offering people greater access to knowledge that is intended to improve the human condition. It is about an information technology devoted to equipping people for political participation in the determination of their lives and communities.

Notes

1. John Willinsky, *Technologies of Knowing: A Proposal for the Human Sciences* (Boston: Beacon, 1999). Parts of this chapter first appeared in this book.

2. "Successful careers depended upon the continual application of scientific thoroughness to limited, specific tasks at specific stages in the course of an occupational lifetime"; Burton Bledstein, *The Culture of Professionalism: The Middle Class and the Development of Higher Education in America* (New York: Norton, 1976), 328.

3. National Science Foundation, "SBE Overview," http://www.nsf.gov/sbe/sbeovrvw.htm.

4. What do SBE projects that advance "our understanding of social processes and social structures" look like? Recent "investments" range from the development of Geographical Information Systems, which aid market research, facility site selection, and emergency responses, to

the role of Balinese Water Temples in managing complex irrigation systems. The NSF website: http://www.nsf.gov/sbe/sber/features/29.htm and http://www.nsf.gov/sbe/sber/features/27.htm.

5. For the NSF budget, see: http://www.nsf.gov/bfa/start.htm. The federal government also funds research in education to the tune of $86 million for 1996, with an additional $48 million for The National Center for Education Statistics "in order to promote and accelerate the improvement of American Education," according to its Web site (http://nces.ed.gov/). In addition, if faculty members at four-year institutions devote roughly one third of their time to research, with average salaries for 1996 at $50,000 and approximately 170,000 faculty in the social sciences and related fields; this amounts to an investment by students and benefactors of public funds of $2.8 billion dollars in salaries, on top of which needs to be added the infrastructure costs of support staff, building, etc. (figures drawn from *Chronicle of High Education*; see its Web site: http://chronicle.com).

6. Andrew Trotter, "Taking Technology's Measure," *Education Week* (November 10, 1997): 11.

7. Cited by Neal Kumar Katyal, "National Testing's Pedigree," *New York Times* (September 12, 1997): A19.

8. Chava Frankfort-Nachmias and David Nachmias, *Research Methods in the Social Sciences*, 5th ed. (New York: St. Martin's Press, 1996).

9. Frankfort-Nachmias and Nachmias, *Research Methods*, 66. For a description of the U.K.'s Social Science Research Council (SSRC) Open Door program, in which "client users" (including unions, managers, and professionals) initiate and define SSRC-funded research projects in collaboration with social scientists, see John Gill, "Research as Action: Experiment in Utilizing the Social Sciences," in *The Use and Abuse of Social Science,* Frank Heller, ed. (London: Sage, 1986).

10. Frankfort-Nachmias and Nachmias's book includes an Appendix written by Nina Reshef, with additional advice on choosing a topic, recommending: "Avoid topics that have been extensively researched, . . . " among other things. Frankfort-Nachmias and Nachmias, *Research Methods,* 558.

11. Richard M. Lerner and Lou Anna K. Simon, *University-Community Collaborations for the Twenty-First Century: Outreach Scholarship for Youth and Families* (New York: Garland, 1998).

12. Rogers Smith, "Still Blowing in the Wind: The American Quest for a Democratic, Scientific Political Science," *Daedalus* 126, no. 1 (Winter 1997): 276–277.

13. Smith, "Still Blowing in the Wind," 254.

14. Smith, "Still Blowing in the Wind, 257, original emphasis.

15. Frankfort-Nachmias and Nachmias, *Research Methods*, 77.

16. Nachmias and Nachmias, *Research Methods*, 91–95.

17. Gary T. Marx, "Of Methods and Manners for Aspiring Sociologists: 37 Moral Imperatives," *American Sociologist* 8, no. 1 (1997): 102–125.

18. Marx, "Of Methods," 103.

19. Marx, "Of Methods," 122.

20. Marx, "Of Methods," 123–124. Cf. Maureen Hallinan, "A Sociological Perspective on Social Issues," *American Sociologist* 28, no. 1 (1997), 11, who holds that sociology falls short of developing "powerful theory" due to "a lack of faith in the power of the discipline and a weakness of will to take on the task."

21. Herbert London, "Resisting Frivolity in Academe," *Chronicle of Higher Education*, May 22, 1998, B7.

22. Cited by Thomas Haskell, "Justifying the Rights of Academic Freedom in the Era of 'Power/Knowledge,'" in *The Future of Academic Freedom,* Louis Menand, ed. (Chicago: University of Chicago Press), 57–58.

23. Richard Rorty, "Does Academic Freedom Have Philosophical Presuppositions," in *The Future of Academic Freedom,* Louis Menand, ed. (Chicago: University of Chicago Press), 20.

24. Rorty, "Does Academic Freedom Have Philosophical Presuppositions," 28.

25. Rorty, "Does Academic Freedom Have Philosophical Presuppositions," 27.

26. Rorty, "Does Academic Freedom Have Philosophical Presuppositions," 34. Rorty is citing from Dewey's *The Quest for Certainty.* Dewey's position was challenged, it is worth noting, by Thorstein Veblen, who held that science, and no less social science, accrued from "idle curiosity." Veblen countered his own theory of the leisured (academic) class with a technocratic faith in society's ability to eliminate inefficiencies and waste; see Dorothy Ross, "Social Science and the Idea of Progress," in *The Authority of Experts: Studies in History and Theory,* Thomas L. Haskell, ed. (Bloomington, IN: Indiana University Press, 1984), 165–185.

Patti Lather

RESPONSIBLE PRACTICES OF ACADEMIC WRITING
Troubling Clarity II

This essay troubles the call for plain speaking by addressing Walter Benjamin's (1989) words, "Nothing more subtle than the advice to be clear in order at least to appear true" (6). By "trouble," I mean to interrogate a commonsense meaning by revealing a constitutive moment of "originary disunity," what Derrida (1972) terms the "irreducible excess" of any concept within itself, its difference from itself, the "*this* that comes with so much difficulty to language" (172): deconstruction. Within the context of this essay, then, to trouble is to mobilize the forces of deconstruction in order to unsettle the presumed innocence of transparent theories of language that assume a mirroring relationship between the word and the world. To ground my remarks, I turn to reviews of my book *Getting Smart*, on feminist research and pedagogy (Lather 1991) and to the efforts of my coresearcher, Chris Smithies, and myself to write a multivoiced text that speaks to a broad audience about the experiences of women living with HIV/AIDS (Lather and Smithies 1997).

Using the example of *Getting Smart*, Gaby Weiner writes of the politics of language of feminist poststructuralism and Marxist feminism as:

highly complex and "difficult," utilizing terminology such as discourse, subjectivity, power-knowledge, drawn from mainstream postmodernist and poststructuralist writing. In my view, McWilliam (1993) is rightly critical of what she terms PMT (postmodernist tension) of such writers as Lather who on the one hand, argue for openness and self-reflexivity, yet in using highly complicated writing styles, seem implicitly to deny that possibility to their readers. As McWilliam suggests, "it is not that there is nothing worthy here . . . the difficulty is that one doesn't so much read this text as wrestle with it." (Weiner 1994, 70)[1]

That this critique of the language of *Getting Smart* is a more general concern in feminist work is exemplified by the editors of *Signs* (Joeres 1992). In "On Writing Feminist Academic Prose," Ruth Ellen Joeres states that "accessibility is essential to the feminist message" against "the increasingly complex language that many of us seem to feel is required of academic work" (702). "Alarmed" about "separatist language," "increasing parochialism," and the institutionalizing pressures that women's studies faces, Joeres (1992) insists that "accessibility and clarity" are key to the sort of work that can "animate" feminist praxis and interrupt its corruption by the academy (703).

Diane Elam (1994), in *Feminism and Deconstruction*, addresses those who worry that academic feminism is esoteric, "not sufficiently mainstream," hopelessly removed from "everyday praxis" (91). Against either/or framings of the accessibility/inaccessibility issue, Elam argues that challenging disciplinary boundaries and interrupting disciplinary procedures are political work that has to be both within and against disciplinary standards of discourse, especially renegotiating the limits of philosophy. I made similar arguments in response to a review of *Getting Smart* by Stephanie Walker (1994) that asked Jane Gallop's question: "How do we do the most good as [academic] feminists?" (176). Addressing Walker's concerns regarding "the interminable intricacies of Lather's theoretical arguments" and the "exclusivist salon" of postmodernists drawn on in the book (174), I wrote the following:

> To be heard in the halls of High Theory, one must speak in the language of those who live there. . . . Believing strongly that we all can't do everything and that the struggle demands contestation on every front, I think my answer to Gallop's question seems to be, for me, at the time of [*Getting Smart*], Dada practice at the site of academic High Theory. Presently involved in a study of women living with HIV/AIDS, I keep coming back to Marge Piercy's poem, "To Be of Use" (1973). What [academic] High Theory has to do with being of use in this new project intrigues me. (Lather 1994, 184–185)[2]

I will return to the issue of the relationship between academic theoretic authority and feminist practice later in this essay. To conclude my introductory comments, I am not uninterested in how academic work can enter common parlance and contribute to the struggle for social justice. My goal is not a facile "for or against" widespread cultural dissemination of ideas, but rather an exploration of its possibilities in the face of limit questions. Limit questions are both insistent and indeterminable, such as the theory/practice relationship which is always both urgent and unanswerable in any context-free way. My objective, then, is to enact a double reading, to think opposites together in some way that is outside any Hegelian reconciliation that neutralizes differences. In order to enact such a double reading of the insistent and interminable question of accessible language in academic writing, I proceed according to deconstructive moves. First, I perform an oppositional reading within the confines of a binary system by reversing the binary accessible/inaccessible.[3] Second, I perform a reflexive reading that questions the inclusions/exclusions, orderings/disorderings, and valuations/revaluations of the first move of reversal, as an effort to reframe the either/or logic that is typical of thinking about the issue at hand. It is here that I delineate Chris and my textual and interpretive moves in *Troubling the Angels* in the paradox of writing that is both accessible to a broad audience and troubling of the uses of transparent language. Using what Gayatri Spivak (1987) has termed "scattered speculations on the question of value," I conclude with some thoughts on the work of theory in thinking the multiple (im)possibilities for thought outside the normalized, routinized, commodified structures of taken-for-granted intelligibility.

The Reversal: Troubling Clarity

> One makes oneself accountable by an engagement that selects, interprets, and orients. In a practical and performative manner, and by a decision that begins by getting caught up, like a responsibility, in the snares of an injunction that is already multiple, heterogeneous, contradictory, divided. (Derrida 1994, 93)

In an essay on "responsibility," Gayatri Spivak writes "as a practical academic" about Derrida's use of "a language that must be learned" as an attempt to push his thesis of complicity. Spivak situates Derrida's language as a "teaching language" that "may be accessible to a reading that is responsible to the text" (1994, 27). Concerning Spivak, Toril Moi (1988) writes:

> Here, for once, is a woman who is not content to leave "high theory" to the men, but who, on the contrary, clearly wants to take it over for her own feminist and anti-imperialist purposes. . . . The Spivak style, then, is not at all an effort to write in a vulnerable or unauthoritative way. On the contrary, her

texts are packed with trenchant statements and unambiguous political and theoretical positions. . . . There can never be one correct feminist style.[4] (20)

Moving to Simone de Beauvoir, Moi (1988) writes:

At the time, her [de Beauvoir's] deliberate assumption of traditional discursive authority represented a massive invasion of previously patriarchal discursive terrain for subversive purposes. Her tone and style not only irked the patriarchs, who would clearly have liked to keep high philosophy to themselves, but also forced them to take her arguments seriously. (21–22)

Hortense Spillers (1994), writing from an African-American subject position, argues that intellectuals cannot be embarrassed out of the advantage of being able to probe the contribution that theory can make to exposing and illuminating oppression. This is what she calls "the question for theory" (107), as she writes against outcries that scholars of color must always write so as to be readable by some general public. Wahneema Lubiano (1991) concurs, as she urges marginalized intellectuals to "elbow" themselves into the site of postmodernism in order to "figure out what happens when the idea of metanarratives is up for grabs" (152). Using Catherine Belsey to argue that realism is about "a world we already seem to know" that "offers itself as transparent" (165), Lubiano urges the use of other practices of representation that decenter traditional realistic narrative forms. Such urgings are about the relationship of theory and practice, language and power, and the need for new languages to create new spaces for resistance and the (re)construction of knowledge/power relations.

Patrick McGee (1992), in *Telling the Other,* his book on postcolonialism and ethnographic practice, writes that to aim at transparent meaning is to inscribe one's ideas within the immediate understanding that resides in the register of the real. Against this, he quotes Lacan to posit a writing that "is not to be understood. . . . Reading does not oblige us to understand anything. It is necessary to read first" (69). Reading without understanding is required if we are to go beyond the imaginary "real" of history. Truth is what cannot be said, what can be only half said: "truth is what our speech seeks beyond meaning" (71). Refusing to substitute one semblance for another, with various people contending for positions as the police of truth, Lacan argues that what is speakable is coded and overcoded. As disruptive excess, the unspeakable cannot be reduced to the easily understood. To speak so as to be understood immediately is to speak through the production of the transparent signifier, that which maps easily onto taken-for-granted regimes of meaning. This runs a risk that endorses, legitimates, and reinforces the very structure of symbolic value that must be overthrown. Hence, for Lacan, not being understood is an ethical imperative.[5]

This is not to deny that the mystifying effects of academic language support the illusion that those institutionally situated as "in the know" are, and that "those who cannot understand have been legitimately excluded from understanding" (McGee 1992, 121). But neither is the transparent use of language innocent. Clear speech is part of a discursive system, a network of power that has material effects.[6] Premised on incorporating a particular form of everydayness into public statements as tools of circulation and naturalization, charges of "not in the real world" or "too academic" (Miller 1993, 164) have particular kinds of effects. For example, the easy to read is positioned against the unreadable by a "get-real press" rife with journalistic intolerance for deconstruction in the face of information overload and "get to the point impatience" (Nealon 1993b, quoting Stephens, 176).

Such calls for clear speech from the "real world" charge that academic "big talk" about "high theory" is a masturbatory activity aimed at a privileged few (Spivak, interviewed in Winant 1990, 90–91).[7] Against such calls, the example of Sigmund Freud serves to illustrate how a clinician's turn to theory can safeguard the practitioner against the immediacy of the demands of clinical practice. Freud gave a weight to client utterances that carried the charge of questions posed to theory, and as a result brought practice and theory to productive crisis. Hence psychoanalytic theory works in the clinical encounter as a need for rigorous questioning, not as an avoidance of the call of suffering, but as an attempt "to allow it the time of another hearing" (Shamdasani 1994, xiv). This revaluation work of folding back on practice of another hearing outside the safe assurance of a pregiven interpretation is far closer to the demands of practice than is first supposed. In Freud's work, theory and practice interpenetrate one another into a discontinuity that calls each other into question. Theory itself becomes pragmatic, even as the pragmatic action of therapy becomes theory.

Sometimes we need a density that fits the thoughts being expressed. In such places, clear and concise plain prose would be a sort of cheat not untied to the anti-intellectualism rife in American society (Giroux 1992). Hence "the politics of clarity," to use Giroux's title, is a central issue in the debate over the relationship of theory and practice. Positioning language as productive of new spaces, practices, and values, what might come of encouraging a plurality of theoretical discourses and forms and levels of writing in a way that refuses the binary between so-called "plain speaking" and complex writing? What are the issues involved in assumptions of clear language as a mobilizing strategy? What are the responsibilities of a reader in the face of correspondence theories of truth and transparent theories of language?[8] What is the violence of clarity, its noninnocence?

In a talk at Ohio State's Wexner Center for the Arts,[9] Steven Melville spoke of Stanley Cavell's (1976) questions: What is the problem in "not getting it"? Who is on trial: the receiver? the sender?[10] The dilemma cannot be solved, Melville argued;

there is no referee, but the dilemma can be insisted on. Just as the photograph is particularly dangerous for its purported realism, and painting less so, Melville delineated practices that juxtapose traditional and uncanny forms. The uncanniness is due to attention to the act of appearing, to the layers and filters that are the conceptual frames that are the conditions of an object's appearing. What is the claim of the mirror, he asked. Is it a false promise of verisimilitude, where the "real" message is that the appearance of the same is not the same? What is the political bite of such practices of layers of wandering, gestures toward styles, practices that cancel themselves to work against the emergence of directedness, that run the risk of knowledge in texts that work over and through themselves, within "the dream of doing history's work"?

Building on Melville's questions, in the face of pressing problems around language, knowledge, and power, across multiple publics and diverse levels of intelligibility, how might we expand the possibilities for different ways of writing, reading, speaking, listening, and hearing?

The Reflexive Move: Troubling the Angels

What follows is a sort of "autotranslation," a textual self-speculation that is both necessary and impossible about Chris's and my book on women living with HIV/AIDS. My move assumes that to make ethnography reflexively is to think philosophically, given that philosophy is about always trying to comprehend its own thought and practice (McDonald 1985). What it means to pose the problem of the text as a way to interrogate the status of ethnography is to stage the problems of representation as an effort to perform what knowing has become in the postmodern. Here *Troubling the Angels: Women Living With HIV/AIDS* is situated as a point of departure from which to track shifting investments in its historical and social production and effects (Weems 1997). The goal is to work out a kind of economy that is other to mastery in both writing and reading—to produce other ears.

In *Troubling the Angels,* my coresearcher and I attempt practices that move across different registers into a sort of hypertext that invites multiple ways of reading. Unlike the artists that Melville speaks of, our task from the beginning was to produce what the participants in our study called a Kmart book, a book widely available to HIV-positive women like themselves and their families and friends.[11] Combining this with my gnomic and abstruse ways of knowing has been a source of both energy and paralysis. The result is a book shaped by the doubled charge of creating a book that would do the work the women wanted, while taking into account the crisis of representation.

This description is from a publicity flier for the book:

Based on an interview study of twenty-five Ohio women in HIV/AIDS support groups, *Troubling the Angels* traces the patterns and changes of how the women make sense of HIV/AIDS in their lives. Attempting to map the complications of living with the disease, the book is organized as a hypertextual, multilayered weaving of data, method, analysis, and the politics of interpretation.

Because of the book's unconventional narration, it invites multiple entries and ways of reading. Interspersed among the interviews, there are [angel] inter-texts, which serve as "breathers" between the themes and emotions of the women's stories; a running subtext where the authors spin out their tales of doing the research; factoid boxes on various aspects of the disease; and a scattering of the women's writing in the form of poems, letters, speeches, and e-mails.

Enacting a feminist ethnography at the limits of representation, *Troubling the Angels* mixes sociological, political, historical, therapeutic, and policy analysis along with the privileging of ethnographic voice.

By refusing to produce a "tidy" text that maps easily onto our usual ways of making sense, Chris and I reach toward a generally accessible public horizon while moving from a "realist" to an "interrogative" text. Rather than seemingly unmediated recounting of participant narratives or unobtrusive chronicling of events as they occur, we "both get out of the way and in the way" (Lather and Smithies, 1997, xiv) in a manner that draws attention to the problematics of telling stories that belong to others. In what follows, using Nietzsche's textual style to ruminate on the question of audience, I try to make sense of what Chris and I have done in the name of creating a multiply coded text on women, AIDS, and angels.

In *Nietzsche's Philosophy of Science*, Babette Babich (1994) argues that the key to Nietzsche's style of philosophy is a resolute provisionality that moves from skepticism to affirmative experimentation with illusion, via a style that is multivalent, heterogeneous, and multivoiced, even choral. Challenging even the credibility of its doubt (21), the Nietzschean text works "to spur what would be the best reader, whether or not this reader could ever exist" (23). Via a kind of "oblique search for the right reader," the text disrupts what in itself is available to the general reader in order to spur the "right reader" (23). Quoting Nietzsche in his "slow search for those related to me" (23), Babich delineates how Nietzsche puts into play the hermeneutic polyphony and ambivalence of reception. Knowing the power of the reader to make the text, Nietzsche's practice was to affect, forearm, and disarm the reader. Putting the author's style up against the reader's style, the Nietzschean text issues a kind of "herald call" that challenges any easy reading via shifting styles/masks, "seeking the reader who would be caught in this way" (24). "Lured by the shifting of such a multifarious text," the engaged reader "is the reader conceived as a thinker" (24).

This reminds me of a woman who approached me at a conference to urge me to keep the angels in the book, to not eliminate them in the name of not imposing what is, unarguably, my own investment in the work of the angels in this text. Telling a story of being a woman outside of formal education, hungry to feed her mind but not knowing where to turn except the book racks at grocery stores and Kmarts, she troubles any easy notions of a reader "willing to confront and answer the challenge of philosophic thought" (Babich 1994, 24). Babich asks: What is on the inside/outside of accessibility, and how can we tap this and evoke in readers a complicity toward troubling the taken-for-granted? What audience is there for a kind of "skewed hermeneutic nexus of romance and rapture, conflict and accession [which] transcends critique? . . . Who can have ears for such an author?" (25). I think also of a First Nations woman, a student in a class I taught, who wrote:

> I believe that the readership has the capabilities to understand the purpose of the troubling angel and thereby trouble the notion of HIV/AIDS for themselves. I also believe that the academy has shortchanged the capabilities of everyday people to be able to grasp the complexities of how dichotomous the world we live in is. The arrogance of the academy . . . maintains and sustains their place of privilege in order for them to be able to be the omnipotent interpreters of other people's lives. This sustains the notion of value free positivist research and prevents us in the academy from troubling our places of privilege.[12]

Situating the text as a kind of doubled gauntlet, both a challenge to read and a course to be run, the Nietzschean text serves as an active filter that "draws and then evades . . . seducing the reader with 'ears to hear'—that is, the reader who can think—by means of the mutable allure of a shifting text" (Babich 1994, 27). Creating a text, then diverting it in a way that returns the question from reader to author, undercutting both authority and tradition and the reader and the author, Nietzschean textuality effects a multiregister movement, "interior to the discourse that is not only self-reflexive but self-subverting" (27). This is a writing for the reader able to understand, but it is also an active filter aimed at eliciting differing capacities for understanding.

Within Nietzsche's textual practice, reading becomes rumination and fosters brooding, a way of reading that produces a reading and then, "within the reflective memory of the first reading, read[s] again" (Babich 1994, 28). This is Nietzsche's signature: advance and demurral, deliberate inscription and covert subversion (28), a double valencing that constructs both a broad appeal and a kind of "renewedly new" reading with each reading. This concept of "coded coding" that has it both ways (33) helps me to locate myself in the problematic of a text that works toward a practice that erases itself at the same time as it produces itself. Such a practice makes space for returns, silence, interruptions, and self-criticism and points to its own incapacity. Such a practice gestures beyond the word via a textual practice that works at multiple levels to construct an audience with ears to hear.

Enacting the tensions between broad accessibility and the complicated and complicating moves of Nietzschean textuality, *Troubling the Angels* is a hypertextual pastiche that is a "warping of comfort texts" (Meiners 1994) aimed at opening up possibilities for displaying complexities. Given the critical practices at work in this text that require more of readers, why could not *Troubling the Angels* have been a "simple" text, a "realist tale" (Van Maanen 1988)? Such a tale would tell the stories that the women want to tell and would not risk displacing their bodies and their stories with high theory, what a University of British Columbia student termed the "akademic krime" of eliding material contexts, a kind of soma, vanity research that loses the women's stories.[13] Why did I feel I had to read Nietzsche in order to proceed? How do I reconcile myself to palpable costs in terms of time and the ethics involved in using the site of this inquiry to wrestle with what it means to move toward a less comfortable social science? As one of the women in the study wrote, "When are you guys going to publish? Some of us are on deadline, you know!" And as Simon Watney (1994) notes, much writing on AIDS in the social sciences is "taking the scenic route through an emergency" (221).

Such questions and cautions push my own motives and form the basis for this second reading of the politics of accessible language. This second reading is a reflexive move that addresses what was absent in the first move of reversal of the accessibility/inaccessibility binary. That reversal troubled calls for clarity in academic writing in order to denaturalize such calls, to situate them as noninnocent. This second reading explores possibilities in the face of limit questions about the kinds of knowledge and reading practices that reinscribe the relation between accessibility/inaccessibility so as to change not only the terms but also the ordering structure of relations.

With Ears to Hear: The Monstrous Text

Let's say I was trying to produce texts that produce other ears, in a certain way—ears that I don't see or hear myself, things that don't come down to me or come back to me. A text, I believe, does not come back. (Derrida, in McDonald 1985, 156–157)

Derrida (in Kearney 1984) writes of "the text [that] produces a language of its own, in itself, which while continuing to work through tradition emerges at a given moment as a *monster*, a monstrous mutation without tradition or normative precedent" (123). While *Troubling the Angels* has precedent,[14] it is an effort to "perform what it announces" through its textuality. What helps me to navigate the (necessarily) troubled waters of this inquiry is a movement between, with, and across academic "high theory" and the reactions of various readers of the book. In what follows, these reactions are presented within an argument that an ending commensurate with the complications of such a study is enriched by the "fold" (Deleuze 1993) of this sort of "response data" (St. Pierre 1997). Hence I begin with excerpts from the Epilogue, which recounts the HIV-positive women's reactions to a prepublication version of *Troubling the Angels*.[15]

Patti: Were there any parts of the book that you didn't like?

Barb: The format. I wanted to read it all from one end to the other, and it was hard to do because I was reading two different things. I would have liked to read one part or the other in sequence.

Patti: So the top/bottom split text was irritating. And it never got easier while you were reading along?

Barb: No.

Lori: I've given the book to four people, and they all said they had a problem with the layout. Some people won't see a movie with subtitles.

Rita: I liked that part where the bottom was a little story, alongside the top part. It made it more interesting, very much more interesting, but I had a hard time with the middle part about angels. It's just a little bit above me, I think.

Lori: I'll be honest, I skipped a lot of the angel stuff. I didn't get why it was in there and I was really into the stories about the women. I was enraptured by the women's stories, and I didn't want to waste my time at that point with the angels. Now that I've seen the play *Angels in America*, I'm going back to read it cover to cover. But at the time, it did not captivate me at all. You're getting into a whole big thing about angels and in a selfish way, I think it takes away from our stories.

Sarah: The angelology part was really interesting. To me it was just interesting to know about angels in our culture and different cultures, and then to tie it in with the struggle with the disease and how we think about it. . . . I felt like I learned some things from the inter-texts. I hope that if you get it published, they don't massacre it!

Heather: It has to have angels in it. That's the whole context. I usually don't buy into such stuff, but as I do this AIDS work, it's a feeling.

Amber: I hope this takes off and they make a little mini-series about it.
Patti: You could be the consultant.
Sarah: I think she wants to be the star!

And from the subtext of the Epilogue:

Patti: The earlier self-published version of this book was no first faint draft. While re-orderings, updates and additions have been made, this version is no radical departure from its earlier incarnation. This is not out of some sense of the great sufficiency of what we have done, but rather out of our puzzlement as to how to proceed differently. For example, in the case of our continued commitment to the split text format in the face of participant reservations, we encountered publishers who also wanted us to get rid of it in the name of appealing to a broader range of readers. We tried other options. We knew we didn't want our commentary to come before the women's stories as we wanted to give pride of place to their words. We knew we didn't want our words to come after their stories as that set us up as the "experts," saying what things "really meant." We tried the idea of "asides," where we would put our comments in sidebars. But all of these efforts renewed our commitment to the kind of "under-writing" that we had stumbled onto in our efforts to find a format that didn't smother the women's stories with our commentary and yet gestured toward the complicated layering of constantly changing information that characterizes the AIDS crisis. Trying to find a form that enacts that there is never a single story and that no story stands still, we practiced a kind of dispersal and forced mobility of attention by putting into play simultaneously multiple stories that fold in and back on one another, raising for readers questions about bodies, places and times, disrupting comfort spaces of thinking and knowing.

Our charge was simple: get the story out. The deliberately discontinuous mosaic that we have settled on may be a case of putting style ahead of story and, seemingly, we could have found a publisher more easily without this complicated and complicating format. But we risked this practice in order to bring to hearing matters not easy to make sense of in the usual ways. Forced to deal with two stories at once, the split text format puts the reader through a kind of "reading workout," a troubling exercise of reading. It stitches together discontinuous bits and multiples of the women's stories through seemingly disconnected narrative worlds, angelology, e-mail and journal entries, letters, poems, interview transcripts, academic talk about theory and method, and autobiography. Multilayered, it risks a choppiness designed to enact the complicated experiences of living with the disease, layers of happy and mournful, love and life and death, finances, legal issues, spirituality, health issues, housing, children, as people fight the disease, accept, reflect, live and die with and in it.

The following turns from the reactions of the HIV-positive women in the study to student writing from a course on AIDS where the book was previewed.[16]

I couldn't follow along regarding the women's identities . . . divided pages . . . and angels . . . unsettling. . . . I wanted to find out about the women, but I felt like there was always something in my way: either random boxes, lines across the page, or angels floating by.

All most people expect is a kind of voyeurism into lives usually unseen . . . book kept my attention. I did struggle with the format, but it was survivable. I found myself pondering the points made in the angel inter-texts. . . . It may be that I am not being sufficiently post-modern when I see the need to connect the layers of meaning. If struggling with the text is the entire point, point taken!

. . . frustrated . . . angry, at the structure and some of the content of the book. . . . I had tried to actually KNOW who each of the women is. . . . However this aspiration to understand who each woman is was perhaps stifled. . . . Maybe we aren't supposed to form attachments to the individual women, to imply that they are merely representatives of the thousands of women living with HIV/AIDS, but I don't find this as effective as portraying them as whole and real people.

I did not at all understand the significance of the angels . . . they really were in no way related to most of the book. Sadly enough, the angel chapters seemed to resemble commercials. I started to flip the pages as one would flip the channel. . . . The work was supposed to be on women speaking their minds in support groups, but before you know it, we're introduced to the personal lives of the authors and sit in on conversations during car rides.

[It was] quite difficult for me to stay focused on any one aspect of the book . . . my attention was never fully where it *should* be.

The poignant and richly informative [stories in the book are] about women and AIDS for women with AIDS, [but the text] violated my traditional reading patterns. The layers of meaning and detail were simultaneously literal and metaphorical . . . intentionally simultaneous . . . esoteric but at the same time wildly interesting . . . [where] I found myself getting lost in those levels of discourse all too often.

. . . angel concept seems kind of out there for me . . . but by the end it did make the ending of the work more meaningful and beautiful . . . tie it all together for us . . . there were so many little meanings around, that I couldn't figure out which one I was supposed to apply here. And maybe that's the point.

. . . like any other college student, [I] read it all the night before we were to discuss it in class. And while this reading style would have worked for any other book, it was difficult to do for this book. The difficulty arose in part due to the fragmentary style of the book, but mostly from the trouble I had trying to refrain from stopping and thinking about what I had just read.

I felt lost. . . . I actually feel this is a disservice to all the women who participated in this book . . . intellectualized and theorized . . . I had many expectations that were not met and were actually contradicted.

How does this "response data" help to trouble Chris's and my effort? Maybe it is a matter of something like Maurice Blanchot's (1982) "This work is beyond me" (126). Maybe the book is not respectful of its sources, putting style ahead of ethics and substance. Perhaps it falls over the edge of "vanity ethnography" (Van Maanen 1988) in not avoiding the self-indulgence that "goes too far" in efforts to bring the researcher into the narrative as an embodied knower (Mykhalovskiy 1996). And what of the problems with the translator as betrayer, intercepting rather than relaying the women's stories? In our desire to address what it means to know more than we are able to know and to write toward what we do not understand, how do we deal with what Renato Rosaldo (1993) terms "the vexed problem of representing other lives" (117)?

"Easy to spot the problem hard to supply the ethic!" Serres (1995a) writes, in addressing a code of practice for messengers (101). His answer is quite useful here, in all its density: that the task of the translator is to fade out behind the message once the incomprehensibility of the message is communicated, once philosophy herself appears in the flesh. Becoming visible as an intermediary, the task becomes to empty out the channel while still foregrounding the productive and distorting effects of the channel, a kind of presence, and absence, and presence again (104). The only way to break free from this is to invent new channels which will soon become blocked again as we derive importance from the channels we create, but the goal is to disappear in delivering the word of the something else which the word signals and gestures toward.

Serres helps me situate myself and follow the relations of the between, with, and across of a text that layers the women's stories of living with HIV/AIDS, researcher interpretive moves, and "factoid" boxes, all juxtaposed with angel inter-texts that bring moments of sociology, history, poetry, popular culture, and "determined policy talk" into a network of levels and orders. Deleuze and Guattari (1983) have termed such an assemblage a *rhizome,* an open trajectory of loose resonating aggregates, as a way to trace how the space of knowledge has changed its contours. Serres (1995b) writes,"we must invent the place of these relations" (137), as ground for practices of academic writing that are responsible to what is arising out of both becoming and passing away. Such practices of writing call out an audience with ears to hear. It is here that the response data is of use to me, in forming resources for thought in what it means to pose the problem of the text.

Reception, of course, takes on a momentum of its own, and moments of failure are particularly important in tracing the kind of work that something does. It is this that draws me in the response data, particularly the references to how *Troubling the Angels* defies "our narrative urge to make sense of, to impose order on the discontinuity and otherness of historical experience" (Hansen 1996, 298). In a space where untroubled witnessing will not do, the text undercuts any immediate or total grasp via layers of point-of-view patterns. Working toward a broad public horizon to present traumas that cannot be approached directly, a sort of resolute materialism is performed via a "flood" or "blizzard" of too much too fast, data flows of trauma and shock and asides of angel breathers, breaking down the taxonomic principles we bring to reading (Ellison 1996, 358). Here the angel functions somewhere "between theory and embarrassment" (368), renegotiating the limits of philosophy in staging the problems of representation.

Hybrid ethnographic texts are nothing new; neither is the effort to popularize and reach a broader audience. Ruth Behar (1995a) points this out in her introduction to *Women Writing Culture,* calling on the work of Zora Neale Hurston. "Writing hurts," Behar goes on to say, telling the story of Esperanza, her informant in *Translated Woman,* who refused to take a copy of the book that Behar had traveled to Mexico to give to her. "Please, take this back, too. We can't read it, anyway" (Behar 1995b, 77).[17] Preoccupied with fieldwork and rhetorical strategies, Western feminist ethnographic traditions of romantic aspirations about giving voice to the voiceless are much troubled in the face of the manipulation, violation, and betrayal inherent in ethnographic representation (Visweswaran 1994). Such tensions have moved me to practices of ethnography as "a site of doubt" (Britzman 1995, 236), practices that have produced a book written out of a kind of rigorous confusion. Here the heroic modernist imaginary is displaced so that something might be seen regarding the registers in which we live out the weight of "hard-borne history" (Serres 1995a, 293).

Refusing textual innocence and an untroubled realism, representation is practiced as a way to intervene, even while one's confidence is troubled. The task becomes to operate from a textual rather than a referential notion of representation, from persuading to producing the unconscious as the work of the text, working the ruins of a confident social science as the very ground from which new practices of research might take shape. In this move, I have come to think of the book as an unauthorized protocol developed in the face of our unbearable historicity, a sort of stammering relation to what it studies that exceeds the subjectivity and identity of all concerned. Here we all get lost: the women, the researchers, the readers, the angels, precipitating an "ontoepistemological panic" (Derrida 1994) aimed at opening up present frames of knowing to the possibilities of thinking differently.

In using the response data to locate myself in this text of responsibility, I am paradoxically attracted to wandering and getting lost as methodological stances. Trying "to stay lost, bewildered, suspended, and in flight" (Serres 1995a, 264), I am simultaneously stuck against the humanist romance of knowledge as cure within a philosophy of consciousness, while turning toward textual innovations that disrupt humanist notions of agency, will, and liberation. In this doubled space, trying to elicit differing capacities for understanding, Chris and I send out possibilities for a different kind of thinking about representation. The nonarrival of such messages is part of the play of the network (Nealon 1993a, 233). Working out of the place and necessity of representation, Derrida advises "knowing how not to be there and how to be strong for not being there right away. Knowing how not to deliver on command, how to wait and to make wait . . . " (Derrida quoted in Nealon 1993a, 234).

Enacting a rhizomatic thinking in a text that peforms what philosophy has become in the postmodern, Chris and I cannot reconcile the contradictions that traverse this book about bodies of knowledge and knowledge of bodies. Rather than resolution, our task is to live out the ambivalent limits of research as we move toward something more productive of an enabling violation of its disciplining effects. Inhabiting the practices of its rearticulation, "citing, twisting, queering," to use Judith Butler's words (1993, 237), we occupy the very space opened up by the (im)possibilities of ethnographic representation.

The Work of Theory: Scattered Speculations
on the Question of Value

[Efforts toward practicing a representation responsible to a different way of thinking] go beyond understanding in some way, they go past the usual understanding . . . indeed, they just don't quite go. It is a question, in truth, of the impossible itself. And that is why I took the risk of speaking a moment ago of aporia. It would have to fail in order to succeed. In order to succeed, it would have to *fail*, to fail *well*. . . . And while it is always promised, it will never be assured . . . a work that would have to work at failure. (Derrida 1996, 173–174)

To conclude, I return to the work of theory in thinking the multiple (im)possibilities for thought outside taken-for-granted structures of intelligibility. In reinscribing the parameters of responsible practices of academic writing, I find Spivak's (1993) complicated and complicating thought on the politics of representation particularly useful. Thinking her way out of the philosophy of consciousness of humanism, Spivak probes the kinds of narratives that are of use in a postfoundational era. Advancing Jean-François Lyotard's idea of paralogical legitimation, innovations leading to new forms, Spivak's interest is in "the responsible study of culture [that] can help us chart the production of versions of reality . . . the responsibility of playing with or working with fire [that does not] pretend that what gives light and warmth does not also destroy" (Spivak 1993, 282–283).

Hence this essay is an account of staging the problems of representation within a posthumanist frame (Spanos 1993). Like Spivak, my investment is to negotiate with an enabling violence attentive to frame narratives that works against the terrain of controllable knowledge. Positioned within the incomplete rupture with philosophies of the subject and consciousness that undergird the continued dream of doing history's work, the text marks the limit of the saturated humanist logics which determine the protocols through which we know (Melville 1986). Stubbornly holding on to the rhythms of the unfoldings of a book that as much wrote me as the other way around, I turn to the theory that helps articulate the investments and effectivities of what Chris and I have wrought. Here I read the affirmations and critiques of our effort as troubling thought about what it means for a book to interrogate, through its particularity, transparent theories of language and, consequently, the status of ethnography.

In sum, working from, with, and for women living with HIV/AIDS, like Fiske (1996) in his juxtaposition of black voices and Foucault as a white theoretical discourse in regards to the differential spread of AIDS, I have doubts about Chris's and my achievement. Unsure as to whether the book is symptom, index, or intervention, it is a risky business, this mining of discursive resources toward a kind of knowledge that jolts us out of our familiar habits of mimesis, referentiality, and action (Cohen 1996). My reach has exceeded my grasp, and that is just fine, this awkwardness, given that much of the book is about what Rilke (1989) termed the "Too Big." As Derrida (1978) says about Nietzsche, I might well be "a little lost in the web of [my] text . . . unequal to the web [I have] spun" (101). And I do not need people always to like my work. My sense of responsibility is not to seduce or persuade some audience as much as it is to implicate by setting up the obligation to see how we see. Such a text is doubled in imposing radical complications that enact the desire for interpretive mastery while surrendering the claim to simplicity of presence.

The danger, as Fiske notes, is to steal knowledge from others, particularly those who have little else, and to use it for the interests of power. This is so even when the intended goal is to extend the reach of the very counterknowledge upon which the book is based, the stories entrusted to those "who enter such alliances from the side of privilege" in order to transform the ubiquitous injustices of history into a readable place (Fiske 1996). Here the work of theory is to help us think through our enabling aporias as we move toward responsible practices of academic writing.

Acknowledgments

Part of this chapter was previously published as Lather, 1996. For the present publication, I have retitled, updated and substantially changed the second half of the essay in order to use *Troubling the Angels: Women Living With HIV/AIDS* (Lather and Smithies 1997) to interrogate normalized structures of intelligibility.

Notes

1. McWilliam's (1993) coining of PMT is more about the tensions implicit in negotiating "the questioning text," with its theoretical and methodological uncertainty, than it is about the sort of contradiction to which Weiner points. Actually referring in this case to Giroux, McWilliam argues that such texts are useful despite their density, although they require some "representing" in a form accessible to students (201).

2. By "Dada practice," I mean a heteroglossic excess, with "one language inhering in and decentering another; one form of discourse invading, subverting, citing, framing, and parodying or dismantling another: a staged contestation of discourses" (Welchman 1989, 64). Unable to be reduced to any one text, such textual practice guards against homogenizations via a linguistic density that produces a "constellation of . . . discursive forms that circulate, play and dissolve," a tangle of codes and systems of signs that "offer a literal invitation to expand our reception and analysis beyond the genres and divisions that have been perpetuated (and guarded)" (70). This is "Dada practice": to mix and collide incommensurable discourses as a way to situate research as a gesture, a performance, a staging of the problems of representation that disrupts the traditional signifying economy.

3. While Derrida insists that "deconstruction is not a method," (in Kearney 1984, 124), it

can be used to inform an-other logic of critical methodology. At the risk of "methodologizing" it, identifying and then reversing the binary oppositions that structure a text or an argument are the first two steps of deconstruction. The third step is to use the energy of the reversal to think one-self into some third space, some space of "both and" and "neither nor" that exceeds the opposing terms of the binary. Deconstruction, then, is an operation of, first, inversion and then reinscription, a rewriting of the relation between the binary terms toward a more fluid conceptual organization of terms which interrupts a binary logic. Working against reinscription into some familiar recipe, Barbara Johnson (1981) suggests deconstruction is about some fourth space that displaces the triangular, dialectical foundations of Western thought (xxxii). And Derrida, famously, proclaims deconstruction as not "a technical operation used to dismantle systems," but something which happens, always already (McDonald 1985, 85).

4. In a 1993 interview, Gayatri Spivak says, "My words are becoming simpler. They are becoming simpler because I can't do anything with the more complicated machinery. It's getting in the way, you know . . . when I'm pushed these days with the old criticism—'Oh! Spivak is too hard to understand!'—I laugh, and I say okay, I will give you, just for your sake, a monosyllabic sentence, and you'll see that you can't rest with it. My monosyllabic sentence is: *We know plain prose cheats.* [laughter] So then what do you do? Shut up? Don't you want to hear some more? And then it becomes much harder" (Danius and Jonsson 1993, 33). Thanks to Bettie St. Pierre for bringing this interview to my attention.

5. At a 1994 session of the annual conference of the American Educational Research Assocation on "But Is It Research," Deborah Britzman concluded her comments with the hope that educational research would become unintelligible to itself. This phrase has "worked like a virus," to quote Kate McCoy quoting performance artist Lauri Anderson. Britzman's statement situates unintelligiblity as an ethical imperative and a political intervention in terms of disrupting the ways we make sense.

6. Arguments regarding the material effects of language are rooted in Althusser's 1971 essay, "Ideology and Ideological State Apparatuses." Althusser writes: "An ideology always exists in an apparatus, and its practice or practices. This existence is material" (166). Demonstrating the material existence of ideological beliefs was Althusser's move against the idealism of Hegelian Marxism, with its focus on consciousness. His move was, rather, toward the immanence of ideas in the irreducible materiality of discourses, actions, and practices. Hence the materiality of ideology "interpellates" or "hails" historical subjects so that consciousness becomes an effect rather than cause. This thesis of the materiality of language is key in poststructuralism; see, for example, Montag, 1995.

7. "High theory" refers to the male pantheon of philosophical writing of those such as Kant and Hegel, their critics Nietzsche and Heidegger, and the Marxist variant kept alive in the Frankfurt School, a tradition today carried on by Habermas. In France, the names include Lacan, Althusser, Foucault, Derrida, and Deleuze. Samuel Delany (1994) talks of the "difficult discourse [that] stems historically from the German academic tradition. . . . As that tradition moved to France and, finally, produced structuralism and poststructuralism [it] picked up a particularly

French accent" (241). Delany goes on about the pleasures of such texts, for example Derrida: "The reason it's complex is because it's not so much an idea as it is a repeated demonstration of a process, in situation after situation, where meanings that at first glance seem clear, total, and masterable are shown to be undecidable, incomplete, and full of slippage and play" (243).

8. Usher and Edwards (1994) write of correspondence theories as "the powerful modernist position that truth is a matter of 'correspondence' with an outside 'reality'. . . . Poststructuralist texts contain within themselves running commentary on and critique of . . . the possibility of knowing the world in a direct and unmediated way—'as it really is'" (18–19).

9. Albert Oehlen and Christopher Williams, joint presentation, Oehlen Williams 95, Wexner Center for the Arts, Ohio State University, January 26–April 9, 1995.

10. Many of these questions are appoached in Melville, 1986.

11. As a feminist qualitative researcher, I was invited into the project by Chris Smithies, a Columbus feminist psychologist, who organized a support group whose members wanted to publish their stories of living with HIV/AIDS.

12. Elaine Herbert, writing for the University of British Columbia course, "Analyzing Qualitative Data in the Crisis of Representation," Summer, 1995. This and subsequent student work is quoted with their permission.

13. Diana Hodges, from the same class as in note 12.

14. Models I drew from include Bennington and Derrida (1993) and two books by the Canadian journalist Brian Fawcett (1986, 1994). Another influence was Joseph McElroy's novel *Women and Men* (1987), where angel inter-texts function as "breathers" and eventually expand in length to take over the text. I was also instructed by the contrasting analyses of the return of angels in postmodernism of McHale (1990) and Bloom (1996).

15. In the fall of 1995, Chris and I desktop-published an early version of the book and mailed it to the twenty-five women we had interviewed in their support groups in four major cities in Ohio. We met with the support groups in early 1996 to get the women's reactions, which have been included in the Epilogue of *Troubling the Angels*.

16. "Constructing AIDS: The Epidemic's Second Decade," a course taught by Dr. Ruth Linden, Stanford University, Anthropology Department, Winter, 1996.

17. Behar (1995b) writes of the scene leading up to Esperanza's refusal of the book: her greater enthusiasm for the television that Behar had brought her; tensions around a money order Behar had sent at the family's request; and Esperanza's interest in a possible Spanish version of the book. Perhaps most importantly, "I understand that not acceping the book is my *comadre's* way of refusing to be the translated woman" (77).

References

Althusser, Louis. 1971. "Ideology and Ideological State Apparatuses." In L. Althusser, *Lenin and Philosophy*. B. Brewster, trans. New York: Monthly Review Press.

Babich, Babette. 1994. *Nietzsche's Philosophy of Science*. Albany, NY: SUNY Press.

Behar, Ruth. 1995a. "Introduction: Out of Exile." In *Women Writing Culture*. R. Behar and D. Gordon, eds. Berkeley, CA: University of California Press, 1–32.

Behar, Ruth. 1995b. "Writing in My Father's Name: A Diary of *Translated Woman's* First Year." In *Women Writing Culture*. R. Behar and D. Gordon, eds. Berkeley, CA: University of California Press, 65–84.

Benjamin, Walter. 1969/1939. "Theses on the Philosophy of History." In *Illuminations*. H. Arendt, ed. New York: Schocken Books, 253–264.

Benjamin, Walter. 1989. "N [Re the Theory of Knowledge, Theory of Progress]." In *Benjamin: Philosophy, History, Aesthetics*. Gary Smith, ed. Chicago: University of Chicago Press, 43–83.

Bennington, Geoffrey, and Jacques Derrida. 1993. *Jacques Derrida*. Chicago: University of Chicago Press.

Blanchot, Maurice. 1982. "Rilke and Death's Demand." In M. Blanchot, *The Space of Literature*. Ann Smock, trans. Lincoln, NE: University of Nebraska Press, 120–159.

Bloom Harold. 1996. *Omens of Millennium: The Gnosis of Angels, Dreams and Resurrection*. New York: Riverhead Books.

Britzman, Deborah. 1995. "The Question of Belief: Writing Poststructural Ethnography." *Qualitative Studies in Education* 8, no. 3: 233–242.

Butler, Judith. 1993. *Bodies that Matter*. New York: Routledge.

Cavell, Stanley. 1976. *Must We Mean What We Say?* Cambridge, UK: Cambridge University Press.

Cohen, Tom. 1996. "The Ideology of Dialogue: The Bakhtin/De Man (Dis)connection." *Cultural Critique* no. 33: 41–86.

Danius, Sara, and Stefan Jonsson. 1993. "An Interview with Gayatri Chakravorty Spivak." *boundary* 2, 20, no. 2: 24–50.

Delany, Samuel, 1994. *Silent Interviews: On Language, Race, Sex, Science Fiction and Some Comics*. Hanover, NH: Wesleyan University Press.

Deleuze, Gilles. 1993. *The Fold: Leibniz and the Baroque*. T. Conley, trans. Minneapolis, MN: University of Minnesota Press.

Deleuze, Gilles, and Felix Guattari. 1983. *On the Line*. J. Johnson, trans. New York: Semiotext(e).

Derrida, Jacques. 1978. *Spurs: Nietzsche's Styles*. Barbara Harlow, trans. Chicago: University of Chicago Press.

Derrida, Jacques. 1994. *Specters of Marx*. Peggy Kamuf, trans. New York: Routledge.

Derrida, Jacques. 1996. "By Force of Mourning." *Critical Inquiry* 22: 171–192.

Elam, Diane. 1994. *Feminism and Deconstruction: Ms. en Abyme*. New York: Routledge.

Ellison, Julie. 1996. "A Short History of Liberal Guilt." *Critical Inquiry*, 22: 344–371.

Fawcett, Brian. 1986. *Cambodia: A Book for People Who Find Television Too Slow*. New York: Collier Books.

Fawcett, Brian. 1994. *Gender Wars: A Novel and Some Conversation about Sex and Gender*. Toronto: Somerville House Publishing.

Felman, Shoshona, and Dori Laub. 1992. *Testimony: Crises of Witnessing Literature, Psychoanalysis, and History.* New York: Routledge.

Fiske, John. 1996. "Black Bodies of Knowledge: Notes on an Effective History." *Cultural Critique* 33: 185–212.

Gallop, Jane. 1991. *Around 1981: Academic Feminist Literary Theory.* New York: Routledge.

Giroux, Henry. 1992. "Language, Difference and Curriculum Theory: Beyond the Politics of Clarity." *Theory into Practice* 31(3): 219–227.

Hansen, Miriam Bratu. 1996. "Schindler's List Is Not Shoah." *Critical Inquiry* 22: 292–312.

Joeres, Ruth. 1992. "On Writing Feminist Academic Prose." *Signs* 17, no. 4: 701–704.

Johnson, Barbara. 1981. "Translator's Introduction." In Jacques Derrida, *Dissemination.* B. Johnson, trans. London: The Athlone Press, vii–xxxiii.

Kearney, Richard. 1984. *Dialogues with Contemporary Continental Thinkers: The Phenomenological Heritage.* Manchester, UK: Manchester University Press.

Lather, Patti. 1991. *Getting Smart: Feminist Research and Pedagogy with/in the Postmodern.* New York: Routledge.

Lather, Patti. 1994. "Dada Practice: A Feminist Reading [Response to Stephanie Kirkwood Walker's Review of *Getting Smart*]." *Curriculum Inquiry* 24, no. 2: 181–188.

Lather, Patti. 1995. "The Validity of Angels: Researching the Lives of Women with HIV/AIDS." *Qualitative Inquiry* 1, no. 1: 41–68.

Lather, Patti. 1996. "Troubling Clarity: The Politics of Accessible Language." *Harvard Educational Review* 66, no. 3: 525–545.

Lather, Patti, and Smithies, Chris. 1997. *Troubling the Angels: Women Living with HIV/AIDS.* Boulder, CO: Westview Press.

Lubiano, Wahneema. 1991. "Suckin' Off the African-American Native Other: What's 'Po-Mo' Got to Do with It?" *Cultural Critique* (Spring): 49–186.

McDonald, Christie, ed. 1985. *The Ear of the Other: Texts and Discussion with Jacques Derrida.* Lincoln, NE: University of Nebraska Press.

McElroy, Joseph. 1987. *Women and Men: A Novel.* Normal, IL: Dalkey Archive Press.

McGee, Patrick. 1992. *Telling the Other: The Question of Value in Modern and Postcolonial Writing.* Ithaca, NY: Cornell University Press.

McHale, Brian. 1990. *Constructing Postmodernism.* New York: Routledge.

McWilliam, Erica. 1993. "'Post' Haste: Plodding Research and Galloping Theory." *British Journal of Sociology of Education* 14, no. 2: 199–205.

Meiners, Erica. 1994. Course Writing for Education 508B, Data Analysis in the Crisis of Representation, University of British Columbia, Summer.

Melville, Steven. 1986. *Philosophy Beside Itself: On Deconstruction and Modernism.* Minneapolis, MN: University of Minnesota Press.

Melville, Steven. 1996. "Positionality, Objectivity, Judgment." In *Seams: Art as Philosophical Context.* Jeremy Gilbert-Rolfe and Steven Melville, eds. The Netherlands: G&B Arts, 68–88.

Miller, Toby. 1993. *The Well-Tempered Self: Citizenship, Culture, and the Postmodern Subject.* Baltimore, MD: The Johns Hopkins Press.

Moi, Toril. 1988. "Feminism, Postmodernism, and Style: Recent Feminist Criticisms in the United States." *Cultural Critique* 9: 3–22.

Montag, Warren. 1995. "'The Soul Is the Prison of the Body': Althusser and Foucault, 1970–1975." *Yale French Studies* 8: 53–77.

Mykhalovskiy, E. 1996. "Reconsidering Table Talk: Critical Thoughts on the Relationship between Sociology, Autobiography and Self-Indulgence." *Qualitative Sociology* 19, no. 1: 131–151.

Nealon, Jeffrey T. 1993a. "Thinking/Writing the Postmodern: Representation, End, Ground, Sending." *boundary* 2, 20, no. 1: 221–241.

Nealon, Jeffrey T. 1993b. *Double Reading: Postmodernism after Deconstruction.* Ithaca, NY: Cornell University Press.

Piercy, Marge. 1973. *To Be of Use: Collected Poems.* Garden City, NY: Doubleday.

Rilke, Rainer Maria. 1989. *The Selected Poetry of Rainer Maria Rilke.* S. Mitchell, ed. and trans. New York: Vintage International.

Rosaldo, Renato. 1993. "After Objectivism." In *The Cultural Studies Reader.* Simon During, ed. London: Routledge, 104–117.

Serres, Michel. 1995a/1993. *Angels: a Modern Myth.* Francis Cowper, trans. Paris and New York: Flammarion.

Serres, Michel, with Bruno Latour. 1995b/1990. *Conversations on Science, Culture, and Time.* R. Lapidus, trans. Ann Arbor, MI: University of Michigan Press.

Shamdasani, Sonu. 1994. "Introduction: The Censure of the Speculative." In *Speculations after Freud: Psychoanalysis, Philosophy and Culture.* Sonu Shamdasani and Michael Munchow, ed. London and New York: Routledge, xi–xvii.

Spanos, William. 1993. *The End of Education: Toward Posthumanism.* Minneapolis, MN: University of Minnesota Press.

Spillers, Hortense. 1994. "The Crisis of the Negro Intellectual: A Post-Date." *boundary* 2, 21, no. 3: 65–116.

Spivak, Gayatri. 1977. "Translator's Preface." In J. Derrida, *Of Grammatology.* Gayatri Spivak, trans. Baltimore, MD: The Johns Hopkins University Press, ix–xc.

Spivak, Gayatri. 1987. *In Other Worlds: Essays on Cultural Politics.* New York: Routledge.

Spivak, Gayatri. 1993. *Outside in the Teaching Machine.* New York: Routledge.

Spivak, Gayatri. 1994. "Responsibility." *boundary* 2, 21, no. 3: 19–64.

St.Pierre, Bettie. 1997. Methodology in the Fold and the Irruption of Transgressive Data." *Qualitative Studies in Education*, 10(2), 175–189.

Usher, Robin, and Edwards, R. 1994. *Postmodernism and Education.* London: Routledge.

Van Maanen, John. 1988. *Tales of the Field: On Writing Ethnography.* Chicago: University of Chicago Press.

Visweswaran, Kamala. 1994. *Fictions of Feminist Ethnography.* Minneapolis, MN: University of Minnesota Press.

Walker, Stephanie Kirkwood. 1994. "Canonical Gestures." *Curriculum Inquiry* 24: 171–180.

Watney, Simon. 1994. *Practices of Freedom: Selected Writings on HIV/AIDS*. Durham, NC: Duke University Press.

Weems, Lisa. 1997. Candidacy exam, November 25, 1997, Ohio State University.

Weiner, Gaby. 1994. *Feminisms in Education: An Introduction*. Buckingham, UK and Philadelphia, PA: Open University Press.

Welchman, John. 1989. "After the Wagnerian Bouillabaisse: Critical Theory and the Dada and Surrealist Word-Image." In *The Dada and Surrealist Word-Image*. J. Freeman, ed. Cambridge, MA: MIT Press, 57–95.

Winant, Howard. 1990. "Gayatri Spivak on the Politics of the Subaltern." *Socialist Review* 20, no. 3: 81–97.

Jo-Anne Dillabough

DEGREES OF FREEDOM AND DELIBERATIONS OF "SELF"
The Gendering of Identity in Teaching

Introduction

If the self, as defined by an eighteenth century ideology of rights, does not exist, whose freedom are we trying so hard to protect? In any case, are "self" and "freedom" what they used to be?
(Maxine Greene 1995)

Roland had learned to see him*self*, theoretically, as a crossing place for a number of systems, all loosely connected. He had been trained to see his idea of his "*self*" as an illusion, to be replaced by a discontinuous machinery and electrical message-network of various desires, ideological beliefs and responses, language forms and hormones and pheremones. Mostly he liked this. He had no desire for any Romantic self-assertion. Nor did he desire to know *who* Maud *essentially* was.
(A.S. Byatt, *Possession* [italics added])

As Maxine Greene and A.S. Byatt imply in their written words, a deep confusion reigns over the meaning of terms such as "freedom" "identity," and "self" in contemporary life. There is also subtle implication in such words that much of what we come to understand as meaningful within the realm of the "political" takes on forms that either become objectionable to some members of society or relate to one's direct personal experience. As many scholars suggest, such disaffection occurs largely because social forces reconfigure our understandings and experiences of the political and what it ultimately means to "possess" an identity in the contemporary state (e.g., Robinson 1998). Arguably, gender politics, as a political formation, is one such example of this phenomenon.

In this chapter, I explore these issues with a particular concern for the ways in which educational concepts that are now central to the field of teaching (for example, teachers' "professional identity," "teacher professionalism") impute a historically determined, masculine conception of identity onto women teachers' personal and professional lives. In so doing, I take as my primary goal the task of confronting the problematic of "meaning" as it relates to contemporary perspectives on the role of gender politics (and feminism) in social life, and more particularly, with regard to the field of teaching in the U.K. I do this by illuminating how political forces (in particular, liberal democratic discourse) have influenced the ways in which meaning is ascribed to historical terms such as "identity," "self," and gender politics in British teacher education.

A further and related goal will be to demonstrate that questions of gender and the history of male dominance in political thought are central to our understanding of contemporary teaching and its character. To do this, I engage in two related forms of feminist critique which permit an analysis of the role of gender in the formation of the teacher as professional.

The chapter is divided into four main sections. The first, entitled "Gender Politics and the Construction of the 'Self' in Liberal Democratic Theory," draws upon feminist critiques of liberal democracy—in particular, feminist concerns about the rational individual in the state—to assess critically the gendered construction of the modern teacher. The central goal here is to illustrate how liberal concepts that are most closely associated with Kantian and Cartesian notions of the "self" resonate with dominant conceptions of "teacher professionalism" in the fields of teaching and teacher education. I argue that these conceptions not only endorse particular forms of masculinity, but serve, at least in part, to regulate the production of the modern teacher.

The second section, entitled "Women and Teacher Professionalism," deals less with grand theoretical concepts and more with substantive educational concerns about the gender dualisms that lie at the heart of "teacher professionalism." Consequently, seminal feminist critiques of the relation between the concept of rationality and women's marginal position in the teaching profession are described and explored. An additional focus here concerns the relationship between national reform discourses and the marginalization of women teachers.

In the third section, "Gender Politics and the Teaching Profession," I draw upon existing feminist research and my own empirical data to illustrate the ways in which rational and instrumental notions of teaching frame the often exploitative conditions of women teachers' work. Since one aspect of the chapter is based upon research with three different groups of women teachers in the U.K., I refer here to teaching in the broadest sense, including female university teachers in teacher education and female student teachers.[1]

In the final section, "Alternative Feminist Conceptualizations of Identity-Formation in Teaching," I draw extensively upon feminist political and social theory to construct an alternative conceptual model for assessing the role of gender politics in the identity-formation of teachers. I justify the development of this exploratory model on two gounds: first, it is essential to unravel the ways in which dominant knowledge forms in any field bear resemblance to historical narratives that most scholars assume are long-forgotten memories of the past. This involves critique in the first instance rather than simply charting the actual pragmatics and discursive practices of liberal democracy itself. Second, since feminist critiques of male epistemology are linked to questions of women's identity, it is important to draw upon them in order to rethink the part played by gender in the identity-formation of teachers. In this regard, the argument will necessarily provide a broad account of how the gendered teacher is constructed in contemporary educational thought. The section will conclude with a presentation of some preliminary theoretical ideas which could support the development of a more comprehensive theoretical framework for understanding the gendered nature of teaching.

In purely theoretical terms, a concern with issues such as these may seem unrelated to the field of education or indeed the field of teaching. And I must confess that it is not the practice of teaching with which I am most concerned here. However, one must see both education and the field of teaching as gendered forms of state regulation and key elements in the reproduction of gender identities. Perhaps more importantly, teaching resides somewhere near the center of the liberal democratic project and is premised upon very liberal, or to be more precise, neoliberal goals. And the "teaching" self and what (rather than who) it should become are at the heart of questions about gender and gender politics in society. I therefore begin with a brief review of sociological work which critiques the contemporary position on teaching in the U.K. and then go on to highlight the absence, within this critique, of an examination of the gender relations which prefigure it.

The Gender Politics of Teacher Professionalism

In recent years, there has been renewed interest in the notion of the teacher as a professional. This has found expression in a number of ways. For example, Nixon and colleagues (1997) have argued that the "identity category" which has the widest popular support in contemporary teacher education is the notion of the teacher as "professional." Despite this support, however, we should note that a uniform no-tion of "teacher professionalism" does not in fact exist.[2] There is, however, a partic-ular view now which circulates about teacher professionalism, at least in the way it is defined by central government and related agencies in the U.K. (for example, the Teacher Training Agency, TTA) and expressed within teacher education reform ini-tiatives. Broadly speaking, this view of "professional identity" is characterized in terms of the teacher's *rational* capacity to behave competently in the name of stu-dent achievement and social and economic change. This conception tends to be de-fined in terms of the instrumentality of the teacher as reform agent and his or her role in subverting personal interests (for instance, political concerns, personal wis-dom) to accord with objective standards of practice. Carr (1989) writes:

> Technical rationality continues to provide the dominant epistemology of practice, and central government's predilection for technological views of teaching is inevitably creating conditions under which a reflexive approach to professional development becomes impossible. (5)

> Teaching is portrayed as an unreflective technical process and "quality" as synonymous with meeting pre-specified standards through a system of su-pervision, inspection and control. . . . Education is seen as something which serves extrinsic purposes such as national interest, the economic needs of the society, or the demands of the labour market. (2–3)

Within this model of teacher professionalism, the liberal discourse most commonly associated with the modern teacher is that of the *rational, instrumental actor*.

Many sociologists in education have critiqued this rational view of teacher pro-fessionalism, arguing that it represents an attempt by the state to marginalize egali-tarian principles in practice. For example, Mahoney and Hextall (1997) suggest that teachers' notions of professional practice are constrained by the now abstract and so-called "neutral" descriptions of the new "standards teacher." Similarly, Jones and Moore (1993) take the view that a mainstream neoliberal culture of "profes-sionalism" now dominates education and serves to constrain educational profes-sionals' authenticity in practice. This culture serves to undermine the political authenticity of teachers and leads to instrumental forms of "technical control." Jones and Moore go on to assert that

> the effectiveness of "competency" resides in the manner in which it codifies and regulates behaviour through constructs of "skills" and the manner in which its methodology, active within a particular policy and institutional context, facilitates technical control. (1993, 387)

Similar ideas have been put forward by Lawn and Ozga (1981), who suggest that "teacher professionalism" is used by the state as a political device which gives the impression of liberation (for example, collaboration, "empowerment"), but simultaneously deskills and deprofessionalizes teachers to the point of exploitation.

Taken together, this work has exposed the formidable links between teachers' professional identities and increasingly centralized modes of state regulation over teachers' labors. It has also pointed to the underlying ideological orientation of "teacher professionalism" as expressed in educational knowledge and discourse.

Whilst this line of reasoning is valuable, critics within this discourse have ignored questions of gender.[3] Consequently, the stress within sociology on "neoliberal" politics or restructuring as sole motivations for understanding the "professional teacher" is limited insofar as the goal of such scholarship is primarily to expose state practices rather than to relate such practices to broader sociological concerns such as gender relations. In the section which follows, I attempt to redress this imbalance. I do so in the first instance by summarizing feminist political and social theorists' concerns about the gendered nature of "idealized" Kantian and Cartesian inventions such as the "rational, instrumental actor" and their relevance to current debates about the modern individual. An engagement with this body of work is pertinent because it affords the conceptual refinement needed to reinstate gender as a key issue in the construction of teacher professsionalism. Having drawn upon feminist political theory in this way, I shall then be in a position to illuminate some of the gendered tensions which arise as a consequence of relying, within an abstract liberal conception of identity, upon two concepts—rationality and instrumentalism—in the development of the teacher as professional.

Gender Politics and the Construction of the "Self" in Liberal Democratic Theory

The Problem of Rationality in Liberal Democratic Theory

> Like Western thought generally, political theory . . . relies on and reproduces its dualistic foundations, where knowledge and citizenship are equally grounded in hierarchical oppositions that value mind over body, culture over nature, reason over emotion, order over chaos, transparency over opacity. The feminine, a metaphor or identity for the denigrated terms, emerges as anarchic and wild; a threat to clear thought, self-discipline and political order. (Coole 1993, 18)

Theoretical debates that concern the gendering of liberal democratic discourse now have a lengthy history in feminist political and social theory. The most notable of these debates is the now long-standing feminist concern with Kantian and Carte-sian notions of the "rational man"—the "disembedded" political subject—as ex-pressed in liberal democratic theory. For example, as feminist political theorists argue, both the Kantian and the Cartesian view of the rational political subject re-flected a certain disdain for anything "coded as feminine" (see Coole 1993, 1) and conflated femininity with the subjective element of political participation. As a consequence, the objective and reasoned elements of political participation were privileged and thus dominated the construction of the active citizen. In such a con-text, women could not possess political identities because their "emotionality" and sexuality were viewed as a threat to the rational state (see Coole 1993). As a conse-quence, male rationality and reason have thus emerged as normative political ideals in liberal democratic societies.

One contribution of feminist political theory to our understanding of the gen-dered nature of liberal democratic practices comes from feminist critiques both of Kantian and Cartesian philosophies and of the concept of reason. For example, both Coole (1993) and Braaten (1997) have argued that "reason," although a rather ideal-ized political concept, is still revered as the centerpiece of liberal democratic practice and remains central to the success of the modern individual. Its essence is that to possess reason is to know, and to be a knowing subject is to possess political power. However, as feminist theorists argue, in conceding to rationality as the sole founda-tion for a political identity, women must remain (at least in abstract terms) outside the domain of the polity since they are constructed symbolically as that which stands in opposition to rationality. As such, women cannot "know" in the purest sense; they are instead viewed as the medium through which the rational individual is cultivated. Women, in other words, stand outside the political process as Other.

> From Plato to Descartes to Kant the self is the unitary substratum; reason reigns over the passions, the I reigns over the will; otherness must be sup-pressed. (Benhabib, 1997, 198)[4]

Carol Pateman (1992) points to similar problems associated with "othering" women by defining them against a theory of rationality. Within liberal discourse, this othering of women is legitimated normatively. However, Pateman argues that liberal democratic discourse, including the discourse of rationality, is not merely a form of exclusion (that is, identifying and then marginalizing the Other), but is, paradoxically, a matter of inclusion as well. These "inclusions" are not all that they seem. She writes:

> The classical theorists did not completely exclude women from the political order, from "civil society." The creation of modern patriarchy embodied a

new mode of inclusion for women that, eventually, could encompass their formal entry into citizenship. Women were incorporated differently than men, the "individuals" and "citizens" of political theory; women were included as subordinates, as the "different" sex, as "women." (Pateman 1992, 19)

As is evident in Pateman's words, modern patriarchy created the normative conditions for the subordination of women in the dominant gender order. It represented women as oppositional to the male stance, as different, as Other. To justify this legitimization, classical liberal theorists normalized the dominance of men over women whilst continuing to valorize the notion of complementary gender relations in the polity. The inclusion of women on the basis of their ability to complement the work and practices of men has ontological significance; that is, women can exist as citizens only if they operate in relation to, and in support of, men. Within this "rational" concept of citizenship, very particular understandings of men and women emerge. For example, the "man" (as a true Hegelian entity) emerges as all "powerful" and "active" in the state and the woman withdraws as "passive," "emotional," and "subjective" (see Hegel 1973).

If we take this analysis of modern patriarchy seriously, then the very idea of possessing an "identity" (when equated with, for example, Kant's "rational man" or Hegel's powerful man) becomes impossible for women, since their inclusion in the state is based upon the experience of further subordination. To put this another way, in "civil" society women cannot possess a political identity; they are simply incorporated to reproduce the material and symbolic social order that men rely upon to maintain their social dominance. This dominance is reflected in myriad forms. However, it is most visible as a form of knowledge—that is to say, a rationalized knowledge form—which is then taken up as a mode of social operation in the state.

From this it follows that when the modern identity is tied to particular forms of rationalism, whether it be construed as "reason" or "rationality," it cannot pertain to women because the rational actor can be fully realized only as a masculine construction and as a symbolic representation of that which women are not. Therefore, as Pateman (1992) argues, the bias inherent in the classical view of women's political inclusion is twofold: (1) the simple conflation of the modern identity (modern political subject) with "rationality" and (2) women's inclusion as a form of sexual complementarity to that of men. Clearly, such exclusions and legitimized "inclusions" are ideologically driven, in the sense of reflecting the subordination of women. However, these very practices are camouflaged in the gendered "universality" and "neutrality" of concepts such as "rationality."

"Identity," when viewed in this manner, poses acute problems for the development of a women's epistemology (as an identity politics) or the notion that women possess "epistemic" authority in the state. Such problems have profound political implications and are exposed most vividly when one begins to speculate about what women must strive to become in order to find a home in the state. For example, the Kantian view of identity gives rise to a cultural vision of inclusive political participation that favors a masculine conception of the modern subject/individual. It achieves this through the formation of stable gender categories that differentiate, as if natural and legitimate, between the "rational" man and "irrational" women.

Perhaps more significantly, when the term "identity" is invoked in a liberal attempt to suggest that all individuals are "free," as it were, to become "rational individuals," such attempts are mistaken, precisely because they do not acknowledge the masculine (and heterosexual) forms of institutional "power" and the role that rationality plays in shaping the gendered nature of the polity. An overreliance on such terms also reinscribes onto the polity a notion of liberal individualism premised upon epistemological positions constructed and further legitimized by men. This process of legitimization, however, does not stop at the level of abstract political institutions. It also interacts with, and functions within, a broader discourse which centers upon political and economic culture. As a result, the rational identity is further commodified under such popular slogans as "enterprise culture" and intersects with masculinity (and the market) as one of the most modern rational forms.

Finally, this strand of political thought constructs an exclusionary notion of the modern identity which can only justify itself through the practice of reason. In such a case, men stand as legitimate representatives of the public sphere, while women, as Clark (1976) suggests, remain in the "ontological basement" of political life. As a consequence, women can achieve political status on par with that of men only if they fully embrace the symbolic gender dualisms that frame state practice and have their roots in the European philosophical tradition; that is, they must separate from the "self" when it is entrenched in any formal attachment or intimate connection with another (see Weir 1997).

The Instrumental Identity in Liberal Thought

The Kantian focus on the separation of "self" from experience in the search for a legitimate political identity exposes another gendered tension which underlies traditional conceptions of rationality. This tension is best expressed as follows: by conceptualizing the "self" as detached, the individual symbolizes a position of complete independence where he or she no longer appears "to have intrinsic needs for others."[5] Weir (1997) views this strong liberal characterization of the individual as an unrealistic abstraction. Such a view "runs against the structural features of the self as a being who exists in a space of concerns" (Taylor 1989, 51). In this political context, it is the alienated (and arguably less humane), but ultimately productive, individual who functions to eliminate the salience of the social sphere. The notion of the alienated and market-oriented individual therefore takes on an instrumental position in relation to the state. As Kenway and Epstein (1996) argue:

> the ideas underpinning market ideologies [in education] are themselves gendered. The notion of the free-standing and hyper-rational, unencumbered competitive individual who can operate *freely* in the morally superior market can only be an image of middle class maleness. (307, my emphasis)

An overreliance on this instrumental conception of identity (that is, autonomous, disconnected) does, however, lead to three conceptual problems that are central to the reproduction of Weir's (1997) "disembedded subject" in the state.

First, the deployment of the term "identity," as part of the liberal initiative, implies that individuals can only be viewed as agents in the struggle toward the implementation of "freedom" and "autonomy" as the governing principles of the state (regardless of the degree to which human regulation is centralized or decentralized). However, the naturalization of such terminology (for example, free society) in the state takes us away from the simple reality that some "individuals" have greater access to freedom than others. Interestingly, "freedom" is typically treated as a term of political inclusion, yet its silent role in women's subordination serves to expose its exclusive functions.

Second, this view of the modern individual negates the role of social context, structure, and particularity in the formation of gender identities; that is, it fails to view identity as an embedded political construct which "always depends upon larger social meanings"[6] for self-definition.

Third, the language of instrumentalism (for example, detached political subject, freedom, autonomy) falsely implies that women will acquire the necessary freedom to act politically in their own name if they extract themselves from their social experience. Consequently, in this model, the social element of identity-formation is denied and unrealistic expectations are circulated about the capacity for women to be "free," despite the now obvious and well-documented social constraints placed upon them.

Liberal Discourse, Gender, and the Construction of the Modern Teacher

On first examination, feminist critiques that have exposed the idealized modern individual as a masculine entity may seem unrelated to educational concepts and, in particular, to teacher professionalism, teacher education, and women's position within it. However, as discussed at the outset, in recent years "teacher professional-ism" has been redefined by the state to reflect a certain strain of rationality which privileges male theories of the polity. Therefore, on any systematic application of feminist critiques of the modern subject to dominant views of teacher professional-ism, a number of tensions arise which pose particular difficulties for feminists.

The first tension emerges when the part played by Kantian or Cartesian repre-sentations of the "rational man" are rendered visible in contemporary notions of teacher professionalism. For example, state-centred notions of "teacher profession-alism," such as the "Competent Teacher" or the "Standards Teacher," are closely as-sociated with Kant's idea that personal perspectives (for example, emotions, experience) should not inform political action in the public sphere and, in this case, the actions of teachers. Instead, it is advocated that teachers' identities should con-form to a more objective and procedural account of professionalism as expressed by, for example, government agencies (such as the TTA). However, if we accept femi-nist critiques of the Kantian position as valid, one could argue that women's (and men's) diverse emotional experiences and political beliefs (and hence, differences) are repressed in this abstract model of teacher professionalism. As such, this model gives a misleading picture of teaching by attending to what has been traditionally viewed as the masculine sphere of the political spectrum (that is, the rational public sphere). The other sphere—the realm of the private—is not viewed as politically relevant in this model of teaching (see Noddings 1996), at least as far as abstract knowledge structures about professionalism are concerned.[7]

Second, the dominant notion of "professional identity" appears to be premised on a rather simplistic and instrumental model of teacher development. This abstract model of professionalism characterizes teachers as individuals who do not make meaningful connections with students or other "professionals," but instead respond to the instrumental goals of the state (see Mahoney and Hextall 1997). Thus the teaching self is not constituted through complex and meaningful social interac-tions. It simply asserts itself in the name of progress. This notion highlights a

> forging of a concept of profession with the quest for order in a period of rapid social change and with middle-class male anxiety about proving one's self, in ways that are highly reminiscent of the themes of the masculine cultural pro-ject as is already visible in relation to bureaucracy. (Davies 1996, 669)

Since, as Davies (1996) argues, women teachers are typically associated with "femi-nine" codes, they are often excluded from, or controlled by, this "masculine cultural project." Consequently, a discursive notion of the teaching "self" is lost, and the complexity of education and its socializing mechanisms remain unexplored.

A third tension emerges when one considers the instrumental forms of training currently in operation in teacher education. Whereas earlier perspectives on professional teacher training emphasized the idea of meaningful student-teacher relationships, school communities, and progressive pedagogical approaches, current approaches point to a return to traditional assessment methods and idea of the teacher as the transmitter of knowledge (for example, whole class teaching). As Gewirtz (1997) writes:

> there is a decline in the sociability of teaching; and there is pressure on teachers to adopt more traditional pedagogies, with a focus on output rather than the process and on particular groups of high-attaining students. . . . These shifts are in large part a consequence of a deliberate strategy on the part of the policy makers attempting to ameliorate particular problems of the state—problems of capital accumulation, legitimation and control. (230)

Paradoxically, this legitimate "authority" and control are not gained through creative and authentic insight, nor through shared social experience in the classroom. Rather, they are achieved through teachers' and teacher educators' individual efforts to commit to standardized procedures that are created by an objective body of so-called "experts." If a teacher succeeds at this task, she will be labelled "competent." However, such notions are constrained by masculine ideals of professional autonomy and agency, "an ideal that can be achieved—in a world of 'hostile strangers' . . . through impersonal relations that are distant and emotionally detached" (Davies 1996, 672).

Since knowledge about teaching appears to be tied to very particular gender codes and categories, the reproduction of masculine ideals through the concept of teacher professionalism leads to the devaluation of those gender codes that are typically associated with the "feminine." This not only means that gender dualisms are rerepresented in educational thought. It also implies that dominant conceptions of teacher professionalism yield to gendered teaching identities that are always unequal.

Fourth, the political language ascribed to the contemporary professional—the language of neutrality and universality—functions to mask the many barriers to women teachers' freedoms within education and the labor market, thus limiting our understanding of the gendering of professional identity itself. It also discourages an exploration of the gendered conditions of women's work in schooling. It thus becomes clear that liberal political categories serve, at least in part, to underscore the instrumentalist and rationalist premises that underlie what is expected of "men" and "women" in teaching and keep them from questioning the differential positioning of male and female teachers in the education hierarchy. As Acker (1994) writes:

If we consider the modal location of men and women teachers, we observe that men and women typically teach different subjects to different groups of children, hold responsibilities for different functions within schools, and generally have different chances for rewards within the system. Women are more likely to teach younger children, men older ones; women to teach girls, men boys; women to teach domestic subjects and humanities; men technological subjects and physical sciences; women to have pastoral responsibilities, men administrative and curricular ones. As Strober and Tyak (1980) put it, women teach and men manage. The divisions are not of caste-like rigidity, but the probabilities that the sexes will experience differential career lines and typical locations in schools are striking enough to allow us to speak confidently of a sexual division of labour in teaching. (76)

Clearly, Acker's remarks provide the basis for problematizing the generation and circulation of so-called neutral terms such as "professional identity" and point to the realization that any such concept must be linked to a symbolic and material understanding of the broader gender order. They also provide a sociological and political framework for examining the links between women's labor, social structure, and identity formation. In summary, feminist critiques of the modern subject provide the necessary analytical tools for exposing the relation between gender and rationality and their complementary roles in the gendering of professional knowledge. They also problematize the gender dualisms that underlie a notion of teaching as rational, instrumental action. This view reconstitutes the teacher as Kant's individuated "rational man"—a teacher devoid of meaningful connections to those whom she is expected to educate. Feminist critiques of concepts such as "teacher professionalism" also point to the implicit theories of gender identity deployed in educational and professional discourses and their representation within hierarchical systems of educational knowledge.

Women Teachers' Political Identity

As I have attempted to demonstrate in the previous section, there is a case to be made for examining the relationship between feminist critiques of the liberal subject and the gendered language of "teachers professionalism," particularly educational language that emerges from knowledge claims made about gender within the immediate ambit of the state. However, while this approach is a necessary step in assessing the relationship between gender politics and the teaching profession, it remains incomplete as a form of feminist critique. We must therefore get beyond questions about the gendered nature of educational knowledge and discourse to look more closely at the relationship between teacher education reform and the political identities of women teachers. This is an important step if we are to move beyond a simple analysis of epistemological concepts, language, and discourse and identify educational sites that are circumscribing women and subordinating them to men.

In my view, therefore, one central question still remains: What role have recent teacher education reforms played in repositioning the "professional status" of women teachers, particularly as it impinges upon a woman's desire to express her beliefs in feminist educational practice or her own authenticity/difference within the context of a broader gender order (for instance, sexuality, race, or class)? The most common response to this question in the critical policy literature is that women teachers are no longer "autonomous" beings and are thus "deprofessionalized." However, the problem is more complex than a simple case for the deprofessionalization thesis. Clearly, one can only argue that teachers are deprofessionalized if they have been viewed as "professionals" in the past. As I have tried to argue, such a notion is fraught with tensions. These tensions are most clearly expressed in current research that points to the "regulation" of women's professional identity in practice and the exploitation of women's labor in teaching (see Acker 1994, Dillabough 1997, Walkerdine 1990).

Let me turn now to a consideration of the role of reform in the regulation of women's political identities in teaching. If we hold, as I have already discussed, that educational discourse is implicated in the reproduction of gendered identities in teaching, it follows that any related reform initiatives should also play a role in such regulative functions. These regulative functions are subtle but, with some analysis, can be shown to expose a number of conflicts that concern not only women's subordination in educational institutions but also the differences among women themselves. Such is the intersection between educational practice and gender relations, but, in the further marginalization of women teachers, precisely what is the role currently played by rational initiatives in teacher reform?

Gender Conflicts, Teacher Education Reform, and the Question of Nationhood

By including reform as an extension of educational ideals and knowledge in teaching, we can begin to identify gender conflicts that emerge from its implementation. Such conflicts are embedded in national projects which have been designed to reconstitute the "nation" as a powerful and competitive entity worldwide. As I attempt to argue in this section, this particular power is not only gendered but is racialized in ways that serve to reconstitute the state as a homogenous and unified entity. The key question that remains, then, is: What does this trend mean for women teachers and, in particular, culturally oppressed women teachers? And how does the state attempt to regulate the gender identities of culturally oppressed teachers through the implementation of such reforms?

Consider, for example, a black feminist teacher who wishes to express a cultural viewpoint that resonates with her history in the classroom. She may wish to teach (as teacher educator, classroom teacher) black women's history, feminist/antiracist practices, or the intersection of race and gender in her teaching. Yet at the same time, such material is thought to bear no relevance to National Curriculum guidelines and may not, according to the national position on standards, contribute to broader national standards of "excellence." On the face of it, this may not appear to have a direct link to the repression of a particular cultural or gender identity in the classroom or to the question of nationhood, but it is clear that a national project that excludes the study of difference simultaneously functions to repress it. Allison Weir (1997) refers to this kind of state function as a "patriarchal discursive strategy" that has its origins in history but that manifests itself (as is the case in education) in the everyday practice of educational governance and in the language of reform itself.

The Teaching Training Agency in the U.K., for example, has produced numerous documents in recent years advocating that teacher educators (and student teachers) should become more accountable (through inspections and other forms of teacher assessment) for the success of reform measures that pertain, amongst other things, to school "standards" (see Mahoney and Hextall 1997). This has meant that many women teacher educators and student teachers (see Dillabough 1997)[8] have spent an enormous amount of time implementing changes that are, in the main, a reinstatement of traditional liberal values and masculinist/culturalist ideals for the future of teacher education. In their crudest forms, these reform ideals are intimately tied to the drive for expediency, competence, and excellence in schools. It is also the case that many of the reforms, as argued in the previous section, are tied up in the very forms of rationality which I have been discussing at a more theoretical level.

Unfortunately, teachers and teacher educators have been given little choice about whether or not to implement such reforms. For example, in the U.K. the funding of teacher education institutions and schools rises and falls on the success of formal government inspections and student performance. If teacher education faculties or schools fail these inspections, then it is often the women teacher educators/teachers who are constructed as the failures, because in many cases it is they who are largely responsible for the practical implementation of such reforms in university classrooms and schools. This is particularly true in the case of primary schools, as more women teachers are located there than in the secondary sector. Teachers are therefore asked to negate their positionality in relation to culture, class, or, for example, feminism in the education of their students and are instead encouraged to educate in honor of the British nation. Therefore, in implementing such deracialized and "gender neutral" policies, women have little choice but to deny their own authenticity, culture, and gender politics in the teaching task and take up and reproduce various forms of what Connell identifies as "hegemonic masculinity" (see Connell 1990).

It is at this level that we begin to see the role of the state (as nation) in the repression of women teachers' difference more clearly. For example, questions of gender, race, class, and/or sexuality and disability are not addressed in the context of the "standards-competent" teacher and the kinds of national identities he or she is expected to shape. The identities the teacher (as a competent teacher) is expected to cultivate relate most directly to the "competent student," in particular, to the successful future citizen in the nation. There is no cultural profile attached to the competent student; she or he simply performs in the name of the state.

In this context, teachers are not encouraged either to express "difference" as part of their professional practice or necessarily to respect students' differences as part of the world in which they live. As Mahoney and Hextall (1997) argue, to reflect "difference" as part of teacher education reform would be to deny the role of teachers in rebuilding a homogenous and undifferentiated nation. What is critical here is the issue of who becomes responsible for implementing this particular national goal and its gendered functions.

Feminist political theorists have been extremely helpful in understanding how an emphasis on the concept of, for example, the "nation-state" might explain this repression of difference in teaching. Yuval-Davis, a feminist political theorist, writes:

> Women are often constructed as the cultural symbols of the collectivity, of its boundaries, as carriers of the collectivity's honour and as its intergenerational reproducers of culture. Specific codes and regulations are usually developed, defining who/what is a "proper man" and a "proper woman," which are central to the identities of collectivity members. . . . However, as cultures are not homogenous, and specific hegemonic constructions of cultures closely relate to the interests of the dominant leadership within the collectivity, these hegemonic constructions often go against the interests of women, who would therefore find themselves in an ambivalent position towards these hegemonic projects. (1997, 67)

Clearly, the manner in which the nation-state has positioned women, both historically and in relation to contemporary citizenship, is significant. If the female role is one of honorable subordinate, then women are placed in a rather precarious position with regard to the cultivation of a national/cultural identity. They must find a political or social means to cultivate this identity through either a kind of national service or biological reproduction. At the same time, they must also repress their own interests and positionality in such processes. This problem is exacerbated if they themselves reside on the cultural margins of the state or are already defined as Other. More importantly, women are often penalized if their own identities do not conform to such a national project. Yet much of what they are expected to achieve relates to a broader project of national control and regulation. Women are indeed central to the success of this national project.

Yuval-Davis's concern about women's ambivalence toward national projects has important implications for women teachers and, in particular, culturally oppressed female teachers. Clearly, the use of such reform initiatives (for example, Standards Teacher, the removal of "race" issues from the curriculum) to produce a position on national identity points to a false notion of "otherness" in the state. To put this another way, the state has constructed its own mythical national identity through which opposition can be defined and then excluded. For example, if the state cannot accept difference as a fundamental aspect of identity and citizenship, then it must create an identity that stands against difference; hence the power of social reproduction and regulation of identities in a liberal democracy.

It is within such political discourses that "race" (also class and sexuality) can be seen as intersecting with gender to produce and regulate what might be called "double denial of difference"[9] in the production of the professional teacher. This is precisely because the only way to achieve national goals is to implement centralized policies which undermine not only the teachers' cultural position, but that of their students as well. In other words, the "standards teacher" must implement mainstream (and "mainly white and mainly male") government initiatives on how to achieve universal performance standards in schools

In following through on such initiatives, reform discourse comes to symbolize a double-denial of difference precisely because to be a successful teacher means to implement, rather than to question, educational practices which are not only "racialized" and "sexualized," but are bound to certain constructions of, and essentialized notions about, the contemporary citizen and the nation. This notion of the professional teacher, as it is currently represented, makes false claims to universality which function to repress not only the different identities in teaching, but also the differences embedded in particular school contexts. This repression of difference thus becomes a tool for the reproduction of further social inequality, because it may deny the needs of particular teachers, constitute them as Other, and force them to compromise their beliefs about what constitutes "inclusion." It also reinforces the notion of "teacher" as citizen of the "empire" and masks the cultural ambivalence of its members (see Bhabha 1990, Yuval-Davis 1997). Such an approach, as Homi Bhabha reminds us, serves to sustain a mythical construction of the modern identity:

Nations, like narratives, lose their origins in the myths of time and only fully realize their horizons in the mind's eye. Such an image of the nation—or narration—might seem impossibly romantic and excessively metaphorical, but it is from those traditions of political thought and literary language that the nation emerges as a powerful idea in the west. An idea whose cultural compulsion lies in the impossible unity of the nation as a symbolic force. (Bhabha 1990, 1)

As Bhabha indirectly suggests, the idea of a "nation," as expressed in state discourse, is rarely articulated by those who are in a position to contest its mythical boundaries. As a consequence, issues concerning those on the margin disappear, and the notion of "state" identity—as autonomous, culturally homogenous, rational—is therefore articulated as natural. Narrow state-centered assumptions about women as workers and "teachers" as professionals thus become crucial in understanding the relationship between nationhood, the repression of "difference" in professional practice, and the sexual division of labor. In this context, reform discourse becomes a powerful regulatory force that serves to police and constrain the development of women's political/cultural identity rather than being an emancipatory tool for political change. This does not mean that resistance to such forces is impossible. However, the supposed "neutrality" of national reform discourses that concern the nature of teaching effectively masks the easily obscured, but salient, alternative expressions of identity "from which alternative constituencies of peoples and oppositional analytic capacities emerge" (Bhabha 1990). "For the nation, as a form of cultural elaboration (in the Gramscian sense), is an agency of ambivalent narration that holds culture as its most productive position, as a force for subordination, fracturing, diffusing, reproducing, as much as producing, creating, forcing, guiding" (4).

In short, the reform mechanisms through which teaching standards are achieved serve to marginalize those aspects of "identity" that are central in maintaining an affiliation and/or involvement with collective movements that challenge the premises of such cultural and gendered narration. Perhaps what is most important about these reform requirements is that they conform to a rationalized and idealized view of education, which attempts to achieve, yet again, the masculine ideal of the *rational instrumental actor*. However, the cardinal point here is that we are not simply dealing with the exclusion of women teachers in the broadest sense. We are describing the ways in which the state mobilizes citizenship and national identity through the exclusion of particular women teachers (and their female students) on the premise that they are "different." To put this another way, they cannot sustain a "self" in a state which does not recognize it unless it is cloaked in the "objective," the "civilized," or the "rational."

Women and Teacher Professionalism

The contradictions inherent in the liberal concepts of "rationality" and "instrumentality" can be more clearly understood if we examine how their deployment in teacher education over time has led to a diminished view of women teachers as "professionals." Therefore, at this level of analysis, the problem moves beyond that of the simple exclusion of women's knowledge from a dominant and indeed abstract notion of teacher professionalism. Rather, it is concerned more directly with the contradictory and problematic nature of women's inclusion in the teaching profession itself.

Interestingly, not unlike feminist political theorists, feminist educationists are also concerned with rationality and its gendered manifestations. However, their arguments move beyond a concern with political thought to professional knowledge and its implications for women teachers. In this section, therefore, I address the ways in which feminist educationists have critiqued the application of male-centered concepts (for example, rationality) to the teaching profession and, in particular, to the lives of women teachers.

Inclusion, Rationality, and Women Teachers' Experiences

> We are arguing that the proof of masculinity as rational, as possessing knowledge, as superior, has constantly to be reasserted and set against its equal and opposite proof of the failure and lack of femininity. To say this is not to collude with the idea that women, and all other excluded groups, really "are" lacking, but to demonstrate the great investments in proving this to be the case. (Walkerdine and Lucey 1989, 201)

In 1989, Valerie Walkerdine and Helen Lucey published an important book entitled *Democracy in the Kitchen*. In this work, the authors were concerned with the question of how liberal democratic ideals (for example, freedom) framed the lives of girls and women, both normatively and symbolically, outside the domain of rationalism. Consequently, as was the case in feminist critiques of liberal democratic theory, Walkerdine and Lucey argued that women's political identities had been constructed against, and in subordination to, male theories of the rational individual. Women were thus seen as both conditioned and constrained by essentializing images of "irrationality"—an image of women dating back to the Enlightenment.

Their work also served to illustrate just how Enlightenment concepts, as a largely male enterprise, continued to reemerge in education over time. According to Walkerdine and Lucey, for example, it is still the bourgeois male teacher or student who is honored with the title "rational being," because it is he who is "endowed with reason" (1989, 200) in the purest sense. By contrast, women teachers and female pupils cannot possess knowledge in their own right because they are viewed as moral vessels through which liberal democracy and the rational society are cultivated. At the same time, however, women teachers and female pupils are still seen in the abstract as "free" and equal to men in their capacity to explore the possibilities and opportunities of liberal democracy in practice.

It is within these debates that concerns about the role of "rationality" have emerged in the field of teaching and teacher education, particularly as they bear upon the lives of women teachers who work in the "feminized" professions (such as teaching and teacher education). Many feminists have suggested, for example, that an overreliance on "rationality" within dominant educational discourse in both schools and higher education masks the historical constraints imposed upon women teachers and their capacity to be "rational" agents within the profession (see Blackmore 1996). As Casey (1990) and Steedman (1985) argue, the very structure of teaching has been shaped by biologically determined gender dualisms that have led to the coding of women as "feminine" and, hence, to the representation of "women teachers as mothers" (see Casey 1990, 1993). As a consequence, the professional status of women teachers is closely tied to domestic work in the private sphere. This linking of women teachers to the private sphere remains dependent, at least in part, upon traditional distinctions within political consciousness between "public man" and "private woman."

The now seminal work of Walkerdine and Lucey (1989) and others (see Steedman 1985) has been key to feminist critiques of women's social positioning in education. Not only has it pointed to the part played by the rhetoric of "rationality" in marginalizing women teachers (and girls), but it also suggests that women teachers are represented as symbolic of the private sphere and deemed responsible for the cultivation of the "rational" ideal of freedom through their role as moral regulators of the state (see Walkerdine 1990). The historical role of teacher thus becomes one of regulating and governing liberal democratic subjects who uncritically support the "freedoms" that are thought to underlie modern capitalism and its gendered manifestations. Walkerdine (1990) writes:

> the primary school forms an important place where this "free-will" is established. It is in this sense that we can begin to understand the position of the teacher as "the responsibility and the spur of freedom." The freedom which she has to foster is, I would argue, the notion of bourgeois individuality. . . . The teacher, then, is responsible for freedom. (61)

Paradoxically, this responsibility for ensuring the "freedom" of students often contradicts that which is articulated about the professional identity of teachers; that is, the professional is ultimately one who is free to the extent that rational and independent choices about educational practice can be made. However, women teachers are constrained by the very "illusion of freedom" at the same time as they are continually reconstituted as "mothers" and "guardians" of the nation. These constraints are clearly linked to identity narratives that concern women's reproductive capacity rather than their ability, as it were, to be "rational."

As these arguments imply, educational discourse which pertains to women teachers is often essentialized by traditional notions of the female identity. However, at the same time such notions are often construed as irrational, driven by emotions, and/or deemed inappropriate by society (see Blackmore 1996). As such, the social construction of women's professional status points to the naturalization of women's teaching identity as inferior to that of men. It also suggests that women teachers' professional identity can be found only amid the so-called "virtues" of the private sphere, which is ultimately viewed as contemptible in the context of a "real" profession. Consequently, the only remaining option for women teachers is to take up an instrumental stance where "mothering" is replaced with procedural forms of quality control or an identification with masculine forms of competence as the sole mechanism for achieving professional autonomy. Arguably, however, this formal identification with masculinity becomes a position of dominance rather than a position of reflection or female agency: "the self becomes all too proficient at the domination of nature, at the repression of drives, at defending identity against otherness, against difference" (Weir 1997, 66).

Consequently, as was the case with the representation of women in political thought, some of the most difficult questions concerning the significance of women teachers' professional identities are collapsed into an oppositional view of gender categories, which leads to the defense of one essentialized teaching "self" over another. However, the dominance of an essentialized teaching "self" in teacher education—the rational teacher—functions to mask the reality that most women teachers are situated on the inferior side of the gender binary. This position ultimately leads to women's exclusion from the formal language of teacher professionalism yet simultaneously defines their inclusion on the basis of female subordination.

Gender Politics and the Teaching Profession

The dual obsession with polarized identity discourses that concern teacher professionalism—"teacher as mother" or the "rational" teacher—has very specific consequences for understanding the institutionalization of the gender order in the teaching profession. These consequences are bound up in the gender relations and political formations that lead to women's experiences of exclusion in the teaching profession. Within education, the most obvious of these exclusions is the often subtle exploitation of women teachers' labor in education.

At this point, therefore, I turn to a consideration of the many and varied aspects of female exploitation in the teaching profession, drawing upon current examples of feminist educational research together with some preliminary work of my own. In reviewing my own work,[10] I focus largely on women teacher educators and, to a lesser extent, female student teachers since their gendered positioning in teacher education remains unexplored. However, I also draw upon research that concerns the experiences of female academics who teach in the feminized professions. I do this with the intention of forging links between the working experiences of women teachers in those academic professions that institutionalize women's labor and the lives of women (both students and academics) in teaching and teacher education. In so doing, I hope to illustrate how educational institutions function within a broader gender order which supports the essentialization of male and female identities yet remains committed to a rational notion of teacher professionalism in both schools and teacher education.

Gender, Exploitation, and the Contemporary Teacher

There is now a detailed, if limited, body of feminist research which attempts to expose the exploitation of women's labor in the teaching profession, some of which includes the study of women teachers in the academy and the work of women teachers more broadly. Much of this work has exposed the gender hierarchies and Kantian dualisms which continue to shape knowledge production about the role of women teachers and their subordinate status. For example, both Acker and Feuerverger (1997) and Brooks (1997) have provided evidence to suggest that female university teachers are exploited as workers; they are overloaded with administrative responsibilities, encouraged to function as caregivers, and given responsibilities which may lead to their exclusion from an equal chance of success as "professionals." In referring to empirical work conducted with female university teachers, Acker and Feurverger (1997) write:

> [Women academics] experience a "bifurcated consciousness" (Smith, 1987) or "segmented self" (Miller, J. L., 1983) or "outlaw emotions" (Jagger, 1989) as they try to live up to the contradictory prescriptions for "caring women" and productive academics. They see themselves working too hard, with high levels of anxiety, in reward systems that they dislike and without sufficient recognition for the aspects of the work they care about or have to do. Although self-selection may play a part in producing the anxiety and perfec-

tionism demonstrated by many of these women, we have argued that their "outsider status" in academe, combined with narrow institutional criteria for success, result in a situation where they suffer considerable pain. (Acker and Feurverger 1997, 418)

Acker and Feurverger also provide some illustrative and provocative examples of women teachers' concerns about the nature of their own exploitation in practice. They quote Lucille, a female academic in their study:

I sort of am used: as a departmental resource, like the fire extinguisher. . . . And I'm the shoulder for students to cry on. And I'm the person who can be counted on to teach well. Who can be called on to do whatever needs to be done. . . . I don't mind, I mean those are things that I would do anyway because they're what one does. But, certainly, as far as recognition for it, or the rest of it goes, forget it. (quotation from Acker and Feurverger 1997, 414)

Other feminists have pointed to the significance of the gender binary in the exploitation of women teachers' labor. For example, Luttrell (1996) argues that women educators are more often employed in nontenured, part-time, or contractual posts, where teaching and pastoral responsibilities are greater than they would be in permanent positions. This kind of employment status often leads to a situation where women are sometimes overwhelmed by the extent to which they have been conceptualized as service providers in education. Recent evidence for this claim in the everyday work of female teacher educators is also present in my own research. In the words of one female teacher educator participating in an interview which I conducted in the U.K. on educational restructuring and women in teacher education:

I was asked to be a year tutor. I was asked and I remember feeling valued when I was asked. Then I got told that "they only asked you because you're the only one that will do it. Everyone else has said no," but I didn't know that then. . . . A year tutor is like everyone's mother. You'll be stuck with everything. . . . It was difficult to cope with. . . . One set of problems after another. . . . So I was seen as a mother figure. . . . I just didn't realize how I became everybody's dogsbody. . . . So I did that for two years and I wouldn't do it anymore. It stopped me from doing any research. . . . I remember saying I wanted to go back and engage in research. . . . I was getting really fed up with that and I remember sitting in the staff room and somebody said "you're year tutor" and I said "I'm not" but I let them do that to me. Now I think why?. . . . Is it because I'm a woman? (Sylvia, Teacher Transcript 2)

Sylvia's comments speak directly to issues that concern the conflation of the categories "teaching" and "motherhood," where the latter category emerges as symbolic of diminished status and working conditions which further marginalize women. Consequently, any institutional attempts to demonstrate "inclusion" through role status or professional responsibilities such as year tutor may lead to experiences of marginalization, which may ultimately constrain women teachers' professional agency in practice. This is largely because inclusion as a "professional" (that is, the position of year tutor) may be premised upon female submission, male hierarchies of knowledge, or a conceptualization of teaching as "motherhood." It thus becomes clear that certain understandings of "inclusion" take priority over others, such that the exploitation of women's labor is legitimized within a formal political structure.

Sylvia's remarks also expose what Luttrell (1996) identifies as the illusions of "maternal omnipotence" (352) which form part of the structured gender relations of labor in teaching and their conscious and unconscious manifestations in the everyday language of individuals in the workplace. These "illusions" are not restricted to Sylvia's experience. They emerge as significant in the lives of other women teachers. As Helen, another female teacher educator, remarked:

> There is always this feeling that if you're a women I think that you do your work for the sake of your job. Then you wish somebody will appreciate you. But they're (men) not in it for the job. They only appreciate you if you're servicing them. Somewhere there is a serious conflict. I don't know what it means. Because sometimes it's like slavery. (Helen, Interview 3, 1998)

As is evident in Helen's remarks, there is a tendency to invoke very particular and indeed dichotomous understandings of gender identity. However, such understandings serve to elucidate the paradoxical nature of women teachers' work. This paradox emerges when the history of women's service role reemerges in contemporary practices and elicits both conscious and unconscious feelings about one's social positioning more generally. According to Helen, for example, the act of service should lead (at least in theory) to a certain appreciation for the work women do. However, as she suggests, appreciation can emerge only as a response to the conflation of women and service. Women teachers therefore emerge as a devalued entity unless they are serving others. Clearly, this process of devaluation not only has serious consequences for women teachers, but also exposes a particular understanding of the structural dimensions of gender inequality in higher education:

> When I came here (to the university) I still saw a very male, white middle-class power structure which shocked me. It all seemed so male. I went to

exam boards and it was all me and these males making the decisions. . . . All the people who seemed to be in a position of authority were men, like principle lecturers. It seemed that there were very few women, and they were all middle class, and I saw the world as a female tutor and I couldn't believe how few . . . female tutors there were. There were hardly any. . . . But I am still shocked and I am still pretty peeved when I sit in exam boards and meetings where you see who holds the power. (Janine, Interview 2, 1996)

Emergent Feminist Political Identities and the Sociological Constraints of Gender Relations in Teaching[11]

The empirical work cited above reveals some of the complex ways in which the teaching profession is both modeled on, and illustrative of, the broader gender order. In other words, as was particularly noted in the first section of the chapter, women's labor in teaching cannot be separated from the historically constructed knowledge claims that circulate about gender relations in society. However, such assumptions contradict many of the new modes of regulating the "competent" teacher. And so the paradox reemerges: notions of the "good teacher" are premised upon rational action and instrumental forms of expertise. Yet, despite the demands placed upon them to conform to it, women teachers and teacher educators are still constructed outside this dominant view of the professional. Consequently, the search for a meaningful and coherent "professional [and political] identity" becomes a fraught, complex, and ambiguous process:

I'm trying to reclaim my identity now. I felt as soon as I'd come here, I'd been turned into some sort of workhorse and that is a gendered position to be in. . . . So I'm very much trying to reclaim and establish a way of working here that isn't at odds with my political situation. I haven't done it yet but that's what I am trying for. However, I am going about gaining political control in a fragmented way. (Sylvia, Interview 2, 1997)

I was doing an executive job and that was all I could do but I couldn't be responsible for both ends, so then we were inspected for the second time and it was exactly the same situation I realised I was going to have to protect myself. . . . I made it very clear that I was not going to take responsibility for that [inspection results]. I said that's not my job, that's somebody else's job. I learned the second time around not be in the great catchall area. I laid down precisely where I was going to walk and what I was prepared to take responsibility for. (Helen, Interview 3, 1998)

And so the battle for women to assert themselves as "professionals" continues. Yet in many cases, such political assertions appear to be based on women's desires both to protect themselves and to set themselves apart from any blame for institutional failure; in other words, such assertions seem necessary for survival in the teaching profession. The need for self-protection, as expressed by both Sylvia and Helen, points to the struggle women teachers engage in both to resist and to move beyond their marginal positioning in the profession. It is precisely through such struggle that the gender dualisms that have shaped the construction of the professional teacher come sharply into view. These dualisms are represented in multiple forms: women teachers as subordinates, as "mothers," and as scapegoats for what has not been achieved in teacher education. What is significant is that each of these images is consonant with the kind of Cartesian and Kantian dualisms which form the history of women's representation in political thought.

In charting women teachers' struggle to achieve political status, one also achieves some insight into the ways in which gender hierarchies are implicated in the production of knowledge about the "professional teacher" and her role in tackling gender inequality in the school classroom. One also begins to see how gender dualisms are made manifest in the lives of women teachers across diverse domains of education. As one female student teacher, Louise, commented in response to a question about her own "feminist practice" in the classroom:

> I've thought about it. I see it in the classroom, in the sort of cliché of the girls being very conscientious and having beautifully presented pages and taking endless trouble and the boys have got very different agendas. There seems to be a maturity gap so I sort of thought as a teacher of my subject I could overcome that and focus on the boys because one feels it is fairly close to a loss of face to show much willingness with a young woman teacher when they're working hard to establish that they're men and all the rest of it. These poor skinny lads. They're like tadpoles. You have to kind of grace that and do whatever. So the line I've taken on the class really is to try and focus them by subject material that they won't feel is too girlie to talk about or too wet. (Louise, Interview 2, 1996)

As Louise's remarks imply, it is here that the manifestations of gender dualisms—codes of masculinity and femininity—have both influenced, yet rendered problematic, the possibility of feminist practice in teaching. Indeed, the very idea of tackling gender inequality may lead to the reproduction of a professional stance which impugns the significance of women. Such a stance emerges in multiple forms. As Carry, another student teacher, commented:

Carry: The boys always draw more attention to themselves than girls. Girls are a lot more subtle.

JD: How would you describe their tactics of getting attention?

Carry: Well, they're vocal. They call out. . . . The girls are a lot quieter. They tend to talk amongst themselves, whereas boys will shout across a room. They have a more physical presence. They will pull you by the arm and drag you back to their chair. . . .

JD: When the boys do that in the classroom how does it make you feel? If you were monitoring all that?

Carry: Well I tend to get annoyed because my time is being taken up in an unproductive way. . . . I've noticed that if you are not careful and not aware you will spend all your time with the boys, and that's really bad. (Carry, Interview 2, 1996)

Carry's difficulties, of which she herself is well aware, are not confined to the classroom. Even the most politically aware feminist teachers find the struggle to identify with women's concerns a formidable challenge. It is a challenge that not only involves the problem of gender relations but is also a broader political struggle over the recognition of women's work in the labor force. The following extract from an interview with Sylvia, a teacher educator, serves to illustrate this:

JD: How would you characterise your feminist strategies in practice?

Sylvia: Well I don't think on my own I can change anything. I can listen to other women. I do see parts of my job as constantly looking at this. . . . I came into education I wanted to change things and I wanted to say that it's OK to be you and it is OK to recognize that you are you, although you might not be able to effect institutional change. You've got the right to have a personal view and I very much think that has to be fought for. . . . I want to be in a position to say that what you are fighting for is worth fighting for. It's worth having. I see it as a fight.

JD: If there was anything that held you back (constrained your agency) as someone who wanted to express your feminist beliefs, what would that be?

Sylvia: OFSTED for instance. Well they are policing. I stood in front of them and told them there was a race and gender issue and I didn't know how they would react. But I did it anyway. I thought it was the right thing. I was shocked that none of the students could see it. None of them. . . . I am aware that I can't pursue my own agenda here because my agenda is too radical. I am aware that I am working in the market economy. I am aware of the pressure on management. I suppose I am aware of the tensions—the reality is the same. . . . To at least keep a position and still to recognise that my position is not going to be achieved in one institution. (Sylvia, Interview 3, 1998)

The social constraints which limit women teachers' political agency are complex. It appears, for example, as though women construct their political identities (and agency) in relation to broader social structures, including those exploitative structures which equate women teachers with subordination in the polity. More significant, however, is the link between gender relations and capitalist restructuring in the broadest sense, along with the manifestation of market thinking in the everyday lives of women teachers. This link, whilst seemingly peripheral to Sylvia's larger discourse about the maintenance of a feminist position in practice, is absolutely central to both the reconfiguration of the polity and the teaching profession in late modernity.

Alternative Feminist Conceptualizations of Identity-Formation in Teaching

In the previous sections, I have been arguing for a need to understand the complex ways in which historically determined gender dualisms serve as identity-framing devices in the field of teaching. I have therefore sought to illuminate, either through critique or through the representation of data, how gender dualisms that reach back to the Enlightenment continue to inform the construction of the modern teacher. These dualistic forms not only are linked to a crude and abstracted form of gender determinism in political theory, but are also manifest in educational concepts (that is, the rational, competent teacher) which privilege masculine "gender codes" in shaping ideas about modern teachers and their practices. As I have argued, these concepts presume a degendered, "disembedded," and decontextualized notion of teacher professionalism.

I now turn to explore an alternative conceptual framework for assessing the role played by gender in the formation of teachers' identities. Such an approach does not resolve all of the problems identified thus far. It does, however, offer a feminist sociological response to instrumental and rational conceptualizations of the modern teacher. It also makes a case for understanding teachers as discursively formed, as individuals who construct meaning through social mediation, and as agents who are "embedded, embodied, localised, constituted, fragmented, and subject to systems of power and exploitation" (Weir 1997, 184).

As a point of departure, I wish to argue that we move away from an instrumental assessment of teacher identities and focus instead on a social, structural, and political analysis of their development. Such a shift calls for the elucidation of an alternative feminist framework which embraces two antithetical notions in identity theorizing; (1) the postmodern notion of the authentic and discursive self and (2) the modern conception of the embedded or collective self (see Benhabib 1997). Any overarching theory of identity-formation must consider the relationship between, for example, teacher authenticity,[12] the social mediation of gender relations, and the capacity of teachers to reflect critically upon their social positioning as gendered subjects within the state. I would therefore like to posit an intersubjective theory of identity-formation (and "teacher professionalism")[13] whereby teachers can be seen as embedded in relationships "between active subjects"; they are, in other words, bounded individuals who possess some degree of political agency. This approach stands against the now dominant view of the "disembedded" professional as an "object of knowledge" or as a passive and deprofessionalized object of discourse (the "professional") whose identity is merely reconstituted through neoliberal political forces.

This line of argument requires us to move beyond the instrumental study of identity-formation in teaching, in which concepts such as "voice" or "narrative" are drawn upon as the only explanatory tools for theorizing the teaching "self." Instead, I suggest we view identity as something which is not solely determined by subjective narrative, but which is also shaped by social and structural relations both within and beyond education. Such an approach suggests that identity-formation (in education) be studied, at least in part, through an examination of what feminist critical theorists (see Benhabib 1997, Braaten 1997, Weir 1997) refer to as "communicative thinking" or what Habermas refers to as "communicative action." According to Habermas (1993) and his contemporary feminist followers, we can know ourselves and recognize others only when we have come to terms with, and reflected upon, our structural "embeddedness" in formal and informal political and language structures. As a consequence, the "embedded" subject is one who communicates, negotiates, and acts upon difference in relation and in response to meaningful social interactions with others. This social position of the embedded subject is thus said to be situated intersubjectively in social and dialectical relation to others. Gender, both as a social construct and a powerful social force, is therefore also situated "intersubjectively."

In emphasizing an adapted yet novel feminist version of the embedded "self," one might begin to view teachers as political agents who reveal and act upon their differences through a shared and meaningful process of critical reflection. This process does not just imply a negotiation of one's identity with those of others. It also involves the negotiation of larger political meanings in language across a variety of diverse social contexts (Habermas 1974, Weir 1997). A hermeneutic approach reminds us that the meaning ascribed to identity-formation can never be fixed or predetermined (Thompson 1981). It arises out of the relation between those who interpret and ascribe meaning to action, language, and everyday practices in varied social contexts and circumstances. Such a framework provides more complex theoretical tools for challenging two critically important, though opposed, views of the modern teacher, both of which contribute to the socially constructed nature of women's subordination. These are: (1) the teacher as an instrumental and unmediated form of masculinity and (2) the "teacher as mother."

In adopting a more sociologically driven feminist framework, we may get closer to challenging and thereby transforming the "real" existence of the gender binary as expressed through formal knowledge structures in education.[14] This approach might also allow us to see ways forward in theorizing a conceptual understanding of the role of gender in teachers' identity-formation which combines both critical modernist conceptions of the self as reflective agent and postmodern notions of the "self" as authentic and discursive (see also Apple 1996; Gewirtz 1997). In my judgment, three conceptual notions which have their roots in contemporary versions of feminist critical theory are likely to be particularly helpful in rethinking the role of gender in the study of identity-formation in teaching. It is to these themes that I now turn.

Intersubjective Identities

As many feminist theorists have argued, self-definition is contingent upon diverse and sometimes conflicting contexts of meaning (see Weir 1997). Such contexts condition the processes which underlie identity-formation: "my identity is produced through a complex process through which I am identified, and identify myself, in terms of intersubjective contexts of meaning" (Weir 1997, 185). Clearly, such a position on identity-formation begs a more complex story about the modern political subject than that offered by many of the male-centered traditions of philosophy which have preceded it. Such complexity, as expressed through feminist dialogue, has much to offer in understanding the gendered nature of identity-formation in teaching. For example, in applying the notion of intersubjectivity to identity-formation, educational researchers might consider approaching women teachers' political "identity" not as a rational entity, but as a complex, subjective, and multifaceted phenomenon embedded in the tension between the desire for political agency and the necessity for mutual recognition (see Weir 1997; Benhabib 1997) in diverse and sometimes conflicting social contexts.

It is through the study of this tension that we might better understand the gendered nature of "intersubjectivity" as central to identity-formation in teaching. Studying how teachers reconcile multiple and often conflicting gender identities in the struggle to engage in politically motivated educational practice constitues an important contribution to the study of identity-formation in teaching. However, such tensions can be examined only in relation to the institutional and social contexts within which women currently operate and which they have encountered in the past. Such efforts should therefore orient themselves toward a study of the "gender regimes" and hierarchies (Connell 1985, 1990) of educational institutions from diverse perspectives (for example, differently positioned women) together with their impact on the gendered experiences of teachers over time.

I would also encourage researchers to begin thinking about the question of gender identity in teaching as a more existential and phenomenological matter than they have in the past. This implies a concept of gender identity which is socially mediated by experience but is not necessarily constrained by making claims about this experience. In this way, experience serves as a kind of epistemic authority over what one comes to know about oneself in the state and about what kinds of agency an individual might therefore assume in any educational context. However, this notion of identity does not imply domination of others by making identity claims of one's own. Clearly, there are ways to make claims about identity which do not imply domination (for example, I am a feminist, but I respect the different forms of feminism which exist. However, I also know there are limits and constraints placed upon me because I have made a particular kind of commitment to feminism. These constraints are personal, political, and epistemological and are also bound by existing social and gender relations. I must reflect on these constraints and strive to resolve them, knowing that, in this struggle, it is the social process which is most significant).

This kind of mediated existentialism therefore implies an identity which is constrained by gender relations and dominant knowledge forms. However, it does not negate the possibility of possessing an identity in totality, for to do so would be simply to reproduce that which classical political theorists such as Kant have characteristically done, that is, to erase women's potential for "selfhood" and political agency. How one chooses to incorporate women's history into the construction of selfhood is very important in this context because "history," including a women's history which is not directly one's own, is intimately linked both to the "existential experience" of being female (in the teaching profession) and to the transformation of gender relations.

Difference and "Narrativity"[15] as Normative

Difference has become the heralded concept of late modernity. It is posited as the definitive term upon which modern narratives about identity have been crushed. Yet feminist critical theorists have argued that "difference" carries enormous power as a normative concept which explains, theoretically and empirically, how one comes to identify oneself and others within the state. The work of such theorists has important implications for the study of women's political identity in teaching because it assumes that teachers, in order to identify and reflect on their position in the profession, need to recognize others (teachers and students) as different from themselves. This commitment to difference in the study of teaching avoids the difficulty of universalizing the rational teacher as masculine whilst simultaneously recognizing the value of particularity in women's lives. It also avoids the trap of equating difference with marginality and allows for a novel understanding of teaching as an act of social mediation and reflection in which difference sits at the center of identity rather than lurking on the margins. The binary is thus challenged and the category of the teacher and its representations can shift. However, identity is not simply a recognition of difference as a part of oneself—that is, the authentic individual as expressed in liberal theory. It is a recognition that teachers are embedded in a meaningful social and political context where multiple selves meet within a dialectical frame. It is at this moment of "meeting" that one can identify with difference both as part of oneself and in relation to others. At the same time, one can also view difference as a discursive entity which is heavily regulated in fragmenting social spaces.

Within this framework, one might also consider what Benhabib (1997) refers to as "narrativity" in the study of identity. In Benhabib's (1997) view, narrativity—the self telling the story—becomes the medium through which the embedded individual expresses himself or herself as a gendered identity in the state. However, this self must be seen as embedded in a "web of gendered narratives" (Benhabib 1997) which restricts teachers' autonomy to merely expressing a singular and authorial view of their professional role. In so doing, the teacher identity transcends the gender binary and becomes a more complex and multifaceted entity.

Human Agency and Political Identity

One of the most salient yet neglected aspects of identity-formation in education is the assessment of teachers' beliefs about human agency. I would therefore argue for a greater focus on the study of human agency in educational theorizing in relation to gender and the professional lives of women teachers. However, in so doing, we must redefine human agency not simply as a phenomenon which is concerned with the exercise of freedom in the struggle for political status, but as a bounded and gendered construct which can only exist in relation to other social structures and human relations.

As a further step, we may also wish to draw upon feminist critiques of human agency which concern the masculinization of women's freedoms in the state in order to argue that human agency is not simply that which exerts power with some effect but something which cannot be fully exercised without a recognition of others in the act of meaningful communication. My own research suggests that women often see themselves as agents, yet they remain incapable in many social circumstances of achieving the kind of agency they have described themselves as possessing. This observation suggests the necessity for dismantling the liberal notion that agency simply represents unconstrained action. It suggests instead that "agency" be reconstructed to include an understanding of how the gendered "self" is constrained and the ways in which such constraints impact the construction of political identities that make claims to agency as a form of political liberation. This implies identifying, for example, the psychological, political, and sociological forces that influence one's capacity to be a reflective "agent," rather than simply assuming that in a liberal world all individuals are agents in their own right. It also demands attention to the ways in which women teachers reflect upon the contexts in which they work and attempt to resolve the identity conflicts which emerge as a consequence of their contradictory and gendered position within education. This view of agency is similar to Connell's (1985) theoretical assumptions about how identities are shaped by the "gender regimes" of social institutions—the communicative symbols and "gender codes"—of everyday life.

Four general assumptions about agency which could form the basis of a feminist analysis of teacher identities can now be sketched:

First, educational theorists need to return to the idea that the teacher agent may serve, theoretically, both as a form of social constraint and as a reflective and active agent in the process of change (see Apple 1996 and Gewirtz 1997 on the question of simultaneity). However, this conceptualization of agency must take into consideration the gendered positioning of teachers and the role that structural inequality plays in constraining women teachers' agency in practice. It must also consider the many ways in which the teaching profession (and the men and women who work within it) reflects the complex and contradictory nature of contemporary gender relations. It must therefore break with oppositional and narrow-minded conceptions of teacher professionalism such as the caring subject or the abstract and rational object. Such views of teaching should not be conceptualized as separate entities, but instead seen as two of many interdependent forces which condition the formation of teachers' professional identities in practice. Consequently, there is no ultimate need to reject Kant's rational self for Steedman's (1985) "mother made conscious" or vice versa. Rather, one is in the position to theorize a feminist form of teacher identity which cuts across such crude gendered distinctions, thereby providing a theoretical basis for assessing the complex ways in which teacher identities are formed through everyday practices.

Second, women teachers are still constrained by what Arnot (1982) identified almost two decades ago as "dominated gender codes" that are embedded in human interaction. It may therefore be more relevant to study the actual gender codes embedded in the language of political agency and related forms of "communicative action/thinking" than it is to define an abstract, idealized, or universal notion of teacher agency. This implies observing the ways in which teachers construct meaning in everyday action and "internalise the objective structure" (see Arnot 1982) of gender relations rather than simply assessing the ways in which they express themselves in isolation from others (for example, narrative accounts). Such an approach may challenge the notion of the teacher as the "disembedded" and neutral actor and bring into relief the part played by gendered subjectivities in the construction of teachers' political agency.

Third, agents are constrained by new modes of regulation and "governance" (for instance, educational reform) which lead to the development of differently positioned forms of agency and political self-expression. New educational structures and modes of regulation must therefore be assessed in order to expose their gendered manifestations (for example, the gendered nature of new teacher education reforms) and the role they play in shaping teachers' political agency in practice. This suggests a novel interpretation of the agent which accounts for the gendered trajectory of the teaching profession and the "recontextualization" of gender relations over time as taking a leading rather than a marginal role in the formation of teachers' professional identity.

Fourth, feminist educational theorists need to worry less about the difficulties associated with a modernist notion of (teacher) agency and more about the processes that shape and condition men and women as so-called "agents" of the state. As it stands, many feminists are trapped in a debate about the question of agency, with postmodernists arguing for its nonexistence and modernists using it as a political tool for women's transformation in the state. In my view, polarizing the debate any further will merely complicate the issues, because ultimately we end up arguing about whether women teachers really have agency (an impossible question to answer!) rather than understanding (or generating theories about), what novel social and political processes currently constrain women's (and men's) ability to act in, and reflect upon, the state.

It seems useful, then, to consider how we might tap the ways in which different forms of agency are constructed in teaching and how various institutional forces (including those firmly entrenched in the male and female psyche) shape agency over time and across space. Once we begin to distinguish between different kinds of agency, we can then begin to assess the gendered nature of agency. In so doing, we would achieve a position from which to challenge the notion of the teaching self as either "rational man" or "illusory women" and have the basis for a feminist theory of *differentiated agency or differentiated identifications* in the state.

We would also better capture the gendered nature of our embeddedness and dependence upon relationships, which is necessary in seeking out and validating diverse identities both within and beyond our professional contexts. We would also be in a much better position to observe what critical theorists once referred to as the "dialectic of modernity" and its impact on gender relations in teaching. In other words, we might learn more about the impact of modernism on our lives as women teachers instead of simply rejecting its basic principles.

This kind of approach would restore the role of structure in the formation of gender identities (and place responsibility on the state) by deflating the importance of the concept of "nonidentity" or the "illusory self" which now circulates as a form of power in so many feminist and nonfeminist educational theories and would give back to women their "otherness, and this means, in true dialectical fashion, their selfhood" (Benhabib 1991, 143).

Conclusion

In this chapter, I have discussed the gendered conflicts which arise as a result of an overemphasis on what Weir (1997) identifies as the "disembedded subject" and what Taylor (1989) has called "disengaged instrumentalism" in the neutral application of the terms "professional identity" and "teacher professionalism" to teacher education. My goal has been to clarify the ways in which such terms are used to construct modern identities, particularly concerning the gender identity-formation of teachers in the nation-state. The ideas inherent in such a view are not new, as political philosophers such as Charles Taylor tell us. For Taylor, modern forms of individualism:

> involve the stance of disengagement, whereby we objectify facets of our own being, into the ontology of the subject, as though we were by nature an agency separable from everything merely given in us—a disembodied soul (Descartes), or a punctual power of self-remaking (Locke), or a pure rational being (Kant). The stance is thereby given the strongest ontological warrant, as it were. (1989, 514)

Such views, while necessary in sustaining liberal myths about "self," "autonomy," and "freedom," are seriously misconceived. They not only misrepresent the diverse identities of teachers themselves, but are interwoven with the diverse forms of gendered exclusions and relations of domination in the social order. Clearly, however, such terms cannot adequately speak to our feminist political intentions in education and, most notably, to intentions which serve the welfare of those who have been disenfranchised in the state's drive toward economic expediency, narrow constructions of nationhood and identity, and international competitiveness. Instead, such concepts constrain our ability to understand the nature of political identities in teaching (see Dillabough 1997), particularly those identities which reflect the experience of inequality and the desire for its eradication (that is, the feminist political identity).

I have therefore offered a feminist rereading of the concepts of "professional identity" and "teacher professionalism" and have attempted to chart the "exclusivity" of gendered knowledge and practice in the field of teaching. I have also sketched a preliminary conceptual framework for assessing the gendered nature of identity-formation in teaching and teacher education. This work points toward a feminist perspective critical of mainstream conceptions of teacher professionalism as relying too heavily upon traditional liberal concepts, as failing to provide adequate recognition of the multiplicity of potential teaching identities in education, and consequently, as incapable of comprehending the gendered tensions to which they give rise.

What has also become clear is the manner in which an acceptance of the gender order as natural is manifest in, and aggravated by, such mainstream conceptions in the field of teaching. These views not only represent teachers' "professional identity" as a form of human agency closely tied to masculinity, but are also linked to women's contradictory and devalued position in relation to the state. To put this another way, educational concepts which concern the modern teacher are not simply free-floating, degendered entities. They are social constructs that yield to, and are located within, broader and more powerful social structures which serve to legitimize a state committed to instrumental goals and individual progress over and above any concern for marginalized peoples, human exploitation, or the welfare of a community. As a result, identities conditioned by the forces of individualism are, by necessity, operating under a "logic of exclusion" (Butler 1990) where the "other" in teacher education becomes what the prescribed identity is not.

In conclusion, the principles of rationality which underlie state-centered views on the modern teacher may provide an outline of what constitutes teacher professionalism, but simultaneously they also serve to define its epistemological boundaries. A failure to challenge this reality merely justifies, rather than critically examines, what are no more than the educational conceptions of a particular time. Sociologists of education have derided this approach because it commits to an uncritical acceptance of instrumental goals which lead to further, yet newly reconstituted, forms of inequality. But beyond this, as I have attempted to argue, it also leads to a retreat from a feminist analysis of the social and political dimensions of identity-formation in teaching. The fundamental effect is that teachers are no longer seen as political participants and are once again removed from contesting the very meanings which are attributed to their professional identities in practice. It is now up to feminists to reclaim the political and social dimensions of teaching. The ongoing struggle to engage with feminist theory as a way forward in the study of teaching constitutes one vital attempt to achieve this goal.

Acknowledgments

This chapter is an extended version of a paper entitled "Gender Politics and Conceptions of the Modern Teacher: Women, Identity and Professionalism," to be published in the *British Journal of Sociology of Education.*

I am greatly indebted to Madeleine Arnot for her ongoing mentorship in the development of the ideas which underlie the work of this chapter. I am also grateful to Phil Gardner, Wendy Luttrell, and Patrick Brindle for their helpful comments on an earlier draft of this chapter. I also wish to thank the women teachers and teacher educators who participated in this study. Without their commitment, this study would not have been possible. I gratefully acknowledge the financial support of the Social Sciences and Humanities Research Council of Canada.

Notes

1. I refer here to women teachers' lives in the broadest sense. The reasons for this are twofold. First, the women involved in my study were from three different yet related domains of teaching: (1) women teacher educators in the academy, (2) female mentors in schools, and (3) female student teachers. Interestingly, many of the key issues concerning these women teachers were comparable regardless of where they were placed professionally. For example, the intensification of work seemed to be congruous across the groups. Moreover, experiences of exploitation were similar across the three different professional groups.

Second, recent work on women teachers in the academy (in particular, service professions) suggests that the working conditions of female teachers in the education professions are also comparable across different aspects of the teaching profession. As a result, in this chapter I attempt to link this literature to my current work in teacher education.

2. I do not wish to argue that there is only one view of "professional identity" in teacher education. I merely point to the dominant view of the teacher as professional and argue that this view has gained public appeal at the cost of marginalizing women teachers (as will be discussed later in the chapter).

3. I know of only one serious attempt to examine the relationship between teacher professionalism and gender as it relates to educational change (see Mahoney and Hextall 1997).

4. Benhabib is reflecting upon the concerns of feminist political theorists who have been influenced by postmodern critiques of the "self."

5. See Weir 1997.

6. See Benhabib 1997.

7. I do not wish to make distinctions between the public and private spheres as a theoretical goal. However, since such distinctions are made in formal educational discourse, I do wish to map out which "abstract spheres" are neglected in educational knowledge.

8. I do not wish to imply here that men have not been asked to implement such "accountability measures." I refer to women here because they are, in many cases, disproportionately represented in teacher education schools or faculties as senior tutors/lecturers or school-based mentors.

9. The term "double-denial of difference" could be expanded to include other forms of oppressive relations around, for example, sexuality.

10. I do not outline any methodological details of this study here since the representation of quotes from teachers is intended merely to illustrate, in preliminary fashion, issues which concern the relation between gender and teacher professionalism.

11. I do not deal extensively here with the theme of "emergent political identities" in teacher education practice. I am currently exploring these issues in relation to other sociological issues (e.g., race, class). Consequently, the empirical data presented here are merely drawn upon to illustrate a concern about the representation of gender dualisms in the everyday lives of women teachers.

12. I am referring here to what teachers, as authentic individuals, bring to the practice of teaching (history, narrative, subjectivity, positioning).

13. Intersubjective theory is a conceptual position on identity-formation which has its origins in the Frankfurt School of Critical Theory. Within the feminist wing of this school, a form of feminist perspective-taking is argued for, whereby it is assumed that individuals invariably have multiple and competing identities which are grounded in social circumstances and reflected upon through social mediation.

14. Unlike theorists who take an extreme postmodernist position, I argue for the existence and manifestation of the gender binary in historical and contemporary thought. I do so for two reasons. On the one hand, I believe it is essential to chart and critique the representation of gender dualisms in contemporary thought—that is, male power over women and its presence in knowledge forms. I argue such a position on the basis of the now detailed body of work charting women's exploitation in many national contexts. To deny the existence of the binary (as part of the gender order) is, in my view, to deny women's struggles for social and political change.
On the other hand, I also believe it is necessary to expose the fundamentally illusory nature of the binary. In other words, we need to examine representations of the gender binary (male power over women) on multiple levels. On a theoretical level, for example, one can assess how women have been conceptualized historically as noncitizens in traditional philosophical thought. On an empirical level, it is also possible to challenge false representations of the gender binary—the categorical separation of masculinity and femininity—through a study of women's diverse lived experiences. Such approaches oblige feminists to consider simultaneously both the "real" and the illusory nature of the gender binary.

15. The term "narrativity" is taken from a paper presented by Seyla Benhabib, to the Department of Social and Political Science, University of Cambridge.

References

Acker, S. 1994. *Gender Education.* Buckingham, UK: Open University Press.

Acker, S., and G. Feurverger. 1997. "Doing Good and Feeling Bad: The Work of Women University Teachers." *Cambridge Journal of Education* 26(3): 401–422.

Apple, M. 1996. "Power, Meaning and Identity: Critical Sociology of Education in the US." *British Journal of Sociology of Education* 17(2): 125–144.

Arnot, M. 1982. "Male Hegemony, Social Class and Women's Education." *Journal of Education* 164(1): 64–89.

Arnot, M., and J. Dillabough. 1999. "Feminist Politics and Democratic Values in Education." *Curriculum Inquiry* 29 (2).

Benhabib, S. 1991. "On Hegel, Women and Irony." In *Feminist Interpretations and Political Theory.* M. Shanley and C. Pateman, eds. University Park, PA: Pennsylvania State University Press.

Benhabib, S. 1995. "Feminism and Postmodernism." In *Feminist Contentions: A Philosophical Exchange.* S. Benhabib, J. Butler, D. Cornell, and N. Fraser, eds. New York: Routledge, 17–57.

Benhabib, S. 1997. "The Debate Over Women and Moral Theory Revisited." In *Feminists Read Habermas: Gendering the Subject of Discourse.* J. Meehan, ed. New York: Routledge, 181–204.

Bernstein, B. 1978. "Class and Pedagogies: Visible and Invisible." In *Power and Ideology in Education.* J. Karabel and A. H. Halsey, eds. Oxford: Oxford University Press, 511–534.

Bernstein, B. 1996. *Pedagogy, Symbolic Control and Identity: Theory, Research, Critique.* London: Taylor & Francis.

Bhabha, H. 1990. "Narrating the Nation." In *Nation and Narration.* H. Bhabha, ed. London: Routledge.

Blackmore, J. 1996. "Doing 'Emotional Labour' in the Education Market Place: Stories from the Field of Women in Management." *Discourse* 17(3): 337–351.

Braaten, J. 1997. "From Communicative Rationality to Communicative Thinking: A Basis for Feminist Theory and Practice." In *Feminists Read Habermas: Gendering the Subject of Discourse.* J. Meehan, ed. New York: Routledge, 139–162.

Brooks, A. 1997. *Academic Women.* Buckingham, UK: SRHE and Open University Press.

Butler, J. 1990. *Gender Trouble: Feminism and the Subversion of Identity.* New York: Routledge.

Butler, J. 1995. "Contingent Foundations." In *Feminist Contentions: A Philosophical Exchange.* S. Benhabib, J. Butler, D. Cornell, and N. Fraser, eds. New York: Routledge, 35–58.

Byatt, A.S. 1991. *Possession.* London: Random House, UK.

Carr, W. 1989. "Understanding Quality in Teaching." In *Quality in Teaching: Arguments for a Reflective Profession.* W. Carr, ed. London: Falmer Press, 1–20.

Casey, K. 1990. "Teacher as Mother: Curriculum Theorizing in the Life Histories of Contemporary Women Teachers." *Cambridge Journal of Education* 20(3): 301–320.

Casey, K. 1993. *I Answer with My Life.* New York: Routledge.

Clark, L. 1976. "The Rights of Women: The Theory and Practice of the Ideology of Male

Supremacy." In *Contemporary Issues in Political Philosophy.* W.R. Shea and J. King-Farlow, eds. Science History Publications.

Connell, R.W. 1985. *Teachers' Work.* Sydney: George Allen and Unwin.

Connell, R.W. 1990. "The State, Gender and Sexual Politics," *Theory and Society* 19: 507–544.

Coole, D. 1993. *Women in Political Theory: From Ancient Misogyny to Contemporary Feminism.* Hertfordshire, UK: Harvester Wheatsheaf.

Davies, C. 1996. "The Sociology of Professions and the Profession of Gender." *Sociology* 30(4): 661–678.

Dillabough, J. 1997. "Democracy Exposed: Gender Conflicts and the Reform of British Teacher Education." Symposium paper presented to the Gender and Education Conference, University of Warwick, Warwick, UK.

Dillabough, J. 1998. "Theorizing Women's Diverse Feminist Political Identities in Teacher Education." Unpublished manuscript.

Dillabough, J., and M. Arnot. Forthcoming, 1999. "Feminist Perspectives in the Sociology of Education: Continuity and Transformation in the Field." In *Encyclopedia: Sociology of Education.* D. Levinson, A. R. Sadovnik, and D. Cookson, eds. New York: Garland.

Fraser, N. 1997. "What's Critical about Critical Theory?" In *Feminists Read Habermas: Gendering the Subject of Discourse.* J. Meehan, ed. New York: Routledge, 21–56.

Fraser, N., and L. Nicholson. 1990. "Social Criticism without Philosophy: An Encounter between Feminism and Post-Modernism." In *Feminism and Postmodernism.* L. Nicholson, ed. New York: Routldege, 242–261.

Gewirtz, S. 1997. "Post-Welfarism and the Reconstruction of Teachers' Work in the UK." *Journal of Educational Policy* 12(4): 217–223.

Greene, M. 1995. "The Lived World." In *Education Feminism Reader.* L. Stone, ed. New York and London; Routledge, 17–25.

Habermas, J. 1974. "On Social Identity." *Telos* 19: 91–103.

Habermas, J. 1993. *The Theory of Communicative Action.* Vol. 2. Thomas McCarthy, trans. Boston: Beacon Press.

Hegel, G.W. 1973. *Hegel's Philosophy of Right.* T.M. Knox, trans. and ed. Oxford: Oxford University Press.

Horheimer, M. 1947. *Eclipse of Reason.* New York: Oxford University Press.

Jones, L., and R. Moore. 1993. "Education, Competence and the Control of Expertise." *British Journal of Sociology of Education* 14(4): 385–398.

Kenway, J., and D. Epstein. 1996. "The Marketization of School Education: Feminist Studies and Perspectives." *Discourse* 17(3): 310–314.

Lawn, M., and J. Ozga. 1981. *Teachers, Professionalism and Class.* Lewes, UK: Falmer.

Lutrell, W. 1996. "Taking Care of Literacy: One Feminist's Critique." *Educational Policy* 10(3): 342–365.

Mahoney, J., and I. Hextall. 1997. "Social Justice and the Reconstruction of Teacher Education." Paper presented to the British Educational Research Association. York, England.

Mentor, I., Y. Muschamp, B. Nicholls, J. Ozga, and A. Pollard. 1997. *Work and Identity in the Primary School: A Post-Fordist Analysis*. Buckingham, UK: Open University Press.

Nixon, J., J. Martin, J. McKeown, and S. Ranson. 1997. "Towards a Learning Profession: Changing Codes of Occupational Practice within the New Management of Education." *British Journal of Sociology of Education* 18(1): 5–28.

Noddings, N. 1996. "Stories and Affect in Teacher Education." *Cambridge Journal of Education* 26(3): 435–447.

Pateman, C. 1989. *The Disorder of Women*. Cambridge, UK: Polity Press.

Pateman, C. 1992. "Equality, Difference, Subordination: The Politics of Motherhood and Women's Citizenship." In *Beyond Equality and Difference: Citizenship, Feminist Politics and Female Subjectivity*. G. Block and S. James, eds. London, Routledge, 17–31.

Phillips, A. 1991. *Engendering Democracy*. Cambridge, UK: Polity Press.

Robinson, S. 1998. "Individualism, Identity and Community in Globalizing Society." Paper presented to the Meeting of the Canadian Political Science Association, Ottawa, Canada.

Steedman, C. 1985. "'The Mother Made Conscious': The Historical Development of a Primary School Pedagogy." *History Workshop Journal* 20: 149–163.

Taylor, C. 1989. *Sources of the Self: The Making of the Modern Identity*. Cambridge, MA: Harvard University Press.

Teacher Training Agency. 1998. *Initial Teacher Training National Curriculum*. Consultation Documents.

Thompson, J. 1981. *Critical Hermeneutics: A Study in the Thought of Paul Ricoeur and Jürgen Habermas*. Cambridge, UK: Cambridge University Press.

Walkerdine, V. 1990. *School Girl Fictions*. London: Verso.

Walkerdine, V., and H. Lucey. 1989. *Democracy in the Kitchen: Regulating Mothers and Socializing Daughters*. London: Virago.

Weir, A. 1997. *Sacrificial Logics: Feminist Theory and the Critique of Identity*. New York: Routledge.

Weiler, K. 1988. *Women Teaching for Change*. Massachusetts: Bergin & Garvey, Inc.

Whitty, G. 1997. "Marketization, the State, and the Re-Formation of the Teaching Profession." In *Education, Culture, Economy and Society*. A. Halsey, H. Lauder, A. Brown, and A. Wells, eds. Oxford: Oxford University Press, 299–310.

Yuval-Davis, N. 1997. *Gender and Nation*. London: Sage.

Permissions

"Diasporas Old and New: Women in the Transnational World," by Gayatri Spivak, originally appeared in *Textual Practice*, 1996, Vol. 10, No. 2, 245–269 and was reprinted with the permission of Taylor and Francis, Ltd..

"Where a Teaching Body Begins and How It Ends," by Jacques Derrida, originally appeared in French in *Politique de la Philosophie*, edited by Dominique Grisoni, Éditions Bernard Grassert, and was reprinted in English with the permission of the publisher.

An earlier version of "Technologies of Reason: Toward a Regrounding of Academic Responsibility," by Peter Pericles Trifonas, appeared with the title "Reason Unbound" in *Educational Theory*, Vol. 48, No. 4, Summer 1998, pp. 395–410.

An earlier version of "Unthinking Whiteness: Rearticulating Diasporic Practice," by Peter McLaren, originally appeared in *Revolutionary Multiculturalism: Pedagogies of Dissent for the New Millennium*, by Peter McLaren, Westview Press, 1997, pp. 237–293, and was reprinted with the permission of the publisher.

An earlier version of "Multiple Literacies and Critical Pedagogies: New Paradigms," by Douglas Kellner, appeared with the title "Multiple Literacies and Critical Pedagogy in a Multicultural Society" in *Educational Theory*, Vol. 48, No. 1, Winter 1998, pp. 103–122.

An earlier version of "The Social Sciences as Information Technology: A Political Economy of Practice," by John Willinsky, appeared with the title "Social Contract" in *Technologies of Knowing*, by John Willinsky, Beacon Press, 1999, pp. 71–99.

An earlier version of "Responsible Practices of Academic Writing: Troubling Clarity II," by Patti Lather, appeared with the title "Troubling Clarity: The Politics of Accessible Language" in *Harvard Educational Review*, Vol. 66, No. 3, pp. 525–545.

An earlier version of "Degrees of Freedom and Deliberations of 'Self': The Gendering of Identity in Teaching," by Jo-Anne Dillabough, appeared with the title "Gender Politics and Conceptions of the Modern Teacher: Women, Identity, and Professionalism" in the *British Journal of Sociology of Education*, Vol. 20, No. 3, 1999, pp. 373–394, and was reprinted with the permission of Taylor and Francis, Ltd..

Contributors

Michael W. Apple is John Bascom Professor of Curriculum and Instruction and Educational Policy Studies at the University of Wisconsin, Madison. A former elementary and secondary schoolteacher and past president of a teacher union, he has worked with dissident groups, unions, activists, and educators throughout the world to democratize educational research, policy, and practice. Among his many books are *Education and Power*, *Official Knowledge*, and *Cultural Politics and Education*.

Nicholas C. Burbules is Professor of Education at the University of Illinois at Urbana-Champaign. He has written about the educational implications of computers, hypertext, www, electronic publishing, teaching and tragedy, aporia and doubt, theories of difference, and communicative virtue. One of his recent books is titled *Dialogue in Teaching: Theory and Practice*.

Jacques Derrida is Director of Studies at the Ecole des Hautes Etudes en Science Sociales. His most recent texts are *Adieu to Emmanuel Levinas* and *Monolingualism of the Other; or, the Prosthesis of the Origin*.

Jo-Anne Dillabough is an Assistant Professor at the Ontario Institute for Studies in Education at the University of Toronto. Her recent publications include "Feminist Perspectives in the Sociology of Education" with M. Arnot (published in D. Levinson, A. Sadovnik, and J. Cookson's [Eds.], *Education and Sociology: An Encyclopedia*). Her forthcoming book (edited with M. Arnot) is titled *Gender, Education, and Citizenship: International Feminist Perspectives*. She has also published internationally in journals such as *Curriculum Inquiry*, *British Journal of Sociology of Education*, *British Journal of Educational Studies*, and *Theory and Research in Social Education*.

Greg Dimitriadis is a doctoral candidate in the Department of Speech Communication at the University of Illinois at Urbana-Champaign. His work has appeared in *Popular Music* and *The Annals of the American Academy of Political and*

Social Science. His work is forthcoming in *Educational Theory* and the *British Journal of Sociology in Education.*

Henry A. Giroux is Waterbury Chair Professor at Pennsylvania State University. He is the author of numerous articles and books including *Channel Surfing* and *Counternarratives.* His most recent book is *The Mouse That Roared: Disney and the End of Innocence* (Rowman & Littlefield).

Douglas Kellner is George F. Kneller Philosophy of Education Chair in Social Sciences and Comparative Education at the UCLA Graduate School of Education & Information Studies. He has written on the application of neo-Marxism and critical theory to the interpretation of various cultural phenomena such as expressionism and other modernist movements, popular culture (especially film and television), and philosophy and social theory. Among his books are *The Politics of Ideology of Contemporary Film* (with Michael Ryan) and *Postmodern Theory* (with Steven Best).

Patti Lather is Professor of Education and Womens Studies at the Ohio State University. She has written on feminism, critical ethnography and research methodology, postmodernism, critical theory, and the politics of education. Her most recent book is *Troubling the Angels: Women Living with HIV/AIDS* (with Chris Smithies).

Cameron McCarthy is a Research Professor and University Scholar at the Institute of Communications Research at the University of Illinois at Urbana-Champaign. He is the author of *Race and Curriculum* and *Uses of Culture.* He is also co-editor (with Warren Critchlow) of *Race, Identity, and Representation* and *Sound Identities.*

Peter McLaren is Professor of Education at the University of California, Los Angeles. He has written extensively on postcolonialism, postmodernism, and Marxism in their applications to school reform and pedagogy. Among his most recent books is *Revolutionary Multiculturism: Pedagogies of Dissent for the New Millennium.*

William F. Pinar is St. Bernard Parish Alumni Endowed Professor at Louisiana State University. Pinar has also served as the Frank Talbott Professor at the University of Virginia and the A. Lindsay O'Connor of American Institutions Professor College at Colgate University. He is the author of *Autobiography, Politics, and Sexuality* and the editor of *Curriculum: Toward New Identities, The Passionate Mind of Maxine Greene, Queer Theory in Education,* and *Contemporary Discourses.*

Roger I. Simon teaches at the Ontario Institute for Studies in Education at the University of Toronto. He has written extensively in the area of critical pedagogy and cultural studies. Simon's recent work has addressed the formation of public memory and the pedagogical character of various forms of remembrance. His most recent book (with Sharon Rosenberg and Claudia Eppert) is *Between Hope and Despair: Pedagogy and the Remembrance of Historical Trauma.*

Gayatri Chakravorty Spivak is Avalon Foundation Professor in the Humanities at Columbia University and the author of many articles and books including *In Other Worlds: Essays in Cultural Politics* and *A Critique of Postcolonial Reason: Toward a History of the Vanishing Present.*

Peter Pericles Trifonas is Assistant Professor of Social and Cultural Studies in Education at the Ontario Institute for Studies in Education/University of Toronto. He has taught at schools and universities in North America and Europe. He has been published in journals such as *Interchange, International Journal of Applied Semiotics, Social Semiotics, Educational Researcher, Discourse: Studies in the Cultural Politics of Education, Postmodern Culture, Educational Theory,* and *Semiotica.* He also has two forthcoming books, *The Future of Postcolonialism* and *The Ethics of Writing: Derrida, Deconstruction, and Pedagogy.*

John Willinsky is Pacific Educational Press Professor of Technology at the University of British Columbia. Postmodernism, postcolonialism, literacy, critical theory, and technology are among his major areas of interest. His most recent books are *Technologies of Knowing* (Beacon Press) and *Learning to Divide the World: Education at Empire's End* (University of Minnesota Press).

Index